Breathed into Wholeness

Catholicity in an Evolving Universe
Ilia Delio, General Editor

This series of original works by leading Catholic figures explores all facets of life through the lens of catholicity: a sense of dynamic wholeness and a conscious awareness of a continually unfolding creation.

Breathed into Wholeness

Catholicity and Life in the Spirit

MARY FROHLICH, RSCJ

ORBIS BOOKS
Maryknoll, New York 10545

Founded in 1970, Orbis Books endeavors to publish works that enlighten the mind, nourish the spirit, and challenge the conscience. The publishing arm of the Maryknoll Fathers and Brothers, Orbis seeks to explore the global dimensions of the Christian faith and mission, to invite dialogue with diverse cultures and religious traditions, and to serve the cause of reconciliation and peace. The books published reflect the views of their authors and do not represent the official position of the Maryknoll Society. To learn more about Maryknoll and Orbis Books, please visit our website at www.maryknollsociety.org.

All scripture quotations are taken from the NRSV unless otherwise noted.

From *The Collected Works of St. John of the Cross*, translated by Kieran Kavanaugh and Otilio Rodriguez Copyright © 1964, 1979, 1991 by Washington Province of Discalced Carmelites, ICS Publications, 2131 Lincoln Road, N.E., Washington, DC 20002-1199 U.S.A. www.icspublications.org.

Some quotations that appear in this book were written before the current sensitivity to inclusive language. The reader is asked to read the quotations in the inclusive manner in which they were intended, even when the language used is exclusive to modern eyes.

Manufactured in the United States of America.
Manuscript editing and typesetting by Joan Weber Laflamme.

Library of Congress Cataloging-in-Publication Data

Names: Frohlich, Mary, author.
Title: Breathed into wholeness : catholicity and life in the spirit / Mary Frohlich.
Description: New York : Orbis Books, [2019] | Series: Catholicity in an evolving universe | Includes bibliographical references and index.
Identifiers: LCCN 2019017783 (print) | LCCN 2019981031 (ebook) | ISBN 9781626983489 (print) | ISBN 9781608338122 (ebook)
Subjects: LCSH: Spirituality—Christianity. | Perfection. | Catholic Church—Doctrines.
Classification: LCC BV4501.3 .F757 2019 (print) | LCC BV4501.3 (ebook) | DDC 248.4/82—dc23
LC record available at https://lccn.loc.gov/2019017783
LC ebook record available at https://lccn.loc.gov/2019981031

To Martha Curry, RSCJ,
and Rosie Dowd, RSCJ,
women who live in the rhythms of the Spirit

Contents

Acknowledgments

My first thanks go to Catholic Theological Union for the year of sabbatical that allowed time for this writing. Presenting Chapters 1 and 6 at a faculty seminar afforded an opportunity to add depth and breadth to the theological foundations of the project. It is a gift to have faculty colleagues who consistently offer encouragement and support along with their suggestions and critique.

I am also deeply grateful to my religious congregation, the Religious of the Sacred Heart, for providing the space and financial support that made it possible to complete the project in a reasonable amount of time. Despite often feeling that it was interminable, my local community has cheerfully supported me through all the stages of travail. Thank you!

A very special thanks goes to my friend Elisabeth Koenig, spirituality scholar and expert on Julian of Norwich, who took time to read and ponder the entire manuscript. Our lively conversations, and her astute suggestions, have helped to improve the content greatly. Special thanks also to John Albright, the physicist who saved me from errors and misrepresentations in Chapter 5, and to Laurie Brink, the biblical scholar who pointed out the importance of examining more closely the anthropology of Saint Paul. I am also most appreciative of all the others, too many to name, who have offered reflections and affirmations along the way.

An acknowledged limitation of this project is that I write from the point of view of a white middle-class Roman Catholic woman who has had only brief sojourns outside the United States and who is deeply steeped in Western intellectual traditions. Those who have other personal and intellectual horizons will recognize what I have failed to see, and, I hope, use their own gifts to carry the insights into new contexts.

Finally, when Sr. Martha Curry, RSCJ, promised me that she would pray for my work on this project every day, I knew that—despite my own limitations—the Spirit would bring forth its fruit!

Foreword

ILIA DELIO

Catholicity is a word that evokes a consciousness of wholeness that is dynamic and engaging, a spiritual connectedness to the fecundity of life. In this new book by Mary Frohlich we break through catholicity as an abstract concept that is often associated with the institutional church to the inner core of catholicity enkindled by the living Spirit of God. *Catholicity* is a word coined by Greek philosophers to describe cosmic wholeness. It entered into Christianity to describe a new cosmic whole where God is center. By center, I do not mean a circumscribed center but a vital center; as Bonaventure said, "The center is everywhere but the circumference is nowhere." This divine center of vitality is the Spirit of God.

The "breath-less" world that we live in today is in dire need of a renewed center of connectivity, a reawakening of the Spirit as the vitality of life. Mary's approach to this urgent task is to develop "catholicity from within." Building on insights from the early church, contemporary theology, and modern science, she discloses the Spirit as the "forgotten God," marginalized as a divine Person of the Trinity yet deeply present in the everyday world. The Cappadocian fathers brought the Spirit of God into light by arguing in favor of the Spirit as a divine Person equal to the Father and Son. Basil of Caesarea did not think of the divine Persons as "substantive" but as communion, three divine Persons in a communion of love. The Spirit is the bond of interpersonal love who mediates divine communion to creatures. The Spirit is the mediator of love who is both sharer and shared, giver and receiver, lover and co-beloved. Hence the Spirit can never be pinned down to "this" Person or "that" Person, for the Spirit is neither this Person nor that Person but shares in the fecundity of life and its receptivity; hence, the Spirit is the center of personalizing union in love as bond, gift, and breath. Where the Spirit of God is, there is newness and creativity of life. Saint Paul wrote that the Spirit is constantly working through the unfinished beingness of creation into the fullness of life. The Spirit groans aloud in the birth pangs of creation and helps us in our weakness when we don't know how to pray (cf. Rom 8:22–26).

God struggles through our lives where sometimes breathing is labored and difficult, where at times we are running out of oxygen because we fail to breathe in God. The Spirit is God's fidelity to life, forever breathing new life in us, but we must learn to exhale, as Mary indicates. The spiritual life is learning the art of God's breathing and learning to breathe in trust and surrender, in compassion and peace. To be fully alive is to inhale the gift of divine love and to exhale with the gift of one's life. The Spirit of God constantly searches our hearts and invites us to co-create this world in loving freedom where God and creature are entangled in the breath of new life.

This book opens a new window by deepening the meaning of *catholicity* as the basis of the spiritual life. How do we develop a consciousness of wholeness in a breathless world of anxiety and competition? How can we overcome narrow individualism by expanding personhood to include all creaturely life? Mary offers a simple paradigm: breathe in and breathe out. This is God's rhythm, God's Spirit. This breath of life enkindles a consciousness of the very gift of life. God breathes in and all things are created anew; God breathes out and everything dances in its unique personality, filled with God. To live in a spirit of catholicity is to live with deep awareness of God's life everywhere present and filling all things, the life of the whole.

Introduction

The present series, pioneered by Franciscan theologian Ilia Delio, brings a fresh, twenty-first-century perspective on catholicity. She writes: "Catholicity catalyzes the movement *toward* wholeness or universality by way of consciousness. . . . It is what moves (catalyzes) a person to think, move, and orient his or her life toward making wholes from the partials of experience."[1] The term *catholicity*, however, is not one that most people encounter in daily life. The inference most initially make is that it refers to Roman Catholicism. This is a partial truth, since *catholicity* is indeed a venerable theological term—but one whose origins actually antedate any denominational divisions.

The concept of catholicity became established in Christian thought through its appearance in the Nicene Creed, adopted in 381 by the First Council of Constantinople: "I believe in the one, holy, catholic, and apostolic church." The original Greek, *katholou*, meaning literally "according to the whole," was intended to affirm that each particular local church, equally with the entire universal church, makes present the fullness of Christ's ongoing life in the world. While each local church is contextualized in a different era, culture, and circumstance, each bears the "whole" in its essence and is intimately interlinked with every other church. Thus, the actual living church is diverse and one, local and universal, concrete and transcendent, without contradiction.

As part of the series on catholicity, the assigned focus of this book is "catholicity and the Spirit." It is noteworthy that the First Council of Constantinople was also the council that affirmed the equal divinity of the Holy Spirit along with that of the Father and the Son. It is in and through the Spirit that the activity of

---

[1] Ilia Delio, *Making All Things New: Catholicity, Cosmology, Consciousness*, Catholicity in an Evolving Universe (Maryknoll, NY: Orbis Books, 2015), 2.

God permeates the world and promotes all that is life-giving. Our primary aim, therefore, is not so much to develop a new theology of the Spirit (although, inevitably, we must deal with certain themes of pneumatology) as to explore the trajectory of the relation between human spirit and divine Spirit. In doing so, we compare the interaction between divine and human spirits to the rhythm of breathing: God breathes in and all things are made whole and gathered into God; God breathes out and each thing dances forth into its diverse individuality, still filled with God. Catholicity concerns this rhythm of divine "in-gathering" and "diversifying." On that basis we develop a model of the "catholicizing" (wholeness-seeking) spirit and explore how to enhance its life.

Catholicity:
The Whole Body Breathing Together

"Breath of God" was the image of the Spirit most favored by Basil of Caesarea, who was one of the most prominent theologians at the First Council of Constantinople. He saw the Breath of God as always accompanying the Word of God, giving both natural and resurrected life.[2] The Breath of God mediates divine communion to creatures, thus sanctifying them and making them spiritual.[3] When the bishops at Constantinople affirmed the divinity of the Holy Spirit, they chose the language of *personhood* as the best terminology to express the commonality and distinction of each member of the Trinity. Basil, it seems, was not comfortable applying the language of *substance* to the Spirit. Rather than *consubstantiality*—the term that had helped to resolve earlier christological disputes—Basil felt strongly that *communion (koinonia)* was more appropriate. According to John Zizioulas, this implies that Basil wanted to affirm that

---

[2] Denis Edwards, *Breath of Life: A Theology of the Creator Spirit* (Maryknoll, NY: Orbis Books, 2004), 26; Basil, *On the Holy Spirit*, trans. David Anderson (Crestwood, NY: St. Vladimir's Seminary Press, 1980), 16:38; 18:46; 19:49.

[3] Edwards, *Breath of Life*, 26; Basil, *On the Holy Spirit*, 9:23.

personhood, for which both uniqueness and relationality are constitutive, is the foundation of substance, not vice versa.[4]

This revolutionary transformation of Greek ontology lies behind the understanding of catholicity that also emerged from First Constantinople. It is the Spirit that mediates catholicity, bringing unity while at the same time delighting in diversity. In the catholic communion of the churches each is constituted both by its unique local expression of life in the Spirit and by its complete, intimate, Spirit-mediated interconnection with all the other churches. It is the personal character of the Spirit that makes this a "communion" rather than merely a network or even an organism. The image is that of a whole body breathing together, silently invigorating its multitude of organs and processes as they go about their diverse functions in service of life.

The personal character of the Spirit and its communion also have profound implications for our theological anthropology, that is, a biblically based perspective on the very nature of being human. As Dennis Doyle states in summing up the perspective of the great French theologian Henri de Lubac, "The Church is catholic because it knows what lies in the heart of every human person."[5] De Lubac himself employed a musical image, proposing that Catholicism (in this case, the Roman Catholic Church) plays upon the deepest and most intimate chords of which the human "instrument" is capable.[6] His assertion was that Catholicism is catholic because it fully embraces and fulfills what is most foundationally human.

De Lubac was a man of tradition who especially loved the patristic authors and saw himself as calling the church back to what these early thinkers had discovered in its exuberant youth. Perhaps he would be shocked by the approach taken in this book, which may seem to take a very long detour through phenomenology, current events, and science before getting to "real

---

[4] Jean Zizioulas, *Communion and Otherness: Further Studies in Personhood and the Church*, ed. Paul McPartlan (London: T & T Clark, 2006), 183–86.

[5] Dennis M. Doyle, *Communion Ecclesiology: Vision and Versions* (Maryknoll, NY: Orbis Books, 2000), 62.

[6] Henri de Lubac, *Catholicism: Christ and the Common Destiny of Man* (San Francisco: Ignatius Press, 1988), 18.

theology." But what de Lubac understood was that the church was meant to be at least as much an "emergent"[7] of human nature as a supernatural "add on." Thus, perhaps de Lubac could be persuaded to appreciate a project, such as this, that seeks to explore the "emergent" in an intimate dialogue with revelation.

Orthodox theologian John Zizioulas also builds on the patristic heritage to promote the idea that human persons have an intrinsically "catholic" nature that is designed to play an essential role in the coming to fulfillment of the entire natural world. Using rather technical language, he writes: "By being person man was meant to offer to creation the possibility of hypostatic catholicity, that is, the fulfilment of nature's ultimate reference to Being, a fulfillment which would take place as a unity respecting the integrity and diversity *(diaphora)* of beings."[8] By "hypostatic catholicity," Zizioulas meant that the essential nature of all created things as intended to be in communion with one another actually becomes an enfleshed way of life. When we as human beings truly live as "persons," both in the depths of intimate interior communion and in concrete, loving hospitality to all that is other than ourselves, we have the potential to be what he calls "priests of creation" who mediate the fulfillment of this inbuilt orientation of all creatures to a "catholic" communion.[9] Hopefully, this book will contribute to making this happen.

Overview

Part I of the book is entitled "Discovering Catholicity from Within." Chapter 1 explores the theological foundations as well as the methodological implications of the concept of catholicity from within. In Chapter 2, "Discovering Spirit in Human Experi-

---

[7] Theories of emergence propose that the natural processes of evolution can give rise to truly new levels of interaction that could not be predicted simply on the basis of observing the lower levels—for example, the emergence of conscious minds. See Harold J. Morowitz, *The Emergence of Everything: How the World Became Complex* (New York: Oxford University Press, 2004).

[8] Zizioulas, *Communion and Otherness*, 229.

[9] Zizioulas, *Communion and Otherness*, 229, 238.

ence," we apply this method as we engage in a brief phenomeno-logical analysis of a variety of experiences that people assert are "spiritual." We also review the research of Wesley J. Wildman on the classification of religious and spiritual experiences.

Part II, "In Search of Catholic Personhood," includes four chapters. Chapter 3, "The Crisis of the Anthropocene," reviews a wide range of sociological assessments of the impact of moder-nity (and postmodernity) on how people form their sense of self and identity. The aura of these assessments tends to be gloomy, suggesting that humanity is headed toward a dim future—or even extinction. The chapter concludes, therefore, with a brief reflec-tion on whether there are any signs that point toward a different future that could emerge from these conditions.

Chapter 4, "Selfhood and Catholicity," examines briefly the theological proposals for a "catholic personality" that can bear the tensions of both strong individuality and radical inclusivity. This is followed by a deep dive into current debates on the na-ture and formation of human selfhood. The chapter concludes by suggesting that the dialogical view of selfhood proposed by Hubert Hermans and Agnieszka Hermans-Konopka may offer the best resolution of the problems discussed in the chapter and make a helpful contribution to the question of what it may mean to form a "catholic personality."

Chapter 5, "Science, Spirituality, and the 'Greening of the Self,'" surveys how some of the concepts of quantum physics of-fer new perspectives on what it means to be a spiritual being, and how spiritual change may occur. Gregory Bateson's ideas on the four orders of change culminate in the question of whether hu-mans may yet develop capability for a way of life that is radically participative in the ecological patterns of the earth and cosmos. Joanna Macy's notion of the "greening of the self" develops this further. The chapter concludes with a review of proposals by some psychological researchers on how spiritual change occurs.

The more explicit consideration of issues of theological an-thropology takes place in Chapter 6, "Breathing Spirit: A Model of Human Personhood." It begins with a review of Léon Turner's critique of theologians' efforts to articulate an anthropology that takes account of the kind of developments recounted in Chapter 4. This leads to a discussion of apophatic or mystical anthropology, culminating in the presentation of a model of pneumatological anthropology that employs both the "breathing" metaphor and the "field" analogy for Spirit.

In Part III, "Living in the Catholicizing Rhythm of the Spirit," Chapter 7 focuses on the Spirit's "breathing in," which is experienced in human life as being drawn radically beyond oneself into communion. Spiritual practices of emptying, exemplified by John of the Cross, Meister Eckhart, and Jan van Ruusbroec, aim to foster this movement. Chapter 8 focuses on the Spirit's "breathing out," which is experienced by human persons as the necessity of constructing a narrative of the self as the scaffold of action in the world. The spiritual practices of Augustine, Julian of Norwich, Thérèse of Lisieux, and Ignatius Loyola exemplify this movement. The chapter also deals with how trauma interrupts this self-construction but can also clear the way for deep transformation.

In the final chapter, "Breathing with the Spirit into Mission," the fruits of the various chapters are gathered, with a view to what this may mean for spiritual life in the social and ecclesial dimensions. The chapter explores how spiritual experiences can blossom into a sense of vocation and the discovery of personal charisms that contribute to the ecclesial and social projects of building communion among people. Development of skills for prophetic and contemplative dialogue is a key to such projects. The chapter concludes with brief sketches of three people, Etty Hillesum, Howard Thurman, and Pope Francis, whose lives uniquely exemplify the catholicizing rhythms of the Spirit.

Part I

Discovering Catholicity from Within

Chapter 1

Catholicity from Within

This chapter provides an overview of "catholicity from within" and explores how a trajectory toward greater inclusiveness and interconnectivity can emerge in the Spirit-inspired rhythms of the human spirit. This idea builds on Henri de Lubac's conviction, noted in the Introduction, that Catholicism is catholic because it fully embraces and fulfills what is most foundationally human. As such, the trajectory of catholicity belongs to all human beings—and perhaps even beyond that, to all creation. Reading de Lubac today, it is evident that he spoke from an old-style Roman Catholicism that could self-confidently take its primary stand on the "catholicity from above" of a kingly Christ in the midst of his unified church, exuding the rosy scent of heaven. Yet de Lubac also opened the door to what has been termed "catholicity from below."

In *The Catholicity of the Church* Avery Dulles has a chapter with that title in which he briefly reviews the early twentieth-century debate on "pure nature," in which de Lubac was one of the major figures. Defenders of the "pure nature" position argued that God and nature are so radically distinct that, on its own, nature would never move toward God. De Lubac, harking back to some of the great figures of the patristic era, championed the opposing view "that human nature is intrinsically ordered toward the goal of eternal blessedness in God through Christ."[1] The implication is that it could be possible to discover at least

---

[1] Avery Dulles, *The Catholicity of the Church* (Oxford, UK: Clarendon Press, 1985), 57.

the general outlines of an orientation to catholicity by a more empirical or phenomenological approach, rather than requiring a theological framework as a starting point.

From a "Below-Above" Paradigm to a "Within" Paradigm

A traditional "from above" perspective focuses on the revealed action of a transcendent God who is ultimately the creator of life and spirit, while a strictly "from below" perspective, such as that of empirical science or historical-critical research, studies what can be measured, documented, and verified in the physical and/or social worlds. Almost fifty years ago Christopher Mooney noted that all christological doctrines begin "from below"—that is, with people experiencing Jesus and trying to understand him. Mooney's point was that in the modern world, when the developed doctrines that affirm Christ's "from above" status are extremely difficult to explain in terms that make sense to people steeped in an evolutionary and scientific worldview, theologians and preachers need to retrace the route "from below."[2] Awareness of this need has fueled the burgeoning contributions of historical-critical and socio-scientific research to theology over the last hundred years or so.

James Loder, who bases his thought in that of Karl Barth, argues that the Chalcedonian definition of Christ as both human and divine justifies seeing approaches from below and above as forming a "bipolar unity." This, in turn, allows the theologian to enter a dynamic exchange of views between theology and the empirical and human sciences. For Loder, however, theological categories ("from above") always retain "ontological priority," and in some sense they "negate" the view of the secular sciences.[3] Thus, the imagery of "above" and "below" remains problematic

---

[2] Christopher F. Mooney, "Christology and the Contemporary American Experience," in *Catholic Theological Society of America: Proceedings of the 26th Annual Convention, Baltimore, Maryland, June 14–17, 1971* (1972): 38–55.

[3] James E. Loder, *The Logic of the Spirit: Human Development in Theological Perspective* (San Francisco: Jossey-Bass Publishers, 1998), 33–41.

insofar as it suggests that the method of discovering God's action in creation is inevitably a rather fraught "either-or," with no real possibility of meeting in the middle.

Our approach here builds on figures such as de Lubac and Zizioulas, as well as other developments in theology, that open the door to a paradigm of observing God acting "from within" creation. Theologically, this approach is based in the conviction that the Spirit of God has been, and is, active always and everywhere in creation. The "catholicizing" activity of the Spirit can, in some sense, be discovered in aspects of the natural world as well as in all human beings, regardless of their religious affiliation.

It is important to acknowledge that my own perspective and training is that of Roman Catholic theology. Thus, I do not envision the Holy Spirit as an independent character but rather as a Person within the divine Trinity which is always wholly implicated in the acts of any of its Persons. Indeed, the fullness of the activity of the Holy Spirit cannot be envisioned apart from the complete participation of the Father and the Son. However, in this project my entry point will be through the Spirit, meaning that the other Persons of the Trinity come into focus only insofar as the specificity of their contribution appears in the process of exploring the activity of the Spirit. Moreover, my initial focus will be on the universal presence and activity of the Spirit, rather than on its action in the specific stories of salvation history.

This is an unusual approach, since it is more common to focus on the Father or the Son, leaving the Spirit to appear somewhat peripherally. Ultimately, we must affirm that the missions of the Son and of the Spirit are both essential to the rhythms of catholicity. Clark Pinnock suggests that "Christ, the only mediator, sustains particularity, while Spirit, the presence of God everywhere, safeguards universality."[4] By focusing on the Spirit, however, we hope to gain a perspective on Christian spirituality that is more accessible and more inclusive, rather than appealing simply to those who are already deeply ensconced in the worldview of Christianity. The churches (at least in the Western world) are hemorrhaging members these days, and while the reasons are

---

[4] Clark H. Pinnock, *Flame of Love: A Theology of the Holy Spirit* (Downers Grove, IL: InterVarsity Press, 2015), 192.

complex, the stumbling block for many is that church teaching connects with neither their lived spiritual experience nor their scientifically informed worldview. Hopefully, this approach may facilitate some of those connections, thus opening conversations that have too long been closed off.

Teilhard de Chardin on Christ's "Third Nature"

Almost fifty years before Mooney's comments about the need to honor "from below" research, Teilhard de Chardin made the even more radical argument that today's world demands that we resolve the apparent antinomy created by focusing on Christ's nature as either human ("from below") or divine ("from above") by recognizing a third nature, "a cosmic nature, enabling him to center all the lives which constitute a pleroma extended to the galaxies."[5] Teilhard took the Greek term *pleroma*, meaning "fullness" or "completion," from such scriptural texts as: "For in [Christ] all the fullness of God was pleased to dwell, and through him to reconcile to himself all things, whether on earth or in heaven, making peace by the blood of his cross" (Col 1:19–20).[6] For Teilhard, *pleromization* means the evolutionary process of the created universe driving toward the creative union of all in the fullness of the cosmic Christ.[7]

In his book on catholicity Avery Dulles discusses the *pleroma* texts in his chapter on "catholicity from above," thereby suggesting that their import is that Christ's fullness precedes its impact on the created world.[8] As noted, however, for Teilhard, Christ's "third nature" is to be the cosmic Omega Point of the evolving universe, which is itself the *pleroma* or fullness of life.[9] From this perspective the categories of "from below" and "from above" fade into the background in the one dynamic, divinely

---

[5] Pierre Teilhard de Chardin, *Christianity and Evolution*, trans. René Hague (New York: Harcourt, 2002), 236n.

[6] See also Col 2:9–10; Eph 1:22–23; 3:19; 4:10–13.

[7] Teilhard de Chardin, *Christianity and Evolution*, 183, 198.

[8] Dulles, *The Catholicity of the Church*, chap. 2.

[9] Teilhard de Chardin, *Christianity and Evolution*, 180.

constituted process of the cosmos rushing toward its divine fulfillment. Thus, in contradistinction to the Barthian tradition represented by Loder, Teilhard posits an eschatological "from within" principle within Christology.

Considering our earlier discussion of Zizioulas's contention that Christianity's great innovation was a shift from an ontology of substance to an ontology of personhood, it is noteworthy that Teilhard articulated a similar shift while situating it clearly within the evolutionary worldview. The traditional "metaphysics of being," Teilhard observes, posits a God who "monopolizes all that is absolute and necessary in being," thus leaving no place for participated being. The implication of such a position is that all of creation's arduous becoming, and all the suffering of myriads of sentient beings, contribute nothing to God's already-complete perfection. A "metaphysics of uniting," however, posits a God who is eternally both united-in-Godself and uniting-of-multiplicity. Teilhard concludes, "The created, which is 'useless,' superfluous on the plane of being, becomes essential on the plane of union."[10]

A "metaphysics of uniting" could perhaps also be termed a "metaphysics of catholicity," although Teilhard himself did not use that term. As already noted, Teilhard envisioned the cosmic movement of uniting as centered in the cosmic nature of Christ, thus giving "a heart" and "a face" to what might otherwise seem like an impersonal tide dragging creation toward greater complexity and union.[11] Ultimately, for Teilhard, union is the communion of all the multiplicity of creation in the person of Christ. This communion is, in fact, both the deepest reality of the present and the eschatological hope of the future.

"Catholicity from within," then, identifies a dynamism toward unity-in-diversity as built into creation by God. Methodologically, "catholicity from within" has two faces. One is drawn from recent panentheistic theologies that depict God as at work within the natural creative and evolutionary processes of the cosmos. The other is more specific to spirituality, exploring human experience as a source for theological insight.

---

[10] Teilhard de Chardin, *Christianity and Evolution*, 178.
[11] Teilhard de Chardin, *Christianity and Evolution*, 180.

Panentheistic Theologies

Approaches strictly "from below" foster much insight but ultimately become untenable because the Spirit can never be reduced to an aspect of creation. Approaches "from above," however, get into trouble when they cannot find a plausible way to cross the abyss they have envisioned between God and creation. An approach "from within" takes the position that God is genuinely present within all of created reality, although never reducible to it. The technical term for this kind of theology is *panentheism,* a middle way between classical theism, which portrays God transcendently "above" creation, and pantheism, which does not distinguish God from the world. The image of the Spirit breathing within all of creation expresses a panentheistic approach.

Defining *panentheism* as "the claim that the world exists within the Divine, although God is more than the world,"[12] Philip Clayton identifies a range of current panentheistic theologies. Some actually differ little from classical theism, while others shade into a version of naturalistic pantheism. Our approach in this book has some elements in common with what Clayton terms "mystical" or "apophatic" panentheism, which discovers in God the radical interconnection of all things and articulates it by drawing upon scientific as well as aesthetic analogies. His prime example is Catherine Keller's *Cloud of the Impossible.*[13] However, rather than following process philosopher Keller's exuberant (and often delightfully outrageous!) theopoetics, we draw upon approaches like those of Catholic theologians Elizabeth Johnson and Denis Edwards, whose relational theologies are articulated in careful dialogue with classical traditions.

Denis Edwards, for example, applies the poetic line of Gerard Manley Hopkins, "There lives the dearest freshness deep down things," to the Spirit. Then he connects this to Thomas Aquinas, who writes: "Now existence is more intimately and profoundly

---

[12] Philip Clayton, "How Radically Can God Be Reconceived before Ceasing to Be God?: The Four Faces of Panentheism," *Zygon* 52, no. 4 (December 2017): 1045.

[13] Catherine Keller, *Cloud of the Impossible: Negative Theology and Planetary Entanglement*, Insurrections: Critical Studies in Religion, Politics, and Culture (New York: Columbia University Press, 2015).

interior to things than anything else. . . . So God must exist and exist intimately in everything" (ST 1.8.2). Finally, Edwards shows how Karl Rahner brings this tradition into the age of evolution by affirming that God is not only the dynamic cause of the existence of creatures, but also of their becoming. Creation is "actively self-transcending" as it not only manifests continuity and conservation, but also the emergence of truly new things. God does not intervene from without; nor does the interiority of God in creatures overpower the creature's own proper activity. Rather, creatures are empowered and fulfilled by the self-giving interiority of the Spirit within them.[14]

Edwards develops the image of the Spirit that breathes in creation, grace, incarnation, and church. He writes:

> As the universe expands and evolves in an emergent process, it is the Breath of God that empowers and enables the whole process from within. The Spirit enables the emergence of the new at every stage from the first nuclei of hydrogen and helium, to atoms, galaxies, the Sun, bacterial forms of life, complex cells, the wonderfully diverse forms of life on Earth, and human beings who can think and love and praise.[15]

Edwards refers here to scientific theories of "emergence," which assert that over time, natural dynamics can produce new levels of complexity that operate in ways not predictable only on the basis of the lower-level dynamics. The emergence of life from inanimate molecules and the emergence of mind from biological systems are perhaps the two premier examples. In *The Emergence of Everything*, biologist Harold J. Morowitz identified thirty-two distinct emergences during the evolutionary process on planet Earth.[16]

---

[14] Denis Edwards, "Ecology and the Holy Spirit: The 'Already' and the 'Not Yet' of the Spirit in Creation," *Pacifica* 13 (2000): 142–48.

[15] Denis Edwards, *Breath of Life: A Theology of the Creator Spirit* (Maryknoll, NY: Orbis Books, 2004), 43–44.

[16] Harold J. Morowitz, *The Emergence of Everything: How the World Became Complex* (New York: Oxford University Press, 2004).

Theories that endorse only what is called "weak emergence" remain committed to a reductionist metaphysics, asserting that even though new levels emerge, everything can still ultimately be explained by the known laws of physics. Some forms of "strong emergence," however, offer a third way between such reductionist physicalism and more dualistic theories. A "strong emergence" theory is one that asserts that evolution produces genuinely novel phenomena that cannot be fully predicted or explained by previously understood physical laws.[17] Scientists tend to scoff at theological use of theories of emergence when they are employed as a kind of "magic wand"—"a strange mystical power within evolution that constantly works to lift the universe to new levels of reality."[18] Nonetheless, emergence theories do offer a way to envision creation as bearing within itself an endlessly creative potential that is not locked in by what we currently are able to see and understand. From a theological perspective, this is an opening for a theology of the Spirit as working in creation from within.

The theology of "deep incarnation" is a more recently developed approach to articulating a panentheistic, "from within" approach.[19] This is an ecological theology that explores the implications of the fact that, like any human body, the body of the human Jesus participated fully in the necessary fleshly conditions of life. There is a sense in which the boundary of any living body, including the human body of Jesus of Nazareth, is artificial; no living thing can come into existence or survive without interdependent relations with the ecological networks of air, water, soil, and living creatures. The incarnation, therefore, does not implicate simply one historical person's body but overflows to everything his body ever interacted with and to everything those things ever interacted with . . . and so, ultimately, to the extent of the entire physical cosmos. Niels Henrik Gregersen, for example, states:

---

[17] Philip Clayton, *Mind and Emergence: From Quantum to Consciousness* (Oxford: Oxford University Press, 2008), 39.

[18] Clayton, *Mind and Emergence*, 47.

[19] Niels Henrik Gregersen, "Deep Incarnation: From Deep History to Post-Axial Religion," *Hervormde Teologiese Studies* 72, no. 4 (2016): 1–12; Niels Henrik Gregersen, ed., *Incarnation: On the Scope and Depth of Christology* (Minneapolis: Fortress Press, 2015).

"Deep incarnation" is the view that God's own Logos (Wisdom and Word) was made flesh in Jesus the Christ in such a comprehensive manner that God, by assuming the particular life story of Jesus the Jew from Nazareth, also conjoined the material conditions of creaturely existence ("all flesh"), shared and ennobled the fate of all biological life forms ("grass" and "lilies"), and experienced the pains of sensitive creatures ("sparrows" and "foxes") from within.[20]

The theology of "deep incarnation," then, is another way of articulating what Teilhard would call the cosmic nature of Christ as totally implicated in every aspect of the evolving physical universe. One of the methodological implications of this is to affirm the validity of employing scientific research as a theological source. In this book, for example, we review the results of various researchers in such fields as sociology, psychology, and physics. The claim of "catholicity from within" is not that scientific research alone can discover the catholicizing trajectory of the Spirit. As Jan-Olav Henriksen notes, "Unlike pantheism, which identifies God and the world, panentheism maintains a difference between God and the world that does not require us to take the present state of affairs to be one in which the reality of God is fully displayed."[21] The claim, rather, is that giving science its due is an essential aspect of uncovering patterns and tendencies that must then be placed in dialogue with our more traditional theological sources.

Spirituality and the "Within" of Experience

As noted earlier, the panentheistic "deep incarnation" perspective asserts that the incarnation reveals God participating in both the material conditions of earthly existence and the "within"

---

[20] Niels Henrik Gregersen, "The Extended Body of Christ: Three Dimensions of Deep Incarnation," in Gregersen, *Incarnation*, 225–26.

[21] Jan-Olav Henriksen, "The Experience of God and the World: Christianity's Reasons for Considering Panentheism a Viable Option," *Zygon* 52, no. 4 (December 2017): 1081.

experience of all sentient creatures. This leads us to our second methodological consideration, which is more specific to spirituality (as distinct from other academic fields of inquiry). In studying spirituality, attention to experience is not only acceptable but actually constitutive.[22] Spirituality is a lived experience of the human spirit desiring, seeking, and celebrating communion with what is perceived as worthy of love and self-giving. In this quest, every aspect of human life may potentially be subsumed—whether more classical spiritual practices such as singing, meditating, reading, and ritualizing, or supposedly secular activities such as sexuality, family life, sports, and civic participation. These various activities, and the artifacts that they engender, can, of course, be studied by a variety of methods. To study the life of the human spirit, however, one must attend to experience.

Admittedly, attending to experience is far from a simple practice. Experience engages the most intimate dimension of a person and has an intrinsic ineffable quality so that it can never be grasped or articulated with full adequacy. Regardless of the medium persons use to convey their experience to others, it will be interpreted through the lenses of genre, language, culture, and audience expectations. Claims made on the basis of experience cannot automatically be accepted as valid.[23] Nonetheless, experience—including its ineffability—is constitutive of what it means to be spirit.

The perspective of "catholicity from within" is that the Spirit of God in mutual indwelling with the human spirit fuels the spiritual urge to find and participate in ever more profound dimensions of communion with what one perceives as worthy of love. This is true of all human beings, even prior to conscious awareness or intention to seek God explicitly. Of course, as in any relationship, conscious intention and commitment open far greater potential depths of communion in the Spirit. Yet the essential longing and trajectory is built into us; we seek the ecstasy

---

[22] Mary Frohlich, "Spiritual Discipline, Discipline of Spirituality: Revisiting Questions of Definition and Method," *Spiritus* 1, no. 1 (March 1, 2001): 65–78; Mary Frohlich, "Critical Interiority," *Spiritus* 7, no. 1 (March 1, 2007): 77–81.

[23] George P. Schner, "The Appeal to Experience," *Theological Studies* 53, no. 1 (March 1992): 40–59.

of belonging to a greater whole, even when that urge is badly misdirected, as in addictions or communal violence. Although this can be tracked from the "outside" to some degree, it is essentially an inner movement known experientially.

Regarding method, the approach taken here also draws on that proposed by Hans Urs von Balthasar, who argued that the experiences of the saints should be regarded as theological sources because they (the saints) actually participate in the experiences and states of Christ.[24] As Mark McIntosh explains, this is "not so much a bringing forward of the past into the present experience of the believer, but a participation of the believer in the eternal aspect of definitive historical saving events."[25] Thus for von Balthasar, the interior experiences of the saints should be recognized as among the most authentic witnesses to the saving action of God in Christ.

Another quotation from McIntosh's interpretation of von Balthasar will help us transition to the approach employed in this book:

> Because of the creation of all things in Christ, certain patterns of self-giving love are inherent foundational structures in historical existence—rather like the way gravity necessarily structures physical existence; to live according to these habits of life is to live freely, unencumbered by fighting against the grain. But Jesus Christ is the true identity of these structures of existence; they turn out to be not abstract laws but the historical dimensions of a personal being.[26]

As discussed earlier in this chapter, our intention is to talk about the spiritual life with a primary focus on the Holy Spirit rather than on the Father or the Son. Again, the three Persons

---

[24] Hans Urs von Balthasar, "Theology and Sanctity," in *Explorations in Theology I: The Word Made Flesh*, trans. A. V. Littledale and Alexander Dru (San Francisco: Ignatius Press, 1989).

[25] Mark Allen McIntosh, *Christology from Within: Spirituality and the Incarnation in Hans Urs von Balthasar* (Notre Dame, IN: University of Notre Dame Press, 2000), 17.

[26] McIntosh, *Christology from Within*, 22.

of the Trinity are one God, so all are implicated in the activity of any of them. However, by shifting the focus to the Spirit, we gain greater potential for seeing how God is at work always and everywhere—not only when there is explicit and conscious reference to the historical activities of Jesus Christ.

The quotation above refers to von Balthasar's contention that Christ imbues historical existence with "certain patterns of self-giving love" that function like "gravity" in human lives. It is the role of the Holy Spirit, presumably, to mediate and activate these patterns in the actual historical circumstances of people's lives. Claiming that this applies to all human beings, whether Christian believers or not, does not require reducing the action of the Spirit to "abstract laws." With fidelity to a panentheistic perspective, it need not be contradictory to affirm the personal action of divine Spirit as working within patterns that have also in some sense been "built in" to creation.

Methodologically, this has two implications. One is that the spiritual experiences of all human beings (not only "saints") can be taken seriously as a source for understanding the action of Spirit. The second is that, insofar as phenomenological analysis or empirical research can discover patterns in religious and spiritual experiences, these too can be considered as potentially offering insight into how Spirit works in human life. Again, none of this means that one can extrapolate directly from accounts of experience or from empirical research results to full-fledged theological conclusions. Nonetheless, such an approach may be able to offer key insights into what may foster (or impede) the "catholicizing" movement of the Spirit.

Spirit as "Field"

Considering this project's focus on how the rhythms of the Spirit play out in human life, we introduce here a helpful pneumato-logical analogy. The reasons for this choice, as well as its implica-tions, will be developed more fully in Chapter 6.

The Hebrew *ruach* is both the breath of life that God breathed into the human being made from dust (cf. Gen 2:7), and the wind or storm that blows over the formless void at creation (cf. Gen 1:2). While the metaphor of breath evokes the vitality and

intimacy of the Spirit, the metaphor of wind evokes the vastness, variability, and unpredictability of Spirit as always with
us yet implacably "other." Wind has some characteristics that
make it a good analogy to the "field" in field theory, which some
theologians have proposed as a helpful way to think about the
Holy Spirit. The value of field theory is that it shifts focus from
individual particles or objects that exert force upon one another
to a total environment that exerts influence in a manner distinct
from that of objects.

In using the analogy of the field for Spirit, I make no claims
to having the technical scientific background to develop it in
an in-depth dialogue with the physical science of classical or
quantum fields. Indeed, some physicists have severely criticized
such a theological approach as a misinterpretation of what the
science of fields actually says.[27] Wolfhart Pannenberg, who may
be the most widely known theologian to have presented the
field analogy, responds that the broader concept of field theory
is not limited to its meaning in physics, since there are also field
theories in psychology, sociology, and mathematics. Moreover,
he notes, the concept of field actually precedes all these specific
theories, harking back to Stoic philosophies.[28] Thus, as in the
writings of Pannenberg and Michael Welker,[29] *field* is employed
as an intriguing analogy that may have potential to resolve certain issues, to open up new avenues for theological exploration,
and to stimulate further dialogue with scientific perspectives.

Pannenberg argues that a field analogy for Holy Spirit is pref-
erable to those that analogize the Spirit to any kind of localized
entity, even a "mind" or "person."[30] The common element in
the various kinds of field theories (for example, in mathematics,

[27] J. C. Polkinghorne, "Wolfhart Pannenberg's Engagement with the
Natural Sciences," *Zygon* 34, no. 1 (March 1999): 151–58; J. C. Polk-
inghorne, "Fields and Theology: A Response to Wolfhart Pannenberg,"
Zygon 36, no. 4 (December 2001): 795–97.

[28] Wolfhart Pannenberg, "God as Spirit—and Natural Science," *Zygon* 36, no. 4 (December 2001): 783–94.

[29] Michael Welker, *God the Spirit*, trans. John F. Hoffmeyer (Minneapolis: Fortress Press, 1994).

[30] Wolfhart Pannenberg, *Toward a Theology of Nature: Essays on
Science and Faith*, ed. Ted Peters (Louisville, KY: Westminster/John Knox
Press, 1993), 37–41; Pannenberg, "God as Spirit—and Natural Science."

physics, psychology, sociology, and so on) is that the field pervades an extensive environment and produces measurable effects. Whapham proposes that in physics, fields "can be defined as immaterial physical properties of space that interact with matter in ways which can be quantified by measurement."[31] Familiar examples of such physical fields are gravity and magnetism, which measurably move objects without having material presence. In psychology, a field is understood as the total life space encompassing everything that influences a person and that the person influences. In quantum physics the meaning is more complex; the quanta of elementary entities may appear either as a wave-like, non-localized field or as a localized particle, and it is not possible to say that it is only one or the other.

Pannenberg does not claim to use the term *field* in exact correspondence to any of these scientific fields but instead develops it uniquely as a theological analogy. He references ancient Greek traditions such as those of Anaximenes and, later, the Stoics, who understood *pneuma* (Spirit) as "a most subtle matter that penetrates everything and holds the cosmos together by the powerful tension between its different parts."[32] Pannenberg notes that it was because the Stoics envisioned *pneuma* as material that early Christian thinkers (spearheaded in particular by Origen) rejected Stoic metaphysics in favor of a more Platonic approach that understood spirit as immaterial *nous* or "mind." Modern field theories, however, eliminate this idea of a pervasive material substance and instead envision the field of force as strictly immaterial. Pannenberg believes that the statement of John 4:24, "God is Spirit," is actually better served by a field theory of *pneuma* than by the classical concept of the "divine mind."[33]

The Holy Spirit, then, is like a field of force in creation that animates and unites all things and draws all toward consummation. God can give creatures freedom in space and time while being "the ground or the field in which the drama of creation unfolds."[34] The divine Spirit-field is eternal because it is simul-

---

[31] Theodore James Whapham, "Spirit as Field of Force," *Scottish Journal of Theology* 67, no. 1 (2014): 19.

[32] Pannenberg, *Toward a Theology of Nature*, 39.

[33] Pannenberg, "God as Spirit—and Natural Science," 787.

[34] Whapham, "Spirit as Field of Force," 26.

taneously present to all of history and all of life. Thus, the field analogy for Spirit offers a view that combines the independence of creation with God's eternity. It also describes how individuality and radical interconnectedness are both integral to each created being. Whapham summarizes: "The spirituality of God is constituted by the field of being which allows the other to be in its own uniqueness and independence while simultaneously securing the unity of the individuals through their interrelationships."[35]

The next chapter applies this method of "catholicity from within" by exploring human experiences of the Spirit from various vantage points, including poetic and biblical reflections as well as phenomenological enquiries. The focus is on how human beings discover, name, and build their life stories around the catholicizing movements of the Spirit.

---

[35] Whapham, "Spirit as Field of Force," 31.

Chapter 2

Discovering Spirit in Human Experience

On the last day of a recent retreat the spiritual teacher Ishpriya, RSCJ, gave us an exercise that was quite revelatory. She said: "Take fifteen minutes to just sit and do nothing. Don't daydream, don't plan, don't reminisce, and don't say prayers. Just do absolutely nothing." So, I went and sat on a bench in the retreat center garden and did nothing. Of course, my mind continued to churn, but I let each thought go its way and returned to doing nothing. The birds chirped and fluttered. The plants and flowers exuded their perfumes. The trees danced in the breeze. Now and then a cloud brought a moment of coolness, followed by the return of the warmth of sun on my skin. The whole world seemed to glow with an Edenic quality of silence, beauty, and peace. All this, just from doing nothing!

The revelatory aspect of this exercise is the discovery that in itself, the world is already whole and at peace; the problem lies in us human beings, who are caught up in practices and attitudes that generate fragmentation and anxiety. And in this lies the root of all spiritualities: the human longing to come home to an encompassing awareness of peace, authenticity, and tender communion. Ronald Rolheiser's book *The Holy Longing* has sold thousands of copies because he so poignantly and astutely describes how this itch for deep wholeness plays in all our ordinary human pursuits.[1] Later in this chapter we examine examples

---

[1] Ronald Rolheiser, *The Holy Longing: The Search for a Christian Spirituality* (New York: Image, 2009).

of how people receive glimpses and tastes of the wholeness that is always awaiting us, yet seems so elusive.

The "doing nothing" exercise had another fruit. Along with the sounds of birds and the fragrances of plants, the sound and power of wind took on new prominence. Gradually, the body's quiet rhythm of breathing also emerged softly into awareness. As is well known, in both Hebrew and Greek biblical traditions the word translated as "spirit" is the same as the word for breath and wind. Clearly, ancient peoples recognized profound similarities among all three. Reflection on the experiences of wind and breath can give us an initial insight into what we mean by "spirit."

Wind

Wind has many faces, from the whispering breeze to the wild tempest. While a weather report can indicate the prevailing speed and direction of the wind in our area, we rarely experience it as simply a steady draft blowing in one direction. As wind interacts with mountains, bodies of water, buildings, changing air pressures, and anything else that it encounters, it becomes a dance of currents that come and go, now in this direction, now in that. These movements are unpredictable, at least from our viewpoint. Even when we think we are prepared, we are surprised when a sudden gust blows off our hat or the wind in a field dies down just as we are expecting it to launch our kite.

When we are in the mood for it, the capriciousness of the wind can seem playful. The leaves and branches of the trees sway hither and thither, and it is a delight to watch their dancing movements. The wind can be like an artist painting in swaying grass or making music with its pulses of sound and quiet. A strong wind arouses awe as its majestic power flows above and all around us. A soft wind can feel tender as it caresses us and whispers in our ear.

But wind is not only playful; it can also be a most serious matter. A breeze may literally be life saving when the weather is brutally hot. By drying our perspiration, it gives the body a chance to catch up in its efforts to throw off heat. In winter, however, even a relatively gentle breeze can reduce the experienced temperature by enough to greatly increase the risk for anyone who goes outdoors without sufficient protection. A wet body loses heat far more quickly, so a hiker caught in the rain when a chilly breeze is blowing can be surprised by symptoms of hypothermia, even when the ambient temperature does not feel that low.

Then there are the occasions when wind terrifies. On a mountain trail, an unobstructed gale-force gust threatens to send the hiker over a precipice. Even in the city, strong winds channeled down a street by tall buildings can knock over the elderly and others not sure on their feet. At night the sound of wild winds rattling our windows and doors brings turmoil and anxiety into our dreams. Finally, a true storm of wind—a hurricane, tempest, typhoon, or tornado—is almost unparalleled in the devastation it can wreak within a few short moments.

The ancient people, who gave wind and spirit the same name, knew all these faces of the wind. They knew wind as both playful and powerful, life saving and terrifying. Most of all, they knew that it was not under their control. "The wind blows where it chooses, and you hear the sound of it, but you do not know where it comes from or where it goes. So it is with everyone who is born of the Spirit" (John 3:8). This gospel text makes the analogy explicit. Wind and spirit are ever present in our lives, yet we will never cease to be surprised by the patterns of their movement.

Breath

Common to wind and breath is that they both move the air, yet beyond that, many aspects of their fundamental character are different. Most notably, wind impacts us from the outside, while breath moves us from within. A strong wind or a cool breeze is felt by all those within its reach, which could be thousands of square miles; a breath is known fully only by the breather, and can be directly shared only with someone who is physically very close to us. While wind may be unidirectional or fitful, breath must remain basically regular and rhythmic. Wind has an extraordinarily broad spectrum of speeds and patterns of movement; breath is far more limited in its changes. After further consideration of breath, we must ask the question again: Why have many traditions given wind, breath, and spirit the same name?

Breath is our ultimate vulnerability. Deprived of breath for as little as five minutes, our brains may be irreparably damaged; five minutes more, and life is over. The average person breathes twenty thousand or more times in a single day. The constant movement of the breath is an ever-present reminder that everything is impermanent.[2] Still, as long as we are alive, we are never without the pulsation of breath, even when asleep or completely unconscious. Yet, despite its quality of being both ever present and obligatory, it is possible to pass a whole day, or many days, without ever noticing the breath. If we do notice it, most often it is because a sudden change in physical exertion makes us breathe more deeply and urgently than usual. Something that makes us cough or sneeze, such as pollen, dust, or smoke, also draws sudden attention to the act of breathing. The temporary sensation of choking sets off a tremor of alarm, even when we know there is no real danger.

Breath practices are a staple of many spiritual traditions. Watching the breath, counting breaths, and slowing or deepening the breath are all ways of focusing attention and enhancing inner awareness. Intensive practitioners in some traditions may learn unusual feats of slowing the breath or techniques that use it as a path to altered states of consciousness. Professional athletes, too, learn to use their breathing as a tool to maximize achievement in their chosen sport. While cultivation of such practices is sometimes called breath control, the truth is that our own breathing is never fully under our control. It is an autonomic function that the conscious mind can channel and guide only to a certain degree.

Day in and day out, in good times and bad, each breath arrives as a gift and goes forth as a surrender. Whether we find this rhythm of gratuity delightful or unnerving, it continues. Even more than is the case with the wind, we do not know where breath comes from or where it is going. Breathing is perhaps our

---

[2] Maxine Sheets-Johnstone, "On the Elusive Nature of the Human Self: Divining the Ontological Dynamics of Animate Being," in *In Search of Self: Interdisciplinary Perspectives on Personhood*, ed. J. Wentzel Van Huyssteen and Erik P. Wiebe (Grand Rapids, MI: Eerdmans, 2011), 216.

act of greatest intimacy with our own inner depths. Yet, from the point of view of consciousness, the inner origin of breath is a mystery in the sense that we cannot grasp or comprehend it, even if we affirm a conceptual belief that—as Genesis 2:7 tells us—it was God who breathed the breath of life into the nostrils of the earth-creature made of dust.

In Jewish and Christian Scriptures, then, the reception of life-breath may be a direct connection to its divine giver, and the surrender of each outbreath a letting go to the Creator. In the Gospel of John, Jesus is depicted as "breathing out" his spirit on the cross (John 19:30) and then, after the resurrection, "breathing on" the disciples as he says, "Receive the Holy Spirit" (John 20:22). In these stories, the human breath of Jesus actually becomes the outpoured gift of the divine Spirit.

Spirit

Spirit, then, is like wind in its awe-inspiring power, its seemingly serendipitous movements, and its potential to give or take life. Spirit is like breath in its faithful accompaniment of our daily lives, its tender intimacy, and its urgency toward the maintenance of life. Spirit is both within us and beyond us; it both belongs intimately to each one of us and is completely beyond our control.

It is important to recall that neither biblical Hebrew nor biblical Greek uses capital letters, so the convention of translating *ruach* and *pneuma* as "Spirit" with a capital "S" when it appears to refer to divine Spirit is the translator's addition to the original biblical texts. The danger of the capital "S" is that it may lead us to reify God as existing in some other realm, quite distinct from this one that we experience on a daily basis. With all due respect for the unique, irreducible aspect of God's transcendence, the full biblical portrayal does not justify relegating God to another realm. Jürgen Moltmann observes that the Hebrew *ruach* may have originally been an onomatopoeic word for "gale." Thus the *ruach Yahweh* is "a tempest, a storm, a force in body and soul, humanity and nature."[3] It is alive, moving, creative, and full of

---

[3] Jürgen Moltmann, *The Spirit of Life: A Universal Affirmation* (Minneapolis: Fortress Press, 2001), 40.

energy. It confronts people with God's presence, and at the same time it is handed over to living beings as the energy of their own lives. Thus, "it is not wrong to talk about the Spirit as the 'drive' or 'instinct' awakened by God."[4] Moltmann emphasizes that Spirit is found both in God's *immanence* in human experience and in the *transcendence* of human beings in God. Similar to the approach of "catholicity from within," Moltmann concludes that the presence of God's Spirit is in human beings the means by which "the human spirit is self-transcendently aligned towards God."[5]

The Johannine texts quoted above identify the human breath of Jesus with "spirit," thus imaging Spirit as dwelling within his bodiliness in the same permeating way that breath dwells within our own bodiliness. Spirit, then, is a dynamism like breathing in and breathing out. On the one hand, spirit is an inward movement, drawing in what the organism needs and expanding the space within; on the other hand, it is an outward movement, releasing what has been within into the world as it empties the inner cavity of the body. In the life of the human spirit the inward movement is an immediacy of inner communion, while the outward movement interprets that experience so that it can be mediated outward into the person's mental and social networks. These two movements are completely integral to each other; there cannot be one without the other, and the cessation of either is the cessation of life itself. The life of the spirit is a rhythm of inward and outward movements, receiving and giving, expanding and pouring out, over and over. Thus, the dynamism of spirit continually refreshes and reinterprets experience as long as life continues.

Religious and Spiritual Experiences

What kind of human experiences reveal a "catholicizing" movement of the spirit? Before asking that question, we will review a careful phenomenological classification of different types of religious and spiritual experiences that has been developed by Wesley J. Wildman. He begins with the broad, inclusive term

---

[4] Moltmann, *The Spirit of Life*, 42.
[5] Moltmann, *The Spirit of Life*, 7.

"religious and spiritual experiences" because, he says, to refer only to "spiritual experiences" is to "risk emphasizing individual states of consciousness at the expense of the corporate dimensions of experience." Yet to refer only to "religious experiences" risks leaving out people who don't regard their experiences as "religious."[6] Within this broad field he distinguishes several overlapping types of experiences.

A very broad category is *religious experiences*. While acknowledging that *religion* is almost impossible to define with exactitude, he accepts a commonsense meaning and defines religious experiences simply as "experiences people have by virtue of being religious or being involved in religious groups."[7] It is an extremely diverse category that includes some vivid experiences (see below), but also many other kinds of experiences that may even be mundane and routinized. Daily prayer and worship, for example, may lack novelty and excitement, yet nonetheless be an important experiential source of meaning and energy for people.

A partially overlapping, partially distinct category is *vivid experiences*. These are "the relatively unusual, typically colorful states of consciousness that are either of enormous religious or spiritual significance, or else are very strange and of deeply uncertain meaning."[8] They may or may not be religious. Vivid experiences include two major overlapping classes: "anomalous experiences" (the strange and bizarre) and "ultimacy experiences."

Anomalous experiences are extremely diverse. They include hallucinations, out-of-body experiences, alien abductions, uncanny insights, and other "weird" events. Their major characteristic is the sense of subjective strangeness, as they "apparently violate the operations of the world as these are understood in normal life."[9] In some cases strange experiences can be created by the manipulation of light, music, or cultic relationships, but more often they strike "out of the blue." They tend to shake and disturb people, both emotionally and cognitively. While they often

[6] Wesley J. Wildman, *Religious and Spiritual Experiences* (Cambridge, UK: Cambridge University Press, 2011), 4.

[7] Wildman, *Religious and Spiritual Experiences*, 78.

[8] Wildman, *Religious and Spiritual Experiences*, 77.

[9] Wildman, *Religious and Spiritual Experiences*, 82.

arise apart from any association with religion or spirituality, their impact not infrequently includes the development of powerful convictions that are impervious to the more usual methods of verification.

Ultimacy experiences are life-changing, transformative experiences that people feel make a vital difference in the direction of their lives. This may include some anomalous experiences, for example, if a person has a vision of a divine figure or feels that prayer has been answered in an extraordinary way. More often, however, the feelings accompanying ultimacy experiences are ones of comfort, excitement, or joy, rather than strangeness. Ultimacy experiences "bring orientation and coping power, inspire great acts of courage and devotion, underlie key life decisions, and heavily influence social affiliation."[10]

While anomalous experiences are usually here and gone, leaving behind a frisson of uncanniness, ultimacy experiences can be either brief or more extended in time. According to research by Wildman and Leslie Brothers, more discrete ultimacy experiences tend to involve five recurring elements: alterations of sense experience; alterations of the sense of self; an awareness of "presences"; cognitive insights; and strong emotions.[11] They often occur at the beginning of a process of personal transformation and sometimes recur periodically during it. Extended ultimacy experiences, however, are often social processes of orientation and control, for example, formation processes. Wildman notes that "many extended ultimacy experiences serve simultaneously as social experiences of orientation and as provocations to transformation."[12] They may also occur as more informal, gradual processes of personal change.

For Wildman, *spiritual experiences* is a category that includes "the entire range of significant experiences . . . that is,

---

[10] Wildman, *Religious and Spiritual Experiences*, 84.

[11] Wesley J. Wildman and Leslie A. Brothers, "A Neuropsychological-Semiotic Model of Religious Experiences," in *Neuroscience and the Person: Scientific Perspectives on Divine Action*, ed. Robert J. Russell et al., Scientific Perspectives on Divine Action 4, 347–416 (Berkeley, CA: Vatican Observatory Foundation; Center for Theology and the Natural Sciences, 2002).

[12] Wildman, *Religious and Spiritual Experiences*, 84–85.

the ultimacy experiences—as well as a rather large chunk but definitely not all of the domain of religious experiences."[13] Thus, there can be "spiritual but not religious" experiences, for example, the ecstasy of a surfer catching a big wave; there can be "religious but not spiritual" experiences, for example, the routine of attending a catechism class; or there can be "religious and spiritual" experiences, for example, a feeling of joy upon receiving eucharistic communion.

Wildman's particular interest is a subclass of ultimacy experiences that he terms "intense experiences." They involve intensity in the sense of "high activation" but, more important, are of "intense existential significance."[14] Wildman notes that while particular types of intense experiences, such as mystical experiences and "bare consciousness" experiences,[15] have been much studied, few have attempted to look at the entire category. Although these experiences are highly diverse and occur unpredictably, most people have them at one time or another in their lives. People instantly recognize them as important, and they "often serve as touchstones for a person's self-interpretation." While the majority are positive, it is not always so; they can also be intensely disgusting or terrifying, for example. Some are spontaneous, while others are cultivated through spiritual practices or ingestion of chemicals. Religious groups often develop social and intellectual traditions that assist in cultivating, integrating, and interpreting these experiences. Nonreligious people, however, sometimes find them "difficult to assimilate for lack of any conceptual framework or social context for making sense of them."[16]

Wildman goes on to develop theories about how to assess the cognitive reliability of religious and spiritual experiences, as well as perspectives on why they emerged within human evolution and how the brain processes them. Our interest, however, is in exploring whether spiritual experiences actually function in human life in a "catholicizing" manner—that is, as turning points

---

[13] Wildman, *Religious and Spiritual Experiences*, 81.

[14] Wildman, *Religious and Spiritual Experiences*, 93.

[15] This phrase is from Robert K. C. Forman, ed., *The Problem of Pure Consciousness: Mysticism and Philosophy* (New York: Oxford University Press, 1990).

[16] Wildman, *Religious and Spiritual Experiences*, 96–97.

toward a life trajectory that is both more deeply rooted in the authenticity of one's local and individual existence and more widely open to realities beyond the self.

Patterns of Spiritual Experience

While I do not have Wildman's training in phenomenology, over the course of twenty-seven years of teaching spirituality courses in a graduate school of theology, I have engaged in a much more informal kind of exploration of spiritual experiences. In countless courses over those years, I have given some variation on this assignment: "Write a one- or two-page account of a significant spiritual experience that you have had." I purposely do not define *spiritual* for the students, because that is exactly what the assignment aims to discover. Using the range of experiences recounted by the class participants, the students then explore together the characteristics of spiritual experience. In this way we do a simple, nontechnical form of phenomenological research, using an inductive method to look for patterns and commonalities in what people understand as spiritual experience.

In reviewing what we have discovered through this exercise, it is noteworthy that, despite being given no definition of *spiritual,* nearly all the vignettes the students provide fit within the category Wildman so designates. Many are "intense" or "vivid" experiences; rarely are they what he calls "anomalous." Since I do not have permission from the students to retell their stories, the following summary and discussion of what I have learned from listening to these hundreds of accounts uses generalized versions and revised details. In a few cases I have included short quotations, usually those encapsulating the storyteller's feelings or discoveries in response to the event, taking care not to reveal the individual involved.

First, note that these stories come, not from a random sample of the population, but from theology and ministry students in a single graduate school in the United States. In terms of national origin, ethnicity, and culture, they are fairly diverse, with probably less than half being Caucasians born in the United States. Furthermore, over half are members of Roman Catholic religious congregations—a unique and specialized lifestyle that commits participants to a relatively intense focus on the spiritual life. Another 15 to 20 percent are Protestant seminarians or clergy. Despite this, I suspect that the basic characteristics of the spiritual experiences they describe would also be found in a broader sample. Confirming that, however, would be a topic for future research.

First characteristic: Spiritual experience is a singular, supremely memorable event in a unique life narrative. Each year, reading and discussing fifteen or twenty of these accounts, I am always struck by the uniqueness of each one. The stories are anything but formulaic. It would be impossible to list all the circumstances in which the events occur, so the following is just a sampling (again, with a few details revised):

- During a tribal initiation ceremony, an African boy has the sudden realization that he is a man and now has both the gift and the responsibility to bring spiritual consolation to others.
- An older brother feels surprise, awe, and pride at the sudden demonstrated capability of a younger sister everyone thought incapable of caring for herself. He is humbled by the realization that his whole paradigm of the relationship will have to change.
- A woman is riding home on the bus after a difficult day at work. The day is bitter cold, she has a migraine, and the bus is noisy and overcrowded. She desperately wants to be quiet and to get home quickly. The woman in the next seat starts telling her about her own journey of faith. Listening, she gradually realizes that a "word" is being spoken to her that frees her from her focus on her own suffering.
- A lifelong Christian enters a grand Buddhist temple and discovers for the first time what it really means to pray.

Again, these are only samples; all the hundreds of stories are equally singular in their settings. Not surprisingly, most of the stories follow the typical narrative plot structure of recounting a problem or tension, followed by the climactic event that leads to some kind of resolution. The one- or two-sentence summaries above capture only the key turning point, while the students' one- or two-page accounts usually fill in some of what was going on before and after this climax. Important, here, is the observation of how spiritual experiences are so deeply woven into people's mundane lives and narrative identities. Spiritual experience does not occur in some separate track or compartment, parallel to "ordinary life"; it occurs as an event amid the unique specificity of each person's life circumstances.

Second characteristic: Spiritual experience is a turning point or conversion moment in each one's story. This is evident from the samples already given. Each one recounts an event that makes the person and his or her future different. This event becomes embedded in the person's memory as a cherished touchstone of meaning. The story of who they are and why they do what they do can no longer be told without including this nugget. Here are a few examples:

- A retreat director guides a retreatant as she touches deep shame and discovers that it is healed in God's presence. She describes the experience as "a sense of eternal time/ no time."
- A priest's sister invites him to be present at the birth of her child. He is overwhelmed by awe and serenity. From then on he feels a different kind of love for every child he encounters.
- A novice hears the story of his congregation's founder's tender response to a poor person and feels it "like a punch in the face." "This is it!" he exclaims. After that, everything falls into place for him.
- After a time of deep anxiety over choices to be made, out of nowhere comes God's reassurance. "I was caught unawares. The moment seized me. The experience changed me for a lifetime."

The event of spiritual experience is a turning point or *metanoia* in a person's narrative identity. Not only feelings but assumptions, values, and behavior change; relationships and roles are reconfigured.

Third characteristic: Spiritual experience is an event of self-knowledge in the presence of the sacred that frees a person to be himself or herself in a more authentic way. In their accounts of these experiences, people consistently affirm that a profound encounter has occurred that frees them from longstanding inner obstacles to the joy of simply being oneself.

- A woman had left the church, angry at its inauthenticity. Twenty-five years later, she walks into a church on Easter Sunday—and for the first time feels "at home." She realizes that now she is free enough to belong as her true self.
- While praying in church, a young man begins to see clearly how he tries to manipulate and control God through his prayer. He asks God to help him rely solely on faith. From then on, he is free of the compulsion to desire consolation.
- Consumed by a great struggle over whether to be ordained, a young seminarian stands naked under a torrential waterfall . . . and is immersed in the powerful embrace of God. He at last feels free to be himself.
- A woman is very anxious about what next step to take in life. She suddenly realizes that she does not have to have everything under control. She feels a light shining into her deepest being, freeing her to trust.
- A young priest has always experienced God as a judge. One day, gazing at an icon of Jesus, he realizes that Jesus was "truly seeing me as myself without any prejudice in deep silence." His image of God—and of himself—is transformed.

The language that people use to describe the sacred encounter is diverse. They may or may not attempt to name it as the presence of God. Yet the stories make it clear that an event has occurred that healed and liberated them at the deepest level of their being.

Fourth characteristic: Spiritual experience takes a person by surprise; it is "grace" that shifts things in ways that could not have been expected or predicted. This may be the most important of all the characteristics noted. In every story the event identified as spiritual was unplanned and unforeseeable. This is true even when it occurred during a set of spiritual exercises such as a retreat. The stories suggest that while each of us may hope, long, and strive for resolution of what is missing in our lives, whatever is actually achieved by our own labor and planning is different from what we identify as spiritual. The spiritual experience is one that floods in at a different, more encompassing level, resolving our tension or suffering in a way that we could not have envisioned beforehand.

- On a solitary hike on a stormy day by the ocean, a young adult stands shouting angry words at God and everyone else. Suddenly, he becomes aware of "the incredible beauty of that raw, wild place" and sees that God loves him completely in his own rawness.
- On retreat at the end of a difficult novitiate, a young nun takes a walk and suddenly, out of nowhere, feels a "mixed numinous feeling. . . . I never had these feelings before." Her heart is completely filled with light, happiness, joy, love, and tranquility.
- A teenage girl takes a walk on a sunny day and sits down by a small stream. Spontaneously, an "unstoppable desire to praise" takes over her whole being. She is deeply happy and at peace with the world and with herself.
- A woman—normally anxious and fidgety—experiences preternatural tranquility while coping with her husband's extreme illness at the same time that many other highly demanding events are occurring.

The astonishing surprise of spiritual experience is that we are embraced, freed, and made whole at a depth that had previously been inaccessible to us, no matter how much we labored and struggled. It is "amazing grace"—the opening of a door to a new, more peaceful, and integrated way of being. Although often other struggles follow, the decisive significance of that shift is never forgotten.

Fifth characteristic: Although often preceded by a time of difficulty, the dominant feelings and moods of spiritual experience are those of peace, joy, love, light, and liberation. Many of the stories involve very difficult circumstances, such as facing death, illness, loss, or conflict. People often describe painful feelings such as confusion, darkness, fear, anger, or despair. Yet at the moment of spiritual experience, they shift into a register of calm and joy. In some cases, particularly the vocation stories, the positive energy of this breakthrough fuels a definitive change of life setting that enables the newly discovered sense of meaning to permeate the immediate future, or even a lifetime. In other cases—such as a person caring for a dying spouse, or a young man consigned to years of forced labor—little outer change is possible. Yet, on the level of the self, everything has changed.

- After several years in a deeply depleting ministry position, a priest learns he will be sent to one he had always wanted. His spirit instantly rises up, jubilant and joyful.
- A pastor becomes involved in an escalating conflict with a neighbor and writes him a very harsh letter. Later, praying, he feels remorseful and goes to apologize. Receiving the other's forgiveness, he feels lightness of heart and joy.
- A man's parents had both died relatively young and in difficult circumstances—one by suicide. He has lived for twenty years avoiding thinking about or remembering them. Finally, he decides to visit their graves. A deep peace comes over him, and happy memories of them flood his mind.
- Forced to do hard labor by a dictatorial government, a young man realizes that he has a choice: to work sorrowfully or to work joyfully. He chooses joy, thanking God every day for air and water even when there is little food.

Sixth characteristic: Spiritual experience changes a person's way of being in relationship; one becomes more aware of belonging to realities bigger than the self, and eager to give oneself on behalf of these realities. While spiritual change is deeply interior, it is also radically relational. The directionality of change is toward deeper, more positive, more inclusive, and more self-giving relationships.

- A stray cat shows up at a woman's door, followed by another a few days later. The repetition of the experience, along with the intensity of her desire to protect and provide for these animals, sparks the realization that she is called to extend her care to homeless people, too. She joins a project that does this.
- As he learns to sail, a young man experiences a deep communion with nature as he discovers how to keep realigning his body and his boat with the currents and the wind.
- A woman caring for her ill and dying parents is, at the same time, accompanying other friends who are doing the same. She feels more and more connected to the suffering and dying Jesus, and she knows her participation in his solidarity with all those who are suffering.

- On a trip in a desperately poor country a woman falls ill and discovers her own vulnerability and her need to be cared for by those who have next to nothing. Knowing that she is "one of them," she dedicates her life to solidarity with the poor.

Spiritual experience draws people out of themselves and into relationships of participation, care, and communion.

Discovering the Larger Questions

When we compare Wildman's more developed taxonomy to my own informal phenomenological discoveries, most of what my students selected as spiritual experiences fit most closely with what Wildman calls an ultimacy experience. Interestingly, they are often not religious. One of the surprising discoveries from my classroom exercises is how many of the stories do not explicitly mention any elements that are identifiably Christian. From all the stories I have heard over the years, about one-third explicitly refer to a scripture text, Jesus, or one of the sacraments; possibly another third of the stories make more oblique references to God or some sense of divine presence. This is even more surprising considering that the sample of stories comes from a group consisting almost entirely of churchgoing people who pray, study the Bible, and frequent the sacraments at a far higher rate than the general public.

Certainly, if a different question were asked, for example, "Tell a story about a spiritual encounter with Jesus" or "Describe your most profound spiritual experience of one of the sacraments," most of these respondents would have little difficulty providing such stories. However, when simply asked for a significant spiritual experience, those more explicitly Christian encounters were not necessarily what rose to the top of their list as the event they wanted to recount. The stories are far more varied, more deeply and uniquely inserted into the personal and cultural life settings of each person, than might be expected if the question asked were more theologically specific.

Again, neither the solicitation nor the analysis of my sample of stories has been done with scientific rigor, so it is not appropriate to over interpret what people did or did not choose to share. For me, the issue is not so much that people did not regularly reference Jesus or use other Christian language, because I'm quite sure that if each of these people were interviewed more thoroughly about the described events, most of them would ultimately (and sincerely) articulate what happened to them in Christian theological terms. What is fascinating is that, as described, the event of "spirit" breaking into and transforming people's lives is more primal, and more embedded in the singularity of each life, than any institutionalized religious perspective could predict. Even people who are studying theology do not initially feel the need to use higher-level theological language to describe such experiences, because simply telling the story of the event powerfully conveys its vital, transforming significance.

What is happening to people in these spiritual experiences? The general pattern is that life serendipitously presents a unique set of circumstances that are "just right" for that particular person to make an inner leap to discovery of an awareness of an inner stance of integrity, peace, and joy. This inner response engages the whole person, including body, mind, feelings, and the most intimate center of the will. The experience fits with Moltmann's observation that the terms *whole, hale, heal,* and *holy* all derive from the same semantic roots, "meaning roughly speaking: entire, healthy, unhurt, complete, and 'belonging especially' to someone."[17] This transformation is experienced as gift or grace rather than as labor. While the immediate experience of wholeness, peace, and joy usually dissipates over the next hours or days, the memory and its meaning do not. The person's self-story has changed, and other changes—affective, behavioral, relational, and vocational—follow.

Such a spiritual experience—some version of which, I suggest, occurs in every human life—is the experiential face of what Ilia Delio calls catholicity. She writes: "To be catholic is to be aware of belonging to a whole and to act according to the whole, including the galaxies and stars, earth, animals, plants, and human life. . . . It is what moves (catalyzes) a person to think, move, and orient his or her life toward making wholes from the

---

[17] Moltmann, *The Spirit of Life,* 175.

partials of experience."[18] It seems that when people personally experience such an event of inner wholemaking, they recognize it as spiritual.

By this inductive method, then, we can arrive at a pre-theological definition of human "spirit" as the inner dynamism that urges toward the maximum awareness of being interconnected, whole, and in harmony, in relation to oneself and all that is beyond oneself. This dynamism, however, finds its fulfillment not on its own level, but in the surprising grace of knowing one is in communion with a reality greater than the self. This informal phenomenological study has explored a selection of somewhat random human experiences. Nevertheless, such an approach from subjectivity raises larger questions, such as the following: From where does this "spiritual urge" come? Is it a sign or manifestation of something that can be articulated in more objective terms? Are these transformative experiences actually responses to a call or invitation from something beyond the self? Is the character of the transformation that people experience basically an organic development from within, or is it better characterized as a startling gift of new capabilities? Finally, how does the concept of Spirit with a capital "S" elucidate these experiences? These are some of the questions that play through our inquiry.

The Rhythm of Spirit and the Story of Our Lives

As noted earlier, the rhythm of spirit is analogous to the rhythm of the physical breath. The movements of drawing inward to an intimate center and pulsing outward to interact with the surrounding world are distinct, yet also integral to each other. Rather than contradicting each other, the inward and outward movements enhance and support each other. Life itself fuels the ongoing rhythm, sparking the repeated flow of inbreath and outbreath.

---

[18] Ilia Delio, *Making All Things New: Catholicity, Cosmology, Consciousness*, Catholicity in an Evolving Universe (Maryknoll, NY: Orbis Books, 2015), xii, 2.

Of course, as is always the case, the analogy is not exact. The physical breath, on the one hand, is largely unconscious, and the body's needs require that it maintain a stable and relatively rapid alternation of the inward and outward movements. The rhythm of spirit, on the other hand, may involve a good deal of conscious awareness, and the speed and balance of transitions between inward and outward occur far more flexibly than does the physical urgency of breathing. Still, the value of the analogy is to emphasize that spirit is a dynamism that is integral to life itself, and that every spiritual life requires cultivation of both inward and outward dimensions.

This book aims to specify with greater clarity what is involved in the inward and outward rhythm of the human spirit. Starting with the outward direction, as we take this movement to its apogee, we find the person in full activity, physically and publicly engaged in the surrounding world. The person is involved in multiple relationships and social networks, within which the person plays roles that are largely shaped by culture. The person uses language, tools, and performance skills in efforts to exert influence and accomplish goals. This is, in fact, exactly where we normally encounter people and get to know them. We meet them in the context of their roles in institutions or other social groups, for example, as teacher, salesperson, neighbor, family member, or perhaps "unidentified"—the stranger who arouses our anxiety. We perceive and respond to how a person dresses, speaks, and behaves, and we are astutely aware of how these outward manifestations communicate intentions to influence us and others in one way or another—for example, by attracting, shocking, impressing, or simply by fulfilling our expectations.

Yet, to understand a person as spiritual, we must take a step back from the apogee of the outward route. Why is the person presenting himself or herself in this way? What history, what values, what fantasies and assumptions, lie behind the public self-presentation? What mental and psychological process has provided the organizing framework that gives a degree of coherence to the person's selection of goals, relationships, and actions? Both in psychology and in philosophy many recent thinkers have converged on the notion of the "narrative self."[19] Essentially, this is the inner story—partly conscious, partly unconscious—that each of us is continually constructing about our life. Shaped by the events of personal and collective history as well as culture, psychological dynamics, and personal creativity, this ever-evolving story features oneself as hero or heroine. It is this inner narrative that enables us, with greater or lesser success, to integrate our past, make choices in the present, and envision a future for ourselves, all with some coherence and dramatic excitement.

Recalling the brief story summaries recounted earlier in this chapter, it is easy to catch glimpses of the narrative self in action. These capsules are short, but nonetheless they convey the dramatic sense of a "before" state that is suddenly shifted by the spiritual experience, leading to an "after" that is qualitatively different. Take, for example, the story of the woman who described herself as normally anxious and fidgety, but then was amazed to find herself experiencing preternatural tranquility while coping with her husband's terminal illness at the same time that other difficult events were happening in her circle of family and close friends. This woman's story of herself prior to this time—possibly based on both her own experience and the assessments of others—included self-characterization as an anxious, fidgety person who could not handle stress well. Her story now, however, is that, in her time of crisis, she was gifted with an unexpected, unexplainable tranquility that enabled her to cope with a high level of stress with remarkable grace. Her story of who she was, is, and can be has changed significantly because of her spiritual experience.

---

[19] Jerome Bruner, "Life as Narrative," *Social Research* 71, no. 3 (2004): 691–710; Dan P. McAdams, "Personality, Modernity, and the Storied Self: A Contemporary Framework for Studying Persons," *Psychological Inquiry* 7, no. 4 (October 1996): 295; Theodore R. Sarbin, "The Narrative Quality of Action," *Theoretical and Philosophical Psychology* 10, no. 2 (1990): 49–65.

In this chapter we explored metaphors and experiences of spirit, concluding with a basic sketch of how spirit is experienced and articulated within a narrative dynamism. The next chapter is the first of four in Part II, "In Search of Catholic Personhood." The chapter sketches some of the rapidly changing social and environmental circumstances that are currently influencing how people develop a sense of themselves as selves, persons, and spiritual beings.

Part II

In Search of Catholic Personhood

Chapter 3

The Crisis of the Anthropocene

On August 29, 2016, at the International Geological Congress meeting in Cape Town, South Africa, a working group presented a formal proposal to designate the current era as a new geological epoch entitled the Anthropocene. The Anthropocene is defined as that period during which the activity of *Homo sapiens* becomes one of the primary factors affecting earth's geological structures and ecosystems. While some scientists argue that such an epoch began with the initiation of agriculture (10,000 BCE) or the Industrial Revolution (mid-eighteenth century), most point to the middle of the twentieth century as the real tipping point. Since about 1950, the rate at which human activity is reshaping basic earth systems such as climate, wind flow, hydrology, species survival and distribution, and soil composition has skyrocketed. Concomitantly, patterns of human daily life, economics, and communication have undergone equally rapid change. This chapter examines the crisis this engenders for humans as spiritual beings.

In his 2015 encyclical on care for the environment, *Laudato Si'*, Pope Francis uses the word *rapidification* to describe this crisis of intensifying change:

> The continued acceleration of changes affecting humanity and the planet is coupled today with a more intensified pace of life and work which might be called "rapidification." Although change is part of the working of complex systems, the speed with which human activity has developed contrasts with the naturally slow pace of biological

evolution. Moreover, the goals of this rapid and constant change are not necessarily geared to the common good or to integral and sustainable human development. Change is something desirable, yet it becomes a source of anxiety when it causes harm to the world and to the quality of life of much of humanity. (no. 18)

This chapter examines the extreme challenges facing the human project of "catholicity" in the rapidifying conditions of the Anthropocene.

The Early Twentieth Century

To make our discussion more concrete, we begin with a brief review of life in the early twentieth century, prior to the mid-century tipping point into the Anthropocene and "rapidification." This period is still within living memory in that many people who are now grandparents or great-grandparents grew up hearing their parents, grandparents, or great-grandparents telling stories about their own growing up in the first thirty years of the twentieth century. Born in 1950, I am among that bridge generation whose imaginations and values were shaped by those stories that seem to be from an entirely different world than the one in which we live today.

A century ago most of my immediate ancestors lived in small towns in the midwestern United States. My father (b. 1915) grew up in Camp Crook, South Dakota, which is situated among the scrub-brush prairies and buttes of the far northwestern corner of the state. At that time Camp Crook, with a population that grew from 120 in 1910 to 163 in 1920, was the oldest and largest town in thinly populated Harding County. Like many similar small towns of the old Midwest, Camp Crook was the relatively bustling center to which those living on the surrounding farms and ranches trekked regularly to buy, to sell, to have some fun on Saturday night, and/or to go to church on Sunday morning. The town had several churches, several bars, various stores, a bank, and a belvedere for special festivities.

At the time of my father's birth—only a little more than one hundred years ago—well over half of the population of the United States lived on farms and in small rural towns like Camp Crook. Motorized vehicles were considered newfangled inventions, as were telephones, phonographs, electric lights, and indoor plumbing. These modern conveniences were gradually becoming available to the small-town folks, but many were still years from having access. For the most part the music that the people of Camp Crook heard had to be produced at home on musical instruments or by local ensembles—one of which (a few years later) was a trio consisting of my grandmother, my father, and his older brother. To view a silent, black-and-white movie, they would have to make a major expedition of 120 miles to the Elks Theatre in the "big city" of Rapid City (population at that time, about 4,000). Television as a part of daily life was still fifty years in the future. Even as late as the 1950s, when I was growing up in Rapid City, making a long-distance phone call was considered such a big deal that the family only did so at most two or three times a year, accompanied by much awe and trepidation.

Was life better or worse then than it is now? One of the great promises of technological progress was labor-saving devices, and indeed, it is true that most physical tasks require far less exertion today than they did one hundred years ago. My grandmother in Camp Crook rose at 4 am every day to light the wood stove, set loaves of fresh bread dough to rise, get the children up and dressed, and fix a heavy cooked breakfast for her family. She made most of the family's clothes herself, and when they needed washing, she scrubbed them on a washboard. Water had to be pumped and hauled for everything, including the family members' weekly Saturday night bath. A housewife's tasks were full time and physically demanding. Few today are eager to return to such an exhausting lifestyle.

Nevertheless, in hindsight we see other aspects of that time that are more appealing. My grandmother had plenty to do, but the day and week were rhythmically organized with a time for each activity. The expectations placed on her were clear, and the skills needed were ones in which she had been formed from childhood. The same was true for everyone else in the household. Food was locally grown, home cooked, and wholesome. Neighbors knew each other well and could be counted on to help in times of trouble. Children had chores, but they also had plenty of time each day for free and rambunctious play, most of it outdoors.

The point of this brief review is not to conclude that everyone was happy in those days. Life a hundred years ago in Camp Crook and similar small towns was not idyllic. Undoubtedly, domestic abuse, alcoholism, mental illness, petty rivalries, and other human ills existed there, as they have wherever human beings have lived, and people had far fewer options for dealing with these sufferings than many do today. My grandmother was not a particularly happy woman; she tended to have melancholy moods that today might be diagnosed as depression. What we note, however, is the straightforward expectations of her daily life and social identity compared to what many people face today. In view of our focus on catholicity, we might even say that her life had a relatively uncomplicated "wholeness." The radical changes in this aspect of life are at the center of what Pope Francis calls "rapidification." In the remainder of this chapter we survey how some key sociologists and cultural analysts characterize the effects of these changes on people's lives and identities.

Characteristics of Modernity

Many term our era as postmodern, but before understanding *post* we must first examine what characterizes *modernity*. Zygmunt Bauman has proposed that the two most predominant characteristics of modernity are the intense push toward a rationalizing and technologizing order and the absolute willingness to overthrow any tradition to realize that order. Thus, modern life is completely permeated with humanly created technology, and it demands highly structured levels of coordination and control. At the same time it prescribes continual doubt and dissatisfaction with the current state of affairs. As Jean-François Lyotard notes, to be modern means that "everything that is received must be suspected, even if it is only a day old."[1]

---

[1] Jean-François Lyotard, *The Postmodern Explained: Correspondence 1982–1985* (Minneapolis: University of Minnesota Press, 1993), 12.

For Bauman, "heavy modernity" was the period exemplified by the Ford-style factory, with its extreme demands for order, routinization, and the rule of heavy technology. The dangers of this era included totalitarianism and the "mass man" image of faceless people, all dressed alike, all living in identical prefab homes, all marching relentlessly to the tick of the clock and the assembly line. For Michel Foucault, the image of this period was the panopticon: a circular building with a central watchtower and separate cells around the edges, so a surveillant in the watchtower could see all the individuals in their cell while none of them could see each other.[2] The image captured the isolation, surveillance, and control that early modernity sought to impose on its denizens.

The current era, however, is what Bauman calls "liquid modernity."[3] Rather than a factory or a panopticon, the defining image becomes that of a transient mobile home park in which each person or family is wholly focused on managing what is going on in its own mobile home. Ties to others are loose and noncommittal, because everyone reserves the right to move on at any time. People pay little attention to larger systems until, say, the supply of electricity malfunctions; then they complain or just move away. Liquid modernity is less controlling but, paradoxically, more disempowering than the earlier version. Everyone is left on his or her own to manage and to figure out individual economic and psychological survival tactics in a constantly changing landscape. In the era of liquid modernity we have become far more self-reflexive and self-critical, but at the same time less able to understand, care about, critique, or influence the economic and political systems in which we are embedded.

Lest this sound overly grim, some point to more positive aspects of these developments. Michel de Certeau writes that even the most oppressed and marginalized people always find creative ways to exercise power at the micro level. He notes that consumers "make *(bricolent)* innumerable and infinitesimal transformations of and within the dominant cultural economy in order to

---

[2] Michel Foucault, *Discipline and Punish: The Birth of the Prison*, 2nd ed. (New York: Vintage Books, 1995).

[3] Zygmunt Bauman, *Liquid Modernity* (Malden, MA: Blackwell, 2000).

adapt it to their own interests and their own rules."[4] Postcolonial thinkers have developed the concept of hybridity to name the way each person crafts a self and a way of life out of whatever diverse materials are available. In a time of de-territorialization, when all images and practices have been abstracted from their original contexts, circulated elsewhere, and planted in hybridized forms in other cultural traditions, hybridity can be both creative and liberating. Yet it can also be harmful when it destroys local traditions, results in "a false and shallow cosmopolitanism which is aloof from the poor and powerless of our world,"[5] or eliminates any form of personal center.

The philosophical underpinnings of modernity are usually said to begin with René Descartes (1596–1650) and the radical separation of the thinking self from the objects upon which it operates. This prepared the way for the rise of scientific methods that systematically doubt all perceptions and concepts while encouraging intensive technological manipulation of all aspects of the physical world. This, in turn, prepared the way for the Industrial Revolution (mid-eighteenth to nineteenth centuries) and, more recently, the cybernetic revolution (late twentieth and twenty-first centuries), which have repeatedly and radically revamped every aspect of traditional ways of life. The "rapidification" of which Pope Francis wrote identifies how the speed of this continual revamping has increased exponentially to the point of vertigo.

Lyotard proposes that, while traditional societies based their lifestyles on looking backward to myths of origin, modern societies came to be founded on a metanarrative (or "grand story") of progress toward a technologically created utopian future.[6] The commitments to ever-expanding technology, massive control systems, and the casting aside of long-held traditions were

---

[4] Michel de Certeau, *The Practice of Everyday Life*, trans. Steven F. Rendall, 2nd ed., vol. 1 (Berkeley and Los Angeles: University of California Press, 2013), xiv.

[5] Clayton Crockett and Jay McDaniel, "From an Idolatry of Identity to a Planetization of Alterity: A Relational-Theological Approach to Hybridity, Sin, and Love," *Journal of Postcolonial Theory and Theology* 1, no. 3 (2010): 9.

[6] Lyotard, *The Postmodern Explained*, 18–19.

premised on the belief that "progress" would lead to an amazing payoff "just around the corner." What we now call postmodernity is actually the breakdown of belief in these metanarratives of progress. One reason for their breakdown is that modernity has not delivered an easy, anxiety-free, pleasure-filled life as the metanarratives promised. At least for vast numbers of people, just the opposite has been the case. Even many of the well-to-do beneficiaries of the best of modernity's comforts find themselves suffering with anxiety, stress, and malaise. Meanwhile, as industry ravages ecosystem after ecosystem, legions are forced off their land into desperate urban slums where even the smallest crumbs of modernity's largesse are hard to come by.

Another reason for disenchantment with metanarratives is highlighted by Charles Taylor in *A Secular Age*.[7] In contemporary cosmopolitan society, people daily interact with people whose cultures and beliefs are totally different from their own. Media, as well as educational practices, add to people's exposure to widely differing stories and worldviews. It is impossible for a modern person to believe and live by any grounding story without, at the same time, being aware that other people believe and live by completely different stories with equal or greater conviction. Thus, we are forced to realize that our beliefs are a choice—one option among many.

The result is what Taylor calls "cross-pressure": the nagging tension, whether conscious or unconscious, of wondering whether one's chosen worldview is really the best one or not. This, in turn, means that our convictions become fragile. Rather than appearing to have the certainty and immovability of the mountains, they begin to look rather ragged and flawed. The increase in religious and political fundamentalisms, in which people fervently and rigidly commit to a highly defined set of beliefs, might appear to contradict this, but Taylor sees this phenomenon as actually a symptom of the fundamentalist's inability to tolerate pervasive cross-pressure. The anxiety created by the nagging possibility of doubt fuels the urgency of choosing one's view loudly and intolerantly. Increasing "fragilization" of belief leads to an increasingly aggressive denial of that fragility.

---

[7] Charles Taylor, *A Secular Age* (Cambridge, MA: Harvard University Press, 2007).

We will return shortly to another look at postmodern disenchantment and its effects on human identity, but first let us take a deeper look at how modernity and postmodernity shape our lives as spiritual beings. Some of the elements often pointed to include the mechanization of time and its complete detachment from place; the technologization of communication and the utter permeation of daily life by the media; and the commodification of everything.

The Mechanization of Time and
Its Disembedding from Place

For those who have grown up constantly attuned to clocks and watches in order to know when it is time to do whatever we must do, it is hard to imagine life before mechanized timepieces. Without clocks, time remains closely linked to personal, local, and natural conditions. In the Middle Ages, for example, the daylight period was divided into twelve segments, and likewise the period of darkness. Before the mechanization of time, we find that an hour was only loosely defined and was longer in summer than in winter. The time to get up was when the sun rose, or perhaps earlier when called by the needs of livestock or crops. The time to have a meeting was when everyone arrived, and the time to end it was when the business at hand was finished. Agreement about when to meet someone required describing time in its relation to a specific place: "I'll meet you by the lone pine at Anzeville on the first day of the blueberry harvest, at the hour when the pine's shadow is the length of two tall men." Thus, before the mechanization of time, how time was perceived and regulated could not be separated from local customs, needs, and seasons.

Relatively crude mechanical clocks and watches began to appear in sixteenth-century Europe, but originally they were available only to the very wealthy and to the general public in town clock towers. It was not until the nineteenth century that time became fully mechanized and clocks began to permeate daily life. This meant that the day could be divided into twenty-four hours of equal length that do not vary according to local conditions. Time had finally been freed from place. It makes no difference where we are, who we are with, or what is going on right now; it is the clock that tells us what we must do. Only extreme emergencies may override the tyranny of the clock.

The great advantage of universally mechanized time is that millions of people—including those at great distances from one another—can be coordinated in their actions, simply by telling each of them what time to act. Think, for example, of the thousands of intricately interlinked schedules involved in coordinating taking a bus to the airport, buying lunch, boarding a plane to fly to another city, taking public transportation again, and finally checking in to a hotel room. Our massive modern cities, industries, and institutions could not exist without mechanized time. Their growth has more recently been further enhanced by computerized time, which is capable of coordinating millions of variables with precision to the tiniest fractions of a second. On the level of coordinating action, mechanized time is a tremendous boon for human unification.

But an air-travel anecdote also illustrates the negative effects of being completely disembedded from any connection to place. During one period of my life I was taking plane trips several times a month. More than once, during a grueling day of traveling, I became so disoriented that, at least for a few moments, I could not answer basic questions such as "What city are you in?" or "What city are you going to?" Airport terminals are built to seal inhabitants off from the earthy locality of the place—from the soil, flowing water, winds, fragrances, flora and fauna, people, and cultures—substituting instead concrete, steel, glass, and plastic focused toward runways and skies. An airport is a shrine to our liberation from being creatures tied to the habitat and relationships among which we were born.

Most humans of the past, like most other living creatures, formed such deep physical and psychological bonds with the particularities of their local ecosystems that dislocation was extremely traumatic. Of course, this does not mean that humans always spent a lifetime in the same place. The human ability to adapt to an extraordinarily wide range of habitats has been key to our species' success. Yet, until recently, that adaptation normally required very close attention to every detail of the local conditions—where and when the sun shines, early warning signs of storms, what edible flora and fauna are available at each season, how local materials can be used to create shelter, how water can be obtained and stored, and so on. Modern life, however, detaches us from all this. In the modern city, survival depends on being attuned to clocks and screens, not to nature's conditions and rhythms.

The ecological and spiritual cost of this has been massive. Currently, there is no ecosystem on earth, even in the deepest depths of the oceans, that has not been disrupted by human pollution. Every hour of every day human-made machines are clearcutting, bulldozing, and grinding up ecosystem after ecosystem, with no regard for the intricate and delicate interweaving of life-enhancing systems they sustain. While some degree of death and destruction is a normal part of the cycles of life, current levels are leading to irreversible declines in thousands of species as well as in essential systems such as global circulation of air, water, and nutrients. If our polluting and clearcutting ways are not mitigated very soon, it may not be much longer before the earth ceases to be a habitat within which human life can thrive. The spiritual cost has also been heavy, with the numbers of those suffering from depression, addictions, and social isolation climbing ever higher.

The Technologization of Communication and the Permeation of Daily Life by Media

That human communication is mediated is not new. Even voice and gesture are complex methods of mediation, deployed to transfer information across physical and mental gaps between persons. Some evolutionary anthropologists believe that it was the development of the ability to use the voice in complex communication that signaled the speciation of *Homo sapiens* 300,000 years ago. Between 10,000 and 4,000 years ago, cultures in several regions of the world independently developed symbolic recordkeeping and writing systems. These were primarily used in high-level business transactions and government (which at that time included religious functions), and thus, directly involved only a very small fraction of the population.

When ancient cultures needed immediate communication over longer distances, methods such as drums, flashing mirrors, and smoke signals came into play. These media are clearly very limited both in scope and content. If the information to be communicated was complex, or the distance was greater, marathon runners, horsemen, ships, or homing pigeons were employed. The gap between an event occurring and the news of it reaching those concerned could be days, weeks, or even months. This remained the reality until the invention of the telegraph, which became widespread in the mid-nineteenth century. In the latter part of that century the telephone was invented, and by 1920 most parts of the United States had some degree of telephone access. Most people used the telephone as an occasional tool for essential communication with family or business associates, although some also discovered its possibilities for sharing gossip. Long-distance phone calls remained expensive and, for most families, rare, until well into the 1960s.

Meanwhile, radio was also invented and, by 1920, was just beginning to become a popular form of home entertainment. By 1940, 85 percent of homes in the United States had radios, which were sometimes as large as today's television sets. In many areas only one radio station could be clearly heard. It was not until the 1950s, with the invention of the transistor radio, that radios became truly portable. Cathode-ray electronic televisions became available by 1930 but had a somewhat slower acceptance rate. The transmitted images were small, black and white, and, by today's standards, of poor resolution. In the 1950s and 1960s, TVs gradually became more ubiquitous across homes in the United States, although it was still very rare for a family to have more than one. Before the 1970s, when cable TV was deregulated, most TVs had access to at most three network stations: ABC, CBS, and NBC.

The point of this brief review of the development of communication technology is to emphasize how vastly different our experience today is from what was the case even within the lifetimes of many alive today. Today, nearly every person in the United States walks around with a smartphone with instant access to millions of websites and videos, as well as the ability to telephone anyone anywhere in the world on the spur of the moment. News from nearly any part of the world arrives within seconds or minutes, often accompanied by graphic video images. This pocket device can store thousands of musical selections and photographs to be accessed at will. It enables its user to view privately any one of millions of videos at any time of the day or night. The GPS feature guides the user step by step from anywhere to anywhere without the traveler needing to know anything other than an address. One study reported that the average smartphone user accesses it eighty-five times a day.

Meanwhile, not only do many households have televisions in almost every room, but the TVs dominate the room and are able to access hundreds of stations with every imaginable sort of content. Eighty-five percent of homes in the United States also have some type of computer in addition to the family members' smartphones, which are themselves computers. Increasingly, many home functions such as lighting, temperature control, and security are operated by a smartphone or computer. The control of these functions, as well as fans, window shades, printers, and any other moveable part, is wireless. It has reached the point that people are surprised and even annoyed when functions—for example, flushing toilets in public restrooms—require physical action on their part.

There is obviously much to be celebrated in the ease of access to information and the ease of function that the permeation of daily life by technology provides. However, our question here is its effect on how we shape our identity and spirituality. We have already mentioned the role of narrative coherence in identity. As people spend many hours of each day engaged with media, they are (or at least can be) exposed to a range of stories vastly expanded from what was possible two or three generations ago. On a given day a hundred years ago in Camp Crook, South Dakota, a teenager might hear a couple of reminiscent stories from friends or family members and an optimistic cultural story or two from a teacher, then read a novel in the evening. On Sunday, at church, he or she heard commentary on a Bible story or two. More often than not, all these stories came from the same or similar cultural contexts, represented common values and themes, and reinforced each other as the teenager incorporated them into a coherent identity narrative.

Now, in one day a teenager is likely to encounter hundreds or even thousands of different stories about people from every corner of the globe and with every imaginable value system (or lack thereof). Although many of the stories may be presented with a level of narrative coherence in themselves, they arrive in a form that is more collage than narrative. Images flash before our eyes: a viral picture of a cute and silly-looking kitten; a horrifying story about a small child mangled in war; the salacious saga of a pop star's latest girlfriend; a grim account of a politician's warning about the threat of nuclear war; a disgusted review of the local baseball team's botched game the night before; shocking pictures of collapsed buildings in the latest earthquake . . . all this and more within a single minute of casual scrolling on one's smartphone.

The capacity of our devices to scroll or channel surf means that much of what we take in is only impressions, not fully crafted stories. It also means that we can pick and choose what we attend to. We are able to pass quickly over undesired messages, linger over those that entice us, and use hyperlinks to find others similar to those that attract us. Due to our short attention spans, storytellers have learned to rely more heavily on visual images than on text to get our attention. Meanwhile, each of the images and stories is, of course, "spun"; that is, someone has crafted the storytelling to achieve an effect, whether empathy, fundraising, ideological conversion, fan loyalty, or simply giving pleasure. Included in the onslaught of stories that wash over us daily are hundreds of explicit advertisements, each of which is intensively vetted to make it as effective as possible in lodging its image and mini-story into our subconscious. Every sort of the most graphic pornography, which prior to the internet required finding and entering an "adult" store, is now freely available 24/7, and it is reported that most teenagers today form their expectations about sex based on this source.

The effect of this, suggests Zygmunt Bauman, is "a message of the essential indeterminacy and softness of the world: in this world, everything may happen and everything may be done, but nothing can be done once and for all—and whatever it is that happens comes unannounced and goes away without notice."[8] Rather than a more or less singular culturally based narrative that is constantly being reinforced by the stories we hear, we live in a cacophony of often-superficial stories that do not hang

---

[8] Zygmunt Bauman, *The Individualized Society* (Malden, MA: Polity Press, 2001), 83.

together or collectively point toward anything worthy of a life commitment. Kenneth Gergen speaks of this as the "saturated self" whose coherence is overwhelmed by the number and incompatibility of invitations to self-investment that impinge upon it. "As social saturation adds incrementally to the population of the self, each impulse toward well-formed identity is cast into increasing doubt; each is found absurd, shallow, limited, or flawed by the onlooking audience of the interior."[9]

In Gergen's view, postmodern culture has created *Homo optionis*. To be human in this culture is defined by having at each moment a vast array of identity options among which we must constantly pick and choose. People can flit in and out of vast numbers of ever-shifting and often virtual relationships with people and groups around the world. Léon Turner writes: "Ultimately, maintaining a committed (or dedicated) singular identity becomes nearly impossible, and individuals resign themselves to subsisting moment-by-moment in a swirling sea of relations."[10] The result is that rather than having a single narrative self, we develop a plurality of selves or personas so that, chameleon like, we can be adept at shifting our story and modus operandi according to whatever relations we are choosing to engage at that moment. Gergen calls this "multiphrenia," which he regards as having both positive and negative potentials. The positive potential is creativity and adaptability; the negative potential is profound anxiety and psychological disintegration. The task of living in a postmodern, media-saturated culture often seems like walking a tightrope between these two.[11]

The Commodification of Everything

A commodity is something that can be an object of trade. While the negotiated exchange of goods between human groups is undoubtedly ancient, it has taken new forms in modern and

---

[9] Kenneth J. Gergen, *The Saturated Self: Dilemmas of Identity in Contemporary Life* (New York: Basic Books, 2000), 73.

[10] Léon Turner, *Theology, Psychology, and the Plural Self* (Burlington, VT: Ashgate, 2008), 44.

[11] Gergen, *The Saturated Self*, 44.

postmodern society. Capitalism places the means of production in private hands and makes profit the essential value that defines success. As much as possible, markets must be free and regulated by supply and demand. Human labor, as well as natural resources and capital itself, become commodities that are traded according to the rules of supply, demand, and maximization of profit.

Compared to previous systems that involved feudalism or slavery, the capitalistic system gives laborers much more autonomy to negotiate for the sale of their time and skills. At least in theory each person has the opportunity to be an entrepreneur with his or her personal resources. The negative side of this is that capitalism makes a person's labor into just another objectified commodity that business owners deploy to maximize their own profit. Owners are not required to have any relationship or concern for employees as whole persons or any mercy based on consideration of the person's difficult circumstances. There are, of course, many examples of businesses that attempt a "kinder, gentler" version of this regime, yet overall the "bottom line" of profit rules.

While this economic system has prevailed since the Industrial Revolution and has brought a more comfortable life for many, especially in industrialized parts of the world, some of the more problematic aspects of its effect on human lives have escalated in conjunction with the changes we have been discussing above. The mechanization of time and its radical detachment from local conditions are essential features of industrialization. In the context of capitalism our time becomes something that we objectify and dole out (or sell) rather than a living flow in which we participate. Perhaps even more serious is the way we lose vital connection and sensitivity to the living natural world that sustains us.

Today, many people can identify at best a few species of birds (pigeons, robins, cardinals, and crows) and perhaps one or two generic tree species (maple and oak). They have no idea what the specific ecological characteristics or conditions of their local region are or even where their water comes from. They take note of the weather only in relation to its convenience or inconvenience, without regard to how it reflects and influences vital life systems. Although most probably know intellectually that food comes from soil and sun, as far as daily life is concerned it comes in boxes, bottles, and plastic bags. For most, the price of a food item is a far greater concern than the health of the land from which it came or the well being of the people who labored to grow and transport it. Much of the food that is available in modern supermarkets is so heavily processed and doctored with additives and chemicals that it bears little resemblance to anything natural. Choices are made based on responses to colorful packaging covered with images and text rather than through a connection to living creatures, land, or farms.

In short, food—the most direct and pervasive link between our bodies and our ecosystems—is radically commodified. More and more that is true of everything that modern humans use in daily life: clothing, tools, transportation, even air (which must be "conditioned"). Only a hundred years ago many of these items were still made at home, or at least locally; now they arrive in boxes from unknown distant places. But commodification has not stopped with changing our way of relating to the things we use; increasingly, it has crept deeper into the most intimate corners of our beings. Even our identities, our relationships, and our spiritualities have become commodified.

The opening for the commodification of identity comes from the pressure described by Gergen as the "saturated self," who is dogpaddling furiously within what Turner calls a "swirling sea of relations." Moreover, many of the relations on offer in this swirling sea are virtual (not face to face), transient (not stable or long term), and/or commercialized (the other wants to sell you something). Unable to find the conditions necessary to develop a truly coherent and stable identity, the easier and more efficient route is to "buy" an identity from the media. Many commercial enterprises, realizing this, invest significant resources in creating an identity "brand" that will not only ensure a loyal customer base but also make these customers into walking promoters of what the company has to sell.

In *Consuming Faith* Tom Beaudoin describes how companies regard their brand identity as their most valuable possession.[12]

---

[12] Tom Beaudoin, *Consuming Faith: Integrating Who We Are with What We Buy* (Lanham, MD: Sheed and Ward, 2007).

They invest their best resources in building up the brand mythology while at the same time doing their best to outsource, downsize, and otherwise distance themselves from the actual physical operations of production. Thus, the clothes we buy may actually be made in near slave-labor conditions by desperately poor women in Bangladesh, but the identity the companies' ads convince us we are projecting when we wear them is cool, beautiful, confident, and quirky. The brand economy, says Beaudoin, works through forming our imagination, just as a spiritual discipline does. Branding strives to lead us to invest trust in the brand mythology and to feel dependent on its propagators. The brand is built to give us a sense of membership in a community as well as to promise us an experience of being at our best and feeling the full zest of life. While on the physical level contact with a company's products has no power to deliver any of this, the brand functions like a placebo that heals because we believe it can.

For many young people the brand that is most important may be a composite style promoted by an entertainer, a TV show, a social-media influencer, or a musical movement. Such a style choice encompasses clothing, hairstyle, favorite phrases, and attitude (lighthearted, rebellious, absurdist, or eroticizing, for example). Even the professional branders know that no one today is a one-brand person. Even if someone identifies strongly with one brand or style, that person will also subscribe to other brands for other aspects of life or simply for variety. Thus, the effect of constant and pervasive brand promotion is to contribute to the loosening and splintering of identity. A recent review of Zygmunt Bauman's *Liquid Modernity* stated: "We have moved from a period where we understood ourselves as 'pilgrims' in search of deeper meaning to one where we act as 'tourists' in search of multiple but fleeting social experiences."[13]

About twenty-five years ago, at the annual meeting of the Society for the Study of Christian Spirituality, I remember the nervous laughter when one of the speakers commented that any day

---

[13] "Liquid Modernity: Zygmunt Bauman," *Social Theory Rewired: New Connections to Classical and Contemporary Perspectives* (2016), http://routledgesoc.com/category/profile-tags/liquid-modernity.

now we might see spirituality used as an advertising gimmick.[14]
Today, almost no day goes by without encountering ads that play
on themes and images traditionally associated with spirituality.
Inner peace, spiritual masters, spiritual quest, wisdom, healing,
idealized love, joy, perfect fulfillment are all themes deployed to
convince us, as sociologist Bernard McGrane notes, that "life
becomes radiant through consumption."[15] Some of these ads play
upon the irony, for example, a series of humorous commercials
for the South African restaurant chain Chicken Licken that
linked its product to "inner peace." Many others, however, are
completely serious in asserting that the proffered shampoo, car,
or brand of water will assure us of spiritual fulfillment.

The commodification of everything also has a profound effect
on our relationships, especially those of romance and marriage.
Here we find a paradox: on the one hand, there is the permeating mentality of commodification, so that love and sex can
appear as things to shop for and then throw away when a new,
"hotter" option comes on the market; on the other hand, there
is the increasingly desperate search for what sociologists call
the pure relationship. Serious late-modern love seekers want
and expect a kind of utopian intimacy that is centered purely
in the couple itself, without having to answer to any external
criteria. Anthony Giddens writes: "A pure relationship is one
in which external criteria have become dissolved: the relationship exists solely for whatever rewards the relationship as such
can deliver."[16] The confining expectations—and the support
systems—of traditional elements such as kinship, social duty,
family honor, or religious law are eliminated, leaving the couple
to seek a stability based almost exclusively on what they can
generate with each other through mutual self-disclosure and
personal commitment.

---

[14] Bernard McGinn, "The Letter and the Spirit: Spirituality as an
Academic Discipline," *Christian Spirituality Bulletin* 1, no. 2 (1993): 1.

[15] Quoted in Todd Stein, "Zen Sells: How Advertising Has Co-Opted
Spirituality," *Lion's Roar: Buddhist Wisdom for Our Time*, November
1, 1999.

[16] Anthony Giddens, *Modernity and Self-Identity: Self and Society in
the Late Modern Age* (Stanford, CA: Stanford University Press, 1997),
6.

When such a deeply personal, freely chosen, truly mutual relationship works, it can generate a form of partnership more fulfilling and fruitful, perhaps, than any known to previous eras and cultures. Yet the road to success in such a relationship is a minefield. First, a relationship based on mutually delightful feelings has a profound vulnerability to the well-known change-ability of feelings. As anti-marriage activist Dea Birkett notes: "Falling in and out of love is unpredictable. Promising to love someone forever is a promise no honest person would make."[17] Behind this vulnerability is an even more fundamental one. If the essential premise of the pure relationship is that each party is a free and completely unconstrained subject choosing to be with the other, the hidden subtext is that each one is also equally free to stop doing so at any time. The result, as Zygmunt Bauman notes, is that commitment within the pure relationship is actually unilateral; each party must make a choice to commit without any real assurance of what the other, equally free person will do in the future.[18] As in so many other aspects of late-modern life, each person is blessed with entrepreneurial freedom—and cursed with the corresponding vulnerability to failure and isolation.

Can Humanity Survive?

So far we have focused mainly on how life in postmodernity influences the way individuals search for stability and identity. This is taking place, however, within an even larger global crisis, which can be summed up as whether or not the impact of these changes will turn out to be survivable for the human species. The possibility that it will not has two major faces: the skyrocketing rate of ecological decline, and the potential for total war.

That humans may have large and destructive effects on the ecosystems they inhabit is not something new. The human spe-cies is an apex predator and, like others at the top of their food chain, strongly affects the populations of flora and fauna in

---

[17] Dea Birkett, "To See This Hollow Institution as Desirable Is Laugh-able," *The Guardian*, October 3, 2004.

[18] Zygmunt Bauman, *Liquid Love: On the Frailty of Human Bonds* (Malden, MA: Blackwell, 2003).

ecosystems where it is present. Those researching evolutionary history find that whenever humans have arrived in a new environment, extinctions have been likely to follow.[19] Examples are the disappearance of many large mammal species in both Australia and the Americas within a short time after *Homo sapiens* began populating these continents.

In addition to highly efficient hunting techniques, early humans also demonstrated high levels of skill in altering the environment in other ways. Clearing land, diverting water, burning grasslands, and importing species from other locales are examples of ways premodern humans could significantly change the ecosystems within which they lived. Sometimes imprudent human activity led to local catastrophes. Jared Diamond's *Collapse* details how the Easter Islanders, for example, cut down every tree on their islands and in doing so undermined their own society's means of survival.[20] In the bigger picture, though, both the earth and human communities have been resilient. Ecosystem destruction or decline in a given region usually just meant that humans moved elsewhere. That permitted the damaged ecosystem (although perhaps permanently altered) to recover its balance—a slow process that, in some cases, could take centuries.

Modernity and its effect of spiraling rapidification have changed this scenario. The philosophical ideology of modernity, as noted, treats everything—living things and ecosystems included—as essentially objectified commodities to be used for human profit, with profit usually narrowly defined in monetary terms. Scientific and technological advances have given humans the capacity to manipulate the physical world at the micro and macro levels, from transgenic DNA splicing to hydrogen bombs. Consequently, the speed, range, and level of destruction of ecosystems are climbing exponentially. Pollution—most notably, at this moment, carbon dioxide, a main contributor to climate change, and plastic, which is befouling even the depths of the

---

[19] J. M. Diamond, N. P. Ashmole, and P. E. Purves, "The Present, Past, and Future of Human-Caused Extinctions [and Discussion]," *Philosophical Transactions of the Royal Society of London. Series B, Biological Sciences* 325, no. 1228 (1989): 469–77.

[20] Jared M. Diamond, *Collapse: How Societies Choose to Fail or Succeed* (New York: Penguin Books, 2011).

oceans—is changing the dynamics of every ecosystem on earth, from the depths of the ocean to the movements of air and water around the globe. While scientists are working day and night to understand and mitigate some of these effects, many believe that the scale of these destructive impacts by humans is already past the point where any mitigation is possible.

Meanwhile, medical advances, as well as increased food supply, have led to a human population explosion. With human numbers approaching eight billion, there is little available space to which to move when a community's current locale becomes unlivable. The two most common causes of major population displacement are violence and environmental collapse. These two causes are often intertwined, since the decline of available ecosystem resources inevitably leads to conflict as different groups vie for limited land, fuel, water, and other necessities of life. Moreover, modern war is disastrously destructive to the environment.

In 2017, the United Nations Refugee Agency reports, more than 68.5 million people were forcibly displaced from their homes, with 25.4 million of them counted as refugees.[21] This does not include tens or perhaps hundreds of millions more who have voluntarily left their home countries because life has become unsustainable there. Sadly, as the numbers of people seeking a fresh start balloon, so does anti-immigrant sentiment in the countries to which they attempt to move. Currently, tens of millions of people are essentially stateless, stuck in long-term refugee camps or in "illegal alien" status in countries that do not welcome them. Before the end of the twenty-first century there could be as many as a billion people on the move as the effects of climate change and other forms of environmental pollution continue to instigate ecosystem catastrophes and violent conflicts.[22]

While war, even in the days of knives and spears, is ugly and destructive, the modern industrialization of war raises the

---

[21] United Nations High Commissioner for Refugees (UNHCR), "Global Trends: Forced Displacement in 2017" (Geneva: UNHCR, June 25, 2018), 2.

[22] David Wallace-Wells, *The Uninhabitable Earth: Life after Warming* (New York: Tim Duggan Books, 2019).

level of destruction exponentially. The possibility of complete nuclear holocaust, which was much more prominent in public consciousness in the 1950s, is unfortunately still very real. The Doomsday Clock kept by the Union of Atomic Scientists (UAS) began at seven minutes to midnight in 1947, reached a low of two minutes to midnight in 1953, then swung to a high of seventeen minutes to midnight when the Cold War ended in 1991. By 2018, it had fallen again to two minutes to midnight, where it remained at the time of this writing.[23]

But even without nuclear weapons, modern warfare leaves behind an astonishing legacy of damage. Between 1962 and 1973, for example, the United States dropped massive quantities of munitions, napalm, and herbicides on Vietnam in the process of destroying or seriously damaging vast swathes of the forests in the South. In addition to the obvious immediate effects of large-scale death and disruption among humans and other species, long-term impacts have included widespread erosion, large numbers of grotesque birth defects, and a permanent loss of forest cover. The war in Vietnam ended almost fifty years ago; we can only imagine how technological "advances" would raise the scale of damage if similar tactics were employed again.

The possibility that humanity does not have a future is a genuinely new element of life in late modernity. Anthony Giddens observes, "There is a good deal of evidence to indicate that unconscious fears of 'an ending to everything' are prevalent among many sectors of the population, and appear with particular clarity in the fantasies and dreams of children."[24] The theme of an apocalyptic future in which bedraggled tribes of humans traverse devastated landscapes while struggling intrepidly to survive transfixes popular culture, played out in numerous movies, books, and video games. In fact, this future is already being lived by people in ecologically devastated places such as the Niger Delta and the war zones of Syria.

---

[23] "A New Abnormal: It Is *Still* 2 Minutes to Midnight: 2019 Doomsday Clock Announcement," *Bulletin of the Atomic Scientists*, Washington, DC, January 24, 2019.

[24] Giddens, *Modernity and Self-Identity*, 183.

Young Adults Today

Books such as *Generation Me* and *Kids These Days* give depressing portraits of ways the realities described above shape the lives of young people in the United States today.[25] Observing how the system of capitalism has reengineered all of life in view of increasing profits, Malcolm Harris writes: "The growth of growth requires a different kind of person, one whose abilities, skills, emotions and even sleep schedule are in sync with their role in the economy."[26] The children of his generation (born between 1980 and 2000) were constantly supervised in the effort to "optimize" them to fulfill their parents' anxiety for their future success—or, for the less privileged, simply to keep them from "causing trouble." Thus, their childhoods were spent in a constant atmosphere of competition and anxiety. If they could not conform, they were labeled ADHD and dosed with psychiatric medications. If they made it into college, they took on massive debt with the promise that education was the guarantee of success. But once they graduated, they learned that the twenty-first-century work world is brutal, often demanding a constant search for low-paying "gigs" without regular hours or health insurance.

Meanwhile, looking for work, as well as looking for dating partners, requires day-and-night attention to building one's brand on social media. Anne Helen Petersen calls this "the burnout generation" because they are never offline—meaning not only the literally ever-present phone but the never-ending internalized demand to be doing "something" to optimize one's possibilities.[27] Jean Twenge describes how child-rearing styles since the 1990s have encouraged young people to have so much self-esteem that many believe they will almost automatically become rich

[25] Jean M. Twenge, *Generation Me: Why Today's Young Americans Are More Confident, Assertive, Entitled—and More Miserable than Ever Before*, rev. and updated (New York: Atria Paperback, 2014); Malcolm Harris, *Kids These Days: Human Capital and the Making of Millennials* (New York: Back Bay Books/Little Brown and Company, 2018).

[26] Harris, *Kids These Days*, 5.

[27] Anne Helen Petersen, "How Millennials Became the Burnout Generation," *BuzzFeed News*, January 5, 2019.

and famous. They feel so entitled to success that any evidence to the contrary—for example, the critical remarks of a teacher or work supervisor—is boomeranged back as a fault in the criticizer. Twenge's research finds that concern about politics, civic involvement, and environmental issues are declining with each younger cohort. She also details how young people have completely tossed out the sexual mores of previous generations, in many cases preferring multiple hookups with no intention whatsoever of intimacy or relationship.[28] Much more could be said, but the question these studies raise is whether the type of selfhood emerging within the contemporary world has any possibility of sustaining a future for humanity.

Will the Anthropocene flame out as rapidly as it began, as humanity willfully destroys its own habitat? Or is it possible for us to change our predilections sufficiently to create a form of human civilization that is both physically and spiritually sustainable? It is commonly noted that a crisis is also an opportunity. While some look at the realities described above and believe that humanity has little chance of surviving its own destructive predilections, others take the more optimistic view that these are the birth pangs of an era in which humanity will discover a genuinely new way of being in community with one another and with the ecosystems of the earth.

John Paul Lederach observes that, when it comes to working for deep personal or social change, pessimism may actually be a gift. Those who are overly optimistic may not be engaging with the complexity of the situation and the reality of how long it takes for real change to occur.[29] However, if change is to occur, it requires moral imagination that can connect into deep stories and envision relationships afresh. The changes needed for humanity's survival, then, may partially depend upon whether we

---

[28] Twenge, *Generation Me.*

[29] John Paul Lederach, *The Moral Imagination: The Art and Soul of Building Peace* (Oxford: Oxford University Press, 2010), 55.

can envision a deep story of cosmically rooted inclusivity and spiritual catholicity.

The next three chapters engage in that project, specifically from the point of view of searching for grounds for what John Zizioulas calls a catholic personality. First, we explore debates surrounding the questions of foundational subjectivity, the narrative self, and the "no-self" critique proposed by various spiritual and philosophical traditions, in search of a view of selfhood able to answer to both contemporary scholarship and Christian theological concerns.

Chapter 4

Selfhood and Catholicity

The previous chapter described some of the contours of the global crisis facing humanity today. Robert J. Schreiter, focusing especially on the challenges to local cultures created by the rapid rise of globalization and neoliberal capitalism, has proposed that a new development of the theological concept of catholicity may be exactly what is needed to navigate the current crisis with some hope of a positive outcome.[1] He suggests that this "new catholicity" should be marked by an inclusive openness to intercultural exchange and communication, with intensive dialogue to ensure that common meaning is truly achieved across cultural boundaries. He adds that rather than considering these efforts to be catholic as only concerning those within the churches, catholicity can potentially become a heuristic concept—that is, a productive ideal operationalized in a method—for all those who seek a world where both local and universal values are respected.[2]

Schreiter and others have developed norms and guidelines that may help to facilitate such intercultural dialogue. Another question to explore, however, is what kind of person is truly capable of this new catholicity? Given that one of the most salient characteristics of the contemporary crisis is the softening and fragmentation of personal identity, along with a concomitant tendency to react to outsiders with violence and/or hardened

---

[1] Robert J. Schreiter, *The New Catholicity: Theology between the Global and the Local*, Faith and Cultures Series (Maryknoll, NY: Orbis Books, 1997), 132–33.

[2] Schreiter, *The New Catholicity*, 120.

boundaries, what will it take to form people who are able to embrace catholicity fully as a real and joyful interculturality? And, more specific to this project, how do spiritual experience and practice play into such formation?

The idea of a catholic personality has been explored by several theologians, especially John Zizioulas (whose ideas were reviewed in the Introduction) and Miroslav Volf. Volf writes that such a person is radically hospitable to the future that God is bringing into being. This spiritual hospitality breaks open the personality's self-enclosure so that truly different others can be welcomed. Volf concludes that "a catholic personality is a personality enriched by otherness, a personality which is what it is only because multiple others have been reflected in it in a particular way. The distance from my own culture that results from being born by the Spirit creates a fissure in me through which others can come in."[3]

For Volf, a "catholic person" is theologically defined by the indwelling of the Holy Spirit, which brings with it the fullness of Christ and the church.[4] We will explore this theological perspective more fully in Chapter 6. In view of our "catholicity from within" approach, however, we first explore the viewpoint of contemporary psychology and philosophy. In this chapter we search for a model of human selfhood that can encompass trends in contemporary thought as well as potentially creating an opening for fresh theological approaches.

Helpful Categories

Léon Turner observes that there is no agreement on the terminology of *self, person, ego, I,* and so on. Some claim that there is nothing "there" to be discussed. In any case, "the study of the self is the study of a variety of different issues, which cannot be

---

[3] Miroslav Volf, *Exclusion and Embrace: A Theological Exploration of Identity, Otherness, and Reconciliation* (Nashville, TN: Abingdon Press, 1996), 51.

[4] Miroslav Volf, "Catholicity of 'Two or Three': Free Church Reflections on the Catholicity of the Local Church," *The Jurist* 52, no. 1 (1992): 542–43.

captured by a single overarching reductive theory of what the self essentially is."[5] To begin, Turner proposes a basic distinction between the inner representations of the self (images and concepts) and the experiential "sense of self."[6] This is similar to William James's classic distinction between "me" (the self as known) and "I" (the self as knower).[7] One key dimension of selfhood, as we will see, is the inner narrative that plays constantly in the background of our minds, full of images and drama that are shaped by elements of culture and psychology. This is easier to study than the more profound question of who, or what—if anything—"owns" this drama in the sense of giving it an experiential and moral center.

Another helpful set of categories is offered by Hermans and Hermans-Konopka when they delineate characteristics of the traditional, modern, and postmodern models of the self.[8] The traditional model is based on a worldview of "totality, overarching unity, and purpose." People experience themselves as living on a "lower" level while trying to connect with "a higher, better kind of life which can only be achieved if one is able to realize one's proper telos or purpose in the cosmos."[9] Traditional society is hierarchical, with leaders receiving power from above. One does not dialogue with those above one; one obeys.

The modern model moves the self to a separate interior space, over against its world. This is the "sovereign self" who "finds its justification in its own ground."[10] Such a "container self" maintains strict boundaries, excluding the other and always seeking control. The modern, inner-directed self emphasizes "personal goals, inner strength, overcoming resistance, personal

---

[5] Léon Turner, *Theology, Psychology, and the Plural Self* (Burlington, VT: Ashgate, 2008), 66.

[6] Turner, *Theology, Psychology, and the Plural Self*, 77.

[7] William James, *The Principles of Psychology*, vol. 1 (New York, Henry Holt and Company, 1890: reprint New York: Dover, 1950).

[8] Hubert J. M. Hermans and Agnieszka Hermans-Konopka, *Dialogical Self Theory: Positioning and Counter-Positioning in a Globalizing Society* (Cambridge, UK: Cambridge University Press, 2010), 84–101.

[9] Hermans and Hermans-Konopka, *Dialogical Self Theory*, 84.

[10] Hermans and Hermans-Konopka, *Dialogical Self Theory*, 87.

achievement and heroism, masculinity, autonomy, future-orien-
tation, progress, and control of the situation."[11]

The postmodern model, finally, eliminates both metanarratives
and the self's inner core in favor of "fragmentation and superficial play with an endless stream of images and sensations."[12]
Life becomes a protean process of change, flux, and a multiplicity of disconnected relationships that require constant rewriting
of the self's story. In the last chapter we saw many of the forces
leading to this result.

Anthony Giddens observes that with the demise of traditional
cultures and the rise of modernity, "the self becomes a reflexive
project."[13] This means that, whereas in traditional cultures a
person's identity is typically ascribed to him or her by the group
and undergoes few changes other than those programmed into
life stages, in modernity each individual is handed the responsibility of constructing a unique identity. In postmodernity the
challenge increases as one must continuously adapt one's identity
to arising circumstances that are themselves malleable and under
construction. Hermans and Hermans-Konopka argue that in the
"glocalizing" (that is, both globalizing and localizing) reality of
late modernity, the "project of the self" actually draws upon elements of all three models. As we will note, their "dialogical self
theory" is an effort to theorize this. First, however, let us examine
the ongoing debates on this topic.

Critique of the Modern Substantial Self

A predominant theme today is criticism of the concept of the
"substantial self" that had emerged in the early modern era.
In brief, this was the view that beneath the transience of our
thoughts, images, feelings, and relationships lies a core of consciousness where our real personhood and agency reside. This
view originated in the influential writings of René Descartes
(1596–1650), who identified the human being as a rational, free

---

[11] Hermans and Hermans-Konopka, *Dialogical Self Theory*, 89.

[12] Hermans and Hermans-Konopka, *Dialogical Self Theory*, 91.

[13] Anthony Giddens, *Modernity and Self-Identity: Self and Society in
the Late Modern Age* (Stanford, CA: Stanford University Press, 1997),
32.

mind allied with a mechanistic body. The Cartesian project, says Fergus Kerr, was to arrive at an absolute point of view by eliminating everything having to do with one's local, embodied viewpoint and presence. The result was a picture of a "self-conscious and self-reliant, self-transparent and all-responsible individual."[14]

For Descartes, all matter, body included, is "mere extension" that in no way participates in the spiritual dimension represented by the human mind. To live rationally and objectively, with interior freedom, is the highest human dignity. Meanwhile, whereas the ancient and medieval world largely regarded the world beyond the self as having a reality whose "forms" or true nature one could discover by encountering them, the post-Cartesian view is that knowledge consists only of mental insights constructed according to the mind's own rules of engagement. In this view "transcendence" resides, not in openness and surrender to God (or, for that matter, to any reality beyond the self), but in the human mind's capacity to transcend and objectify the world. Thus the human mind becomes almost godlike in its capacity to stand apart from the world and to reconstruct it (both mentally and physically) according to its own lights. This modern perspective, then, affirms that what Léon Turner called the existential "sense of self" is borne by a substantial, conscious, experiencing entity that is transcendent to any of the contents of its consciousness.

As Philip Rolnick notes, this belief that the self's bedrock is its self-consciousness led to the self becoming "an object to itself, even an imprisoning obsession, as it goes to great ends to evaluate and analyze itself, and now, quite commonly, to be analyzed."[15] He is pointing, of course, to the psychoanalytic movement founded by Sigmund Freud (1856–1939). Freud sought to take the Cartesian turn to its logical climax by developing methods that would liberate people from suffering as they learned how to objectify themselves and thus gain insight into how they internally construct their individual perspective on the

---

[14] Fergus Kerr, "The Modern Philosophy of Self in Recent Theology," in *Neuroscience and the Person: Scientific Perspectives on Divine Action*, ed. Robert J. Russell et al., Scientific Perspectives on Divine Action 4 (Berkeley, CA: Vatican Observatory Foundation; Center for Theology and the Natural Sciences, 2002), 24.

[15] Philip A. Rolnick, *Person, Grace, and God*, Sacra Doctrina (Grand Rapids, MI: Eerdmans, 2007), 214.

world. Freud, as well as most of the schools of modern psychology that followed, located the possibility of transcendence and liberation squarely within the human realm, eliminating any need for divine or ecclesial intervention.

While Descartes himself remained a believer in God and at least nominally a member of the Christian church, when he replaced the centrality of transcendence-into-God with transcendence-into-self, he set in motion what would eventually culminate in Friedrich Nietzsche's radical and contemptuous atheism. Yet Nietzsche's vaunted "death of God," it turned out, was also the death of the modern "substantial self." As Philip Rolnick observes, Nietzsche "would abolish the very notion of the subject. Again and again, he refers to it as a fiction, something of an indexical convenience blown up into a basic metaphysical essence, an effect confused with a cause."[16]

Nietzsche, then, was a key figure in what is today called the postmodern movement of deconstruction. This is the view that all our relationships and structures, whether physical, mental, or linguistic, are arbitrary and transient. A radically postmodern view of the self is that there is no such thing; human life, like the existence of anything at all, is only a constant restless flux of experiences and temporary relationships that emerge and fall away until death calls an end to the process. This view asserts that, in reality, the play of the narrative or representational self has no center of experience or continuity; in Gertrude Stein's much-quoted words, "There is no 'there' there."[17]

The No-Self Debate

The view that there really is no such thing as a self has become popular among avant-garde academics, but it also has deep roots in certain longstanding spiritual traditions, most notably

---

[16] Rolnick, *Person, Grace, and God*, 107.

[17] Gertrude Stein, *Everybody's Autobiography* (New York: Cooper Square, 1971), 289. The original statement referred to her childhood home in Oakland, California, which had been demolished. Her words have entered popular culture, however, as a summary of the postmodern view of reality.

Buddhism. In a review of a book in which Western philosophers debate with Buddhists on the question of self, John Spackman proposes that there are actually three possible stances: substantialism, non-substantialism, and "no-self" views.[18] Substantialism is the modern Cartesian/Kantian view, described above. Non-substantialist views assert that while there is no permanent ontological entity called a self, we can rightfully identify an experiential self with some form of consciousness, continuity, and agency. The most radical no-self views deny even this much, claiming that the sense of having a self is simply an illusion created by brain processes.

Almost every discussion of the no-self question quotes a widely known passage from philosopher David Hume (1711–76), who scoffed that no matter how hard he looked, he could not find a "self" anywhere in his mind or body. He writes: "We are never intimately conscious of anything but a particular perception; man is a bundle or collection of different perceptions which succeed one another with an inconceivable rapidity and are in perpetual flux and movement."[19] Thus Hume applied his "bundle theory" (that objects do not have substance but are only a bundle of properties) even to human selfhood. Daniel Dennett is a more recent philosopher who argues similarly. Our experience of the world and of ourselves actually has no innate coherence, but we confabulate the story of the self as a "narrative center of gravity"—a fiction that helps us coordinate our activity more effectively.[20]

No-self *(anatta)* is a central doctrine of Buddhism. Buddhists affirm that there is no permanently abiding self or soul, but only the ever-changing flow of thoughts, feelings, perceptions, and so on. Ever since the time of the Buddha, however, what this means has been greatly debated. As the volume reviewed by Spackman

---

[18] John Spackman, "Self, No Self? Perspectives from Analytical, Phenomenological, and Indian Traditions," *Mind* 125, no. 499 (July 2016): 923.

[19] David Hume, *Treatise on Human Nature* I, IV, sec. 6.

[20] Daniel Dennett, "The Self as a Center of Narrative Gravity," in *Self and Consciousness: Multiple Perspectives*, ed. Frank S. Kessel, Pamela M. Cole, and Dale L. Johnson (Hillsdale, NJ: Lawrence Erlbaum Associates, 1992).

indicates, the variety of different Buddhist interpretations of "no-self" rivals the numerous philosophical positions on offer today. An example of the most radical view is offered by one of the volume's editors, Mark Siderits, who denies the reality of consciousness itself. He affirms that not only is the self an illusion, but so is our belief that we are aware of ourselves. Siderits goes so far as to propose that true Buddhas are those who know that, in fact, they are zombies—mere cogs in an "undead" societal information processing machine.[21]

Many Buddhists, however, interpret the no-self doctrine in ways that are more compatible with a middle or non-substantialist position. They affirm that while there is no ontological self or soul, the empirical and psychological self has a certain level of reality. Buddhist teacher Martin Verhoeven, for example, asserts that Buddhists affirm the ordinary sense of "person" as one who has experiences and is responsible for his or her actions. He also notes that the Buddha explicitly rejected the views of the nihilists of his own time, who taught that human actions are meaningless, and therefore, we have no moral responsibility for our behavior.[22]

When it comes to human selfhood, however, Siderits is not alone in arguing that there is no "there" there. This assertion that what appears to be consciousness and agency is actually only the buzzing and beeping of impersonal neural networks represents the culmination of the postmodern deconstructionist approach. Such an extreme no-self position would be difficult to reconcile with basic tenets of Christian theology. A moderated non-substantialist position, however, presents more possibilities.

Reclaiming the Self in Postmodernity

Today, much debate revolves around these contrasting views of the self. Is there ultimately a core of responsible consciousness

---

[21] Mark Siderits, "Buddhas as Zombies: A Buddhist Reduction of Subjectivity," in *Self, No Self? Perspectives from Analytical, Phenomenological, and Indian Traditions*, ed. Mark Siderits, Evan Thompson, and Dan Zahavi, 308–31 (New York: Oxford University Press, 2011).

[22] Martin J. Verhoeven, "Buddhist Ideas about No-Self and the Person," *Religion East and West* 10 (October 2010): 98–101.

capable of grounding the "blooming, buzzing confusion"[23] of our inner experience, or is the most intimate reality of our own being actually nothing but flux and death? Various philosophers have attempted responses. Dan Zahavi, for example, offers helpful clarifications when he explains why we should reject a Kantian approach, that is, the idea of the self as a "pure identity-pole" to which "any episode of experiencing refers back." This would be the concept of a pure subject, unsullied by any element of being an object. Such a pure self is discovered only as a presupposition of experience, not as a "given" within experience.[24] Despite being non-substantial, it retains the aura of the "essential self" of modernity.

The alternative that Zahavi offers is the phenomenological self, described as "the self as an experiential dimension" emerging within the stream of consciousness.[25] The phenomenological self is not over against the stream of consciousness; rather, it is an essential part of its structure. Zahavi writes: "To have a self-experience [is] simply the acquaintance with an experience in its first-personal mode of presentation, that is, from 'within.'"[26] Rather than talking about a "subject of experience," he asserts, we should instead speak of the "subjectivity of experience." This approach accounts for the diachronic continuity of our life experience because the first-person givenness of the self carries through all the diverse experiences constituting a life history. The narrative self, he observes, depends on the underlying reality of the phenomenological self.[27] Dan McAdams takes a similar stance when he uses *self* as a verb, writing: "To self—or to maintain the 'stance' of an 'I' in the world—is to apprehend

---

[23] James, *The Principles of Psychology*, 488. James was describing the impact of the world on an infant who has not yet developed the capacity to discriminate among perceptions.

[24] Dan Zahavi, "Phenomenology of Self," in *The Self in Neuroscience and Psychiatry*, ed. Tilo Kircher and Anthony S. David (Cambridge, UK: Cambridge University Press, 2003), 57; idem, *Subjectivity and Selfhood: Investigating the First-Person Perspective* (Cambridge, MA: MIT Press, 2008).

[25] Zahavi, "Phenomenology of Self," 59.

[26] Zahavi, "Phenomenology of Self," 61.

[27] Zahavi, "Phenomenology of Self," 62–63.

and appropriate experience as a subject, to grasp phenomenal experience as one's own, as belonging 'to me.'"[28]

Calvin Schrag is another philosopher who wants to split the difference between the substance-self of modernity and the completely deconstructed self of postmodernity. In John Spackman's terms, he affirms a non-substantialist view rather than embracing no-self. In an interview question about his book *The Self after Postmodernity*, Schrag chided postmodernists "for failing to realize that the basic truth of deconstruction resides in the fact that no complete deconstruction is possible." He continued, summing up his perspective as follows:

> The self, I argued, is not an unchanging substance, or a transcendental ego, or a universal entity of some sort, or an abstract assimilation of attributes and properties. No, the self is a concrete, life-affirming, sensing and perceiving lived body, dynamically changing and developing in its struggle for self-knowledge and self-constitution. The self is a wayfarer along life's way who is able to understand and constitute itself in its discourse, its action, its community, and its encounters with transcendence.[29]

While Schrag affirms the postmodern view that the self is not separate from the body and that it is always on the move and in process, he takes from the modern view the concept of the self's capacity to seek genuine values, to make choices, and to constitute itself through its acts and relationships. He calls this "a praxis-oriented self, defined by its communicative practices."[30] Schrag and others seeking to mediate the modern/postmodern debate are eager above all to emphasize that the self does not stand in solitary splendor apart from its own relationships and actions but is genuinely constituted by them. As Pamela Cooper-White

---

[28] Dan P. McAdams, "The Case for Unity in the (Post)Modern Self: A Modest Proposal," in *Self and Identity: Fundamental Issues*, ed. R. D. Ashmore and L. Jussim (New York: Oxford University Press, 1997), 56.

[29] Laureano Ralón, "Interview with Calvin O. Schrag," *Figure/Ground*, January 24, 2011.

[30] Calvin O. Schrag, *The Self after Postmodernity* (New Haven, CT: Yale University Press, 1999), 9.

notes, "The problematic aspect of a 'core' or essential self is not so much what it contains, but what it excludes, i.e., the inherent relationality and interdependence of persons."[31] By defining the self as an active agent of communication, Schrag identifies human selfhood as constitutively embedded in relationships.

The Contribution of Relational Psychological Theories

It is noteworthy that despite Freud's focus on Cartesian self-objectification as a path to liberation, his most revolutionary discovery was that the most liberating of all methods is "interpretation of the transference," that is, alert attention to the actual dynamics occurring in a live relationship between a patient and a therapist. It is in embodied intersubjective dialogue that the life of the self—including its most profound self-knowledge—comes most fully into being. Even as they employed this intersubjective method in clinical practice, however, Freud and much of the psychoanalytic movement that followed him embraced a more impersonal instinct-based model to explain psychological dynamics and structures.

Certain schools of post-Freudian psychology, however, developed the insight into relationality more systematically. One approach that became popular in the 1980s and 1990s among those interested in employing psychology to understand the spiritual life better was object relations theory. The term *object relations* is rather off-putting to the uninitiated, but in fact, its basic thrust is a shift from the mainstream Freudian instinctual model to a more interpersonal model. This theory focuses on development occurring within the earliest caregiver-infant bond rather than on the Oedipal phase (ages three to six) that Freud regarded as so decisive. An *object relation* is an intrapsychic structure resulting from the internalization of early relationships with people, especially the mother (or another primary

---

[31] Pamela Cooper-White, "Reenactors: Theological and Psychological Reflections on 'Core Selves,' Multiplicity, and the Sense of Cohesion," in *In Search of Self: Interdisciplinary Perspectives on Personhood*, ed. J. Wentzel Van Huyssteen and Erik P. Wiebe (Grand Rapids, MI: Eerdmans, 2011), 150.

caretaker). Michael St. Clair defines *object* as "a mental image of a person . . . colored with feelings."[32] On this basis Cooper-White develops a view of the human subject as "a web or network of self-states . . . formed in identification with objects or part-objects we have internalized from our experiences of other persons since birth."[33]

While object relations theory focused on psychological content (for example, internalized images of self and others in relationship), Heinz Kohut's "self psychology" sought to articulate the psychology of the underlying existential "sense of self." Kohut defined the self as a fundamental psychological structure that is not knowable in itself (as content would be) but nevertheless can be tracked and interpreted through observable data. He writes:

> The self . . . is, like all reality—physical reality (the data about the world perceived by our senses) or psychological reality (the data about the world perceived via introspection and empathy)—not knowable in its essence. We cannot, by introspection and empathy, penetrate to the self per se; only its introspectively or empathically perceived manifestations are open to us.[34]

Consequently, Kohut offers a psychological theory that can substantiate Schrag's middle way between the substantial self of modernity and the dissolved self of postmodernity. When asked to further define the self, Kohut answered with a phenomenological description of selfhood as it is experienced:

> There are a number of things that define this experience. The self is the center of initiative. We experience ourselves as the center of initiative. We know we are influenced, we know we listen to other people's opinions, we consider choices. And yet somewhere there is a sense of comparative independence, of assertiveness, of initiative. That's one feature.

---

[32] Michael St. Clair, *Object Relations and Self Psychology: An Introduction*, 4th ed. (Belmont, CA: Thomson/Brooks/Cole, 2004), 126–27.

[33] Cooper-White, "Reenactors," 143.

[34] Heinz Kohut, *The Restoration of the Self* (Chicago: University of Chicago Press, 2009), 311.

Another feature is cohesion in space and continuity in time. There is also a sense of cohesion versus fragmentation; a sense of the harmony of oneself versus the chaos of oneself; a sense of strength about the self versus a sense of weakness, lack of vitality; a sense of feeling alive. We must feel alive. Part of being less than a self (amusing as that sounds) is not to feel alive. . . . Now when you may say you have a fragmented self, you still say "self." But if it were totally fragmented, it wouldn't be a self.[35]

Kohut's approach, like that of object relations theory, is also radically relational. He developed the concept of the "selfobject," which, strictly speaking, is not a person, but rather the self's internalized perception of another being's participation in building up the self. The two most important types of selfobject relations are "mirroring," in which the other gazes admiringly on the self, and "idealizing," in which the other is admired by the self. Kohut is reported to have often said that "there is no self without a selfobject,"[36] meaning by this that the internalization of both types of relationship is essential for the construction of a viable self. The very young child needs to feel admired, praised, regarded as desirable and competent, *and* to feel admiration for someone who is beneficent, powerful, and provides a sense of safety and belonging. These selfobject experiences are internalized as story templates that the person can utilize throughout life to form increasingly mature relationships that both support the self and sustain thriving communities.

The Storytelling Self

Our internalized images and stories derive from our past experience, yet their function has more to do with shaping our

---

[35] Heinz Kohut and Charles B. Strozier, *Self Psychology and the Humanities: Reflections on a New Psychoanalytic Approach* (New York: W. W. Norton, 1985), 234–35.

[36] Marshall L. Silverstein, *Self-Psychology and Diagnostic Assessment: Identifying Selfobject Functions through Psychological Testing* (New York: Routledge, 1999), 212.

future choices and actions. Neurophysiologist Rodolfo R. Llinás proposes that selfhood arises from the need of even the most rudimentary motile creatures to be able to make predictive assessments of cognitive input in order to act on behalf of their own survival. This input arrives through many channels but must be centrally coordinated so that the creature can make an organized physical response. He sums up: "Self is the centralization of prediction."[37]

Much of this centralization and assessment occurs at a level of awareness that does not require consciousness. Llinás gives examples: blinking one's eye before being conscious of an approaching insect, and a boxer who can react far faster than he can consciously evaluate what he perceives. As evolution produces creatures with capacities for more complex kinds of controlled movement, however, it has also generated self-awareness and thinking minds.[38] With an interplay of unconscious and conscious mentation, humans can ruminate, fantasize, think, or plan. Although an approach like that of Llinás is physiologically reductionistic, it is noteworthy that it accords well with the developing consensus that human selfhood is both a centralized "being present" and a guiding, predictive narrative.

This consensus, then, understands the representational self both as fundamentally relational and as constructing itself through storytelling. As Jerome Bruner notes, "Self-making is a narrative art." He described this art as drawing on an inner dimension of "memory, feelings, ideas, beliefs, subjectivity," but also on the outer dimensions of "the apparent esteem of others and the myriad expectations that we early, even mindlessly, pick up from the culture in which we are immersed." While we are not slaves of culture, "all cultures provide presuppositions and perspectives about selfhood, rather like plot summaries or homilies for telling oneself or others about oneself."[39] Thus our story selves are both highly individualized and deeply shaped by the cultures, languages, and literatures to which we are exposed.

---

[37] Rodolfo R. Llinás, *I of the Vortex: From Neurons to Self*, A Bradford Book (Cambridge, MA: MIT Press, 2002), 23.

[38] Llinás, *I of the Vortex*, 50.

[39] Jerome S. Bruner, *Making Stories: Law, Literature, Life* (Cambridge, MA: Harvard University Press, 2003), 65–66.

The pervasiveness of the storytelling impulse was explored in the 1940s when psychologists conducted experiments in which they presented people with shapes such as triangles and circles moving around randomly or in meaningless patterns. The test subjects consistently used stories to describe the shapes and movements in terms of agents, intentions, and plots. For example, the random movements of a circle and a triangle might be recounted as a comedy in which a man romantically pursues a woman who repeatedly evades him. These experiments demonstrated that humans instinctively construe movement through time and space as having a narrative structure.[40] Even when there is actually no pattern to the movement that we see, our minds want to emplot it as a drama full of intentional action, crisis, and efforts to bring about resolution.

Not surprisingly, this applies above all to how we make sense of events in our own lives. Whether casually chatting about what happened today or very seriously trying to explain the meaning of our life, we tell stories. Gustav Freytag (1816–95) delineated a five-part, pyramidal model of dramatic structure: (1) exposition (introduction of protagonists and goals); (2) rising action (conflict and counter-action); (3) climax (turning point; protagonist's fate changes); (4) falling action (working toward resolution); (5) denouement (resolution).[41] Even simple stories tend to be emplotted along these lines. The psychoanalytic movement revealed how deeply this storytelling impulse structures not only conscious discourse, but even the unconscious. While the exact source and meaning (if any) of nighttime dreams remain disputed, they exemplify the brain's compulsion to create exciting dramas out of whatever impulses are coursing through it.

More important for our spiritual lives, however, is the way internalized stories subconsciously govern our choices. Psychologists have studied in detail how each of us creatively weaves early life experiences into a template for a personal drama in which we ourselves are both author and "hero." This template, however,

---

[40] Theodore R. Sarbin, "The Narrative Quality of Action," *Theoretical and Philosophical Psychology* 10, no. 2 (1990): 50–51.

[41] Gustav Freytag, *Freytag's Technique of the Drama: An Exposition of Dramatic Composition and Art*, trans. Elias J. MacEwan 6th ed. (1923; Andesite Press, 2015).

can help or hinder us as we move through life. For example, one storyline may be that of the abandoned and wounded child who is repeatedly rejected. All future events will be emplotted in terms of this storyline, leading to a life of failed relationships and a deeply embedded conviction of victimhood. A more positive storyline would be that of the admired child whose accomplishments bring pride and honor to the family. This story can fuel great achievement on behalf of family and community. However, if the story is held on to rigidly, such a person may feel compelled to overwork in the expectation of greater and greater acclaim. Moreover, the person may have no way to make sense of times when life delivers rejection, conflict, or failure.

These examples are, of course, somewhat oversimplified. As we will see in the next section, our inner repertoire is not limited to just one storyline. Moreover, humans are endowed with an element of freedom and creativity such that the plot of our story can evolve in ways not wholly predetermined by early life experience. The goal of much psychotherapy is to awaken this freedom so that a person who has felt constrained to live out a self-destructive storyline can discover the potential to choose a different way of constructing his or her life story.

The key point for our purposes, though, is that a helpful way of defining the representational self is as a dynamic storytelling process through which a person interprets events, selects actions, and seeks to create a future. The self is not so much a structure, in the sense of something established and stable, as an ongoing process of construing experience narratively. Theodore Sarbin compared the self to an author who "composes a script, a drama, a scenario, using imaginative skills to create order out of disconnected or chaotic events."[42] This includes using poetic license to ignore some inputs, emphasize others, or bend the plot toward desired outcomes. It also involves negotiating with others, since ultimately our self-narratives have to be performed in shared social spaces. In this regard Sarbin recalls James Thurber's story of Walter Mitty, whose highly heroic inner self-narrative dissolved into a very different story when he faced the real people

---

[42] Sarbin, "The Narrative Quality of Action," 59.

in his life.[43] The story has great humorous appeal because we all recognize this disjunction between our fantasies and our actual behavior.

The comparison with narrative dynamics gives important insight into both continuous and labile elements of the self. Stories require a strong thread of continuity as past characters and events must contextualize the emerging drama, yet stories can also have surprising plot twists or reconfigurations of their cast of characters. In fact, the best stories do all of these things—they maintain recognizable coherence from beginning to end while also delighting us with suspense and surprise. The same, perhaps, could be said of the healthy human self. Still, as Bruner notes, "self-making through self-narrating is restless and endless, probably more so now than ever before."[44]

The Plural Self

Indeed, it is common to argue today that the very idea that we have a single "self," even at the level of representations and narratives, should be replaced with a more complex view. Feminists and postcolonialists, among others, point to the problematic political implications of the modern urge to postulate a unified self. Pamela Cooper-White asserts:

> A solitary construct of what it means to be human participates in an exaggerated heroic narrative, which cannot be disentangled from the myths of conquest that undergird both imperialism and colonialism. . . . Devotion to oneness benefits the "One" who masquerades as the universal, whereas multiplicity makes space for the marginalized, those constructed as "Other" in the binary dualism of One versus Many.[45]

---

[43] "The Secret Life of Walter Mitty," in James Thurber, *Writings and Drawings*, Library of America 90 (New York: Literary Classics of the United States, 1996); Sarbin, "The Narrative Quality of Action," 59–60.

[44] Bruner, *Making Stories*, 84.

[45] Cooper-White, "Reenactors," 151.

The plural self concept asserts that human beings do not form just one, unified representational self but, rather, a shifting network of alternative selves with which to negotiate the varied circumstances they encounter. As Fernando Pessoa states: "Each of us is more than one person, many people, a proliferation of our one self. . . . In the vast colony of our being, there are different kinds of people, all thinking and feeling differently."[46] Recalling Turner's distinction between the inner representations of the self (images and concepts) and the existential sense of self, the argument that inner representations of self are multiple may be less radical than the argument that the "I" itself lacks unity. Even in less pluralistic cultures people grow up participating in various relationships and roles that give alternative experiences of self. For example, self-with-mother may be affectionate and playful, while self-with-teacher may be nervous and perfectionist. There is a certain commonsense quality to the recognition that we can be different people in different circumstances.

Nevertheless, the plurality of the self may remain masked in premodern or traditionalist cultural situations that offer—or impose—clearly defined, unified guidelines and supports for how people are to form their identities. Today, however, daily life typically involves engaging in ever-changing relationships with people of widely differing ethnicities, cultures, and value systems. Zygmunt Bauman, as noted earlier, delineated "the essential instability" of the conditions within which people today must compose and maintain their sense of self.[47] Under these circumstances, Léon Turner observes, "each new social interaction carries with it a multiplicity of novel passageways into the future, and no common rules exist to help the individual adjudicate between different courses of action."[48] Not only must people be engaged in a permanent process of reconstructing their sense of world and self, but they must also have a chameleon-like ability to bring forth new forms for new circumstances. Bauman goes so far as to state that a common result is a "palimpsest identity" in

---

[46] Fernando Pessoa, *The Book of Disquiet*, ed. Maria José de Lancastre (London: Serpent's Tail, 1991), 11.

[47] Zygmunt Bauman and Rein Raud, *Practices of Selfhood* (Malden, MA: Polity Press, 2015), 121.

[48] Turner, *Theology, Psychology, and the Plural Self*, 46.

which independent "snapshots" pile upon one another without any attempt at unification.[49]

Psychologists confirm the multiplicity of inner representations but emphasize distinctions between healthy multiplicity and pathological fragmentation. Object relations theory describes a range of internalized objects with associated emotions providing a repertoire of potential responses to new situations. In his concept of self psychology Kohut argues that, in normal development, a "nuclear self" is formed that lives out the stance of relation to a primary selfobject—typically patterning itself according to either the mirroring or idealizing styles.[50] Kohut notes: "This structure is the basis for our sense of being an independent center of initiative and perception, integrated with our most central ambitions and ideals and with our experience that our body and mind form a unit in space and a continuum in time."[51] Chronic fragmentation of self, however, occurs when the nuclear self is weak or nonexistent, and the person is unable to attain any sense of coherence, continuity, or vitality. This is a dangerous psychological condition in which the person is likely to be subject to bouts of rage, severe sexual dysfunction, repeated relationship failure, and other personally and socially distressing symptoms.

Nonetheless, postmodernists argue that not all self-multiplicity is pathological. Rather, it can be playful and emancipating. While modernists looked for the one "authentic self" hidden behind inauthentic versions, postmodernists take delight in the vertigo of leaving behind all fixed reference points.[52] Gregory Peterson captures this when he writes that the self is a body-based process that "resembles more a surfer on the sea than a ship and its captain."[53] Joseph Davis concludes, "In these celebratory versions

---

[49] Zygmunt Bauman, *The Individualized Society* (Malden, MA: Polity Press, 2001), 83.

[50] Note that Kohut's "nuclear self" is not understood as "a constitutional, inherent essence," but as an internalized template for relationships (see Cooper-White, "Reenactors," 147).

[51] Kohut, *The Restoration of the Self*, 177.

[52] Turner, *Theology, Psychology, and the Plural Self*, 56–57.

[53] Gregory R. Peterson, "Do Split Brains Listen to Prozac?" *Zygon* 39, no. 3 (2004): 555.

of postmodernism, the performative ability to transcend and reconstitute one's self is the very definition of freedom."[54] The question remains, however: Is this playful multiplicity fundamentally at the level of the "me" or self-representations, or does it go so far as to dissolve the very consistency of the "I"? While some clearly affirm the no-self position, most theorists aim for the middle-ground, non-substantialist view of a fluid and plural self that nonetheless retains a capacity for centered consciousness and responsibility.

The Dialogical Self

The dialogical self theory of Hubert Hermans and Agnieszka Hermans-Konopka offers a way to bring together much of what has been discussed.[55] They draw on the work of Russian literary critic Mikhail Bakhtin (1895–1975), who analyzed works of literature as expressing a multiplicity of voices. Bakhtin's basic insight was that every word or phrase that we employ has an intrinsic quality both of being addressed to certain other persons and of calling forth from them a response. This is not a simple two-person exchange, however, because we are always involved in multiple relationships at once. Moreover, our words themselves have been acquired from the multiple conversations in which we are embedded, so when we make any utterance we resound echoes in all those conversations even as we create new ones. All discourse, then, is dialogic in multiple and complex ways. Whenever we speak or write, we engage a complex play of voices both within our inner world and in the world that we address.

Hermans and Hermans-Konopka transpose this from the world of literature to the psychology of the self. Like language, the self is intrinsically oriented to communicating with others and seeking a response from them. Through the relationships that it experiences, the self develops a range of "positions," that is, styles, roles, and communicative strategies. It then deploys them in creative interior and exterior dialogues to sustain itself

---

[54] Joseph E. Davis, ed., *Identity and Social Change* (New Brunswick, NJ: Transaction Publishers, 2000), 57.

[55] Hermans and Hermans-Konopka, *Dialogical Self Theory*.

and to achieve its goals. The self's dialogues, however, are not simple, but always involve "a dynamic multiplicity of I-positions or voices in the landscape of the mind, intertwined as this mind is with the minds of other people." In a globalizing society, Hermans and Hermans-Konopka note, the position repertoire of the self must consider "an unprecedented density of positions," which are "more heterogeneous and laden with differences, oppositions, and contradictions."[56] The self must frequently change and adapt to the emergence of unexpected positions, both internally and externally. These multiple identities are not necessarily harmonized, but remain labile and restless as I-positions hybridize, split, reform, and contend with one another.

It is important to note that Hermans and Hermans-Konopka are not proposing a no-self view that sees this flux simply as random and unanchored movement. They affirm: "It is our view that the notion of multi-voicedness or multi-positionality can coexist very well with a self that acknowledges the working of the I as a guardian of a certain degree of unity and continuity in the self."[57] The other key point to emphasize is that the dialogical self is relational to the core. It is complex, contentious, and restless, but all in the interests of engagement in multiple dialogical relationships. Thus, it is far from the image of the solitary modern self, which surveys the world from an interior vantage point in order to use objectivity and reason to seize control and "integrate" its world. Hermans and Hermans-Konopka's view of the self as essentially a dynamic, complex, embodied, and relational process accords with Spackman's middle group of non-substantialist theories of the self.

For our goal of developing insight into a catholic way of being, an important insight offered here by Hermans and Hermans-Konopka is that the intrinsic dynamism of the self has both centering and decentering tendencies. Movements to localize—that is, to root oneself more fully in a particular place and community—can stabilize the self's sense of coherence but may also risk closure to new potentials. Movements to globalize—that is, to engage with diverse and discontinuous cultures—energize innovation but risk fragmenting the self. In the postmodern context

[56] Hermans and Hermans-Konopka, *Dialogical Self Theory*, 31–32.
[57] Hermans and Hermans-Konopka, *Dialogical Self Theory*, 146.

the dialogical self operates as a "pendulum swinging between the decentering movements of globalization and the centering movements of localization."[58] Keep in mind, however, that as it swings, the dialogical self "pendulum" is not just shifting from one position to another but, rather, creating new coalitions of positions with each swing.

To clarify this concept, consider a teenage Mexican youth who crosses the border into the United States. Prior to this trip his identity was formed by a fairly local, centered coalition of positions including "I as son of my hardworking parents," "I as indigenous Purepecha from Michoacán," "I as Catholic," "I as farmer," and "I as the one who can save my family from poverty." When he arrives in the United States, he is decentered from all these positions and instead has to deal with deeply destabilizing ones including "I as illegal alien," "I as despised brown, Spanish-speaking person," "I as pressured by drug traffickers," "I as day laborer," and "I as almost starving." As he tries to make his way, he strives to re-center by connecting with other Mexican immigrants from his original locality who can affirm some of his earlier positions as well as empathize with the fragmenting forces in his new reality. Yet he cannot rely totally on his country mates; he has to learn a new language, adapt to new cultural customs, and develop new work skills. The cycle between taking in new, decentering positions and striving to find a localized center may continue for some time before the young man is able to establish a new identity, perhaps by making new coalitions such as "I as proud Mexican and Texan," "I as belonging to a small evangelical church where we all help each other survive," and "I as skilled construction worker who can send money home to my family."

Hermans and Hermans-Konopka also introduce another concept that is helpful in thinking about the question of how people can develop a catholic personality. Describing a variety of types of expanded awareness and mystical experiences, they propose that such events can actually "deposition" the self so that, at least temporarily, it is simply a field of awareness rather than being identified with specific, socially mediated positions. The depositioned self is characterized by open receptivity, permeable boundaries,

---

[58] Hermans and Hermans-Konopka, *Dialogical Self Theory*, 62.

and awareness of being part of a larger whole. Such experiences, they observe, are not limited to "gifted mystics" but occur rather commonly in various contexts. Often, such an event triggers a change of direction and/or the discovery of new possibilities for future identity. They conclude: "In our view, an increasingly globalized, interconnected world society is in need of a self that learns to be part of an expanded field of awareness. That is, self-contained identities are not well suited to work on such problems, because their strict boundaries are too sharp and their extensions too limited to feel solidarity with people and the environment on a global scale."[59] We will develop this idea of the "catholicizing" role of depositioning events more extensively in Chapter 7.

Psychologist John A. Teske adds his voice to this perspective as he discusses the discovery of brain scientists that some aspects of the functioning of the human brain and of our cognitive system are inherently modular. Modularity means that many cognitive functions are managed by specific brain areas and may have evolved separately from one another. This creates a fundamental "integrity problem," since a fragmentation of the self is our default state. Religion and spirituality, then, have emerged in human life because they function to solve this integrity problem.

Teske suggests that while "integrity of belief" and "integrity of emotion" may be desirable, the integrity problem is not really solved except by an "integrity of relation"—that is, a profound sense of belonging to a whole greater than oneself. The self, which is "not an interior entity but an intersubjective mode of being,"[60] must learn to identify with larger and larger intersubjective entities. This culminates, Teske suggests, when the self gives itself up for the benefit of the whole. He writes:

> This is not a vitiation of the self but its transformation, its kenosis. . . . The final level of spirituality involves participation in a transindividual world, transformation by it, and even sacrifice to it . . . to surrender the very sacredness of self that is maintained by fantasies of individual immortal-

---

[59] Hermans and Hermans-Konopka, *Dialogical Self Theory*, 171–72.
[60] John A. Teske, "The Spiritual Limits of Neuropsychological Life," *Zygon* 31, no. 2 (June 1, 1996): 218.

ity. What is involved is a sacrifice of the boundaries that once defined self, not to lose oneself but to gain the whole world beyond.[61]

In this chapter, we explored some perspectives on selfhood from contemporary psychology, neurophysiology, and philosophy in order to lay the groundwork for a fresh theological approach to a "catholic personality." What has emerged is a view of the self as both a centering presence and a dynamic, complex storytelling process, oriented not only toward survival but also toward belonging to ever more comprehensive wholes. In the next chapter we will review some perspectives and new visions deriving from the world of science.

---

[61] Teske, "The Spiritual Limits of Neuropsychological Life," 230.

Chapter 5

Science, Spirituality, and the "Greening of the Self"

This chapter explores how radical shifts in the scientific perspective on reality have the potential to revolutionize our understanding of ourselves as spiritual and social beings, as well as our approach to spiritual change and growth. Like most revolutions, this one does not wipe away everything that went before, but rather introduces new models and values that have the effect of restructuring and reprioritizing elements that were previously stagnant.[1]

To begin, I acknowledge my limitations in understanding and explaining many of the scientific developments of the last hundred years or so. While I regularly peruse popular science books and websites, I have no real expertise in any of the hard science disciplines. Physics, which is the discipline that has been most revolutionized and that is most foundational for revolutionizing one's perspective on the world, is arguably the most difficult for a non-expert to penetrate. In this chapter we confine ourselves to a general overview of key characteristics of the shift from a Newtonian worldview to one shaped by quantum physics and

---

[1] Thus, in Part III we will examine how some very classical Christian spiritual practices, such as John of the Cross's approach to contemplation and Ignatius of Loyola's *Spiritual Exercises,* can be revitalized by this kind of recontextualization.

relativity theory, and how these make a difference as a background for our spirituality.[2]

Many aspects of Newtonian physics have the appearance of being a science of common sense. The Newtonian or "classical" approach begins with what our senses can perceive and measure, within proportions of size that are relatively accessible to us. Its discoveries are explained using images compatible with our own way of acting upon the world. For example, the "billiard ball" metaphor of particulate objects bumping up against one another and thus exerting effective force fits well with our commonsense experience of pushing one thing (for example, our body, or a tool) against another to make something happen. With the aid of early microscopes and telescopes the reach of the senses was expanded, and Newtonian science eventually became sophisticated enough that it could sometimes demonstrate that measurements show a different reality than common sense had long assumed. Newton himself, for example, was able to explain the movements of the planets with great exactitude, thus sending several millennia of previous theories to the dustbin. The counterintuitive insights of chaos theory, which explores complex nonlinear phenomena, are a more recent extension of Newtonian principles.

Newtonian science laid the foundations for the astounding technical innovations of the industrial revolution that have transformed the lives and habitats of every species on earth in a mere 250 years. Eventually, however, attempts to push the boundaries of exploration in the direction of both the unimaginably small and the unimaginably large led to problems. The evidence stopped fitting with the basic metaphors of Newtonian science, such as the "billiard ball" particles that push one another around. The fundamental Newtonian assumptions that reality functions like a machine, that matter is particulate, that everything that happens is caused by a physical force exerted upon an object, and that the universe is a closed system (and thus fully

---

[2] For those interested in a far more detailed study of these issues as they affect key aspects of Christian theology, I recommend Heidi Ann Russell, *Quantum Shift: Theological and Pastoral Implications of Contemporary Developments in Science* (Collegeville, MN: Liturgical Press, 2015).

explainable) began to look flawed.[3] Newtonian science was brilliant and world changing, and it still produces excellent results at the daily-life level where so many of our vital mechanistic technologies operate. It has become increasingly clear, however, that it does not offer a good model or method for understanding the most foundational realities of the cosmos.

Before reviewing the characteristics of the emerging quantum worldview, we must consider another aspect that is central for our topic. Newtonian science was constructed within the philosophical frame of modernity, which is usually identified as beginning with the thought of René Descartes. Descartes envisioned material reality as completely distinct from human mind and will. The material world consists essentially of inert "stuff" that human intelligence is free to manipulate and use in any way we desire. For Descartes, even animals are completely on the other side of the divide from human consciousness. This gives a free hand to a worldview in which the natural world and other-than-human living creatures have no intrinsic rights in the face of our scientific prowess. It also separates us from our own bodies, which potentially become alienated and deadened.

This modern dualism is actually far more radical (and destructive) than ancient dualism. Platonic philosophy, for example, saw matter as the most diluted, least real manifestation of being. Yet, despite its inferiority, matter still remained in essential continuity with the supreme reality of the One from which it emanated. Ancient ascetical spiritualities based on this type of dualism may appear to treat the body harshly, yet such discipline actually aimed to bring the body along into a transformed state that is completely permeated with the deeper reality of spirit. An example is this well-known desert saying: If you will, you can become all flame![4] The implication is that the whole embodied

---

[3] For a summary and critique of basic principles of Newtonian science, see Robert E. Ulanowicz, *A Third Window: Natural Life beyond Newton and Darwin* (West Conshohocken, PA: Templeton Foundation Press, 2009), 20–24.

[4] John Wortley, ed., *The "Anonymous" Sayings of the Desert Fathers: A Select Edition and Complete English Translation* (New York: Cambridge University Press, 2013).

person can be "deified" by participation in divine life, thus visibly flaming with the Holy Spirit.

Modern dualism, however, places such a complete divide between body and soul that it engenders a perennial conundrum as philosophers and theologians try to figure out how to reintegrate the two. Spiritualities based on modern dualism are more likely to envision the "saved" soul as dispensing with the body completely. Rather than disciplining the body to transform it, asceticism deriving from such a mentality applies force to pacify the body as a means of liberating the soul. When modern dualism places God wholly on the side of mind or soul, God's presence and action in the world become inexplicable. Faced with the inability to envision the material and spiritual dimensions as integral to each other, many modern people came to the conclusion that, in fact, all that exists is what we can see and touch, that is, the physical dimension. Reductionist materialism became not only a respectable position but often was even considered the normative one, particularly among professional scientists and other members of the educated classes.

Newtonian science thrives within the objectifying, reductionist paradigm of modern dualism. The discoveries of quantum physics, however, are more difficult to reconcile with that worldview. This does not mean that it is impossible to reconcile them, and many scientists are quite content to interpret the quantum discoveries in ways that remain compatible with their reductionist and materialistic worldview. Many others, however, see these discoveries as opening the door to a radically different insight into the nature of reality.

Quantum Reality

Quantum physics undermines the comfortable assumption that matter consists of tiny particles that behave something like the larger particles we can see and measure. Investigations of the fundamental particles—such as atoms, electrons, molecules, and even smaller micro entities—reveal that it is only possible to account for their behavior by recognizing that they have a wave character as well as a particle character. In fact, it seems that the more foundational and (relatively) enduring condition of microphysical entities is the wave state, in which they remain until they are drawn transiently into a particle state by interaction with other entities.

Waves form fields that behave very differently than particles. For example, at a given time a particle has to be located in one place and only one place, while a wave is spread out in space so that it is "everywhere"—or perhaps one must really say "nowhere."[5] A particle encountering an obstacle must either rebound in one direction or find a hole to pass through, while a wave may bend around the obstacle and create complex interference patterns that continue to propagate in multiple directions. In quantum physics the wave form of microphysical entities is more like a set of potentials or forms than it is like a physical manifestation. Even though these potentials are not yet manifested in physical form, they are "real" because the entity's behavior cannot be explained without accounting for them.

Quantum physics gets its name from the discovery that when the wave states of fundamental entities manifest momentarily as particles, they do so not randomly but in defined energy levels called *quanta*. The way this is typically explained (although with many caveats about the inadequacy of the image) is to envision electrons orbiting around an atomic nucleus and to define numerically the various energy levels at which it is possible that these electrons could be found. For example, suppose that for a given atom these levels are 1, 2, 4, and 16. The electrons, then, are guaranteed never to be found at energy levels 3, 5, 6, or any other number not listed. Since the electrons require energy to jump to higher levels, the probability that an electron will be on any given level varies with the energy available. Perhaps at a temperature of 10 degrees centigrade, the probability of the electron being at level 1 is 90 percent while the probability for level 16 is 0.01 percent. Consequently, it is possible, although unlikely, for the electron to manifest as a particle in the level 16 state. In fact, there is no way of predicting when that unlikely state will occur—except that, statistically, it will happen at a rate of one in ten thousand measurements. The electrons' shifts are truly

---

[5] Lothar Schäfer, *Infinite Potential: What Quantum Physics Reveals about How We Should Live* (New York: Deepak Chopra Books, 2013), 239.

random and unpredictable, although over time a probability curve can be sketched to show how often each state will occur.

One of the implications of observing that fundamental entities are more like waves than like particles is the realization that all things are radically interconnected. Wave patterns do not have boundaries; they propagate indefinitely, meanwhile interacting with, and changing the patterns of, all the other waves they encounter. If reality is an infinite ocean vibrating with interacting wave patterns, all of them are having an impact on all the others. An even "spookier" aspect of this has been discovered in the phenomenon called *entanglement*.[6] Experiments have discovered that when two electrons have been paired (entangled) so that when one has a positive spin the other has a negative spin, they retain that pairing no matter how far apart they later are placed. If the spin on a paired electron in Chicago flips from positive to negative, instantaneously the spin on its partner in Beijing flips from negative to positive. This instantaneous shift is "impossible" in classical physics. Since nothing can travel faster than the speed of light, it ought to take at least 0.035 seconds for any communication to happen between two localities at such a distance. The fact that it does not means that on some more fundamental level reality has a nonlocal aspect. No communication is necessary because the "two," although appearing in different physical localities, are already actually "one."

The above paragraphs, of course, are a highly simplified layperson's summary of a few aspects of a supremely complex science. My goal here is not so much to explain the science as to reflect on how it opens up the potential of a new worldview that has important implications for our spirituality. Quantum physics describes the foundation of reality not as particulate and mechanistic, but as flowing and (in some ways) indeterminate. It affirms that individual foundational events are truly random and unpredictable, although en masse they are predictable according to probability curves. It explains how certain types of extremely unlikely events (for example, those with minuscule probabilities)

---

[6] Einstein is reported to have called entanglement "spooky action at a distance." For discussion, see Heidi Russell, *Quantum Shift: Theological and Pastoral Implications of Contemporary Developments in Science* (Collegeville, MN: Liturgical Press, 2015). chap. 3.

actually will occur, albeit rarely. It affirms a level of radical interconnection and nonlocality that contradicts some of our most basic assumptions about how the world works. Thus, the new physics undermines the assumption that the nature of reality is such that it can be fully understood by us. Even some of the more hard-nosed scientists, who urge damping down over-enthusiastic attempts to draw spiritual implications from quantum physics, agree that quantum reality has an intrinsic quality of mystery.[7]

Some cautions are indeed in order. The most important one is that we cannot extrapolate directly from the quantum level of reality to the everyday level, as if they operate in the same way. A criticism of popular interpretations of quantum physics is that they sometimes intimate that anything can happen—for example, that large and complex physical entities could pop in and out of the time-space dimension and manifest radically new potentials as readily as micro particles appear to do. In fact, in everyday life, the rules of classical physics still apply. Complex physical entities are not going to "blink in and out of the empirical world"[8] or be moved from place to place by invisible magic forces. We must particularly beware of quantum profiteers who want to sell therapies (whether physical, psychological, or spiritual) that defy the limitations of normal physical reality.

Nevertheless, some aspects of quantum theories do crack open doors that in classical physics were firmly shut. For example, while the quantum experiments that demonstrate nonlocal entanglement at the level of electrons are not, in and of themselves, proof of the reality of paranormal psychological nonlocality (such as mental telepathy) or of spiritual nonlocality (such as the instant effectiveness of intercessory prayer at a distance), they do raise the question of whether such experiences might participate in a dimension of fundamental reality that is only beginning to be understood by scientists. Of course, the crack in the door cannot be taken as carte blanche to affirm whatever sort of occult and bizarre possibility one finds fascinating. Still, with due caution—and with the clear recognition that such affirmations

---

[7] Carl S. Helrich, "On the Limitations and Promise of Quantum Theory for Comprehension of Human Knowledge and Consciousness," *Zygon* 41, no. 3 (September 2006): 563.

[8] Schäfer, *Infinite Potential*, 256.

are not directly implied by the science (which deals with simple microphysical entities, far from the complexity of brains, psyches, or souls)—these quantum discoveries are providing rich grounds for further theological and spiritual exploration, as recent books by John Polkinghorne and Kirk Wegter-McNelly demonstrate.[9]

Lothar Schäfer

Lothar Schäfer, a quantum chemist, is an example of a scientist who has taken the route of speculating on philosophical and spiritual implications of quantum theories. He contends that quantum physics unveils a "transcendent" realm of reality,[10] meaning that the invisible world of wave forms and their potentialities is like an ocean of virtual potential whose transient whitecaps are the physical things we perceive with our senses. Referring to the particle state as "matter" and the wave state as "form," he writes:

At the level of atoms and molecules, a frantic dance is constantly going on: out of matter and into form, out of form and into matter. From such considerations the view evolved that all visible things are emanations out of a field of forms that is spread out through the entire universe. When material particles dissolve in fields of mathematical forms and patterns of numbers—when they *become* such patterns and forms—they transcend the domain of matter: They become *transmaterial*. From this arose the notion that *the basis of reality is a domain of transmaterial forms, images, or elementary thoughts.*[11]

Schäfer, then, proposes a "new idealism" to replace the reductionist materialism that has reigned as the predominant cultural ideology of the modern period. The transmaterial forms

---

[9] Kirk Wegter-McNelly, *The Entangled God: Divine Relationality and Quantum Physics*, Routledge Studies in Religion 15 (London: Routledge, 2011); J. C. Polkinghorne, ed., *The Trinity and an Entangled World: Relationality in Physical Science and Theology* (Grand Rapids, MI: Eerdmans, 2010).

[10] Schäfer, *Infinite Potential*, 267.

[11] Schäfer, *Infinite Potential*, 237–38.

exist in the cosmic potentiality of what physicist David Bohm called the undivided wholeness that is foundational reality. Our consciousness, too, emerges from this wholeness, and so we are born with an insatiable spiritual longing to reclaim the wholeness that is our grounding state.[12] Even our moral wisdom derives from this transmaterial dimension of radical wholeness. Schäfer writes: "Morality is the manifestation of a transempirical, tacit moral form that exists in the realm of potentiality and appears spontaneously in our consciousness when it is needed, offering its advice to our judgment and free will."[13]

Not surprisingly, Schäfer's ideas are criticized by many scientists.[14] They see him as extrapolating much too far beyond the confirmed science of microphysical entities when he makes these assertions in the realms of philosophy, psychology, and ethics. Yet even those who criticize him acknowledge that the science does raise these kinds of questions. The critics' view is that the questions ought to be left unanswered until science makes more progress, while Schäfer counters that the crisis of our times cries out for a fresh, inspiring vision that is built on the latest developments in science.

Gregory Bateson and Cosmic Wisdom

Although he died almost forty years ago, Gregory Bateson (1904–80) left a legacy of writings that offer resources that may tie together some of the ideas we have been harvesting throughout these chapters.[15] Bateson shares with Schäfer a new form of

---

[12] Schäfer, *Infinite Potential*, 23–29.

[13] Schäfer, *Infinite Potential*, 188.

[14] Helrich, "On the Limitations and Promise of Quantum Theory for Comprehension of Human Knowledge and Consciousness"; Stanley A. Klein, "Order from Virtual States: A Dialogue on the Relevance of Quantum Theory to Religion," *Zygon* 41, no. 3 (September 2006): 567–72; Ervin Laszlo, "Quantum and Consciousness: In Search of a New Paradigm," *Zygon* 41, no. 3 (September 2006): 533–41.

[15] For an overview of Bateson's life and work, see Noel G. Charlton, *Understanding Gregory Bateson: Mind, Beauty, and the Sacred Earth*, SUNY Series in Environmental Philosophy and Ethics (Albany: SUNY Press, 2008).

idealism, grounded in the conviction that reality is "mindlike." By this he does not mean that world process is directed by some kind of gigantic, invisible mystical consciousness. Rather, his insight is that the world is shaped by "information," which he defines as "a difference that makes a difference."[16] When no mind is active, all is one and without differences; but even the most rudimentary mind (such as a machine) responds to the differences that are information.

Mind, in this perspective, is not equivalent to consciousness. For Bateson, the basic character of mental process is simply to receive, interpret, and respond to information. Intelligent activity of that sort is going on around us in the natural processes science describes as shaping landscapes, climates, the growth of living creatures, evolutionary development, and ultimately the movements of stars and galaxies. In our own bodies, for example, the digestive system, the respiratory system, the immune system, and many other functions operate intelligently with little or no conscious awareness on our part. Bateson believed that an ecosystem, especially one that has had many millennia to develop a wide range of mutually sustaining networks among its diverse inhabitants, is the best model of mind at work in nature.

Bateson understood the world as consisting of a series of nested levels of mind. Again, we can think about this in terms of our own participation in the world. In Western cultures we tend to imagine our "self" or "I" as located inside the body, often in the head or chest, and mainly defined by consciousness and personal agency. Yet, in reality, for human beings to survive, they must be in a living and supportive relationship with a viable galactic system, a sustainable ecosystem (climate, foodstuff, water, and so on), and many different kinds of functional human groupings (family, workplace, transportation systems, city, nation, and so forth). Many levels of systems must be cooperating intelligently within their body (cellular, blood, organs, hormones, psyche, and so on). What we consider our conscious mind is actually only a very small component of these many nested systems, all of which are only able to maintain their functions through intelligent and mutually supportive interdependence.

---

[16] Gregory Bateson, "Double Bind, 1969," in *Steps to an Ecology of Mind* (Chicago: University of Chicago Press, 2000), 271–72.

A central tenet of Bateson's schema is that purposive consciousness is only one part of the much larger set of nested forms of intelligence that contribute to the human capacity for knowledge. There is far more wisdom available to us in drawing upon the unconscious minds of ecosystems, human communions, and body knowledge than in limiting our sense of self to our overconfident conscious mind. In reality, all these nested minds are ours, too; as he notes, in the pronoun *we* should be included "the starfish and the redwood forest, the segmenting egg, and the Senate of the United States."[17] As long as we human beings rely on solving problems by using our ability to understand consciously and to manipulate parts of the world, we are doomed to create even worse problems despite the best of intentions.

For Bateson, the reason our conscious minds so often botch ecological problem solving is that human beings tend to think linearly, while the world operates nonlinearly, that is, through a complex and holistic network of connections. The term he often used for this was *cybernetics,* which refers to the science of systems controlled by complex interconnected feedback loops. As he states:

> The cybernetic nature of self and the world tends to be imperceptible to consciousness, insofar as the contents of the "screen" of consciousness are determined by considerations of purpose. The argument of purpose tends to take the form "D is desirable; B leads to C; C leads to D; so D can be achieved by way of B and C." But, if the total mind and outer world do not have this lineal structure, then by forcing this structure upon them, we become blind to the cybernetic circularities of the self and the external world. Our conscious sampling of data will not disclose whole circuits but only arcs of circuits, cut off from their matrix by our selective [purposive] attention. Specifically, the attempt to achieve a change in a given variable, located either in self or environment, is likely to be undertaken without

---

[17] Gregory Bateson, *Mind and Nature: A Necessary Unity* (Toronto: Bantam Books, 1980), 4.

comprehension of the homeostatic network surrounding that variable.[18]

The self, then, is not simply that small wisp of consciousness shimmering in our head and chest, but a participant in a vast living network of intelligence whose roots reach back to the ancient origins of the universe, the beginnings of life, the billions of species in the chain of evolution, and the intricate interweavings of life in millions of ecosystems, as well as all that the billions of our own species have ever known, loved, and created. Linking this to Rodolfo Llinás's assertion that from a neurophysiological point of view "self is the centralization of prediction,"[19] we can see how openness to these depths of interconnection can make available a level of wisdom that is sadly lacking in so many of our personal and societal choices.

Here we begin to get a glimpse of a new vision of the truly catholic personality. Recalling Hermans and Hermans-Konopka's ideas about the dialogical self whose life unfolds as an ongoing dialogue of I-positions, imagine the possibilities if these inner positions of the self can draw upon not only imagined human roles but also the living wisdom of wild creatures, ecosystems, ancient human communities, and even the galaxies! While such an expanded vision of selfhood may seem far-fetched to the narrowed mindset of the typical Western urbanite, cosmically connected participatory consciousness has a venerable history in indigenous communities and is being redeveloped today by many who are trained in both indigenous and Western lifeways. Stephen Harrod Buhner, for example, draws on both science and indigenous herbal medicine practice as he describes in detail the process of opening one's heart to let a plant communicate its healing capacities.[20] Robin Wall Kimmerer, a member of the Citizen Potawatomi Nation and a distinguished professor of ecology, writes movingly of her own

---

[18] Gregory Bateson, "The Effects of Conscious Purpose on Human Adaptation," in *Steps to an Ecology of Mind*, 446–53.

[19] Rodolfo R. Llinás, *I of the Vortex: From Neurons to Self*, A Bradford Book (Cambridge, MA: MIT Press, 2002), 23.

[20] Stephen Harrod Buhner, *The Secret Teachings of Plants: The Intelligence of the Heart in the Direct Perception of Nature* (Rochester, VT: Bear and Company, 2004).

lifelong exploration of what it means to belong to the community of plants, animals, mountains, and stars.[21]

Many efforts are being made to bridge the indigenous perspective and Western science. When a group of psychologists led by Eric Bergeman asked people what they think spirituality is, they found that the answers converged on "a knowing or awareness of the interconnectedness of all things in nature."[22] Bergeman and his coauthors, then, propose that, whereas Western people tend to begin from a stance of feeling separate and finite, what they call spirituality is whatever moves them toward the "open possibility" and "dynamic web of interactions" that quantum physics has shown us is reality. Spiritual practice frees us from the illusion of separateness to rediscover the radical attunement of matter and mind in "an awakened sense of an interdependent whole self."[23]

In *World as Lover, World as Self*, Joanna Macy eloquently describes such a "greening of the self":

> We know that we are not limited by the accident of our birth or the timing of it, and we recognize the truth that we have always been around. We can reinhabit time and own our story as a species. We were present back there in the fireball and the rains that streamed down on this still molten planet, and in the primordial seas. We remember that in our mother's womb, where we wear vestigial gills and tail and fins for hands. We remember that. That information is in us and there is a deep, deep kinship in us, beneath the outer layers of our neocortex or what we learned in school. There is a deep wisdom, a bondedness with our creation, and an ingenuity far beyond what we think we have.[24]

---

[21] Robin Wall Kimmerer, *Braiding Sweetgrass: Indigenous Wisdom, Scientific Knowledge, and the Teachings of Plants* (Minneapolis: Milkweed Editions, 2013).

[22] Eric Bergeman et al., "Neuroscience and Spirituality," in *In Search of Self: Interdisciplinary Perspectives on Personhood*, ed. J. Wentzel Van Huyssteen and Erik P. Wiebe (Grand Rapids, MI: Eerdmans, 2011), 84.

[23] Bergeman et al., "Neuroscience and Spirituality," 94.

[24] Joanna Macy, *World as Lover, World as Self: Courage for Global Justice and Ecological Renewal* (Berkeley, CA: Parallax Press, 2007), 192.

These authors expand our concept of what it means to be a catholic personality, hospitable to and rooted in both the wisdom of the cosmos and the earthy, interconnected networks of our local environment. It is noteworthy in this context that the biblical Wisdom traditions closely identify wisdom *(hokma)* and Spirit *(ruach)*, thus offering a potential connection between these views of cosmic wisdom and life in the Spirit.[25] But how can we move toward becoming such catholic personalities? This would clearly require a remarkable spiritual transformation of both individuals and communities.

Bateson's Four Levels of Change

In an essay entitled "The Logical Categories of Learning and Communication," Bateson strives to lay out a scientifically based theory of how this could happen. Drawing on Bertrand Russell's theory of logical categories, Bateson identifies four increasingly comprehensive levels of human change. He called these Learning I, Learning II, Learning III, and Learning IV.[26] Bateson's explanations for these levels of transformation are difficult to follow, but a more accessible overview has been offered by Bill Buker. Buker found a correlation (based to some degree on an earlier sketch by Bateson[27]) between Bateson's first three levels and the stages alcoholics must go through in order to address fully their addiction.[28] The example of substance addiction is apt for our purposes because, as Gerald May detailed in *Addiction and Grace*, it is also a paradigm for the spiritual struggle of every human being.[29]

---

[25] Jürgen Moltmann, *The Spirit of Life: A Universal Affirmation* (Minneapolis: Fortress Press, 2001), 46.

[26] Gregory Bateson, "The Logical Categories of Learning and Communication," in *Steps to an Ecology of Mind*, 279–308.

[27] Gregory Bateson, "The Cybernetics of 'Self': A Theory of Alcoholism," in *Steps to an Ecology of Mind*, 309–37.

[28] Bill Buker, "Spiritual Development and the Epistemology of Systems Theory," *Journal of Psychology and Theology* 31, no. 2 (2003): 143–53.

[29] Gerald G. May, *Addiction and Grace: Love and Spirituality in the Healing of Addictions* (San Francisco: HarperSanFrancisco, 2007).

Addiction involves an inability to change a pattern of behavior that gives a person certain immediate rewards but, at the same time, blocks the person from reaching goals that are even more important to his or her life and well being. At the stage of Learning I (first-order change) an alcoholic tries to reduce or stop drinking, but without changing anything else in his or her attitude or way of life. This is an attempt to change a deeply embedded and compulsive behavior by sheer will power. When that leads to repeated disastrous crises, the person may eventually recognize the need to move to Learning II (second-order change). This is when the person realizes that the problem is not just an isolated behavior but a complete package of interconnected attitudes and behaviors that is called alcoholism. With this insight the person is ready to accept the guidance of those who have a personal and/or professional understanding of alcoholic psychology. By entering therapy and/or attending Alcoholics Anonymous meetings, the alcoholic may be able to gradually make changes in the syndrome of problematic behaviors.

The problem of addiction to alcohol (or anything else) is not really resolved, however, unless the alcoholic arrives at Learning III (third-order change). Here the person begins to realize that his or her personal struggles with alcoholism are really only the tip of the great iceberg of coming to terms with his or her true spiritual condition. Third-order change, therefore, is a deep, systemic change of consciousness that surrenders to the limitations and opportunities of one's participation in the nested "minds" of the cosmos. Bateson calls this "an involuntary change in deep unconscious epistemology, a spiritual experience."[30] Alcoholics Anonymous puts it in terms of opening to the reality of profound interdependence with a "Higher Power."

Bateson asserts that even third-order change (let alone fourth-order change, as we will see below) is, in fact, not that common among human beings. The reason for this, in his view, is that, in the first two or three years of life a form of second-order change takes place that forms the basic character out of which we will instinctively respond for the rest of our days.[31] The very young human being, then, does not just react to things or absorb

---

[30] Bateson, "The Cybernetics of 'Self,'" 331.
[31] Bateson, "Logical Categories," 297–301.

external patterns, but at some point makes a choice to "lock in" a particular paradigm that will guide future responses.[32] Earlier we referred to this as a person's basic story template—for example, the story of being a victim, or the story of always succeeding, or the story of only caring about having fun. Bateson himself does not use the language of story but refers to "the punctuation of experience," that is, a paradigm for how to identify a stream of events as a particular context and then know how to negotiate one's way through it successfully.[33] The problem is that this early story template is so deeply embedded in a person's psyche that it becomes very difficult to change.

Third-order change, however, requires not just changing the story but radically loosening its grip so that one realizes that it is "just a story" and that one is truly free to choose a way of being rooted in deeper wisdom. Ultimately, this is the shift from being able to identify a context and deploy a paradigm for how to punctuate it, to recognizing one's living participation in "the context of contexts"—the great cosmic series of nested minds. Most alcoholics have to undergo one or several experiences of catastrophic "hitting bottom" before they are open even to second-order change, let alone to the far more profound refounding of consciousness that is third-order change. Bateson notes that even with intensive psychotherapy the most common result of efforts to change is not a new level but a revision of premises at the same level.[34] The one previously trapped in the story of victimhood now calls herself a survivor, which may be a more empowering story but is not necessarily an indication of third-order liberation. Here is how Bateson describes the passage from Learning II to Learning III:

---

[32] Loder describes this as the "No!" which emerges at about fourteen months, setting ego boundaries and delineating space. James E. Loder, *The Logic of the Spirit: Human Development in Theological Perspective* (San Francisco: Jossey-Bass Publishers, 1998), 92–94.

[33] Gregory Bateson, "Social Planning and the Concept of Deutero-Learning," in *Steps to an Ecology of Mind*, 163.

[34] Bateson, "Logical Categories," 302; Robert Kegan's model of the progressive disembedding of the self from its subjective assumptions may have some parallels with Bateson's approach. Robert Kegan, *In Over Our Heads: The Mental Demands of Modern Life* (Cambridge, MA: Harvard University Press, 1997).

If I stop at the level of Learning II, "I" am the aggregate of those characteristics which I call my "character." "I" am my habits of acting in context and shaping and perceiving the contexts in which I act. Selfhood is a product or aggregate of Learning II. To the degree that a man [*sic*] achieves Learning III, and learns to perceive and act in terms of the contexts of contexts, his "self" will take on a sort of irrelevance. The concept of "self" will no longer serve as a nodal argument in the punctuation of experience.[35]

He then describes the potential fruit of such a shift as "a world in which personal identity merges into all the processes of relationship in some vast ecology or aesthetics of cosmic interaction. . . . Every detail of the universe is seen as proposing a view of the whole."[36]

In much of his writing Bateson only describes these first three levels. Occasionally, however, he refers to a Learning IV (fourth-order change) that takes place on a collective level. According to Robert Dilts, "Learning IV would involve the establishment of completely new behaviors that do not fit *any* current system of classes of behavior."[37] Perhaps an example from prehistory is the emergence of complex language capabilities in the human species, making ever larger and more complex social groupings possible. Christians could argue that another example is the coming of Jesus, who offered the entire human race a radically new potential for union with God and with one another.

Again, Bateson did not spell out very clearly what he meant by this Learning IV.[38] We might speculate, however, that since he described Learning III as the individual transcending all previous definitions of self in favor of participation in the cosmic mind, Learning IV might be the emergence of a society whose collective

---

[35] Bateson, "Logical Categories," 304.

[36] Bateson, "Logical Categories," 306.

[37] Robert Brian Dilts, *From Coach to Awakener* (Scotts Valley, CA: Dilts Strategy Group, 2003), 271.

[38] Michael Welker's assertion that Bateson falls into a "vague holism" may refer especially to this undeveloped fourth level. Michael Welker, *God the Spirit*, trans. John F. Hoffmeyer (Minneapolis: Fortress Press, 1994), 38.

mores and behaviors are intrinsically based on that participation. It would be what Thomas Berry called the Ecozoic Era, in which human cultures live in intelligent, sustainable mutuality with the systems of the natural world.[39]

Sam Mickey is a philosopher who is trying to develop conceptual categories to facilitate such a transformation to an ecologically based human society. He builds on the work of Gilles Deleuze and Félix Guattari, whose geophilosophy sees humans as immersed in "intimate contact with the profound life of all forms or all types of beings" and gives them responsibility "for even the stars and animal life."[40] Recognizing that the environmental crisis is, fundamentally, "a crisis of the integration of human and earth systems," Mickey searches for how to be a midwife for a "planetary civilization."[41] Whereas what is currently developing is a global civilization that homogenizes cultural differences and crushes local ecosystems in order to enhance the wealth of a few global corporations and their stockholders, a planetary civilization would tend the health of each locality at the same time as complexifying the ecological networks of mutual support.

Mickey suggests that midwifing such a planetary civilization connotes "the possibility of becoming otherwise, the possibility of inventing new modes of togetherness, intensifying the vibrant coexistence of humans with one another and with all the habitats and inhabitants of earth."[42] All these thinkers—Gregory Bateson, Joanna Macy, Thomas Berry, Sam Mickey, as well as Gilles Deleuze and Félix Guattari—hold out hope that this radical transformation to a planetary society based in ecological and cosmic wisdom truly is a possible human future. But we still wonder: How?

---

[39] Thomas Berry, *Thomas Berry: Selected Writings on the Earth Community*, ed. Mary Evelyn Tucker and John Grim, Modern Spiritual Masters (Maryknoll, NY: Orbis Books, 2014), 134–44.

[40] Gilles Deleuze and Félix Guattari, *Anti-Oedipus: Capitalism and Schizophrenia* (New York: Penguin Books, 2009), 4.

[41] Sam Mickey, *On the Verge of a Planetary Civilization: A Philosophy of Integral Ecology* (London: Rowman and Littlefield International, 2014), 5.

[42] Mickey, *On the Verge of a Planetary Civilization*, 8.

Science and Religious Experience

Surely these visions of a planetary civilization or an ecozoic age are intriguing. Yet they may seem like little more than "pie in the sky" unless humans change radically—and soon. The question this project asks is what spiritual experience and practice may have to do with such processes of transformation. In the coming chapters we examine how theology can respond to this challenge. In recent decades, though, many secular researchers have also begun to study it. Although from the viewpoint of theology and Christian spiritual practice their theories may be incomplete, much can be learned by taking into account their research and proposals.

Neurologist Patrick McNamara has developed a theory of how religion may foster brain processes that enable people to develop "enhanced moral sensibilities, greater internal freedom, greater self-control, deeper insight into Self and others, empathy and compassion for others . . . generativity, and prosocial behaviors in general." These qualities, he suggests, have evolutionary survival value because they foster skills of long-term social cooperation in diverse groups that are not simply kin-based.[43] The mechanism that McNamara proposes is the development of a "strong executive self" through repeated processes of "decentering." Like many other postmodern theorists, he sees the self as naturally tending toward plurality and fragmentation. Yet evolutionary survival would favor a stronger and more unified self with the capacity to promote group bonding.

Religion, McNamara suggests, provides a set of practices that temporarily inhibit the self's sense of agency, thus placing the existing self-structures "offline." In this way the self is decentered and, for the moment, disempowered. A subconscious search then begins to find "a more integral version of the Self that can encompass deeper, more optimal solutions to internal and external conflicts and problems." Eventually, what remains of the old self is integrated into the larger, more complex, more cosmically ordered "ideal self" that religion offers.[44] If such a process of

---

[43] Patrick McNamara, *The Neuroscience of Religious Experience* (Cambridge, UK: Cambridge University Press, 2014), 164.

[44] McNamara, *The Neuroscience of Religious Experience*, 47.

decentering is successful, the resulting self is more effective in achieving unifying relations with diverse human groupings as well as in being wily enough to evade predators and enemies.

Thus, McNamara presents a theory of why religious practice and religious doctrine were positive and perhaps even necessary adaptations for the historical survival of the human species. Central is the concept of the decentering of the self through religious practice and religious experience. He finds support for this part of his theory in research on the neurological correlates of religious experiences. Much complex research is summed up when he writes: "At the neurochemical level, the reduction in agency/intentionality is mediated by a reduction in serotonergic activity in the prefrontal and anterior temporal cortices, thus transiently inhibiting prefrontal/temporal cortical function."[45] In greatly simplified terms this means that when religious experience involves reducing intentionality or "turning over the will to God," it is accompanied by a reduction in the production of serotonin, which is one of the main chemicals that mediate brain activity. This reduction is specifically in the regions of the brain most responsible for thought and volition (prefrontal lobes) as well as those involved in more ecstatic religious experiences (temporal lobes). The result seems to be reduced thought and volition, sometimes accompanied by the release of blissful or ecstatic feelings.

McNamara as well as numerous other researchers have presented detailed and highly nuanced reviews of these and other brain processes accompanying various kinds of religious experience. Eugene D'Aquili and Andrew Newberg, for example, detailed the brain correlates of a type of experience they term Absolute Unitary Being (AUB).[46] These are experiences in which the self seems to melt away and merge completely into a sense of oneness with the cosmos (if interpreted more impersonally) or God (if interpreted more personally). Usually, such experiences are blissful and are subjectively felt as more "real" than ordinary sense experiences. Persons who have experienced AUB

---

[45] McNamara, *The Neuroscience of Religious Experience*, 143.

[46] Eugene G. D'Aquili and Andrew B. Newberg, *The Mystical Mind: Probing the Biology of Religious Experience* (Minneapolis: Fortress Press, 1999).

often report lifelong enhancement of peace and happiness, as well as reduced fear of death. For our purposes, the specific brain mechanisms that their research outlines are less important than their science-based affirmation of the self-transcendence function of religion. Like McNamara, they find a decentering or temporary dissolution of the self at the center of the attraction that spirituality and religion exercise upon human beings.

D'Aquili and Newberg also propose a second, balancing mechanism that is involved in religion. They propose that the brain is structured with a "causal operator" whose function demands the postulation of a cause for everything that is observed to happen. This causal operator has evolved because understanding the causes of things is essential to having a sense of control of one's environment. Thus, when no cause is empirically observed, the causal operator brain function will insert one—often in the form of gods, spirits, or mystical forces. Religious practices such as prayer, ritual, and sacrifice are oriented to attempts to control the environment, especially in aspects that do not seem controllable by ordinary human action.

Left to itself, the causality function and its orientation toward control may lead to magic, superstition, and/or hegemonic religion. Conversely, the self-transcendence function and its orientation toward surrender into wholeness could descend into orgiastic, hallucinatory, or "navel-gazing" tendencies. In religions, the two typically work in tandem, balancing each other. Although McNamara does not refer extensively to the work of D'Aquili and Newberg, his idea of the "strong executive self" that only emerges on the basis of having been repeatedly decentered would be a way of explaining the potential fruit of this balancing of surrender and control.

Wesley Wildman, whose phenomenology of religious and spiritual experiences we reviewed in Chapter 2, also builds on McNamara and discusses a related dynamic of surrender and control. He asserts that, although what he calls intense experiences seem to come upon us without our exercise of intentionality, they are "prodigiously efficient information-processing and meaning-making neurocognitive operations."[47] The "knowing"

---

[47] Wesley J. Wildman, *Religious and Spiritual Experiences* (Cambridge, UK: Cambridge University Press, 2011), 137.

resulting from intense experiences sometimes cannot be expressed adequately in words yet may represent a more complete awareness of the depth and complexity of reality than sense awareness or ordinary mentation can achieve. This kind of knowing necessarily involves movement back and forth between a firmer-boundaried self with clear subject-object distinctions and a hazy-boundaried self that merges with its "others." As with McNamara's "executive self," this requires being able to relax the boundaries enough to discover and create new possibilities in one's interaction with the environment. Wildman suggests that this alternation requires more sophisticated cognitive equipment than only doing one or the other.[48]

Wildman, who is a convinced secularist, carefully explains that he is not asserting that all intense experiences can simply be taken at face value. Each must be discerned, he believes, according to criteria that deploy a naturalistic cosmology, an ecological-semiotic theory of dynamic engagement with reality, and a symbolic account of religious cognition. A naturalistic cosmology excludes supernatural explanations. An ecological-semiotic theory affirms that "our impression of the real is a socially cooperative endeavor built on the perception-action dialectic in engagement with an ambient environment that opens up to our understanding only in the respects in which we are prepared to engage it."[49] Finally, a symbolic account of religious cognition affirms that our deeper and more complex experiences of value can only be expressed in symbols.

Wildman concludes that if "intense experiences" are understood as an in-depth engagement with reality that draws upon culturally available symbols for expression, some of them may be "nothing less and nothing more than perception of the depth structures of nature in all their intricate differentiation and grading. . . . [They] are the means by which we engage the valuational richness of reality, just as sense perception is the way that we engage the sensible aspects of our ambient environment."[50] Thus, he affirms that even from a strictly secular viewpoint, spiritual experience can be understood as unlocking deeply grounded

---

[48] Wildman, *Religious and Spiritual Experiences*, 177.
[49] Wildman, *Religious and Spiritual Experiences*, 176.
[50] Wildman, *Religious and Spiritual Experiences*, 183.

wisdom that could reshape social, political, and ecological relationships.

In this chapter we explored how the research and insights of a
variety of scientists contribute to fresh perspectives on the value,
character, and transformative potential of spiritual experiences.
Now, finally, we bring all this more explicitly into dialogue with
aspects of Christian theology.

Chapter 6

Breathing Spirit: A Model of Human Personhood

In previous chapters we reviewed some contemporary views of the psychology of selfhood and the science of religious experience in search of a perspective that is both relevant within the broader cultural conversation and helpful in thinking about how to form catholic personalities, that is, persons capable of deep dialogue, intercultural living, inclusive hospitality, and an ecozoic way of life. In this chapter we finally bring Christian theology explicitly into the conversation.

As Léon Turner's *Theology, Psychology, and the Plural Self* has shown, Christian theology, generally, has not found it easy to absorb the views of selfhood offered by postmodern thinkers.[1] Christian thinkers typically criticize the "modern self" insofar as it is presented as isolated, autonomous, and strictly rational, but they have also tended to be defensive in the face of postmodern proposals of a plural, decentered, process-based self. The conviction that fidelity to scripture and tradition requires retaining some kind of essential substrate—a soul created by God and destined for eternal life—has been strong. The difficulty is that this substrate often ends up looking something like a stripped-down (or, perhaps souped-up) version of the "substantial self" of

---

[1] Léon Turner, *Theology, Psychology, and the Plural Self* (Burlington, VT: Ashgate, 2008), chap. 1.

modernity.[2] In order to engage a debate among these views, first let us briefly review the development of early Christian thought on personhood.

The Christian Notion of the Person

The word *person* has roots in Etruscan and Roman theatrical cults. First, the mask used by a character was called a *phersu*, and later the character who speaks through the mask became known as a *persona*. In the first century this term merged with the Greek term *prosopon* (face), which has to do with seeing and being seen, or being hidden and unveiled.[3] This pre-Christian history is particularly interesting since the term's origins in theater highlight the gap between what is behind the mask and what is being presented by the mask. In theatrical presentations, roles and faces are not fixed realities but a play of illusions in which an ever-shifting story is gradually unfolded. One mask or one character may even change roles or play many roles. The masks are quite explicitly presented as mediators of dialogue, both among the characters and with the drama's audience. Thus, it seems as if this early history of the term *person* could offer resources for thinking about the plural, labile, dialogical self of postmodernity.

Early Christian theology, however, went in a different direction. Kenneth Schmitz notes that in the early Christian era a search was ongoing to find a name for the most profound reality of the human being, and the term *person* emerged as the best. Thus, it came to refer to "the manifestation of meaningful depth, the distinctiveness of the individual, the intimacy of direct personal encounter, and the dignity associated with the divine and the specifically human."[4] As is typical in the history of language,

---

[2] Fergus Kerr, "The Modern Philosophy of Self in Recent Theology," in *Neuroscience and the Person: Scientific Perspectives on Divine Action*, ed. Robert J. Russell et al., Scientific Perspectives on Divine Action 4 (Berkeley, CA: Center for Theology and the Natural Sciences, 2002).

[3] Kenneth L. Schmitz, "The Geography of the Human Person," *Communio* 13, no. 1 (1986): 27–48.

[4] Schmitz, "The Geography of the Human Person," 31.

some earlier meanings then fell away or into the background as the term became established with this new meaning.

Over the next few centuries this term played a greater and greater role in emerging Christian doctrines. This involved a complicated, centuries-long, often highly contentious and politicized process that every beginning theology student must study in excruciating detail. Rather than review all that here, we focus on the core issues and choices that led to the establishment of fundamental Christian doctrines. Our concern today is which aspects of the terminological or philosophical choices that were made almost two millennia ago are still open to further development in our radically different world, and which must remain as irrevocable foundation stones.

The essential revelatory data that the early theologians were working with included the Hebrew scriptures, the story of Jesus, and the ongoing life of the church communities. In the communities, especially at the eucharistic liturgies, Christians found the most intimate depth of reality in an experience of communion with Jesus and with one another. This fueled the bedrock convictions that Jesus was resurrected and that he was divine. These beliefs clashed, however, with basic tenets of both established Jewish tradition and the dominant Greek and Latin philosophical schools. The bishops had to find a way to articulate the communities' core beliefs in a way that would make sense to people trained in these earlier traditions—and that could, therefore, facilitate mass conversions to Christian faith.

The starting point, of course, had to be Jesus, since claims about his identity and role were what defined the Christian movement. The fundamental claim was that Jesus was a human being like us, and that he was also God—just as much so as the God who is creator of all that exists. Eventually, the term *person* was developed in ways that resolved the host of thorny issues arising from this formidable claim. Jesus was a person, with all the characteristics that Schmitz noted were beginning to be ascribed to persons: depth, individuality, capacity for intimacy, and dignity. But Jesus was (and is) a divine Person. While this divine Person has a human nature as well as a divine nature, it is not his nature(s) but his divine Personhood that unifies and defines him. Thus, *person* became the primary term for characterizing God.

At the same time, Jesus's humanity reveals that human beings are also only fulfilled in becoming persons according to his model.

If Jesus is a divine Person, and persons are defined by their capacity for fully mutual intimacy, it followed that he must be in relationship with another divine Person who has equal capacity. Both the Hebrew scriptures and the gospel stories of Jesus's relationship with God as *Abba* point clearly to this other divine Person: God the Father. A similar combination of community experience, scriptural exegesis, and logic eventually led to the affirmation of the Holy Spirit as the third divine Person, and thus the fleshing out of the complete doctrine of God as Trinity. This doctrine, says Catherine LaCugna, is based in the conviction that "God is absolutely personal, that God's being originates in love, ecstasis, self-diffusion, and fecundity. . . . God alone exists at every moment in perfect communion."[5]

Zizioulas observes that, in addition to the christological reflections noted above, another revelatory datum contributing to this affirmation is the doctrine of *creatio ex nihilo* (creation from nothing) derived from chapter one of the Book of Genesis. This doctrine interprets Genesis as depicting God freely choosing to create all that exists and to be intimately present to it in a paternal manner. The world, then, is a product of freedom (rather than of necessity), and it is founded in a living personal relationship with its divine Creator.[6] Everything that exists is dependent on this free and personal relationship for its origin, its sustenance, and its fulfillment.

What was really revolutionary about this development, says Zizioulas, was that it affirmed an ontology in which "person" is more foundational than "substance." In the ancient world the main ontological options were monism—in which God and the world are one—or gnostic dualism, in which there is an ontological and moral abyss between God and the world. Christians,

---

[5] Catherine Mowry LaCugna, *God for Us: The Trinity and Christian Life* (San Francisco: HarperSanFrancisco, 1991), 245, 301.

[6] John D. Zizioulas, *Being as Communion: Studies in Personhood and the Church* (Crestwood, NY: St. Vladimir's Seminary Press, 1985), 41.

however, asserted that "the ultimate ontological category which makes something really *be*, is neither an impersonal and incommunicable 'substance,' nor a structure of communion existing by itself or imposed by necessity, but rather the *person*." The implication, says Zizioulas, is that "true being comes only from the free person, from the person who loves freely—that is, who freely affirms his being, his identity, by means of an event of communion with other persons."[7]

Catherine Mowry LaCugna has helpfully summed up the essential "notes" of personhood.[8] The most central characteristic of personhood is that persons exist only in a relationship of communion with other persons. This is true for the divine Persons in the Trinity, and it is also true for human beings insofar as human fulfillment is destined to be found in the *ecclesia*—the communion of human beings with one another and with God. She also notes that persons are catholic in two aspects: they are created to be inclusive of everything that exists, and "each human person uniquely exemplifies what it means to be human just as each divine person uniquely exemplifies what it is to be divine."[9] Finally, she describes a person as "an ineffable, concrete, unique, and unrepeatable ecstasis of nature." This is quite a mouthful, but the key points include the constitutive tension between a non-objective ("ineffable") and an objective ("concrete") dimension, as well as the affirmation that personhood is constitutively directed outward toward others ("ecstasis").

For our purposes the most portentous affirmation emerging from early Christian thought is the characterization of both God and human beings as "persons." Persons are free, capable of loving, and fundamentally designed for mutual intimacy. Persons are never static or reified beings who can be known objectively; rather, they are intrinsically relational creatures who can only be known relationally. This is true from their beginning in receiving life as a gift from a personal God, to their end in fulfilled communion with divine and human persons.

---

[7] Zizioulas, *Being as Communion*, 17–18.
[8] LaCugna, *God for Us*, 289–92.
[9] LaCugna, *God for Us*, 290.

The Theologians' Problem

As previously noted, Christian theologians have found it challenging to articulate a view of human personhood that is faithful both to the core convictions of Christianity and to emerging contemporary perspectives that endorse plurality and lability as basic characteristics of the self. According to Léon Turner, Alistair McFadyen's *The Call to Personhood* makes one of the best attempts, yet still falls short. McFadyen proposes that our most important, core relationships form in us a "deep self" that serves as a basis of stability and continuity, while other "local selves" carry on a variety of relations at a more surface level.[10] Turner criticizes this as a return to the modern "essential self," albeit with a foundation in relationality and with at least some recognition of plurality (for example, the "local selves").

Another valiant effort, says Turner, is found in Wolfhart Pannenberg's *Anthropology in Theological Perspective*. Pannenberg proposes that human life is created to be fundamentally exocentric, that is, oriented to a wholeness centered beyond itself. Selfhood, he suggests, arises out of the human being's intrinsic exocentric orientation toward becoming radically whole.[11] This orientation is ultimately eschatological, opening human persons to our destiny as images of God in communion with God. In infancy, the psychological foundations of this come to birth in the symbiotic relationship of basic trust with caregivers. Pannenberg writes: "The wholeness of the self, which infinitely transcends the limitations of life at any given moment, finds its present manifestation as personality."[12] It is the self, then, that provides the basic structure of unity and continuity for human persons. The ego or "I" arises later and, in Pannenberg's view, is concerned mainly with holding life together in each succeeding present moment. Egocentrism, then, is an inbuilt tension in human life that resists the deeper orientation to exocentrism.

---

[10] Alistair I. McFadyen, *The Call to Personhood: A Christian Theory of the Individual in Social Relationships* (Cambridge, UK: Cambridge University Press, 1990), 102.

[11] Wolfhart Pannenberg, *Anthropology in Theological Perspective* (Philadelphia: Westminster Press, 1985), 220–42.

[12] Pannenberg, *Anthropology in Theological Perspective*, 235.

For Turner, the problem with the theological anthropology of both McFadyen and Pannenberg is that they conflate theological and psychological criteria in defining the self. Theologically, it is essential to affirm that the totality of the person is in relationship with God, and that this totality—the person's entire life history—will be eschatologically redeemed. Both McFadyen and Pannenberg then place this singularity into the structure of the self, arguing in different ways that (at least ideally) human psychological development results in a single unified self that is able to carry on this relationship with God over the course of an entire lifetime.

Turner argues that this conflation is not necessary, if one recognizes that there is a fundamental distinction between the "self" as a set of self-representations and the more basic "sense of self" that is the center of experiencing and being present. William James named these the "me" or self-as-object and the "I" or self-as-subject. A second important distinction is between a sense of diachronic unity—that is, the sense that I can trace "my" life experience from birth to death—and the structure of synchronic unity—that is, how a person at any given moment maintains some sense of self-coherence. Turner's key point is that having a sense of diachronic unity (continuity over time) does not necessarily require having a single, relatively unchanging represented self who "holds" that unity through time.[13] There are other theoretical options, he believes, that can maintain what is essential theologically while more effectively taking account of current scientific data and cultural convictions.

The option to which Turner gives most attention is that of the narrative self. As discussed in Chapter 4, this is the view that *unity* is an ongoing constructive process of interpreting the diversity of one's experiences as an emplotted narrative. The story one tells today will be different from the story told tomorrow, or in a different context, and some life events will never be included in any of these stories. Yet in the storytelling process one experiences and represents a sense of the coherence of one's life through time. A second option is to locate the ability to have a sense of diachronic unity in the "sense of self" or "I" rather than in the represented self or "me." This is the approach taken by Dan Zahavi, who argues

---

[13] Turner, *Theology, Psychology, and the Plural Self*, 157.

that the phenomenological sense of first-person givenness necessarily precedes the development of the narrative self.[14]

Yet the theological challenge remains. Do any of these approaches offer sufficient gravitas to bear the weight of Christian theological convictions about the ethical capability and the eternal value of the human person? This requires a different approach—one that allows both the "me" and the "I" to be as thoroughly contingent and labile as contemporary psychology and philosophy insist, yet recognizes a third dimension of human personhood that is explicitly theological.

The Apophatic Self

In his study of mystics Bernard McGinn discovers that many point to a third dimension that is beyond both the consciousness *of* objects and the self-presence of the agent *in* acts of intention. In this third dimension "God becomes present in inner acts, not as an object to be grasped or explained, but as a direct and transforming presence."[15] From the point of view of our ordinary consciousness of both objects and ourselves, this dimension is apophatic—that is, it is ungraspable and, literally, unknowable. It is the infinity of God in us, giving us our being and life.

Gregory of Nyssa was one of the first Christian mystics to articulate such an apophatic anthropology.[16] Gregory's key insight drew upon the biblical verse, "All of us, gazing with unveiled face on the glory of the Lord, are being transformed into the same image from glory to glory, as from the Lord who is the Spirit" (2 Cor 3:18, NABRE). Gregory, who had already affirmed the

---

[14] Dan Zahavi, "Phenomenology of the Self," in *The Self in Neuroscience and Psychiatry,* ed. Tilo Kircher and Anthony S. David (Cambridge, UK: Cambridge University Press, 2003), 62–63.

[15] Bernard McGinn, "Reflections on the Mystical Self," in *Cahiers Parisiens/Parisian Notebooks,* ed. Robert Morrissey, vol. 3 (Paris: University of Chicago Center in Paris, 2007), 110–30.

[16] Bernard McGinn, "Hidden God and Hidden Self: The Emergence of Apophatic Anthropologies in Christian Mysticism," in *Histories of the Hidden God: Concealment and Revelation in Western Gnostic, Esoteric, and Mystical Traditions,* ed. April D. De Conick and Grant Adamson (New York: Routledge, 2014), 87–100.

infinity and incomprehensibility of God, realized that the image of God in humans must likewise be infinite and incomprehensible, but in humans the restoration of this image is necessarily a temporally prolonged process. This is the basis of Gregory's famous doctrine of *epektasis*, which posits that each time we receive a taste of fulfillment in God, it will awaken in us an ever deeper thirst for more, since God is infinite and we ourselves are created to be the vessels of this infinity.[17]

Martin Laird finds that in Gregory's commentary on the *Song of Songs* he goes even further. As the bride enters ever more deeply into the unknowing of apophasis, the Holy Spirit moves directly within her mind to distill mystical truths. Laird writes: "While all thoughts are at some point abandoned in order to enter the divine sanctuary or to grasp the Beloved in union by faith alone, the result of this contact is that truth bedews the mind with obscure insights; the Holy Spirit breathes on the mind and causes waves of thought to move upwards."[18] Even more striking, however, is how God moves within her whole being to give direct witness of God's Word to others—a process that Laird terms "logophasis." He summarizes: "As a result of apophatic union, in which concepts, words and images have been abandoned, characteristics of the Word are taken on; the Word indwells the deeds and discourse of the one in apophatic union. Hence a new discourse emerges: the Word says itself (hence the term *logophasis*) through deeds and discourse."[19]

Laird also makes connections between Gregory of Nyssa's insight and postmodern thought, specifically that of Catholic philosopher Jean-Luc Marion. While Husserl argued that phenomenological practice can discover the constituting "I"

---

[17] Gregory of Nyssa, *The Life of Moses: Gregory of Nyssa [Gregorius Nyssenus]*, trans., intro., and notes by Abraham Malherbe and Everett Ferguson, foreword by John Meyendorff, The Classics of Western Spirituality (New York: Paulist Press, 1978), paras. 219–39.

[18] Martin S. Laird, *Gregory of Nyssa and the Grasp of Faith: Union, Knowledge, and Divine Presence*, Oxford Early Christian Studies (Oxford: Oxford University Press, 2004), 144.

[19] Martin S. Laird, "'Whereof We Speak': Gregory of Nyssa, Jean-Luc Marion, and the Current Apophatic Rage," *Heythrop Journal* 42, no. 1 (January 2001): 3.

behind all that appears, Marion counters that what we can actually discover is only that all things—including ourselves—are "given." We are in the world not so much as those who can grasp and control our world or ourselves, but rather as those who are called to respond to what is given to us. Thus, there is a fundamentally apophatic quality to human life and vocation. Laird argues that, for Marion as for Gregory, "abandonment of language, image and concept . . . leads to an encounter, indeed union, with the Word, as a result of which Marion's theologian, in abandoning discourse, is paradoxically said by the Word: theo*logy* becomes *theo*logy."[20] Rather than theology being done by a human being who speaks in interpretation of God, it is God who speaks directly through the "empty" theologian.

Indeed, Marion has written a book in which he interprets Saint Augustine in terms of such an apophatic anthropology. In the *Confessions*, says Marion, Augustine begins by asking "Who am I?" and ultimately is forced to conclude that it is impossible for him to know himself, because he has no "place" of his own in which to stand or from which to depart upon a search for himself. His only remaining option is to indwell this *aporia* (irresolvable dilemma) of placelessness. This leads Augustine, says Marion, to the conclusion that "if, therefore, something like a self remains possible for me, I will never find it in my own nonplace but solely there where a place is found, even if it is not situated in my own domain." It turns out that this place "outside my domain" is, in fact, God. Marion continues: "This place without me, before me, but only thus *for* me, who remains essentially outside and foreign to it, God alone is found there."[21] In short, God, who is both more intimate to me than my own self and infinitely beyond my self, is my "place"—a place that the self will never be able to grasp, understand, or claim as its own. The self does not "take place" except as sheer gift of God, and living this receptivity radically is the closest that one can come to self-knowledge.

---

[20] Laird, "'Whereof We Speak,'" 6.
[21] Jean-Luc Marion, *In the Self's Place: The Approach of Saint Augustine*, trans. Jeffrey L. Kosky, Cultural Memory in the Present (Stanford, CA: Stanford University Press, 2012), 283.

John F. Crosby, in reviewing Marion's book on Augustine and the self, expressed appreciation for his non-metaphysical, radically theocentric view of the human person, but also raised the question of whether Marion had gone too far. Personhood, suggests Crosby, is defined both by radical relationality *and* by a certain "belonging to oneself" such that one can exercise real agency. He wishes that Marion would address this "paradox of a *creaturely person*, that is, a being who though existing through God is nevertheless established in himself to the point of being able to dispose over himself—a being who is not only a creature of God but also a partner of God, existing in a dialogical relation with him."[22]

This, then, is our challenge. How can we understand the human person as fundamentally grounded in God yet also having genuine integrity as a person in his or her own right?

Pneumatological Anthropology: Biblical Perspectives

Without claiming to be able to develop a full-fledged new approach to theological anthropology, some version of a "Spirit anthropology" may be helpful in resolving the issues discussed in this chapter. As briefly introduced in Chapter 1, this approach draws on biblical perspectives (especially Paul) and recent attempts to use the analogy of a field to think about the Spirit.

Although an adequate review of relevant biblical texts would require another book (or several!), a few key texts offer additional perspectives on these issues.[23] In Genesis, creation is described in terms of the *ruach* (wind or spirit) that blows over the *tohu vabohu* (formless wasteland). The Harper Collins Study Bible translates Genesis 1:2 as "the earth was a formless void and darkness covered the face of the deep, while a wind [*ruach*] from God swept over the face of the waters." This is followed by the progression of "days" as creation takes form, culminating in humankind on the sixth day and the sabbath of God's rest on the seventh day. There are, of course, innumerable interpretive

---

[22] John F. Crosby, "Called by Him," *First Things* 236 (October 2013): 64.

[23] F. W. Horn, "Holy Spirit," in *The Anchor Bible Dictionary*, ed. Hans Dieter Betz et al. (New York: Doubleday, 1992), 262–63.

perspectives that draw different nuances of meaning from these texts. For our purposes, however, the key image is that of the living wind or breath of God progressively animating and giving form to the materiality of creation. This image underlies the analogy of Spirit as a nonmaterial and nonlocal "field" that nonetheless organizes, unites, and gives direction to all created entities. This image also underlies the notion of the apophatic self—the human person as emergent within the formless abyss of the Spirit.

People are often taken aback by the diversity and plurality of perspectives on how the Spirit is conferred on human beings in the Hebrew Bible. Daniel Castelo suggests that we should not think of this as a problem of incoherence but rather as the gift of the diversity that is needed for diverse situations.[24] Sometimes the Spirit is given to a judge or a leader for a limited time so the person can accomplish a specific task (for example, Othniel in Judg 3:10, or Samson in Judg 14:6). There are groups of ecstatic prophets, although often their "frenzy" is regarded with some suspicion (for example, 1 Sam 10:10; 19:23). With the kingship, the belief develops that the Spirit is conferred along with the anointing and laying on of hands for office (for example, 1 Sam 16:13). In the classical period many of the prophets do not claim the power of the Spirit but present themselves simply as God's messengers and defenders of the covenant.[25] It is the Word of God that fills them with zeal to demand justice and reform of corrupt structures.[26] In the postexilic period an eschatological vision develops of the Spirit as poured out in fullness upon all the people at the end of times (for example, Isa 44:3; Ezek 39:29).

In the Gospels the Holy Spirit is named as appearing at key initiatory moments in Jesus's life, such as his conception (Matt 1:20; Luke 1:35) and his baptism (Mark 1:9–12; Matt 3:16; Luke 3:22). John 19:29 portrays Jesus "giving up his spirit" at the moment of death. Finally, in John 16:7, 12–15, the Spirit is

---

[24] Daniel Castelo, *Pneumatology: A Guide for the Perplexed* (London: Bloomsbury T & T Clark, 2015), chap. 2.

[25] Robert R. Wilson, "Early Israelite Prophecy," *Interpretation* 32, no. 1 (January 1978): 3–16.

[26] Sigmund Mowinckel, "The Spirit and the Word in the Prophets," in *The Spirit and the Word: Prophecy and Tradition in Ancient Israel*, trans. K. C. Hanson (Minneapolis: Augsburg Fortress, 2002), 83–89.

presented as the *Paracletus* or Advocate sent by Jesus to complete his mission after his historical life has ended. These texts portray the Spirit of truth as a character in the ongoing narrative of Jesus's life, for upon his departure the Advocate will come to stay with the disciples and lead them in fulfilling his mission. The Spirit's role is future oriented, guiding the disciples to understand and to live out the glory eternally intended by the divine Father and Son. Luke portrays this promise as fulfilled when the Holy Spirit descends upon the disciples with "a sound like the rush of a violent wind" at Pentecost (see Acts 2:1–4).

For Saint Paul, it was arguments with his opponents that required him to refine his understanding of the human person and its relation to the divine Spirit. In the context of his struggle with the Corinthians, who resisted his authority because he did not seem to manifest the signs and miracles they expected from a "superapostle," Paul strove to articulate as clearly as possible how God works in, and transforms, human beings. Scripture scholar Hans Dieter Betz details how in 2 Corinthians 4:5—5:10, Paul asserts that God can work powerfully through a person even though that person remains a "clay jar" that is subject to all the weaknesses and assaults that are endemic to physical life in a contingent world.[27]

> For we do not proclaim ourselves; we proclaim Jesus Christ as Lord and ourselves as your slaves for Jesus's sake. For it is the God who said, "Let light shine out of darkness," who has shone in our hearts to give the light of the knowledge of the glory of God in the face of Jesus Christ. But we have this treasure in clay jars, so that it may be made clear that the extraordinary power belongs to God and does not come from us. (2 Cor 4:5–7)

Betz notes that, here, Paul does not say that the person's knowledge of God derives from the nature of an immortal soul, or

---

[27] Hans Dieter Betz, "The Concept of the 'Inner Human Being' (o Esō Anthrōpos) in the Anthropology of Paul," *New Testament Studies* 46, no. 3 (July 2000): 315–41; idem, "The Human Being in the Antagonisms of Life according to the Apostle Paul," *The Journal of Religion* 80, no. 4 (October 2000): 557–75.

from possession by the divine spirit, or even from the indwelling of Christ. Rather, Betz states, "the treasure is the heart illuminated by the spirit."[28] By being illuminated by the Spirit and encountering "the glory of God in the face of Jesus Christ," the embodied person is gifted with regaining the integrity that the first human being, Adam, lost by sinning. Still, the human person remains a contingent being, and God's power remains God's. The transforming effect of the Spirit is not seen in the person becoming extraordinary or performing miraculous deeds but in the fruits of the gospel being conveyed through that person on behalf of others.

Rejecting dualistic anthropologies that would require the exterior body to be shed in order for the inner "soul" to unite with God, Paul affirms the fundamental goodness and integrity of created human beings. He also takes care to affirm the human being as participant in the ongoing historical process.[29] Although through illumination by the Spirit a Christian is already sharing in the life and death of Jesus, who is the "second Adam," this participation does not remove the person from the vagaries of history—or from the painful contradictions within the person's own being. What it does do, however, is provide "the freedom to take a courageous look at the ugly inside at its deepest level. The believer is able to endure the freedom of this insight because of the simultaneous experience of overcoming it."[30] The heart illuminated by the Spirit finds God always at work in history, drawing it toward its fulfillment, even when what is visible is weakness, destruction, and death. Nonetheless, life in the Spirit will not be completely fulfilled until the end of time in the resurrection—"a building from God, a house not made with hands, eternal in the heavens" (2 Cor 5:1). Paul concludes that God, who has created and prepared human beings for this end, "has given us the Spirit as a guarantee" (2 Cor 5:5).

---

[28] Betz, "The Human Being in the Antagonisms of Life according to the Apostle Paul," 566. Note that Betz does not capitalize *spirit* even when it refers to the divine Spirit.

[29] Betz, "The Concept of the 'Inner Human Being' (o Esō Anthrōpos) in the Anthropology of Paul," 340–41.

[30] Betz, "The Human Being in the Antagonisms of Life according to the Apostle Paul," 572.

It would take a few hundred more years of reflection and debate for Christians to articulate clearly the momentous insights of the doctrine of the Trinity and the Personhood of the Spirit, based on such texts as those we have reviewed, as well as many others. What we can observe in this biblical trajectory is increasing personal intimacy in how the Spirit is at work to bring humanity (and all creation) to the fulfillment intended by God. Eugene Rogers has suggested that the best way to articulate this is to say that with the coming of Jesus, human persons are offered full incorporation into the narrative of the Word. The Spirit often seems elusive, yet actually is "seeking to make herself known, in the only way possible: by incorporating subsidiary persons, human persons, into the trinitarian life, where alone the Spirit's personhood could be experienced, by reading them into the text, narrating them typologically into the stories she shares with Jesus and the Father."[31] Henceforth the Spirit is to be a living character in a disciple's self-narrative, and the primary role of that character is to guide the disciple in how to belong to Jesus and how to participate in completing his mission. One who accepts the identity of a Jesus disciple is gifted with all the cornucopia of biblical symbols and stories—and especially those of Jesus and his Spirit—as resources for the construction of a new self-narrative.

Contingency, Wholeness, and the Field of the Spirit

In considering Spirit anthropology within our postmodern world, we can envision human persons as created within a nonmaterial and nonlocal Spirit field that always and everywhere animates, unites, and draws toward consummation. In its own divine integrity the Spirit field is, of course, infinitely more than a mere part or dimension of the human person. Yet the human person has no existence apart from the power of that animating, uniting, consummating field, so from the viewpoint of the created person, the Spirit is the most utterly foundational dimension of his or her

---

[31] Eugene F. Rogers, *After the Spirit: A Constructive Pneumatology from Resources outside the Modern West*, Radical Traditions (Grand Rapids, MI: Eerdmans, 2005), 46.

existence. A weak analogy might be the dynamic pattern of iron filings that emerges when a magnet is held under the paper upon which they lie. As long as the magnetic field is there, the charged pattern of relationships among the various filings holds steady, even while the magnet moves around under the paper. Take away the magnet, and the pattern—and all its inherent relationships— ceases to exist. Similarly, the Spirit brings human persons into existence, dynamically holds them amid all their activities, and guides them with its nonmaterial orientation toward consummation. As Robert Davis Hughes states, "All spiritual qualities, including life, soul, consciousness, sociality, virtue, human spirit, and eternal life are . . . relational terms between the dust we are on the one hand, and the Holy Spirit on the other."[32]

In this view the Spirit is, in fact, the apophatic dimension described above under apophatic anthropology. What is apophatic is, by definition, unknowable and ungraspable yet at the same time existentially foundational. The spiritual seeker progressively discovers that the self is labile, pluralistic, and even illusory, yet in doing so also encounters hints and glimpses of the apophatic abyss as the "direct and transforming presence" of God.[33] The divine Spirit moves within the contingent human person, gifting him or her with the only "wholeness" that is possible for such a creature.

At one stage in writing this book, I found myself resisting the use of the term *wholeness* in the title. It seemed that this term could too easily evoke either the modern "myth of progress," which imagines the trajectory of life as heading toward ever-greater perfection, or a romanticized ideal of "integration" as an achievable psychological state. My present view is that a biblically informed Spirit anthropology does not envision human life in terms of an arrival point of "wholeness" at some time in our future. Rather, the nature of our human existence is to be contingent, always becoming, and inevitably crisis ridden. The only wholeness possible for us is found in surrender into the reality of being breathed by the Spirit. In that sense we are

---

[32] Robert Davis Hughes, *Beloved Dust: Tides of the Spirit in the Christian Life* (New York: Continuum, 2008), 7.

[33] McGinn, "Reflections on the Mystical Self."

equally whole when we are "broken," and equally broken when we are "whole."

African American theologian Romney Moseley made a related critique of the stage theories of moral and religious development (such as those of Lawrence Kohlberg and James Fowler) that were immensely popular in religious education circles in the 1980s and 1990s. These theories trace an upward path toward culmination in "universalizing" faith. Moseley was particularly concerned about these theories' elitist appeal to an economically secure, upwardly mobile, dominating culture that screens out the ways in which it contributes to the devastation of poor, nonwhite, marginalized communities. A person may feel whole and integrated within such a culture while oblivious to the brokenness inflicted on others:

> Attention needs to be paid foremost to what we consider to be normative forms of self-world equilibrium. What we perceive as integration . . . is more likely the result of action taken in response to crises and doubts, which are themselves indicative of the absence of synchrony in inner or outer relations. . . . In other words, what we take to be wholeness might very well be a defensive posture against alienation. What is secure in one arena of life is merely a temporary platform for attending to the discontinuities in other arenas.[34]

Moseley emphasizes that his key point, similar to mine, is that "the past, present, and future are situated in relation to eternal life."[35] Within the course of our temporal lives we will never be freed from the reality of woundedness—our own, and that of others—and the consequent calling to engage in what he calls "kenotic emancipatory praxis," which "opens the conclaves of power to the powerless."[36] Aldo Tassi puts it this way: "The 'calling' toward wholeness is an invitation to conduct the life of the

---

[34] Romney M. Moseley, *Becoming a Self before God: Critical Transformations* (Nashville, TN: Abingdon Press, 1991), 71.

[35] Moseley, *Becoming a Self before God*, 72.

[36] Moseley, *Becoming a Self before God*, 129.

spirit in a way that leads to an acceptance of the destabilized situation of being as a possible theater for God's creative work."[37]

No doubt, the expansive visions of an "ecozoic society" (Thomas Berry), a "planetary civilization" (Sam Mickey), or the "greening of the self" (Joanna Macy) must be submitted to the same critique. On the one hand, insofar as they play into an upwardly mobile expectation that human action can achieve a kind of future state of perfection, they may be problematic. On the other hand, insofar as they honor the catholic principle of the Spirit breathing responsiveness to cosmic wholeness into persons and communities that remain completely earthy, local, and subject to contingent conditions, they may motivate us to engage in the kind of emancipatory praxis to which we are called.

A Model of Personhood

In sum, the model of personhood being proposed is that the foundation and source of human selfhood are apophatic, that is, literally grounded in God.[38] This explains the failure of all efforts—whether secular or theological—to locate a stable, autonomous core self. While affirming that the Spirit is a divine *Person,* and therefore enters as a *character* in each human person's construction of the narrative self, the communication of the Spirit is very different from that of my embodied neighbors or friends who can literally whisper in my ear or offer me a proposal for my future. The more seriously a disciple seeks to know the Spirit and to attend to its promptings, the more the apophatic dimension becomes the predominant experience. This is articulated as an *un*knowing in which one has a conviction of knowing truth and being moved at a depth never experienced before, yet without knowing in the usual cognitive and intellectual sense.

---

[37] Aldo Tassi, "Spirituality as a Stage of Being," in *Divine Representations: Postmodernism and Spirituality*, ed. Ann W. Astell (New York: Paulist Press, 1994), 30.

[38] For a discussion of apophatic anthropology in the medieval context, see Denys Turner, *The Darkness of God: Negativity in Christian Mysticism* (New York: Cambridge University Press, 1998), esp. chap. 6.

As we are marked with ashes on our foreheads on Ash Wednesday, we hear, "Dust you are, and to dust you shall return." Not only our bodies, but our selves, too, are fundamentally fragile, protean, and transient. The secular discovery of this reality, not recognizing the Spirit, names it with the language of deconstruction, fragmentation, and confabulation. A theological perspective, however, names it with the language of apophaticism. Jesus is reported to have said, "Those who want to save their life [*psyche*] will lose it, and those who lose their life for my sake will find it" (Matt 16:25; see also Luke 9:24; Mark 8:35; John 12:25). The emptiness of the self is the space in which God can come to fullness.

Yet, just as our bodies are made of dust and yet exist as solid (though ever-changing) structures, the self does have real existence as a psychological structure that is essential to human survival and flourishing. The psychological absence of a self is a severe pathology. The general consensus today is to understand self-making as an ongoing narrative process that strives to bring sense and coherence to the multitudinous experiences occurring in one's life. Self-making combines elements of the documentary and the fictional. There are usually threads of continuity throughout life, but also significant rewritings. According to dialogical self theory, people are typically at work on more than one plotline at a time. A simple example is a plotline for the good mother, another for the hard-nosed prosecutor, and a third for the mountain climber. Other, more obscure plotlines are also likely to exist, rumbling at or just below the surface of consciousness. At each choice point, tensions and alliances among parts of the self must be renegotiated. All this occurs within a thoroughly relational context of responding to the actions, desires, expectations, and stories of others.

From a secular viewpoint the drama of selfhood is driven primarily by psychological dynamics as well as political considerations. (Political in this context refers to negotiations of influence or power between persons and within groups.) From the theological viewpoint, however, an additional factor is at work. The nonlocal, nonmaterial field of force that is the divine Spirit operates like a magnet drawing self-making toward relationships and responses that are shaped by the narrative of the Word. This is not an impersonal or coercive magnetism, however, because the Spirit's essential character is that of a divine Person. A better analogy might be the magnetism of charismatic persons whose radiation of love draws others to want to be with them and to be like them. The Spirit is an apophatic field of divine personal love that draws human persons to desire to "write their stories" in ways that enhance the outpouring of that love.

A common debate in discussions of the divine Spirit is the relationship between the Spirit in creation and the Spirit in redemption. In relation to the current discussion, this is the question of the relation between the Spirit as present always, everywhere, and to all persons, and the Spirit as uniquely conferred upon some persons through sacrament and/or charism. Even more specifically, it has to do with the Spirit's relationship with Jesus. For example, is an explicit discipleship relationship with Jesus necessary for a person to receive the fullness of the Spirit? Insofar as the Spirit is present as source and fount of life always, everywhere, and to all persons, spiritual practices deriving from all the religions and cultures of the world may offer pathways of access to deeper awareness of Spirit. Christian theology, however, has traditionally affirmed that since the three Persons of the Trinity are one God, they are necessarily a "package deal." While this does not completely exclude access to the Spirit in other-than-christocentric milieus, it is usually interpreted to mean that the fullness of the Spirit comes through Christ.

The hypothesis developed here is that the field of the divine Spirit is operative always and everywhere; it is not exclusive to Christians or to those who explicitly seek God. Wherever anyone finds the grace to love selflessly, the magnetism of the Spirit is at work. Christians believe, however, that God has provided not only the attractive force of the Spirit but also a human incarnation of the completely Spirit-filled life. Jesus is the Word of God, or perhaps we could even say the Story of God. His life, death, and resurrection incarnate the story of divine selfless love. The stories of his life—including both the stories told in the Gospels, and those untold but nonetheless inscribed in the history of humanity—are given as templates or paradigms for our own self-making. To follow Jesus is to seek to make one's life a new version of his story of selfless love.

Doing this has never been simple for humans, because each person faces unique personal, cultural, and political challenges that do not line up straightforwardly with those faced by Jesus during his earthly life. The Jesus template, therefore, cannot be applied like a cookie cutter that automatically produces the result of a Jesus-like life. Rather, it is more like a handbook of scenarios that one can search to find those that offer suggestive possibilities to one's imagination. These possibilities must then be discerned by attention to where the attractive force of the Spirit is strongest and most authentic. Making a conscientious choice and then courageously performing the next action in one's personal drama remain the creative prerogative of each individual.

All this has seemingly become more complex in the context of the contemporary world, however. Most previous generations of human beings lived in social and cultural contexts that provided much more stability and guidance in the choices needed to create one's personal drama of the self. Such cultures could often be coercive in their expectations for how people would live their lives. Even within such situations, though, people have always had choices to make, and occasionally individuals broke free of cultural expectations in startling and courageous ways. We might think of Joan of Arc, Francis of Assisi, or Meister Eckhart. Yet even such as these selected their breakout models from a relatively slim slate of available cultural templates. Joan of Arc, for example, modeled herself on the warrior; Francis of Assisi first chose the way of the hermit; and Eckhart maintained his roles as preacher and professor even while confounding all expectations. What is different today is that, both during the childhood developmental process and in adulthood, options are multiple and, at the same time, rapidly evolving. The dynamics of the potentially fragmented dialogical self, with its many part-selves that may or may not be able to negotiate a satisfactory truce, become far more prominent than in situations where the design of selfhood is more strongly channeled by culture and peer pressure.

Implications for the Rhythm of Spiritual Practice

The analogy of breathing points both to the role of the divine Spirit and to the rhythmic dynamism of divine life as it creates, redeems, and sanctifies. The Spirit breathes our very life into us; the Spirit *is* our life, and it is the ground of any wholeness that we can ever hope to have. The life that the Spirit breathes in us, however, goes forth into the created lifeform of human person-hood that has the responsibility to co-create itself by writing and performing its own story of the self.

In comparison to the wholeness of the divine Spirit, our stories are rather ragged, jumbled concoctions that more often than not look as though they would never stand up in the court of divine judgment. Yet, fortunately for us, the Spirit has never been absent in the process of our struggle to create ourselves. The inward and outward rhythm of the physical breath of life has a correlative in the breath of the Spirit in us. Breathed inward, we glimpse the apophatic ground, and selfhood melts in the abyss of love. Breathed outward, we struggle amid adversity and complexity to create a life at least half worthy of the love we have witnessed. This rhythmic movement is the breathing of the Spirit in us. The wholeness of our lives, such as it is, is not our own, but God's.

Our spiritual practices are meant to intentionally embody this rhythm of inward and outward movements. Some practices are more concentrated on the outward movement, that is, on the Spirit's participation in our work of creating and living out our self-story. Other practices are more concentrated on the inward movement, that is, on our touching into the apophatic reality of the Spirit as ground of our being. Every authentic spiritual practice, however, includes elements of both movements.

In the next two chapters we examine these two types of practices, and how they may contribute to the development of the catho-lic personality needed for our time, as well as proposing some elements of spiritual practice appropriate to this late modern reality. The overarching metaphor is that of being breathed into catholicity by the Spirit.

Part III

Living in the Catholicizing Rhythm of the Spirit

Chapter 7

Breathed In: The Way of Emptying

The Spirit breathes. The breathing of the Spirit is a metaphor for the dynamic, rhythmic movement engendered in creation by the pervading field of the Spirit. The Spirit is the force of infinite love breathing us inward to the apophatic depths of the Father and outward into participation in the Son's salvific action. Just as the field of gravity inexorably draws weighted objects downward toward the center of the earth, so the Spirit field draws every created being along in its inward and outward rhythm. The human person is created with a unique capacity to participate freely and totally in that rhythm of selflessness and self-creating.

We now explore the implications of these perspectives for spiritual practice. In this chapter our focus is the "way of emptying"—in classical terms, the apophatic way—beyond all images and words. Although in our physical breathing it is breathing out that empties the lungs, this spiritual way of emptying is our response to the indrawing breath of the Spirit, who urges us to let go of every possession, up to and including our very selves. While this path typically involves contemplative practices such as concentrated interiority, stillness, and various forms of meditation, it is noteworthy that the most apophatic mystics often are also the strongest proponents of finding God in everyday life rather than simply in special interior experiences. The apophatic path is, ultimately, the way of non-dualism. What is discovered on this path is that God is both nowhere and everywhere. In Christian terms, the seeker arrives at the joyful insight expressed by Saint Paul: "It is no longer I who live, but it is Christ who lives in me!" (Gal 2:20).

The contemplative practices associated with the way of emptying are often arduous, guiding the seeker to be progressively stripped of all attachment to words, images, feelings, and desires. The great paradox of the apophatic path is that it is frequently taught as the most excellent way, yet ultimately it cannot be practiced or achieved by any action or effort. In the end, the very image of self-emptying fails; it is as impossible to empty oneself completely by one's own actions as it is to lift oneself off the ground by one's own bootstraps. The breakthrough of realization, when it comes, is always a surprise and a grace. It is awakening into a knowing beyond knowing, which those who know call unknowing. In Christian theological terms it is the realization that we participate in the very life of God.

Denys Turner and Experience

We must briefly address a major challenge in any discussion of apophaticism. In his acclaimed monograph *The Darkness of God* Denys Turner explores in great detail why any approach that considers the apophatic as engendering an experience is problematic.[1] The apophatic is, precisely, the affirmation that both God and the most foundational reality of our own being cannot be experienced. Turner argues strongly that modern approaches to mysticism that regard it as a special kind of experience fundamentally misinterpret the patristic and medieval sources upon which they draw.

These classical sources, including those we discuss in this and the next chapter, are all deeply imbued with the dialectics of Neoplatonic epistemology. Turner outlines the Neoplatonic approach as a two-level dialectic. On the first level it describes experience with alternating affirmative and negative language as a means to facilitate a hierarchical process of "ascent to God." The second level of the dialectic, however, is a critique of experience itself. Turner writes that "in the highest, apophatic negations, we know only what affirmations we deny; but we

---

[1] Denys Turner, *The Darkness of God: Negativity in Christian Mysticism* (New York: Cambridge University Press, 1998).

know nothing of what our denials affirm."[2] Turner argues that the modern rejection of this dialectical approach tends to leave us wallowing in the assumption that everything the mystics write about is an "experience" to which we might aspire.

Turner's point is well taken; the way of emptying is not a path to a certain type of experience but rather a practice of openness to the Holy Spirit—who, of course, is ultimately beyond our capacity to experience. In this book, however, we employ the approach of catholicity from within, which affirms that the Holy Spirit does, in fact, leave traces in our experience. One of the effects of these traces is that they motivate us to take up practices that may open us even more deeply to the Spirit's transforming power in our lives. This chapter traces how long-term commitment to such practices will, indeed, require us to let go of our search for experiences. We begin, however, from where we are, as creatures glimpsing something of God within our experience and recognizing this as a call to go further.

One of the characteristics of spiritual experience, as noted in Chapter 2, is that it comes upon us by surprise, seeming to transform us—if only for a moment—without our having planned it or even actively participated in it. This is the grace of the Spirit's rhythms, not putting any conditions on its gifts of a tantalizing taste of divine communion. When we speak about a "way," however, we move into the realm of active and intentional participation in collaboration with the Spirit. One of the fruits of a spiritual experience is often that the person begins to search for practices and communities that can support movement toward committed and stable living of the vision glimpsed in that experience.

The exemplars presented later in the chapter offer the way of emptying as a mystical way. It must always be remembered, however, that within early Christianity the *mystikos* (mystery) was not understood as an esoteric or ecstatic experience available only to a spiritual elite. It was, rather, the saving presence of the life, death, and resurrection of Jesus mediated by the scriptures and the sacraments—and thus, equally available to all. What distinguishes those tradition has named mystics is that they followed the path of the mystery all the way to the end. In doing

---

[2] Turner, *The Darkness of God*, 271.

so, they gained wisdom from which those of us still on the way can benefit.

Union: Devotional or Ontological?

The end to which the way of emptying leads is traditionally called union with God. One of the great debates about such union has been whether it is fundamentally a matter of love and will or of knowledge and intellect, since various mystics emphasize one over the other. Bernard McGinn concludes that "in Christianity at least the contrast between intellectual and affective mysticism is too general to be helpful," since in reality all Christian mystics include elements of both.[3] Louis Dupré adds that to call the *unio mystica* "cognitive *or* affective is to treat an essentially unified and unifying consciousness as a divided and oppositional one. Unless consciousness is both cognitive and affective, it misses the very wholeness characteristic of the final union."[4]

Dupré then discusses how this relates to the paradoxes of mystical language: those who describe union typically insist on its non-dualistic, ontological character, yet at the same time they are drawn to employ the affective language of love, which by nature is dynamic and dualistic.[5] Given the conclusion of earlier chapters that human psychological selfhood is formed as a dialogical narrative while being spiritually grounded in God, this makes sense. The way of emptying is the discovery of one's foundational grounding in God. Along the way the narrative self is in many ways deconstructed, but it is not destroyed. As we note in the next chapter, the transformative process both reconstructs and deconstructs. Even when traversing the apophatic way, the

---

[3] Bernard McGinn, "Love, Knowledge, and *Unio mystica* in the Western Christian Tradition," in *Mystical Union in Judaism, Christianity, and Islam: An Ecumenical Dialogue*, ed. Moshe Idel and Bernard McGinn (New York: Continuum, 1996), 84.

[4] Louis K. Dupré, "*Unio mystica*: The State and the Experience," in Idel and McGinn, *Mystical Union in Judaism, Christianity, and Islam*, 21.

[5] Dupré, "*Unio mystica*," 23.

narrative self never completely loses its need for elements of devotional language that retain the dualism and dialogical character of love to express and foster its vocation.

When a seeker relates devotionally to God as one who loves and is loved, the sense of being stripped and emptied is likely to be envisaged, first, as a surrender of the will to God. For Howard Thurman, this is "to give up the initiative over your own life; to yield at the core of one's self, the nerve center of one's consent to God."[6] In his book on catholicity Hans Urs von Balthasar describes one who is totally open to the Holy Spirit as being willing to take the grace God offers into oneself "in a Catholic, all-embracing way, without conditions or limitations . . . as a placing of one's whole life at God's disposal, as a Yes without limits."[7] While this "unlimited Yes of faith" may at times be felt as the joy, relief, or even bliss of resting with complete trust in the arms of God, it may at other times be accompanied by feelings of sorrow, rage, or terror as one's most intimate desires and expectations have to be relinquished. The struggle to let go of one's self-will in favor of openness to the Spirit is often prolonged and painful.

For Christians, the interpersonal or devotional style of piety is in many ways normative, since our theology affirms God as personal and Jesus as mediating our salvation. Yet, as Dupré has indicated, "to articulate the goal and final stages of this loving communion, many mystics introduced expressions of ontological union that are hardly compatible with the duality of love."[8] It is here that the fully apophatic way emerges. This union is a state of being that is beyond experience, or at least beyond the capacity of the mind to reflect and use language. Those attempting to speak about it insist that it is not simply an experience, but rather a transformation of the substance or center of the soul. It is here that language such as the "annihilation of the self" may come into use. Dupré sums up by saying: "Consciousness here

---

[6] Howard Thurman, *Temptations of Jesus: Five Sermons Given by Howard Thurman in Marsh Chapel, Boston University, 1962* (Richmond, IN: Friends United Press, 1978), 67.

[7] Hans Urs von Balthasar, *In the Fullness of Faith: On the Centrality of the Distinctively Catholic* (San Francisco: Ignatius Press, 1988), 81.

[8] Dupré, "*Unio mystica*," 23.

merely appears to reverberate at the impact of an ontological reality that surpasses it. . . . The center of the mind has turned from self-consciousness to God-consciousness."[9]

With this introduction we now consider three Christian wisdom teachers who are exemplars of the way of emptying. Of these three, perhaps we could say that Meister Eckhart offers the deepest explanatory perspective while Jan Ruusbroec provides the most inspiring and evocative imagery. It is John of the Cross, however, who most clearly describes the necessary practices—as well as the high cost of making the journey. Historically, John comes after the others, but he is presented first because he most clearly exemplifies the interplay between the devotional path of love and the apophatic way.

John of the Cross

John of the Cross (1542–91) is best known for his teaching on the "dark nights" through which a spiritual seeker must pass. Behind this metaphor is his affirmation that God is infinite love and infinite light, beyond the capacity of both our sensory and spiritual faculties in their ordinary functioning. Just as a light too bright for the capacity of our eyes blinds us, so God is "darkness" to us. Yet God is our true center, toward which we incline as surely as a stone must fall toward the center of the earth.[10] Any time we grasp at something other than God—even if it is as profound as a magnificent insight into God or an experience of ecstatic communion—we impede our movement into God, thus both losing God and cheapening ourselves. The only way to be genuinely fulfilled and integrated in the radical love of God is courageously to enter the darkness by being emptied of all objects, whether sensory or spiritual, that may attempt to capture

---

[9] Dupré, "*Unio mystica*," 10–11.

[10] John of the Cross, "The Spiritual Canticle," 12, 1 and 17, 1 in *The Collected Works of Saint John of the Cross*, rev. ed., trans. Kieran Kavanaugh and Otilio Rodriguez (Washington, DC: ICS Publications, 1991), 515 and 542; idem, "Living Flame of Love," 1, 11–13, in Kavanaugh and Rodriguez, *The Collected Works of Saint John of the Cross*, 644–45.

our attention. Only thus can we advance in union with God in the "dark night" of faith.

It is much easier to understand what John is really teaching, however, if we begin with the poem "The Dark Night," in which he masterfully combines devotional and apophatic imagery.

1. One dark night,
fired with love's urgent longings
—ah, the sheer grace!—
I went out unseen,
my house being now all stilled.

2. In darkness, and secure,
by the secret ladder, disguised,
—ah, the sheer grace! —
in darkness and concealment,
my house being now all stilled.

3. On that glad night
in secret, for no one saw me,
nor did I look at anything
with no other light or guide
than the one that burned in my heart.

4. This guided me
more surely than the light of noon
to where he was awaiting me
—him I knew so well—
there in a place where no one appeared.

5. O guiding night!
O night more lovely than the dawn!
O night that has united
the Lover with his beloved,
transforming the beloved in her Lover.

6. Upon my flowering breast,
which I kept wholly for him alone,
there he lay sleeping,

and I caressing him
there in a breeze from the fanning cedars.

7. When the breeze blew from the turret,
as I parted his hair,
it wounded my neck
with its gentle hand,
suspending all my senses.

8. I abandoned and forgot myself,
laying my face on my beloved
all thing ceased; I went out from myself
leaving my cares
forgotten among the lilies.[11]

In this poem John of the Cross presents the "night" as fundamentally the night of lovers. In this night Lover and beloved seek each other, encounter each other, are united, and abandon themselves into each other. This night is secure, graced, glad, guiding, and lovely. It is also a time of being unseen, stilled, disguised, concealed, and secret. Paradoxically, the Lover appears "in a place where no one appeared." As the Lover sleeps on his beloved's breast, she is wounded by the sweet breezes and all her senses are suspended. Finally, "all things cease" as the beloved abandons and forgets herself.

The poem provides a beautiful and moving portrait of the way of emptying as, ultimately, a practice of love. Yet it also awakens our awareness that this practice of love requires going far beyond all that is visible, clear, well defined, and controllable. It requires actively going out from one's customary places and behaviors, following a light that burns only in the heart, and finally allowing one's senses, one's cares, and even one's very self to fall away into the divine Lover.

In his books *The Ascent of Mount Carmel* and *The Dark Night* John comments on the "Dark Night" poem as he goes step by step through all that is involved in this process of emptying

---

[11] John of the Cross, "The Dark Night," in "The Poetry," in Kavanaugh and Rodriguez, *The Collected Works of Saint John of the Cross*, 50–52.

and purification. However, somewhat strangely (at least to modern sensibilities), he employs a highly discursive and intellectualized style that frequently seems far from the poetic imagery and narrative on which he is purportedly commenting. These books describe the spiritual "night" in terms of four stages: an "active night of the senses," in which seekers do all they can to wean the sense faculties from their inordinate pleasures; a "passive night of the senses," in which God completes the purification of the senses; an "active night of the spirit," in which seekers learn to let go of the attachments of the higher faculties of intellect, memory, and will; and a "passive night of the spirit," in which God purifies persons of the deepest roots of all their imperfections.

The reader who picks up these books without having been introduced to the poetic heart of John's spirituality often finds them daunting, as well as, at times, tediously repetitive. It is the *Ascent*, in particular, that has shaped John's popular reputation for demanding an almost inhuman level of asceticism. The majority of this book is devoted to detailed consideration of the active night of the spirit, spelling out numerous types of natural and supernatural mental contents and affective responses that must be released into the "night" so that the seeker can become empty enough to welcome the touch of God. The following passage provides a summary of the teaching of the *Ascent* on the active nights of sense and spirit:

> I affirm, then, that if people take faith as a good guide to this state [of supreme contemplation], not only must they live in darkness in the sensory and lower part of their nature (concerning creatures and temporal things) . . . but they must also darken and blind themselves in that part of their nature that bears relation to God and spiritual things. . . . Since this transformation and union is something that does not fall within the reach of the senses and of human capability, the soul must perfectly and voluntarily empty itself—I mean in its affection and will—of all the earthly and heavenly things it can grasp. It must do this insofar as it can.[12]

---

[12] John of the Cross, "The Ascent of Mount Carmel," II,4,2, in Kavanaugh and Rodriguez, *The Collected Works of Saint John of the Cross*, 159.

The key to interpreting John's asceticism is to focus less on what he says we must let go of, and more on what he asserts is the fruit of these practices. In the passage above he observes that "this transformation and union is something that does not fall within the reach of the senses and of human capability." Harking back to the "Dark Night" poem, the union with the divine Lover is the deepest and most ardent longing of the soul; yet no human thought, imagination, feeling, or action can approach the infinity of God. We must be completely emptied, our "house now all stilled," so that the divine Lover can appear "there in a place where no one appeared."

It is also crucial to understand that the ascetical practices of the active nights are not actually central for John of the Cross. The active nights still depend upon what Denys Turner calls "the self constructed upon anxiety" that strives to make itself into a hero of ascetical practice.[13] The active nights are, therefore, only a necessary prelude to the far more important "passive nights" in which God becomes the active agent in the deconstruction of the hero self and the ultimate realization of union with God.[14] In Book I of "The Dark Night" John describes the signs for recognizing when the crucial transition from the active to the passive night of the senses is taking place:

> The first [sign] is that since these souls do not get satisfaction or consolation from the things of God, they do not get any from creatures either.
>
> The second sign . . . is that the memory ordinarily turns to God solicitously and with painful care.
>
> The third sign . . . is the powerlessness, in spite of one's efforts, to meditate and make use of the imagination, the interior sense, as was one's previous custom.[15]

---

[13] Turner, *The Darkness of God*, 243.

[14] For a detailed exposition of the path to union as presented by both John of the Cross and Teresa of Avila, see Edward Howells, *John of the Cross and Teresa of Avila: Mystical Knowing and Selfhood* (New York: Crossroad, 2002).

[15] John of the Cross, "The Dark Night," I, 9, #2, #3, #8, in Kavanaugh and Rodriguez, The *Collected Works of Saint John of the Cross*, 377–80.

One much-debated question is whether the dark nights John describes are common or rare experiences. Related to this is the question of whether they apply only to people deeply committed to a life of prayer. The key to responding to these questions is to remember that, for John, the darkness to which he refers is specifically the incapacity of the human person to perceive God with any of our ordinary faculties of knowledge and the consequent necessity of faith. Even for people who intentionally seek to relate to God in faithful prayer, however, the dark night is not limited only to issues occurring during prayer. Moreover, if indeed the Spirit is at work in all human lives, even when unacknowledged, some "shadow" of the night would appear to be a principle of growth in every life, challenging people to seek meaning beyond the superficialities of perception and feeling.

The "active night of the senses," for example, may flow into many ordinary acts of letting go of one desired thing in favor of another of higher value, for example, giving up sleeping in every morning in favor of going to work so one can feed one's children. The "passive night of the senses" appears when a person undergoes an unchosen loss—such as the death of a loved one or a humiliating failure—and asks in agony, "How can this be?" The active night of the spirit is present whenever people are struggling with crises of meaning or conscience. Some aspects of the passive night of the spirit may correlate with the profound undoing of the self that results from severe trauma (as we see in the next chapter).

However, for John, the full impact and value of the dark nights occur within the concentrated pursuit of the contemplative life, when a person longs to know and belong to God. In this context the full expression of the passive night of the spirit, in particular, does not seem to be a common experience. In "The Dark Night" John describes it as the final deconstruction of the self in transition to union with God:

> Poor, abandoned, and unsupported by any of the apprehensions of my soul (in the darkness of my intellect, the distress of my will, and in the affliction and anguish of my memory), left to darkness in pure faith, which is a dark night for these natural faculties, and with my will touched

only by the sorrows, afflictions, and longings of love of God, I went out from myself.[16]

Later, he adds that in such a moment the soul suffers "an oppressive undoing and an inner torment. . . . Sometimes this experience is so vivid that it seems to the soul that it sees hell and perdition open before it."[17] The twentieth-century spiritual writer Thomas Merton, for whom John of the Cross is a primary source, uses the more modern language of the "self" to describe this final spiritual transition, observing that "the only full and authentic purification is that which turns a man completely inside out, so that he no longer has a self to defend."[18] Denys Turner describes this transition explicitly in terms of going beyond all experience: "The *negative experiences* of the dark nights are but the perplexity of the soul and the desolation of desire at the *loss* of its self-of-experience."[19] This loss, however, is far greater gain; as John says, "Having been made one with God, the soul is somehow God through participation."[20]

Meister Eckhart

Among Christian spiritual teachers and theologians Eckhart may be the most radical example of the way of emptying. He also exemplifies the paradoxical and hyperbolic language that is needed to speak of what transcends all words and all imagining. Here is one example of his description of the inner reality of the human being:

> I have sometimes said that there is a power in the spirit that alone is free. Sometimes I have said that it is a guard

---

[16] John of the Cross, "The Dark Night," II, 4, 1, in Kavanaugh and Rodriguez, *The Collected Works of Saint John of the Cross*, 400.

[17] John of the Cross, "The Dark Night," II, 6, 6 , in Kavanaugh and Rodriguez, *The Collected Works of Saint John of the Cross*, 405.

[18] Thomas Merton, *Contemplative Prayer* (New York: Image Books Doubleday, 1996), 109.

[19] Turner, *The Darkness of God*, 251.

[20] John of the Cross, "Living Flame of Love," 3, 78, in Kavanaugh and Rodriguez, *The Collected Works of Saint John of the Cross,* 706.

of the spirit; sometimes I have said that it is a light of the spirit; sometimes I have said that it is a spark. But now I say that it is neither this nor that, and yet it is a something that is higher above this and that than heaven is above the earth. And therefore I now give it finer names than I have ever given it before, and yet whatever fine names, whatever words we use, they are telling lies, and it is far above them. It is free of all names, it is bare of all forms, wholly empty and free, as God in himself is empty and free. It is so utterly one and simple, as God is one and simple, that man cannot in any way look into it.[21]

Eckhart has a (not undeserved) reputation for being difficult to understand. His penchant for abstractness, his unconventional approach to common tropes, and his frequent use of shocking or paradoxical language all make his thought difficult, especially for those seeking a more conventionally logical and coherent approach. However, these challenges come into a different focus when we remember that even as he valued philosophical and theological precision, Eckhart's more profound interest was in actually awakening people to the life in God that he had discovered. The people who flocked to his preaching and spiritual teaching were not limited to professors and clergy but came from all walks of life. The key to this popular appeal probably lay partially in his personal charisma, but even more important was the spiritual effectiveness of certain aspects of his rhetoric. As Reiner Schürmann notes, Eckhart was more invested in being a preacher with an "imperative" style that calls the hearer to change, than he was in being a writer in an "indicative" style that aims for description and analysis.[22] While he certainly engages in the latter, he seems always ready to break out with innovative terminology or shocking paradoxes that reveal his intent to have a spiritual impact.

---

[21] Meister Eckhart, *Meister Eckhart, the Essential Sermons, Commentaries, Treatises, and Defense*, trans. Edmund Colledge and Bernard McGinn, The Classics of Western Spirituality (New York: Paulist Press, 1981), 180.

[22] Reiner Schürmann, *Meister Eckhart: Mystic and Philosopher* (Bloomington: Indiana University Press, 1978), 29–30.

Michael Sells analyzed apophatic mystics across traditions and found that they typically use language so that "unnameability is not only asserted but performed."[23] Examples from Eckhart might be startling sayings such as "God loves my soul so much that His life and being depend on His loving me, whether He would or no";[24] or "Man's last and highest parting occurs when, for God's sake, he takes leave of God."[25] Such koan-like sayings can jolt the reader out of the complacency of merely intellectual understanding and instigate a momentary event of "mystical" insight. Apparently the original hearers of Eckhart's preaching came in search of just that—and today, eight hundred years later, many still avidly read his written texts for the same reason.

Along these lines Bernard McGinn (following the lead of several important German scholars) calls Eckhart's central concept of *Grunt* (ground) "an 'explosive metaphor' in the sense that it breaks through previous categories of mystical speech to create new ways of presenting a direct encounter with God."[26] For Eckhart, "God's ground and the soul's ground is *one* ground."[27] In this simple and preachable term, Eckhart innovatively fused concepts of the inmost depth of the soul and of the most utterly transcendent reality of God. The practical implication is clear as he writes: "For whoever would enter God's ground, his inmost part, must first enter his own ground, his inmost part, for none can know God who does not first know himself."[28] But this "ground" type of self-knowledge is by no means to be found in concepts, images, or feelings. Utterly prior to any distinction of subject and object, the

---

[23] Michael Anthony Sells, *Mystical Languages of Unsaying* (Chicago: University of Chicago Press, 1994), 3.

[24] Meister Eckhart, "Sermon 65," in *The Complete Mystical Works of Meister Eckhart*, trans. Maurice O'C Walshe (New York: Crossroad, 2009), 62.

[25] Meister Eckhart, in *Meister Eckhart: A Modern Translation*, trans. Raymond Blakney (New York: Harper and Row, 1949), 204.

[26] Bernard McGinn, *The Mystical Thought of Meister Eckhart: The Man from Whom God Hid Nothing* (New York: Crossroad, 2001), 38.

[27] Eckhart, "Sermon 15," in Colledge and McGinn, *Meister Eckhart, the Essential Sermons, Commentaries, Treatises, and Defense*, 192.

[28] Eckhart, "Sermon 54b," in Walshe, *The Complete Mystical Works of Meister Eckhart*, 251.

ground is so radically apophatic that even God cannot "know" it in the usual sense of that term. Eckhart writes:[29]

> This little town [the ground] . . . is in the soul so one and so simple, far above whatever can be described, that this noble power about which I have spoken [the intellect] is not worthy even once for an instant to look into this little town; and the other power too of which I spoke [the will] . . . it also does not ever dare to look into it . . . if God were ever to look upon it, that must cost him all his divine names and the properties of his Persons; that he must wholly forsake, if he is ever once to look into it.

Eckhart is coy about explicitly teaching methods of prayer or meditation. He is adamant that the way to the "ground" is not defined by any particular practice. He counsels that whatever we do must come forth from that apophatic inner ground, "without asking, 'Why?'" He continues, "when people think that they are acquiring more of God in inwardness, in devotion, in sweetness and in various approaches than they do by the fireside or in the stable, you are acting just as if you took God and muffled his head up in a cloak and pushed him under a bench. Whoever is seeking God by ways is finding ways and losing God, who in ways is hidden."[30] Another favorite Eckhartian theme is that we pray wrongly when we pray for specific persons or intentions rather than simply becoming one with God. "When I pray for nobody and for nothing, then I am praying most truly, for in God is neither Henry nor Conrad."[31]

Eckhart does, however, sketch a series of processes that must occur if a person is to discover oneness with God. The underlying philosophical framework within which Eckhart is working is his

---

[29] Eckhart, "Sermon 2," in Colledge and McGinn, *Meister Eckhart, the Essential Sermons, Commentaries, Treatises, and Defense*, 181; McGinn, *The Mystical Thought of Meister Eckhart*, 140–41.

[30] Eckhart, "Sermon 5b," in Colledge and McGinn, *Meister Eckhart, the Essential Sermons, Commentaries, Treatises, and Defense*, 183.

[31] Eckhart, "Sermon 65," in Walshe, *The Complete Mystical Works of Meister Eckhart,* 64.

own version of Platonic *exitus-reditus* (emanation and return).[32] The *exitus* phase consists of the "boiling up" *(bullitio)* of the Trinity out of the One, followed by the "outflowing" *(ebullitio)* of creation. The two themes described below constitute the *reditus*, the return of spiritual beings to the One.

The first theme, and perhaps the most basic, is detachment *(abescheiden)*. Other related terms include releasement or letting go *(Gelassenheit)*, unforming *(entbilden)*, unbecoming *(entwerden)*, freedom, emptiness, dispossession, and nakedness.[33] Eckhartian detachment is far more radical than simply letting go of material possessions, or even of the inner contents of one's consciousness. Only by forsaking one's very self can one become empty enough to be filled with God. Eckhart writes, "Truly, if a man renounced a kingdom or the whole world but held on to himself, he would not have renounced anything."[34] When the soul reposes in this "naked nothingness," then "God can work upon it in the highest place and according to his highest will."[35]

In recent decades it has been popular to claim that Eckhart's "naked nothingness" is more Buddhist than Christian, and/or that he ultimately shares the a-theistic views of some strains of contemporary philosophy.[36] A complete analysis of these interpretations is beyond the scope of this project. There is no doubt, however, that Eckhart himself interpreted his views in strongly trinitarian and christological terms. This is especially evident when he writes about the second *reditus* theme, giving birth *(Geburten)* to the Son in the soul. Detachment, or "un-forming the created form of the soul," is the prerequisite to Christ being born in us. In fact, McGinn notes, "detaching and birthing

---

[32] Bernard McGinn, "Theological Summary," in Colledge and McGinn, *Meister Eckhart, the Essential Sermons, Commentaries, Treatises, and Defense*, 30.

[33] McGinn, *The Mystical Thought of Meister Eckhart*, 133.

[34] Eckhart, "Counsels on Discernment 3," in Colledge and McGinn, *Meister Eckhart, the Essential Sermons, Commentaries, Treatises, and Defense*, 249.

[35] Eckhart, "On Detachment," in Colledge and McGinn, *Meister Eckhart, the Essential Sermons, Commentaries, Treatises, and Defense*, 292.

[36] For discussion, see Beverly Lanzetta, "Three Categories of Nothingness in Eckhart," *The Journal of Religion* 72, no. 2 (1992): 248–68.

should be seen not as successive stages in a mystical path but as two sides of the same coin."[37]

Rather than following longstanding Christian tradition that describes three distinct births of Christ—the first in eternity from the Father, a second in history from Mary, and a third in the present in the believer's heart—Eckhart asserted that the birth of the Word is the same in eternity and in us. He writes: "As truly as the Father in his simple nature gives his Son birth naturally, so truly does he give him birth in the most inward part of the spirit, and that is the inner world. Here God's ground is my ground, and my ground is God's ground."[38] This birth of the Word in us is not mediated in any way by images, concepts, or actions that we can perform. Eckhart affirms: "When the powers [for example, intellect, will, and memory] have been completely withdrawn from all their works and images, *then* the Word is spoken."[39] Although Eckhart affirms that this birth will only take place in those who have mastered the ordinary virtues, he also insists that it is only by this birth, which enables us to share completely in the Son's relationship to the Father, that humans may become capable of living truly just lives.[40] Once one has thus become stripped of one's very self, says Eckhart, "*whatever* is born in you or touches you, within or without, joyful or sorrowful, sour or sweet, that is no longer yours, it is altogether your God's to whom you have abandoned yourself."[41]

For Eckhart, then, there are two levels of perfection: one of utter dispossession, the other of God being born in us. The first occurs when the soul breaks through to the ground and "grasps the pure absoluteness of free being, which has no location, which neither receives nor gives: it is bare 'self-identity' which is

---

[37] McGinn, *The Mystical Thought of Meister Eckhart*, 138–39.

[38] Eckhart, "Sermon 5b," in Colledge and McGinn, *Meister Eckhart, the Essential Sermons, Commentaries, Treatises, and Defense*, 183.

[39] Eckhart, "Sermon 1 [Q. 101]," in Walshe, *The Complete Mystical Works of Meister Eckhart*, 33.

[40] Amy Hollywood, "Preaching as Social Practice in Meister Eckhart," in *Mysticism and Social Transformation*, ed. Janet Ruffing (Syracuse, NY: Syracuse University Press, 2001), 76–90.

[41] Eckhart, "Sermon 3 [Q. 104]," in Walshe, *The Complete Mystical Works of Meister Eckhart*, 51.

deprived of all being and all self-identity. *There* she grasps God nakedly in the ground, where He is above all being."[42] But even higher than that is the possession of both body and soul by the person of Christ—the fruit of the birth of the Word in the soul. Of this he says: "Just as the inner man, in spiritual wise, loses his own being by his ground becoming one ground, so too the outer [physical] man must be deprived of his own support and rely entirely on the support of the eternal personal being which is this very personal being."[43] In other words, having abandoned personal identity into the ground, the entire embodied human being is claimed by the personal being of Christ. In the context of our discussion these two phases share some elements in common with our images of the Spirit's breathing in and breathing out.

Eckhart then explores more deeply what this means for us as created persons, whose ground is God. First, he says explicitly that there are two kinds of being: the "bare substantial being" of the Godhead, and "personal being." Here he alludes to a distinction that he sometimes makes between Godhead and "God." While the ground is bare substantial being, Christ is eternally born into personal being. Eckhart then goes on to assert that Christ's personal humanity is exactly the same as ours—not, of course, in its individual and historical manifestation, but in our shared human nature. This means that "by grace, I am one in that personal being and *am* that personal being." The personhood of Christ literally lives in me. He sums up: "So, since God dwells eternally in the ground of the Father, and I in him, *one* ground and the same Christ, as a single bearer of my humanity, then this (humanity) is as much mine as his in one substance of eternal being, so that the being of both, body and soul, attain perfection in one Christ, as one God, one Son."[44] As Julie

---

[42] Eckhart, "Sermon 70 [Q. 67]," in Walshe, *The Complete Mystical Works of Meister Eckhart*, 358.

[43] Eckhart, "Sermon 70 [Q. 67]," in Walshe, *The Complete Mystical Works of Meister Eckhart*, 359.

[44] Eckhart, "Sermon 70 [Q. 67]," in Walshe, *The Complete Mystical Works of Meister Eckhart*, 359–60.

Casteigt notes, one finds that regarding personal identity, "one's own supposite is not oneself, but an other—the Christ."[45]

The French philosopher Maurice Blanchot claimed that mystics such as Eckhart violently reduce the person to an impersonal ground as they "explode" the fundamental cognitive and psychological structure of subject and object.[46] Casteigt, however, refutes Blanchot's claim by pointing to Eckhart's assertion that both bare substantial being and personal being are "one 'substance.'"[47] Eckhart's way of explaining this is trinitarian and christological: the Trinity is both One (radically indistinct) and Three (distinct Persons), and Christ is both God (radically other than creation) and human (an embodied person in the created world). McGinn notes that this dialectic is typical of Eckhart's theology; it is "a way of speaking about God as simultaneously totally immanent to creatures as their real existence and *by that very fact* absolutely transcendent to them as *esse simpliciter* or *esse absolutum*."[48] In a "negation of negation," Eckhart affirms that God is both radically distinct and indistinct from creation.

Casteigt sees Eckhart employing this dialectic as he develops an anthropological model in which persons are able "to exist body and soul and simultaneously to break through towards the ground where I dwell in the one, because I am the one in the other, the personal in the a-personal."[49] For Casteigt, we only grasp this dialectic existentially when we enter it as the

---

[45] Julie Casteigt, "'Ni Conrad, Ni Henri': Le Fond de La Personne Est-Il Personnel, Impersonnel Ou sans Fond Dans Les Sermons Allemands de Maître Eckhart?," *Archives de Philosophie* 76, no. 3 (July 1, 2013): 437. All translations from this essay are my own.

[46] In Casteigt, "'Ni Conrad, Ni Henri': Le Fond de La Personne Est-Il Personnel, Impersonnel Ou sans Fond Dans Les Sermons Allemands de Maître Eckhart?," 426.

[47] Eckhart, "Sermon 70 [Q, 67]," in Walshe, *The Complete Mystical Works of Meister Eckhart,* 359.

[48] McGinn, "Theological Summary," 34.

[49] Casteigt, "'Ni Conrad, Ni Henri': Le Fond de La Personne Est-Il Personnel, Impersonnel Ou sans Fond Dans Les Sermons Allemands de Maître Eckhart?," 440.

dynamic mutual interiority of love, in which "the one is in the other totally and reciprocally."[50] This returns it to a more practical level and points to the fact that it is in the realm of loving relationships that most human beings may have their best opportunity to partake of such "mystical" moments.

Eckhart's anthropology makes a powerful contribution to our project of understanding how life in the Spirit involves growth in catholicity, that is, in the ability to have deep personal and local roots at the same time as being open and inclusive of a wide range of diversity. A rustic image that Eckhart proposes is that of a door's hinge, which stays in one place while the door moves widely. The hinge is like the "inner person," who reposes in the utter simplicity of the ground, while the door is like the "outer person," who moves about in the world and deals with all kinds of multiplicity and turbulence.[51] His example is Mary at the foot of the cross, her outer person wailing in sorrow while her inner person reposes in God. Elsewhere he explains: "The more purely simple a man's self is in itself, the more simply does he in himself understand all multiplicity, and he remains unchangeable in himself."[52]

In yet another sermon Eckhart states explicitly that the person who has broken through into the nakedness of the ground becomes capable of the widest and most inclusive hospitality:

> Whoever is to remain in the nakedness of this nature without any medium must have gone out beyond all persons to such an extent that he is willing to believe as well of a man far beyond the seas, whom he never set eyes on, as he does of the man who lives with him and is his closest friend. For so long as you think better of your own people than you do of the man whom you never saw, you are

---

[50] Casteigt, "'Ni Conrad, Ni Henri': Le Fond de La Personne Est-Il Personnel, Impersonnel Ou sans Fond Dans Les Sermons Allemands de Maître Eckhart?," 439.

[51] Eckhart, "On Detachment," in Colledge and McGinn, *Meister Eckhart, the Essential Sermons, Commentaries, Treatises, and Defense*, 291.

[52] Eckhart, "Sermon 15," in Colledge and McGinn, *Meister Eckhart, the Essential Sermons, Commentaries, Treatises, and Defense*, 191.

going astray, and you have never had a single glimpse of this simple ground.[53]

Interestingly for our purposes, Eckhart uses the metaphor of a magnet to describe how God draws the plural (and potentially fragmenting) powers of the soul into unity.[54] In sum, Meister Eckhart may be the best example of a Christian thinker and spiritual teacher who offers a view of personhood that corresponds, at least in substantial measure, with postmodern philosophical and psychological views while at the same time offering a profound spiritual vision of how one grows into ever-deeper catholicity.

Jan Ruusbroec

After this rather heavy going with Eckhart, some readers may be wondering what has become of our focus on practical implications of the view we are developing. A brief consideration of the Flemish mystic Jan Ruusbroec (1293–1381) may be helpful, as he shares some elements of Eckhart's approach while developing his teaching in images and practices that are both warmer and more down to earth.

In medieval debates Dominicans typically took the position that union with God occurs in the intellect and is a form of knowledge, while Augustinians and Franciscans regarded union as occurring in the will and being more fundamentally characterized by love. As a Dominican, Eckhart emphasized intellect and knowledge, although, in his case, union appears as a transcendent "unknowing." Ruusbroec, however, leaned toward the Augustinian-Franciscan side of the debate.[55] Ruusbroec

---

[53] Eckhart, "Sermon 5b," in Colledge and McGinn, *Meister Eckhart, the Essential Sermons, Commentaries, Treatises, and Defense*, 182.

[54] Eckhart, "The Book of the Parables of Genesis," in Colledge and McGinn, *Meister Eckhart, the Essential Sermons, Commentaries, Treatises, and Defense*, 111–12.

[55] Rik Van Nieuwenhove, "The Franciscan Inspiration of Ruusbroec's Mystical Theology: Ruusbroec in Dialogue with Bonaventure and Thomas Aquinas," *Ons Geestelijk Erf* 75, no. 1 (March 2001): 102–15.

apparently did not know Eckhart's work directly, although a possible contact came through a reported encounter with Eckhart's disciple John Tauler. A more important commonality is that both men lived and worked within a broader German-Flemish community of spiritual discourse, much of it oral, vernacular, and developed by women. There is considerable evidence that the imagery and concepts of the beguine Hadewijch influenced both Eckhart and Ruusbroec, although it is not certain that Eckhart actually read her texts.[56] Hadewijch, like Ruusbroec himself, drew strongly upon the works of the Cistercian William of St. Thierry, who followed Augustine in describing union in terms of love. To a much greater degree than Eckhart, Ruusbroec drew on the Low Country tradition of *minnemystik* (love mysticism), of which Hadewijch is one of the most outstanding examples.

The key to Ruusbroec's spirituality is what Bernard McGinn calls his dynamic trinitarianism. Like Eckhart, Ruusbroec's framework is the Christian Neoplatonic tradition of *exitus-reditus,* or flow from and return into God. An intensely dynamic rhythm of outward and inward motion, flux and reflux, pervades every aspect of Ruusbroec's thought. In *Spirit of Life*, Moltmann notes how surprisingly compatible this Neoplatonic imagery of flowing outward and inward can be with a panentheistic pneumatology.[57] Love, which is God, eternally both contracts into unity and expands into the distinction of persons.[58] Bernard McGinn observes that one of the most original aspects of Ruusbroec's theology is that he portrays the love of the Holy Spirit as the dynamic force not only in the outflowing of God into creation, but also in the inflowing and "drawing inwards" of the divine persons into unity.[59] Of the Trinity, Ruusbroec writes: "In

---

[56] Bernard McGinn, ed., *Meister Eckhart and the Beguine Mystics: Hadewijch of Brabant, Mechthild of Magdeburg, and Marguerite Porete* (New York: Continuum, 1994); idem, *The Varieties of Vernacular Mysticism: 1350–1550,* The Presence of God: A History of Western Christian Mysticism 5 (New York: Crossroad, 2012), 5.

[57] Jürgen Moltmann, *The Spirit of Life: A Universal Affirmation* (Minneapolis: Fortress Press, 2001), 211–12.

[58] Louis K. Dupré, *The Common Life: The Origins of Trinitarian Mysticism and Its Development by Jan Ruusbroec* (New York: Crossroad, 1984), 56.

[59] McGinn, *The Varieties of Vernacular Mysticism*, 17–19.

the relations of the [divine] persons there is mutual knowledge and love, flux and reflux between the Father and the Son by means of the love of the Holy Spirit, who is the love between them both."[60] Thus, his imagery clearly reinforces the model that is being developed throughout this book.

This is how Ruusbroec describes the life of a person who is "established firmly in the bond of love":

> This person . . . will see how God himself richly and gener-
> ously flows forth with glory and incomprehensible delight
> to all his holy ones, in accordance with the desire of every
> spirit. He will also see how they themselves flow back,
> with all that they have received or could accomplish, into
> that same rich Unity from which all delight comes forth.
> This flowing forth of God constantly demands a flowing
> back again, for God is a flowing and ebbing sea which
> ceaselessly flows out into all his beloved according to their
> needs and merits and which flows back with all those upon
> whom he has bestowed his gifts in heaven and on earth,
> together with all that they possess or are capable of.[61]

A person's participation in this ebb and flow of divine life leads to a rhythm between outgoing, active love *(minne)* and inward-drawing, passive repose or enjoyment *(ghebrucken)*. Ruusbroec observes: "You should understand that God comes ceaselessly to us both with intermediary and without intermediary, and calls us both to blissful enjoyment and to activity in such a way that the one will not be hindered by the other but rather constantly strengthened by it."[62]

Ruusbroec describes the spiritual itinerary as having three phases: the active life, the interior life, and the contemplative life. This is traversed by a human person who has three natural levels of inclination to unity that can become supernaturally "adorned

---

[60] Ruusbroec, *The Twelve Beguines*, quoted in McGinn, *The Varieties of Vernacular Mysticism*, 19.

[61] Jan van Ruusbroec, "The Spiritual Espousals," in *John Ruusbroec: The Spiritual Espousals and Other Works*, The Classics of Western Spirituality (New York: Paulist Press, 1985), 103.

[62] Russbroec, "The Spiritual Espousals," 134.

and possessed" by appropriately following this itinerary to the fullness of unity in God.[63] The lowest level of inclination to unity is that centered in the heart, which unifies the bodily and affective powers. The second level is that of the spirit, which unifies the higher faculties of memory, intellect, and will. Finally, "the highest unity is that which we have in God. . . . This is the unity from which we have flowed forth in a creaturely way, in which we abide essentially, and to which we are lovingly returning through charity."[64]

It is at the level of our "essential unity" that God gives the human person the capacity to participate in God's own trinitarian "ebb and flow." Ruusbroec affirms that "God works in us from within outward, whereas all creatures work from without inward." At the level of essential unity God gives grace, which calls a person outward to enact works through the employment of both higher faculties and sensory powers. At the same time, God gives God's own self, "above all grace," to draw the person inward to "enjoyment and rest."[65] In contradistinction to Eckhart, Ruusbroec is careful to emphasize that, even here, the human person is not God but rather a created image of God who is gifted with bearing the divine radiance. The fact that the most foundational reality of our being is "in God" means that our being is "essentially relational," that is, we only exist because of and in our creaturely relationship with God.[66]

Ruusbroec's description of the state of modeless passive delight, or "enjoyment," has some elements in common with Eckhart's description of the "naked nothingness" into which the soul sinks in union with the ground. Ruusbroec writes that those in this state of union "lose their spirit, melt away, flow away and become one spirit in God in enjoyment, eternally inclined into the fathomless blessedness of his being."[67] However, Ruusbroec is also concerned to distinguish his view from that of other spiritual teachers—quite possibly including Eckhart—whom he

[63] Ruusbroec, "The Spiritual Espousals," 73.

[64] Ruusbroec, "The Spiritual Espousals," 73–74.

[65] Ruusbroec, "The Spiritual Espousals," 74–75.

[66] McGinn, The Varieties of Vernacular Mysticism, 24.

[67] Jan van Ruusbroec, "The Seven Steps," quoted in McGinn, The Varieties of Vernacular Mysticism, 12.

sees as overemphasizing the value of this bare, imageless state. One of the spiritual deviations that Ruusbroec most strongly condemns is the person who seeks to stay in a "purely natural state of rest" by becoming "bare and imageless in his senses and devoid of all activity," but is not moved by the amorous rhythm of supernatural charity that stirs both affective desire for repose in God and eagerness to go out to serve others.[68]

McGinn observes that, for Ruusbroec, "the goal of the mystical life is to achieve a greater and greater share in the fusion of opposite motions, simultaneous and concomitant in God, but usually experienced in our temporal domain as distinct and successive."[69] Considering our current project, it is particularly noteworthy that Ruusbroec explicitly compares this rhythm of love to the inbreathing and outbreathing of the Holy Spirit. He writes: "The Spirit of God breathes us forth for loving and for working virtues, and he breathes us back into him for resting and enjoying."[70] The Spirit draws us inward to a state of blissful union beyond distinctions, and the same Spirit propels us outward into acts of love for God and others. The two directions of the breath are constant and integral to one another, so that the person who lives in the Spirit is always in motion from one to the other. To live this rhythm of the Spirit is to never stop growing in love, since "the one element is strengthened by the other, for the higher the love, the greater the rest, and the greater the rest, the more fervent the love."[71]

Regarding catholicity, perhaps the best summation of the contribution of Ruusbroec is his concept of the common life. While acknowledging that the term *ghemeyne* (common) has connotations in Middle Dutch that are hard to convey in English, Louis Dupré calls our attention to the fact that the summit of contemplation is described as at the same time the most humble and down-to-earth way of life.[72] The more all three dimensions of the human person (the heart, the faculties, and the essential ground) have reached their true center in God, the more they

---

[68] Ruusbroec, "The Spiritual Espousals," 136.
[69] McGinn, *The Varieties of Vernacular Mysticism*, 10.
[70] Ruusbroec, "The Seven Steps," 13.
[71] Ruusbroec, "The Spiritual Espousals," 127.
[72] Dupré, *The Common Life*, 63–64.

live in common with one another, with the ebbing and flowing Trinity, and with all creation. Life is common, then, when it is completely and openly shared both with the Trinity (in contemplation) and with one's fellow created beings (in humble service).

Christ is the prime model of the common life. Ruusbroec writes that he "went out to all in common in his love, his teaching, and his admonitions. . . . His soul and body, his life and death, and his service to others were and are common to all."[73] Likewise, the true contemplative who lives with God in superessential unity will "flow forth to all who need him, for the living spring of the Holy Spirit is so rich that it can never be drained dry. . . . [This person] therefore leads a common life, for he is equally ready for contemplation or for action and is perfect in both."[74] Ruusbroec's common life, then, is a dynamic and theologically based integration of contemplation and action, grounded in the catholicizing breath of the Holy Spirit.

These spiritual teachers help to fill out the pneumatological model of human personhood developed in Chapter 6. While Gertrude Stein's aphorism "There is no 'there' there!"[75] can be read as a despairing cry of the emptiness of the self, in a Christian framework it can instead be read apophatically: "There's no 'there' there but God." As Julie Casteigt notes in her discussion of Meister Eckhart, "One's own supposite is not oneself, but an other—the Christ."[76] Or, in the classical words of Saint Paul: "It is no longer I who live, but it is Christ who lives in me" (Gal 2:20).

---

[73] Ruusbroec, "The Spiritual Espousals," 107.

[74] Ruusbroec, "The Sparkling Stone," in *John Ruusbroec: The Spiritual Espousals and Other Works*, The Classics of Western Spirituality (New York: Paulist Press, 1985), 184.

[75] Gertrude Stein, *Everybody's Autobiography* (New York: Cooper Square, 1971), 289.

[76] Casteigt, "'Ni Conrad, Ni Henri': Le Fond de La Personne Est-Il Personnel, Impersonnel Ou sans Fond Dans Les Sermons Allemands de Maître Eckhart?," 437.

These teachers also remind us that the path to this wholeness (which, ultimately, is God's alone) can be an existentially challenging one, passing through frightening "dark nights" that will take individualized forms depending on our personal contexts and traumas, and will demand the utmost of each one of us if we have the courage to persist to the end. Still, what may at first appear to be a rather chilly view is "warmed up" when seen within a radically relational framework. The best image for the ultimate depth of life in God is not a cold wind blowing over icy infinitude, but flames or rivers of love leaping up, pulsing, and flowing forth. Hadewijch and Ruusbroec help us here, with their imagery of flow and rhythm and "storms of love." So does the poetry of John of the Cross, the romance of Lover and beloved. Their imagery points us toward the second path, the way of remembering, explored in the next chapter.

Chapter 8

Breathed Out:
The Way of Remembering

In the "way of emptying" one loses oneself in God; all is forgotten as one falls into the abyss of God's heart. In the context of apophatic prayer, forgetting may be bliss. The rhythm of the Spirit, however, does not call us only to forget. The practice of remembering—including remembering God, remembering the stories of God's active presence among the people of God, and remembering one's own story in the presence of God—is equally essential to life in the Spirit. *Remembering* has the connotation not only of situating ourselves in relation to the flow of time, but also of reconstructing the identity that has in some way been taken apart by the impact of God.[1] This chapter explores what happens as the Spirit "breathes out" into co-creation of our psychological selves, our relationships, and our actions.

Memory and Selfhood

Chapter 4, "Selfhood and Catholicity," reviewed many aspects of contemporary understandings of human selfhood, including the general consensus that a key aspect of selfhood is the ability to recount the story of one's life as a more or less coherent narrative. Thus, selfhood and memory are deeply intertwined. Children learn early that hearing and telling stories about what

---

[1] See Iain Matthew, *The Impact of God: Soundings from St. John of the Cross* (London: Hodder and Stoughton, 1995).

has happened is an essential dimension of "being somebody" and building relationships on that basis. Around the age of two or three, toddlers begin learning to form their fragmentary memories into stories by participating in "memory talk" with their parents and others. In memory talk, adults provide a model by telling simple stories about what has happened and thereby coach the youngsters in doing the same. The little ones learn to structure their memory stories according to the accepted cultural patterns that the adults model for them. Thus, from the very beginning, memory (and selfhood) are shaped by the norms of both narrative and culture.[2]

While the study of the neurophysiology of memory has made tremendous leaps in recent decades, here we review only a few basic points that are most relevant to our purposes. Memory scientists affirm that remembering involves many different parts of the brain. Different components of an experience—visual information, emotional arousal, smells, sounds, tastes, touches, body position, spoken words, written texts, and so on—are each processed by different brain areas. Memory of an event involves a neuronal encoding, called an *engram*, that can cue all the involved neurons from the various locations to fire together in order to recall the event. Factors that enhance the likelihood of an event being initially encoded as an engram include novelty, heightened attention, and a moderate (but not overwhelming) degree of emotional arousal.

However, if a memory is to be long-lasting, the initial engram usually has to be more elaborately encoded by strengthening its links to information that we have previously encoded.[3] Oral cultures, including those of medieval Europe, often had strategies for enhancing memory, such as complex "memory castles" where items to be memorized were placed in different imagined rooms that could be systematically retraced. On the everyday level,

---

[2] Paul John Eakin, *Living Autobiographically: How We Create Identity in Narrative* (Ithaca, NY: Cornell University Press, 2008), 25–28; Katherine Nelson, "Memory and Belief in Development," in *Memory, Brain, and Belief*, ed. Daniel L. Schacter and Elaine Scarry, 259–89 (Cambridge, MA: Harvard University Press, 2001).

[3] Daniel L. Schacter, *Searching for Memory: The Brain, the Mind, and the Past* (New York: Basic Books, 1998), 39–63.

however, elaborative encoding happens most easily when the new experience links into our established self-story of meaning. For example, while a vacation day at the beach may be recounted in full that evening over a few beers at the pub, ten years later almost nothing will be remembered—unless it was the day we fell in love, or found out our best friend had cancer, or saw our child reach a new milestone of maturity, or found some other life-marking significance in the events of that day.

Even immediately after an event, though, an encoded memory does not call forth an exact replica of the original experience. Some aspects of what took place will not have been registered at all, while others will be enhanced or distorted—especially if they "cue up" other engrams that are already well established. For example, perhaps I met a man at the beach that day whose face reminded me of my brother. Later I have only a sketchy memory of what we were doing, what he was wearing, or what he said, but I clearly remember the man's face—although in reality, this "memory" may conform his face to my brother's more than is accurate. Memory scientists say that every recalled memory is actually a new construction in the moment of recall, built from a combination of something that cues the engram and the firing of the engram within this particular context.[4] In the example just given, the cue of the face of the man at the beach fires the engram of my brother's face, so that I remember my brother at the same time that I encode a new engram of this man's face. In my future recollections these two closely linked engrams may have a tendency to leak into each other, so that many years hence I might be convinced that on some occasion (which I can't quite remember) I was surprised to meet my brother at a beach!

The point is that even though our self-story of meaning is built out of memories, memory is shiftier than it seems. Anyone who has sat around sharing memories of childhood with adult siblings knows the astonishment each one feels at the totally inaccurate recollections of everyone else at the table! This can only partly be accounted for by the fact that no two people, even identical twins, have had identical experiences. It also has to do

---

[4] Marcia K. Johnson and Carol L. Raye, "Cognitive and Brain Mechanisms of False Memories and Beliefs," in Schacter and Scarry, *Memory, Brain, and Belief*, 38.

with the reality that every time a memory is recalled—that is, every time the neuronal engram fires afresh—it is literally reconfigured within a new context. Over time, as it is linked to various contexts of meaning, the engram evolves until it may in some cases bear little resemblance to its original form. Paradoxically, this is especially true of our most formative childhood memories, which we may have recounted and reflected on frequently over many decades and in many significant contexts.

Memory science does not go so far as to say that there is no connection between our memories and what really happened. Research has found that some memories are fairly accurate, others are very inaccurate, and some are completely false. Jean Piaget once gave an example of an intense and detailed memory of an incident in his infancy that turned out never to have happened. His nanny had told Piaget's parents that someone had tried to kidnap him, and the family repeated the dramatic story frequently during his childhood. Late in life, the nanny confessed that she had made up the story. Piaget speculated that he had probably built up his false memory of the incident by placing authentic memory fragments of commonplace events into the family narrative.[5] His story illustrates how a memory's importance in our story of identity may be unrelated to its connection to real historical events.

If we assume that the purpose of memory is the factual recall of the past, this evidence that memory often has a rather tenuous relation to historical facts can be disconcerting. This shows that we need to rethink the purpose of memory. We may recall that neurophysiologist Rodolfo Llinás says that "self is the centralization of prediction."[6] It is by narratively emplotting our memories—that is, constructing a self-story—that we build a predictive trajectory into our sense of self. The real purpose of memory is to make it possible for us to live a meaningful and deeply relational life in the present moment, with a view to making choices that enhance our chances of fulfilling our future goals. As Chris Westbury and Daniel Dennett state: "Memory in

---

[5] Jean Piaget, *Play, Dreams and Imitation in Childhood* (London: Routledge and Kegan Paul, 1967), 187–88.

[6] Rodolfo R. Llinás, *I of the Vortex: From Neurons to Self*, A Bradford Book (Cambridge, MA: MIT Press, 2002), 23.

the most fundamental sense is the ability to store useful information and to retrieve it in precisely those circumstances and that form which allow it to be useful. . . . What we recall is not what we actually experienced, but rather a reconstruction of what we experienced that is consistent with our current goals and our knowledge of the world."[7]

Jerome Bruner says something very similar about selfhood, affirming that there is no "intuitively obvious and essential self to know" but "rather, we constantly construct and reconstruct ourselves to meet the needs of the situations we encounter, and we do so with the guidance of our memories of the past and our hopes and fears for the future."[8] Bruner calls self-making a "narrative art" in which one weaves one's inner resources of memory, feelings, and beliefs into a story one hopes will enhance one's connections with the persons and social groups one cares about. The story is normed by commitments both to be "true to oneself" and to foster relationships with others.[9] The latter requires that we tell the story according to the cultural and interpersonal conventions that are regarded as appropriate by those who are receiving it.

Does this mean that our autobiographical self-stories are fiction? Most of those who study autobiography say yes, if we accept that the root meaning of *fiction* is "that which is formed, shaped, molded, fashioned, invented."[10] Unlike a novelist, however, the storyteller of the self is limited in the degree of invention his or her hearers will tolerate. John Paul Eakin discusses the cases of James Frey's *Million Little Pieces* and Benjamin Wilkomirski's *Fragments: Memories of a Wartime Childhood*. Both of these memoirs were highly praised when first published but were later found to be riddled with outright fabrications. The books had to be withdrawn from publication and lawsuits

---

[7] Chris Westbury and Daniel C. Dennett, "Mining the Past to Construct the Future: Memory and Belief as Forms of Knowledge," in Schacter and Scarry, *Memory, Brain, and Belief,* 13, 19.

[8] Jerome S. Bruner, *Making Stories: Law, Literature, Life* (Cambridge, MA: Harvard University Press, 2003), 64.

[9] Bruner, *Making Stories,* 65, 69.

[10] Paul John Eakin, "Autobiography, Identity, and the Fictions of Memory," in Schacter and Scarry, *Memory, Brain, and Belief,* 290.

were filed against the authors.[11] In reading an autobiography or hearing someone recount a memory, listeners recognize that there will be interpretive bias, but they still expect that, essentially, the person is aiming to recount what he or she believes happened. In other words, the unconscious aspect of fictionalization is tolerated, but conscious fabrication is not.

Participating in the Memory of the People of God

Life in the Spirit is experienced as a rhythm of losing and finding the self in God. Chapter 7 focused on "the way of emptying," in which selfhood melts away as it is breathed into the oceanic communion of divine love. This chapter focuses on "the way of remembering" in which the self is breathed out and reconstituted within the story of God. In Christianity the story of God is understood to be proclaimed in scripture and performed in liturgy. These are the genres through which God offers the narrative self the possibility of participating in the life that the Spirit breathes into the world.

Scripture, however, is far from offering a single or simple story. In Roman Catholicism, the canonical scriptures consist of seventy-three books. These deploy a wide range of genres including historical narrative, prophetic proclamation, stories, poetry, wisdom sayings, gospel, letter, apocalyptic, and more. Each of the books has a long and complex history, in many cases having been compiled from various fragments and then edited and re-edited many times before arriving at the form in which we receive it. Interpretation of scripture is complicated and often highly contested. A basic principle is that in order to interpret any part of scripture correctly, one must take into account the whole of scripture—that is, one cannot simply take one story, one saying, or one book and use it to assert an idiosyncratic theology. Yet, it is also true that no one can know all of scripture equally well, so a certain degree of selectivity is inevitable. Each ecclesial community, and each individual believer, discovers a somewhat unique "story of God" within this massive, complex, roiling collection of texts that we so blithely call the Bible.

---

[11] Eakin, *Living Autobiographically*, chap. 1.

Again, this does not mean that "anything goes." Just as when we construct our personal stories we are expected to make a good-faith effort to remain grounded in what actually happened, so when we draw upon the stories of scripture we ought to make a good-faith effort to attend to the larger, overall patterns of biblical meaning rather than go off on a tangent. Two of the popular "big story" approaches to scripture in the modern era have been the salvation-history approach and the paschal-mystery interpretation. The salvation-history approach reads the whole Bible as the story of God's redeeming activity as it has been manifested in a series of historical events. The paschal-mystery interpretation focuses on identifying the most profound pattern of God's action, echoing repeatedly throughout the Bible, as that of a passage through death to life. In interpreting the stories of the exodus, for example, the salvation-history approach emphasizes it as a historical event in which God miraculously acted to bring the people to safety in the Promised Land, while the paschal-mystery approach emphasizes the underlying pattern of a journey through deathly danger to astonishing new life. While either of these approaches can come in handy when one is called upon to sum up the story of God in two minutes or less, it is not surprising that both have garnered strong criticism for greatly oversimplifying what the Bible actually contains. The Bible is far too multifaceted to be reduced to the expression of a simple historical or archetypal pattern.

It can be more helpful to think of the Bible as the memory of the people of God. All that has been said about our own individual memories applies, in some analogous way, to the Bible's function in the community of the people of God. What is remembered are the community's stories of its experiences of God's revelation, processed through many genres, repeated editings, and frequent recounting, and handed on to us so that we, today, will be able to know our belonging in the community, articulate our own story of meaning, and make choices in view of God's desired future. Just as the primary purpose of our memory is not so much to show a movie of the past as it is to facilitate a meaningful life in the present and future, so with the Bible. But, also like our own memories, the biblical memory is grounded in the real life of a people; to put faith in the Bible is to believe that those who have constructed it throughout the ages have consistently made a good-faith effort to remember that people's real story of relationship with God.

Of course, this approach also oversimplifies. Who belongs to the people of God? How have people discerned that an event in their experience is a true revelation of God? Why are some stories included and others excluded? What do we do with the contradictions, fictions, and outdated worldviews enshrined in scripture? These are not simple questions. Moreover, the people of God have never been a single community with a single story of their life with God; neither have the many communities that make up the people of God ever actually lived in happy harmony, either within a single community or in relation to all the other communities. But again, all this is not so different from the case of our own memories and our own selves. We, too, struggle to construct our story from memories laced with contradictions, conflicts, and ambiguities.

The dialogical self theory that was discussed in Chapter 4 can help to make sense of this. Hermans and Hermans-Konopka propose that, rather than thinking of the self-story as a straightforward narrative built around a central "I" character, it is more accurate to see it as an evolving repertoire of various self-characters, each of them arising in dialogue with different publics. These self-characters are often in contention with one another, as well as with their dialogue partners. They form coalitions that may remain stable for a time but eventually will shift as life moves on. In the view of Hermans and Hermans-Konopka, selfhood is complex, contentious, and always on the move. The same is true for the people of God.

Augustine's *Confessions*

Life responsive to the Spirit is lived in the rhythm of the way of emptying and the way of remembering, as the two movements call one another forth and deepen one another. The fruit of this rhythm is seen most profoundly in spiritual autobiographies, when an author explicitly strives to tell his or her life story as a story of God.

Augustine's *Confessions* is perhaps the most famous of all spiritual autobiographies. Hundreds of articles have been written detailing the many ways in which Augustine intricately shapes his recollections to suit literary, philosophical, and scriptural ends. Although most commentators give him the benefit of the doubt in assuming that there is a kernel of historical fact in his memories, there is no question that each story has been thoroughly worked over at many levels so that it can serve the purposes of the overall narrative.

To take just one example, Book VII recounts a crucial event in Augustine's conversion when, by reading the Platonists, he grasps the Neoplatonic "method of ascent," which leads him to the inner discovery of the immateriality of God. Philip Cary notes, however, that the way Augustine presents the Platonic teaching here is much more sophisticated than what he presented in his writings from the period he claims to be remembering. Evidently the memory has been reconstituted on the basis of later learning. Cary suggests that, for Augustine, this reconstruction of the memory was for the sake of revealing its "truth," which he had not as clearly understood at the time.[12] In the "present" of writing his autobiographical reflections, Augustine's focus is on showing as fully as possible how God has actually been revealed in every aspect of his life—even though, in the "past" that he recounts, he did not clearly understand that.

While most ordinary readers find the autobiographical stories of Books I–IX most interesting, the key to the *Confessions* lies in Books X–XIII, where Augustine explains his theory of memory and brings his narrative to a scripture-permeated climax as God gives creation "rest" in Godself. As Paige Hochschild explains, for Augustine memory is the dimension of the human person that can hold both the diverse and chaotic experiences of the changing world, and the unifying "sense of the divine presence."[13] Even though the natural memory's knowledge of God remains indirect, Augustine sees it as providing the possibility of stability and unity in the midst of all that is constantly passing away. Put into the terms we are using in this book, the memory's efforts to discover and recount a coherent storyline for a person's life

---

[12] Phillip Cary, *Augustine's Invention of the Inner Self: The Legacy of a Christian Platonist* (Oxford: Oxford University Press, 2003), 36.

[13] Paige E. Hochschild, *Memory in Augustine's Theological Anthropology* (Oxford: Oxford University Press, 2012).

manifest the Spirit-borne unity of one's existence—a unity that actually exists only in God and is always "under construction" within our temporal existence.

Augustine believes, then, that memory is at the center of what it means to say that human persons are created in the image of God. James Giles asserts that, for Augustine, the self is not an inner thing but "a nexus in a field of relations" that images a trinitarian God, and exists only in relation to its creator.[14] Augustine's experience of his own selfhood is that it is always on the brink of flying apart and falling into chaos; but "by being pulled toward God, the self is pulled away from dispersal and distraction."[15] Thus, Augustine understands human persons as constantly in a process of "selving" as the Spirit draws them toward fulfilling their vocation as image of God.

Consequently, human memory becomes the bridge to Augustine's understanding of how Christ's incarnation as the divine Image of God can actually fulfill the promise of bringing peace and order to creatures embedded in history. Hochschild argues that "the decisive moment in Augustine's conversion is the vision of the incarnate mediator . . . [who], in the flesh, manifests what the Trinity as a whole acts out in creation: the mysterious manner in which what is perfectly unified and at peace can be present to, and enter into relation with, what is multiple or ontologically 'other.'"[16] Christ, the image or "story" of God, incarnates the catholic paradox of unity amid seemingly irreconcilable plurality. This is how Christ "saves" us: he enables the potential chaos of our "selving" to find its center in the ordered wholeness of "cosmos."[17]

Based on this paradigm, the *Confessions* is Augustine's demonstration of a practice of memory meditation that is able to perform "a restoration of memory in the form of the memory of the Church."[18] Augustine's personal recollections (Books I–IX)

---

[14] James E. Giles, "The Story of the Self: The Self of the Story," *Religion and Intellectual Life* 4, no. 1 (September 1, 1986): 109.

[15] Giles, "The Story of the Self: The Self of the Story," 111.

[16] Hochschild, *Memory in Augustine's Theological Anthropology*, 186.

[17] Giles, "The Story of the Self: The Self of the Story," 112.

[18] Hochschild, *Memory in Augustine's Theological Anthropology*, 153.

reach a climax in a hermeneutic of scripture as the revelation of God's radical fulfillment, on behalf of the whole people of God, of that "sense of divine presence" that dwells in the memory and that, fired by the Spirit, blossoms into the theological virtue of hope (Books X–XIII). The natural memory (created in the image of God) longs to bring unity and peace to the soul but cannot do so—until the incarnate Image of God, enthroned and revealed in the memory of the people of God (the scriptures), completes its work of bringing the whole creation to unity and peace in God.

Thus, Augustine's *Confessions* remarkably recapitulates an entire process from the chaos and fragmentation of personal memory to a cosmic vision of the salvation of the universe. It is no wonder that this book is such a perennial favorite of spiritual seekers, who need not grasp all this theoretical background in order to be captivated by following Augustine in his practice of transformative memory meditation.

Julian of Norwich

Another text that demonstrates how memory mediates the relationship with God is *Showings* by Julian of Norwich.[19] This is not an autobiographical text, strictly speaking, since it includes only the most minimal information about the trajectory of Julian's life. It does, however, deal with her memories of religious experience. The text consists of two parts, the "Short Text" and the "Long Text." The Short Text is a recounting of fifteen visions that Julian received during a near-fatal illness when she was thirty and a half years old. The Long Text, which she asserts she wrote twenty years later, reviews these visions in greater detail and with a more mature and well-developed theological commentary. The Long Text also adds a sixteenth vision, the parable of the Lord and the Servant, with an exceptionally long theological commentary.

The visions took place as Julian, seemingly on her deathbed, looked up at the processional cross carried by a little boy

---

[19] Julian of Norwich, *Showings*, ed. Edmund Colledge and James Walsh, The Classics of Western Spirituality (New York: Paulist Press, 1978).

accompanying the curate who came to give her last rites. The core of all the visions is Jesus's face, crowned with thorns, with "red blood trickling down from under the crown, all hot, flowing freely and copiously, a living stream."[20] According to her own testimony, Julian spent the next two decades of her life praying with the memories of the divine face and the "precious blood" that descends to hell, then "overflows all the earth, and is ready to wash from their sins all creatures who are, have been and will be of good will."[21]

Commentators have discussed in great detail the differences between the Short Text and Long Text versions, even raising the question of whether someone other than Julian wrote the later text. Wai Man Yuen, however, proposes that the two versions are a remarkably clear instantiation of the process that occurs in a person who has a genuine experience of God.[22] Such a religious experience has a quality of atemporal "infinity" so that, by its nature, it cannot be fully understood. Yuen is referring here to the impact of the apophatic, which (as we saw in the previous chapter) is beyond our capacity for experience and yet leaves a memory trace that is remembered. These traces may be blurred and fragmentary, yet they are planted in self-memory as constituting an event of the utmost significance. Thus, an authentic religious experience initiates a lifelong process of rumination on its memory, seeking to bring the experience to coherent articulation, to honor it, and to understand it.

Since the original experience derived from an atemporal and infinite reality, rumination continues to be on the memory's "present" as well as its "past." Although a true experience of God will never be able to be exhaustively understood, the one who ruminates in this way matures and develops in theological insight. Yuen's interpretation suggests that, in fact, such a sequence of experience of God, followed by a period of rumination on the memory (or memories), eventually bearing fruit in

---

[20] Julian of Norwich, *Showings*, chap. 3.

[21] Julian of Norwich, *Showings*, chap. 12.

[22] Wai Man Yuen, *Religious Experience and Interpretation: Memory as the Path to the Knowledge of God in Julian of Norwich's* Showings, Feminist Critical Studies in Religion and Culture 1 (New York: Peter Lang, 2003).

theological elaboration, may be the unacknowledged root of all authentic theological insight.

As an example of this process, let us examine Julian's parable of the lord and the servant.[23] Very briefly, the parable is the story of a great lord and a servant who is deeply devoted to him. The lord sends the servant on a mission, but in his overeagerness the servant trips, falls into a ditch, and is severely injured. He is left there for some time, in great pain and feeling utterly abandoned. His greatest suffering is that he cannot turn his face to look upon his lord—who, in fact, has never stopped gazing on him "most tenderly . . . with great compassion and pity." Then Julian understands that the lord, showing absolutely no sign of blame for the servant's failure to fulfill his mission, will lift up his servant and place him "immediately before the Father, richly clothed in joyful amplitude, with a rich and precious crown upon his head."

As previously mentioned, Julian did not even include this vision in her Short Text, yet twenty years later it became the centerpiece of the Long Text as well as of her most striking theological insights. Whatever the original experience was that became articulated in this parable, it must have been exceptionally confusing or difficult for her—so much so that she initially did not "remember" it as a distinct event within her sequence of visions. Perhaps this aspect of her experience was originally encoded at an affective or somatic level rather than in language. Those who study memory make a distinction between implicit, largely unconscious memories and the explicit memories that we can more easily call into consciousness. Explicit memories are often imagistic, but the person can talk about the images and develop a more or less coherent story line on that basis—as Julian did in the Short Text with her other fifteen visions. Many formative emotional and somatic memories, however, are largely stored in the nonverbal form of implicit memory, which is difficult to access yet highly influential on our subsequent feelings and responses.

An example of implicit memory is a person's earliest bodily experiences as an infant, long before language can buffer responses to pain or pleasure. A baby who is frequently left to

---

[23] Julian of Norwich, *Showings*, chap. 51.

cry, cold and hungry, is likely to enter adulthood with heavy emotional burdens of fear, rage, and lust that he or she cannot account for in explicit memory. While that example is somewhat extreme, most of us carry a degree of such burdens—the emotions and reactions that we do not understand, yet vaguely sense are rooted in long-ago experiences. Even in adulthood, intense or pervasive emotional experiences can register in implicit memory in ways that baffle the conscious mind.

Philip Sheldrake suggests that the issue Julian was struggling with when she articulated this particular parable was how to reconcile her experience of God's utterly blame-free love with the reality of her sinfulness.[24] Just prior to recounting the parable, Julian had been reflecting on sin, weakness, and "our contrariness [that] makes for us here on earth pain, shame and sorrow."[25] Before they are theological concepts, both love and sinfulness are deeply rooted human experiences. To experience oneself as sinful is to feel overwhelmingly ashamed, impure, rejected, and lost. We do not know the autobiographical origins of the sorrow of sinfulness in Julian, but we do know that her social and theological context enhanced such feelings by promoting an image of an angry God who sees sin everywhere and is eager to cast sinners into hell.

Yet Julian's remembered experience of God engendered a totally different emotional and somatic response: the joy of being completely loved, accepted, embraced, and cherished, without even a glance at her "sin." Perhaps, then, the parable of the lord and the servant is an expression of Julian's story of herself in relation to God. She is the devoted and beloved servant who fell for a time into a ditch of isolation and agony, only to discover that the love of God had never abandoned her. Each moment of this story parallels real moments in her own life experience— even though the story as told is fictional.

Julian's repeated rumination on this story over many years led her to the discovery of its theological depth. The servant is Adam (all humankind), but he is also the Son (Jesus). The lord

---

[24] Philip Sheldrake, "Two Ways of Seeing: The Challenge of Julian of Norwich's Parable of a Lord and a Servant," *Spiritus* 17, no. 1 (2017): 1–18.

[25] Julian of Norwich, *Showings*, chap. 48.

(God the Father) has never been angry with the servant, even during the time when the servant felt abandoned and suffering. The lord's only desire is to lift up the servant and bring him back close to himself. Julian's discovery, as Elisabeth Koenig notes, was that "God looks at fallen people with the love Julian sees in the lord's face as he gazes at his servant, and with the love of a mother who tends her child even when she stumbles or is covered with mud."[26]

To depict the drama of the soul's relationship to God, Julian masterfully employs intense imagery drawn from traditions of medieval dramatic performances as well as from the erotic Song of Songs traditions mediated to her by William of St. Thierry.[27] Rooted in the vision of Christ's face and copiously flowing blood, much of *Showings* is devoted to the details of Christ's passion: the wounds of Christ, the crown of thorns, his scourging, his agony, his thirst, and so on. For Julian, it is through the passion that Jesus works "to unite human persons' 'sensuality' with their 'substance,' meaning that everything in them that resists God is joined to everything in them that never departed from God."[28] Eventually, Julian's theological ruminations led to the articulation of a remarkably nuanced insight into the human being as one with God even while remaining wholly contingent: "And I saw no difference between God and our substance, but, as it were, all God; and still my understanding accepted that our substance is in God, that is to say that God is God, and our substance is a creature in God."[29]

Thus, despite not being an explicitly autobiographical text, Julian's *Showings* offers rich insight into how contemplative practice enables the narrative self to move from fragmentation to "one-ing" (Julian's favorite term for the effect of God on her soul). The wholeness to which God restores the individual is also a renewed oneness with all humankind, as Julian indicates when

---

[26] Elisabeth Koenig, "Julian of Norwich (c.1342–c.1415): Showings," in *Christian Spirituality: The Classics*, ed. Arthur G. Holder (London: Routledge, 2009), 153.

[27] Elisabeth Koenig, "Julian of Norwich, Mary Magdalene, and the Drama of Prayer," *Horizons* 20, no. 1 (1993): 36.

[28] Koenig, "Julian of Norwich (c.1342–c.1415)," 154.

[29] Julian of Norwich, *Showings*, chap. 54.

she writes: "The love of God creates in us such a unity that when it is truly seen, no man can separate himself from another."[30] Yet, this is far from being an instantaneous or simple process; Julian lets us know that her own journey to the wholeness of fully knowing God's love involved many decades of prayer, suffering, meditation, and "remembering."

Commentators Maggie Ross and Vincent Gillespie also find a profound apophatic dimension in Julian's text. The omnipresent, graphic imagery of the self-emptying love of Christ on the cross, they observe, is "a paradigm for the procedures of Julian's text, for her approach to God, for her relationship to her audience, and for the audience's performative relationship to the text. To inhabit the text, the reader must be prepared to inhabit this paradigm."[31] Entering the text by "performing" it in prayer, Ross and Gillespie suggest, leads the reader through the images into "an imageless and apophatic contemplation."[32] Thus, they show that, even though Julian's explicit emphasis is on imagery and remembering, she is a wise teacher of the rhythms of the Spirit.

Whereas those who explicitly emphasize the apophatic way of emptying focus maximally on the deconstructive impact of God on the self, the texts of both Augustine and Julian illustrate how the breaking-in of an experience of God leads to a long process of memory work that reconstructs the self's story to enhance the relationship with a loving God and to undergird the choices involved in a way of life that expresses that fulfilled relationship.

Trauma and the Way of Remembering

In the context of the writings of a long-ago person whom our tradition has lifted up as a great saint or mystic, the phrase *deconstruction of the self* may sound relatively benign. We might assume that it is a strictly spiritual process that a dedicated spiritual seeker can traverse securely, as one would follow a

---

[30] Julian of Norwich, *Showings*, 309.

[31] Vincent Gillespie and Maggie Ross, "'With Mekeness Aske Perseverantly': On Reading Julian of Norwich," *Mystics Quarterly* 30, no. 3–4 (September 2004): 128.

[32] Gillespie and Ross, "'With Mekeness Aske Perseverantly,'" 132.

well-marked trail. In fact, that is exactly the aim of the "way of emptying": to provide a set of spiritual practices that facilitate and, in a sense, cushion the fall into the abyss. Yet that is not the way taken by the vast majority of humanity. It is probably much more common that spiritual change is initiated by life incidents that engender deep confusion and suffering, which then have to be processed at great length in the "way of remembering."

Describing the impact of trauma, Judith Herman writes: "At the moment of trauma, the victim is rendered helpless by overwhelming force. . . . Traumatic events overwhelm the ordinary systems of care that give people a sense of control, connection, and meaning."[33] Memory scientists say that such extreme emotional arousal sometimes leads to a "flashbulb" memory, where every detail of the jolting event is remembered, while much of the larger context is forgotten or distorted. A crime victim, for example, may be able to describe every detail of the gun pointed at his face while being unable to pick the gunman out of a lineup. Another possibility, however, is that emotion thoroughly overwhelms the memory-encoding process so that very little is captured in explicit memory. An accident, for example, may only be remembered as the crashing in of pain and panic, with no ability to recall what led up to it or what happened after.

Regarding the current reflection on memory and selfhood, trauma is a life incident that significantly derails the person's efforts to construct a coherent and meaningful self-story. In that broad sense, no human life escapes some degree of trauma. Examples of "normal" traumas that most people must endure along the way include feeling abandoned or betrayed by someone in whom one had trusted, being humiliated by a public failure, and losing a loved one in death. When a person is able to bear such a trauma within a sufficiently strong interpersonal network of support, trauma can function somewhat like what we have described as the way of emptying; that is, it decenters and deconstructs the self, forcing reconstruction on the basis of deeper roots.

In discussing the spiritual effects of trauma, however, we must not be too glib. Some kinds of trauma are almost unimaginably destructive of human psychological and spiritual well being. It

---

[33] Judith Lewis Herman, *Trauma and Recovery*, rev. ed. (New York: Basic Books, 1997), 33.

has been found that even for a previously well-functioning adult, the sense of identity and selfhood can be completely broken down by severe or persistent trauma such as torture, imprisonment, or the violence of combat. Children, who are still in the process of laying the foundations of identity, are even more vulnerable, especially to long-term sexual, physical, or emotional abuse. Post-Traumatic Stress Disorder is a recognized mental illness, in which a person may suffer for years or even decades with flashbacks, uncontrollable emotional outbursts, abysmal self-esteem, and the inability to form lasting relationships or hold a steady job.

Judith Herman notes that traumatic events are "extraordinary, not because they occur rarely, but rather because they overwhelm the ordinary human adaptations to life."[34] Frequently reported statistics indicate that in the United States one in three females, and one in six males, experience some form of "sexual contact violence" during their lifetime.[35] Child abuse and neglect that rise to a criminal level affect at least 700,000 annually.[36] Millions of children and adults live in neighborhoods where the constant possibility of violent death permeates daily life with anxiety. We can also add combat veterans, those who have been bullied, the incarcerated, victims of extreme natural disasters such as hurricanes and wildfires, victims of mass shootings, the addicted and their families, and others whose life-crushing catastrophes do not make national headlines. Overall, as much as half the population of a relatively prosperous and peaceful nation such as the United States may have experienced events that could qualify as severely traumatic. In some parts of the world where violence and societal breakdown are rampant, this figure may approach 100 percent.

I, Rigoberta Menchú: An Indian Woman in Guatemala, a memoir of horrifying events during Guatemala's civil war, il-

---

[34] Herman, *Trauma and Recovery*, 33.

[35] National Sexual Violence Resource Center, "Get Statistics," citing S. G. Smith et al., "The National Intimate Partner and Sexual Violence Survey (NISVS): 2010–2012 State Report" (2017).

[36] National Children's Alliance, "National Statistics on Child Abuse," citing the US Administration for Children and Families, "Child Maltreatment 2014" (January 25, 2016).

lustrates how trauma can affect autobiographical memory.[37] In a book-length critique David Stoll proved that Menchú had claimed as her own experiences several incidents that she could not have witnessed or that did not take place as she described.[38] In her discussion of this Leigh Gilmore attributes Menchú's "fictionalizing" to the fact that when trauma fragments the self, it shifts the driving question of autobiography from "How can I tell my heroic story within the conventions of the reigning cultural narrative?" to "How can I reinvent myself beyond the limits of this oppressive, violent narrative?" For the traumatized subaltern, then, elements of fiction become essential and constitutive.[39]

Interestingly, Stoll also expressed willingness to forgive Menchú's fictions on the grounds that she "had often achieved a larger symbolic truth."[40] As Gilmore notes, every autobiographer is expected to be "both unique and representative,"[41] and when the representative function involves courageously witnessing on behalf of oppressed others, it may be seen as acceptable to testify to events one has not actually witnessed. In Menchú's case, those who most avidly welcomed her memoir were those who supported political movements on behalf of the oppressed native peoples of Guatemala, so her "public" affirmed that her representative function was more important than her unique experience.

While the experience of trauma described by Menchú is at the extreme end of the spectrum, there may be a sense in which all traumas, whether public and political like hers or seemingly more individual and personal, effect a similar shift in the norms for how the story must be told. As noted earlier, the purpose of memory is not so much exact factual recall as projecting a coherent path to a desired future. Trauma creates a massive

---

[37] Rigoberta Menchú, *I, Rigoberta Menchú: An Indian Woman in Guatemala* (London: Verso, 1984; published in Spanish in 1983).

[38] David Stoll, *Rigoberta Menchú and the Story of All Poor Guatemalans*, exp. ed. (Boulder, CO: Westview Press, 2008).

[39] Leigh Gilmore, *The Limits of Autobiography: Trauma and Testimony* (Ithaca, NY: Cornell University Press, 2001).

[40] Gilmore, *The Limits of Autobiography*, 4; Stoll, *Rigoberta Menchú and the Story of All Poor Guatemalans*.

[41] Gilmore, *The Limits of Autobiography*, 8.

stumbling block because its terrifying emotional and physical impact shatters one's previous self-story and hijacks the memory into a hypersensitive tendency to flashbacks. A return to psychological thriving requires finding a cohort of others who share similar experiences and, with them, searching for a way to tell the story as a heroic path beyond traumatized victimhood to a new life. This typically involves a long traverse through the "way of remembering," as we see in the cases of Julian of Norwich and Thérèse of Lisieux.

Julian, as we have seen, underwent the extremity of a life-threatening illness and saw herself immersed in "woe," especially at the time of writing the Short Text.[42] Perhaps a better example comes from Thérèse of Lisieux's *Story of a Soul*, a text that is far more explicitly autobiographical. Before she was ten years old, Thérèse (1873–97) traumatically lost three "mothers." Her birth mother could not nurse her, so Thérèse spent most of her first fifteen months being mothered by a peasant wet nurse. After she was brought home, her birth mother died of breast cancer when Thérèse was only four years old. When she was nine, Pauline, the older sister whom Thérèse had claimed as her new mother, entered a strictly cloistered Carmelite monastery. Not long thereafter, Thérèse became ill with weakness, paralysis, and hallucinations. She began to recover only when she saw the smile on a statue of the Virgin Mary come alive, embracing her with heaven-sent motherly love.[43] Although this vision provided the wherewithal for Thérèse to regain stability, she returned to the intense practice of the way of remembering in young adulthood as she wrote *Story of a Soul*. We can read this text as her reconstitution of identity in radical relationship with God.

Tragically, many trauma victims remain trapped in the destructive patterns that trauma has imprinted. Even the lesser

---

[42] Julian of Norwich, *Showings*, chap. 20; Kerrie Hide, *Gifted Origins to Graced Fulfillment: The Soteriology of Julian of Norwich* (Collegeville, MN: Liturgical Press, 2001), 10–12.

[43] Thérèse de Lisieux, "The Distressing Years (1881–1883)," in *Story of a Soul: The Autobiography of Saint Thérèse of Lisieux*, trans. John Clarke, 3rd ed. (Washington, DC: ICS Publications, 1996), 51–68.

traumas of life, if they are not worked through, can stall growth. Yet many spiritual writers, classic as well as contemporary, have realized that if the pain, confusion, and instability generated by trauma are courageously faced and accepted, such events may be precious openings to a life far more deeply rooted in God. Psychiatrist Gerald May details how the "sacred illness" of profound suffering may prepare a person to become a wisdom guide for others.[44] Trauma can function as a somatic and social instantiation of the deconstructive way of emptying, calling forth the reconstructive way of remembering that offers a path through trauma to reclaimed wholeness. Other contemporary clinicians and writers who trace this path include Robert Grant and Arthur W. Frank.[45]

Julian and Thérèse, as well as many other Christians, find their saving "narrative of the Word" in the gospel stories of Jesus's violent death followed by his being raised to resurrected life. John of the Cross develops this theme with the paradoxical image of a divine "cautery of love" that is applied to all the soul's wounds, thus transforming them into "wounds of love" that, paradoxically, heal the soul. In ancient times doctors often cauterized wounds by burning them with a hot iron, believing that this facilitated healing. John writes: "Whether a soul is wounded by other wounds of miseries and sins or whether it is healthy, this cautery of love immediately effects a wound of love in the one it touches, and those wounds deriving from other causes become wounds of love."[46] In this way, John, one of the most widely known masters of the way of emptying, affirms the potential role of the many kinds of wounds and traumas that life effects in opening our hearts to God's love.

---

[44] Gerald G. May, *Addiction and Grace: Love and Spirituality in the Healing of Addictions* (San Francisco: HarperSanFrancisco, 2007).

[45] Robert Grant, *The Way of the Wound: A Spirituality of Trauma and Transformation*, private publication (1996); Arthur W. Frank, *The Wounded Storyteller: Body, Illness, and Ethics* (Chicago: University of Chicago Press, 1997).

[46] John of the Cross, *Living Flame of Love*, trans. Kieran Kavanaugh and Otilio Rodriguez, rev. ed. Collected Works of Saint John of the Cross (Washington, DC: ICS Publications, 1991), para. 7.

Ignatius of Loyola

Eugene Rogers observes that, while the Spirit often seems elusive and invisible, she actually seeks to make herself known by "reading" people "into the text, narrating them typologically into the stories she shares with Jesus and the Father."[47] He is describing how, in the way of remembering, the Spirit co-creates with us our selfhood as completely implicated in the story of God. There may be no one in the history of the church who has offered a more practical way of doing just that than Ignatius Loyola (1491–1556).

Ignatius developed his *Spiritual Exercises* as a highly structured method for a retreatant to weave together his or her life story with that of Jesus. Designed to be traversed in thirty days, the *Spiritual Exercises* leads the retreatant through meditation on sin (Week One), commitment to following Jesus (Week Two), joining him in his passion (Week Three), and participation in his resurrection (Week Four). Each "week" (which does not have to be exactly seven days) includes a series of recommended themes and scenes for meditation, including a wide range of scriptural texts. Ignatius says that the purpose of the *Spiritual Exercises* is "seeking and finding God's will in the ordering of our life for the salvation of our soul."[48] The underlying conviction expressed in the *Exercises* is that a person can genuinely encounter Jesus in the present moment, know that one has been "elected" by God in the individuality of one's vocation, and, on that basis, make choices that reshape the direction of his or her life toward wholehearted participation in Jesus's mission.

In his discussion of the *Spiritual Exercises* Jesuit liberation theologian Ignacio Ellacuría observes that by having the personal encounter with the will of God as their goal, the *Exercises*

---

[47] Eugene F. Rogers, *After the Spirit: A Constructive Pneumatology from Resources Outside the Modern West*, Radical Traditions (Grand Rapids, MI: Eerdmans, 2005), 46.

[48] Ignatius, *The Spiritual Exercises of St. Ignatius: A Literal Translation and a Contemporary Reading*, trans. David L. Fleming (St. Louis, MO: Institute of Jesuit Sources, 1991), #1.

"are already a principle of historicization."[49] The *Exercises* assume that a retreatant will not just have an experience or an insight but will be existentially changed in a way that will have an impact on history. Ellacuría notes that the *Exercises* afford an opportunity to weave together three histories: "one's own individual history, the broader history in which it is embedded, and the history of God's redemptive work, with its definitive moment in Jesus' history."[50] Matthew Ashley adds, "[Ellacuría's] point here is that the Exercises do not have as their goal gaining information about God, or about God's will, but of encountering God and God's will, of being confronted with God's will and responding to it here and now."[51]

While Ignatius's explicit instructions focus much more on ruminating on the stories of God and Jesus than on remembering one's own life events, he invites retreatants to enter the themes and stories imaginatively in ways that necessarily lead to remembering and reworking one's own self-story. Ignatius teaches a way of meditating called composition of place, in which the retreatant is encouraged to "see in imagination the material place where the object is that we wish to contemplate."[52] Jesuit directors developed this into the practice of encouraging people to enhance their presence to Jesus by being as elaborate as possible in imagining themselves as participants in each proposed scene. As Nicolas Standaert states, "One encounters in a concrete way the person of Jesus by stepping into the scene and becoming a sharer in what those who were there really saw, heard, smelt and so on."[53] Retreat directors often suggest that one imagine

---

[49] Ignacio Ellacuría, "Lectura Latinoamericana de Los Ejercicios Espirituales de San Ignacio," *Revista Latinoamericana de Teologia* 23 (1991): 113; as translated in J. Matthew Ashley, "Ignacio Ellacuría and the Spiritual Exercises of Ignatius Loyola," *Theological Studies* 60, no. 1 (2000): 16–40.

[50] Ashley, "Ignacio Ellacuría."

[51] Ashley, "Ignacio Ellacuría."

[52] Ignatius, *The Spiritual Exercises of St. Ignatius*, #47.

[53] Nicolas Standaert, "The Composition of Place: Creating Space for an Encounter," *The Way* 46, no. 1 (January 2007): 17.

oneself as one of the characters in the story, or as a peripherally involved onlooker.

Without saying so in so many words, Ignatius's method opens the door to a profound level of personalization of these stories. Clearly, to imagine in detail the sights, smells, and sounds of a gospel story is to engage in elements of fiction, since rarely is any such information provided except in rudimentary form. Even more significant, however, is how the retreatant will inevitably draw upon his or her own internalized stories to re-create imaginatively the dynamics of the relationships and incidents that are recounted. Even though all participants in the *Exercises* are using essentially the same themes and stories for their meditation, what they experience and discover will be highly individualized. In fact, this is the point of such exercises: Jesus will encounter each of us in our own story, in our own wounds, in the very places where we are most engaged in an existential struggle to know who we are and where we are going. This is how the Spirit "reads us into the story" of the Word.

The emphasis on the reality of encounter with Jesus in one's own historical setting raises the question of how this is related to the historical, first-century reality of Jesus. Today, people who have been formed by close attention to the fruits of sophisticated historical-critical research might regard Ignatius as rather naive, since he seems to take scripture stories literally and does not ask whether these things really happened. However, Hans Urs von Balthasar, who spent over twenty years as a Jesuit before leaving to found his own community, offers a different perspective.

Arguing that Christ is eternally open to having humanity enter into his very self, Balthasar writes: "The framework of [the world's] meanings is constructed of the situations (the interior situations) of Christ's earthly existence. Man cannot fall out of this space which is Christ's, nor out of the structural form created by his life."[54] Thus, Balthasar proposes that the interior events of meaning in Jesus's historical life have been permanently imprinted into historical existence so that they are always available

---

[54] Hans Urs von Balthasar, *A Theology of History*, 2nd ed. (New York: Sheed and Ward, 1963), 66.

to those who seek to be united to them. Although relatively little of Jesus's interior life is explicitly recorded in scripture, meditation on the stories that are recorded offers a privileged path to participation in this inner life of Christ. According to Balthasar's approach, then, it is less important to know and replicate the exact actions of the first-century Jesus than to participate, here and now, in the movements of his heart. These movements are genuinely historical, both because they mirror the heartfelt responses of the first-century Jesus, and because they are our way of incarnating those same inner movements within our own historical settings.

In Chapter 1, we noted Balthasar's idea that "because of the creation of all things in Christ, certain patterns of self-giving love are inherent foundational structures in historical existence—rather like the way gravity necessarily structures physical existence."[55] We also connected this to the universal action of the Spirit, who mediates this "gravity" of attraction to self-giving love in all people's lives, without being limited only to those who have already committed themselves as Christian. What is interesting about the way Ignatius designed his *Spiritual Exercises* is that, while they certainly presume a sincere willingness to enter imaginatively into the scriptural themes and gospel stories, they do not necessarily presume that the retreatant is already a fully committed Christian.

In fact, in Ignatius's own social context, participants almost certainly would have been at least nominal Christians, but many probably understood their Christianity primarily in terms of conformity to exterior norms. The design of the *Exercises*, one might argue, is to bring one's self into the "field of gravity" of the Spirit so that, if one is paying attention (and has a good retreat director!), one will be brought to a turning point where one says a deeply interior "Yes!" to Love—and all its concrete implications. Ignatius (and Balthasar) would certainly have understood this as a yes specifically to Christ and his church. In recent decades, some have proposed, however, that

---

[55] Mark Allen McIntosh, *Christology from Within: Spirituality and the Incarnation in Hans Urs von Balthasar* (Notre Dame, IN: University of Notre Dame, 2000), 22.

it is possible to offer the *Exercises* in interreligious settings[56] or even for "seekers"[57] who are not coming with the specific intention of commitment to Christ. The success of some of these experiments suggests that Ignatius did indeed capture something of the Spirit's "field of gravity" that can draw people "from a self-centered mode of being to one fully dedicated to the service of others."[58]

One of the assertions throughout this book is that all spiritual practices manifest a degree of the rhythm between emptying and remembering, even though some practices focus more on one or the other. Although Ignatius does not name the way of emptying as such, its imprint is seen in his insistence on obedience. He writes, "We must put aside all judgment of our own, and keep the mind ever ready and prompt to obey in all things the true Spouse of Christ our Lord, our holy Mother, the hierarchical Church."[59] This self-abdicating attitude also appears, in a more personal and intimate form, in the prayer "Contemplation to Attain the Love of God":

> Take, Lord, and receive all my liberty, my memory, my understanding, and my entire will, all that I have and possess. Thou hast given all to me. To Thee, O Lord, I return it. All is Thine, dispose of it wholly according to Thy will. Give me Thy love and thy grace, for this is sufficient for me.[60]

In this culminating prayer, Ignatius expresses, in devotional form, the movement of self-emptying and receiving oneself back, ready for mission.

---

[56] Sarita Tamayo-Moraga, "A Resource for a Religiously Plural Dialog Juxtaposing the Spiritual Exercises of Ignatius and Buddhist Wisdom," *Buddhist-Christian Studies* 37 (2017): 131–43; Ruben L. F. Habito, *Zen and the Spiritual Exercises: Paths of Awakening and Transformation* (Maryknoll, NY: Orbis Books, 2013).

[57] Roger Haight, *Christian Spirituality for Seekers: Reflections on the Spiritual Exercises of Ignatius Loyola* (Maryknoll, NY: Orbis Books, 2012), 88–91.

[58] Habito, *Zen and the Spiritual Exercises*, xiv.

[59] Ignatius, *The Spiritual Exercises*, #353.

[60] Ignatius, *The Spiritual Exercises*, #230–237.

In this chapter we explored how the Spirit works with us as we remember and co-construct our self-story, which is the framework for our relationships and actions in the world. The concluding chapter brings together the various explorations from all the chapters with a return to the theme of catholicity, now with a focus on implications for personal and ecclesial mission.

Chapter 9

Breathing with the Spirit into Mission

As we conclude this exploration, let us review some of its basic themes. By taking the stance of catholicity from within, we committed ourselves to looking for the Spirit at work within creation. Consequently, both the results of the human and physical sciences and the testimonies of human experience became resources for our quest. More traditional biblical and theological resources were brought into play at a second stage to interpret and amplify the discoveries from "within." This interplay continues as we reflect on what difference the insights developed in this project may make for our own spiritual lives, our churches, and our societies.

The Mission of the Spirit

In Chapter 2, we explored what may be learned of the Spirit through human experiences. A biblical perspective, however, strongly affirms that an experience of the Spirit is not given to a person simply for the sake of having an experience; it is, rather, the urgent impetus of divine life filling one with the vitality, energy, and desire to participate in the Spirit's own mission. If we were to name that mission, it might be *communion*. All the Spirit's work is to bring all creation to an intimate and consummated communion in the loving heart of God. Our personal spiritual experiences afford us a glimpse of that beautiful vision and light a spark in our hearts that may fuel lifelong efforts to do our part, however small, in fulfilling it.

Yet, the beautiful vision of all things in loving communion with one another also presents a problem, when the ever-present reality of our broken and conflict-ridden world overwhelms us. It is difficult to be optimistic about the future of humanity in a time when even the ecological systems that sustain the physical possibility of human life are being driven toward collapse. If the Spirit is at work in all things to draw them toward consummated communion, why are self-centered ambition, destruction, and death so predominant in the structure of the world's workings?

A complete answer to such a question—if it is even possible—is far beyond the scope of this project. The problems of sin and evil are notoriously confounding to every system of thought. However, this series on catholicity does address one aspect of the conundrum presented by the existence of conflict, destruction, and death. Catholicity identifies a key aspect of the mission of the Spirit as dynamically fostering the intrinsic coalition between differentiated particularity and fulfilled participation in the cosmic whole. In the Spirit, unity is always in dynamic counterplay with differentiation. We make a mistake, then, when we oversimplify our concept of the Spirit's mission, as if God's intention were ultimately to melt everything down into harmonious oneness. An oversimplified view of the Spirit's call to unity can lead to either one of two extremes in pastoral practice: an authoritarian approach that strives to impose uniformity, or a laissez-faire approach that laughs off differences as insignificant.

We only need to look around us in the natural world to see that the creator God delights in the creative novelty of burgeoning differentiation—and that this does not always result in harmony. Where there is differentiation, there is pluralism; and where there is pluralism, there will inevitably be conflicts of interest. Moreover, differentiation implies ongoing change, and in living systems this requires death so that life can be renewed. The ongoing differentiation of environments, species, and diverse abilities cannot happen without complex dynamics of both collaboration and conflict. While collaboration manifests the catholic urge toward wholeness and harmony, conflict reflects the equally catholic impetus of competing local needs. The unity that the Spirit engenders is best imaged as a complex "web of differentiated relationality,"[1] in which relationships are diverse, creative, dynamic, and tensive.

In Michael Welker's survey of the Hebrew scriptures he finds a similar complexity as the Spirit is found working in very diverse, strange, and often quite ambiguous ways.[2] While he finds a general tendency of the Spirit to elicit "processes of gathering, uniting, restoring and strengthening the community,"[3] this sometimes takes place amid mayhem, trickery, and other behavior of questionable morality. One of the more shocking examples is that of Jephthah, who is presented as acting in the Spirit when he makes the vow that ultimately requires him to offer up his own daughter as a burnt sacrifice (Judg 11:29–40). The Spirit, it seems, does not shy from being present even within the conflict and ambiguity that permeate the reality of life in the created realm.

Welker finds greater clarity in the New Testament, where Jesus is identified as the public bearer of the Spirit who comes to fulfill the messianic promises of justice, mercy, and knowledge of God.[4] Henceforward, the Spirit who is sent is specifically the Spirit of Jesus Christ, known through its fruits of healing, renewing, unmasking evil, lifting up the marginalized, and drawing all toward the reign of God. It is here that Welker introduces the metaphor of the force field, writing: "The Spirit of God thus generates a force field of love in which people strive so that all things might 'work for good' for their 'neighbors.'"[5]

Welker prefers the force-field metaphor for the Spirit because it allows many different entities to be influenced but in truly different ways. Whereas a more anthropomorphic image may conjure up the idea of an architect with a master plan, a force field does not necessarily synthesize or coordinate its influence. Two things influenced by the same field of gravity, for example,

---

[1] Antje Jackelén, "Emergence Everywhere?!: Reflections on Philip Clayton's Mind and Emergence," *Zygon* 41, no. 3 (September 2006): 629.

[2] Michael Welker, *God the Spirit*, trans. John F. Hoffmeyer (Minneapolis: Fortress Press, 1994), chap. 2.

[3] Welker, *God the Spirit*, 98.

[4] Welker, *God the Spirit*, chap. 4.

[5] Welker, *God the Spirit*, 227.

might nonetheless catastrophically crash into each other. Or we might think of the different ways that items made of plastic, copper, and iron respond to the same magnetic field. Of course, the impersonality of these images makes them not fully adequate to the reality of the Spirit. The value of the image is that a force field can put a directional "lean" on all things, but each thing's response will depend on its particular circumstances, nature, and capability. Within the complex web of differentiated relationality that is the created world, the action of the Spirit is often difficult to discern clearly, even when we are convinced that it is ever present.

Human beings are created with the capacity to respond to the attractive force of the Spirit on a personal and moral level. Yet human beings are extraordinarily complex creatures, both interiorly and exteriorly. Our review of contemporary philosophical and psychological models of human selfhood in Chapter 4 concluded that the best model may be Hermans and Hermans-Konopka's "dialogical self," which recognizes that the psychological self is never a simple unity but bears within itself the dynamic plurality of the "web of differentiated relationality" that is intrinsic to being part of the created world. The implication is that our longing for wholeness and integration is not designed to be satisfied by arrival at a point of completion within our lifespan. In Chapter 6, we placed this model within a theological perspective, proposing that only radical interior openness to the Spirit can afford the human person a wholeness that, in its created manifestations (both psychological and social), nonetheless necessarily remains incomplete and "on the move" as long as we continue in embodied life.

Discovering Our Charisms

In the Greek of New Testament times, *charis* meant "a favor or gracious gift that gives joy and engenders gratitude"; the simplest translation is "grace." In various ways it was incorporated into the theological language of the New Testament to refer to the amazing gifts that God has given to people through the Spirit. Even *Christ*, which means "the anointed one," derives from the same root. So does *eucharist*, which literally translated means "thanksgiving for grace." According to scripture scholar Enrique

Nardoni, Paul used the words *charisma* and *charismata* in various ways. Summing up, Nardoni observes that charism refers to "the concrete form in which the saving action of God's grace is appropriated by each believer."[6]

Thus emerged the idea of charisms as the unique, particularized gifts that the Spirit develops in each member of the church so that each individual can make a personal contribution to the upbuilding of the community. A foundational text for the theology of charisms is 1 Corinthians 12:4–31, where Saint Paul states: "There are varieties of gifts, but the same Spirit. . . . To each is given the manifestation of the Spirit for the common good." He then discusses many types of gifts and develops the analogy of a body with many parts, each of which is necessary for the body's healthy functioning. The giving of charisms is a perfect exemplification of the catholicity of the Spirit's way of operating. The charisms are highly diverse and particular to each individual and local community, but their orientation is toward fulfilling the Spirit's mission of enhancing communion on all levels.

One of the problems with how the language of charisms is often used is that it can sound as if the Spirit is handing out reified "things" to people—that is, as if the Spirit drops a "package" of teacherhood on one person while dropping a "package" of administrative skills on another person. It would be more accurate to say that when a person is open to the Spirit, that person's natural gifts and capabilities can be "in-Spirited" so that they are drawn into fuller participation in the activity of the Spirit's mission. Paul used a different word, *pneumatika*, for the more extraordinary gifts such as speaking in tongues and prophecy; these seem to be given in the moment for the purpose of enhancing worship services, while *charismata* is a broader term that includes gifts evoked on a more long-term basis for many kinds of services and activities.[7]

Bernard Lee makes an important distinction between deep story and charism, observing that the narrative structures of a personal or communal deep story provide resilient continuity of identity but do not become charism until the story comes

---

[6] Enrique Nardoni, "The Concept of Charism in Paul," *Catholic Biblical Quarterly* 55 (1993): 71.

[7] Nardoni, "The Concept of Charism in Paul," 72.

alive afresh to "mediate redemption for the cry of the age." He continues: "The deep story emerges as a charism when it is able to rise to the occasion, and when the occasion—which is the contemporary world in all its concreteness—rises in turn to meet it. When they meet publicly, the world knows it. At that moment redemption has a face and charism is afoot."[8]

Lee's categories help us to understand how charism is brought forth as a concrete manifestation of the Spirit's mission through the inward and outward rhythm of the Spirit's breathing. When the Spirit breathes us in so that we let go of all else and abandon ourselves to divine communion, the concreteness of our historical being is in-Spirited and anointed for charism. When the Spirit breathes us out into the co-creation of our world, the first essential framework that we co-create is the narrative of our deep story. The point that Lee is concerned to make is that as the rhythm of breathing continues, sometimes we lose touch with the concrete urgency of the anointing of the Spirit, which is intended to be given afresh for each new local moment and situation. We may begin to think that it is enough to be faithful to the deep story—the memory of how we have been called and sent forth. This is like practicing the way of remembering while neglecting the way of emptying.

Spiritual Experiences as Expressions of the Spirit's Mission

With this expanded perspective on the Spirit's mission and our participation in it, let us reconsider the characteristics of spiritual experience that emerged from our informal phenomenology of reported experiences. In Chapter 2, the characteristics were described, insofar as possible, without explicitly theological language. Although the group who provided the stories consisted of Christian theology students, our hypothesis is that very similar characteristics would be found if stories of spiritual experience were solicited from a much more diverse population—including people who identify with various religious traditions or no tradition at all. If further research proved this to be true, it would

---

[8] Bernard J. Lee, "A Socio-Historical Theology of Charism," *Review for Religious* 48 (January 1989): 131.

provide an important form of evidence for how the Spirit is at work in all human lives to urge them toward participation in the Spirit's mission.

- *First characteristic:* Spiritual experience is a singular, supremely memorable event in a unique life narrative.
- *Second characteristic:* Spiritual experience is a turning point or conversion moment in each one's story.
- *Third characteristic:* Spiritual experience is an event of self-knowledge in the presence of the sacred that frees a person to be himself or herself more authentically.
- *Fourth characteristic:* Spiritual experience takes a person by surprise; it is "grace" that shifts things in ways that could not have been expected or predicted.
- *Fifth characteristic:* Although often preceded by a time of difficulty, the dominant feelings and moods of spiritual experience are those of peace, joy, love, light, and liberation.
- *Sixth characteristic:* Spiritual experience changes a person's way of being in relationship; one becomes more aware of belonging to realities bigger than the self, and eager to give oneself on behalf of these realities.

This research suggests that the Spirit moves powerfully in the life of each human person at some point (or points), working through the unique interior and exterior contingencies of the person's circumstances to awaken and liberate an awareness of the live possibility of a more joyful, authentic, participative, and self-giving way of being. Although not always articulated as such, these are "vocation experiences." A person who is able to attend to such experiences and unpack their meaning is able to discover, in the oft-quoted words of Frederick Buechner, "the place where your deep gladness and the world's deep hunger meet."[9]

While my theology students mainly recounted experiences that they had indeed attended to, with positive life-changing effects, the sad truth is that in many human lives spiritual experiences occur but their call is not heeded. Such experiences invite a person to deep change, not only in attitudes and values but also in

---

[9] Frederick Buechner, *Wishful Thinking: A Seeker's ABC*, rev. and exp. ed. (San Francisco: HarperSanFrancisco, 1993), 119.

many concrete aspects of their life such as personal relationships, group affiliations, and economic behaviors. Such change is always difficult, but even more so if one does not find a supportive group culture that helps one to pay attention to such experiences, name their significance, and place them within a long-term trajectory of committed practice. Religious groups provide this kind of support—and yet, not always effectively. In the current era young people, in particular, find it difficult to see a connection between their spiritual experiences and the frames of meaning provided by the churches. Discovering how to provide appropriate spiritual companioning and a culture of support for young people, so they will be able to attend to the call inherent in their spiritual experiences, is an urgent need of our time.

The Individual in Community

While the release of joy and vitality that typically accompanies spiritual experience is obviously of great value for the individual, it may be of even greater importance for its enhancement of that person's capacity for relationality and community building. We have focused predominantly on the challenges of spiritual living from the perspective of the individual person, but it must always be remembered that the proposed model of personhood assumes that, both psychologically and spiritually, there is no person apart from participation in relationships. On the psychological level the dialogical model of the self places relationships with others into the very structure of the self, as each "part self" is formed within an ongoing dialogue with other persons, groups, or anthropomorphized beings, real or imagined. From the spiritual perspective there is no person apart from the foundational relationship with the creator-God. Consequently, the authenticity of personal life is not to live simply for oneself, but always with and for others.

Thus, focusing on the individual does not mean downplaying the urgency of community building and communal change. Despite common tropes that suggest that increasing individuality and increasing community centeredness work against each other, the opposite is the case when individuality is developed as the uniqueness of each one's relation to the Spirit. Indeed,

Karl Rahner has noted that even at the subhuman level "the true law of things is not: The more special and distinct in character, the more separated, isolated and discontinuous from everything else, but the reverse: The more really special a thing is, the more abundance of being it has in itself, the more intimate unity and mutual participation there will be between it and what is other than itself."[10] Thus, the greater is the capacity for individual relationship to the Spirit, the greater also is the capacity for intimate relationships and community building at all levels. Even the secular philosopher Félix Guattari included a similar position in his ideas on "ecosophy," writing that what is needed to deal with current planetary crises is "*heterogenesis*, in other words, processes of continuous resingularization. Individuals must become both more united and increasingly different."[11]

Spiritual experiences, then, are manifestations of the mission of the Spirit to foster communion. Their fruit is intended to be the engagement of persons in the work of building concrete communities at all levels from the interpersonal life of families, neighborhoods, and congregations to the politics of cities, nations, and global society. As we saw in Chapter 5, the ultimate vision of communion is to live from the depth of participation in the cumulative wisdom of the entire created cosmos. This would be the fullness of catholicity—to live at one and the same time as individual, locally rooted persons and as members of the cosmic community.

The Spirit and Social Change

In Chapter 5, we presented the visions of Gregory Bateson, Thomas Berry, and Joanna Macy, all of whom point to the urgent need to break through to a different level of cosmic wisdom and ecologically based societal structures. In this time of massive cultural and ecological crisis, we long for equally massive change

---

[10] Karl Rahner, "On the Significance in Redemptive History of the Individual Member of the Church," in *Mission and Grace*, vol. 1 (London: Sheed and Ward, 1963), 118.

[11] Félix Guattari, *The Three Ecologies*, Bloomsbury Revelations (New York: Bloomsbury Academic, 2014), 45.

of human behaviors at the global level. It is easy to despair when more often than not we see social change seeming to move in the exact opposite direction from the proposed vision. Our challenge is to find ways to practice hope, like that of the poet W. S. Merwin, who wrote that he would keep planting trees even if it were the last day of the world's existence.[12]

The most powerful place to begin planting the seeds of the new vision may be at the smallest level, with oneself and one's immediate social relationships. Leadership consultant Margaret Wheatley points out that "most social change initiates or is shaped by a single traceable conversation."[13] A similar comment, often attributed to anthropologist Margaret Mead, states: "Never doubt that a small group of thoughtful, committed citizens can change the world. Indeed, it is the only thing that ever has." In a discussion of painful issues of tribalism and exclusion that act against social efforts to build community, Miroslav Volf observed that the theologian's contribution to resolving such conflicts will usually be not so much in proposing new social arrangements (since most theologians lack real expertise in this area), but rather in "fostering the kind of social agents capable of envisioning and creating just, truthful and peaceful societies, and on shaping a cultural climate in which such agents will thrive."[14]

John Paul Lederach, who is an expert in facilitating reconciliation processes in groups torn by violence, gives many examples of how acts of "moral imagination" on the part of individual, untrained members of conflict-ridden communities have often been far more significant in initiating a movement toward more positive relations than the contribution of highly educated experts like himself. A person with moral imagination, he says,

---

[12] See W. S. Merwin, "Place," in *The Rain in the Trees* (New York: Knopf, 1988).

[13] Margaret J. Wheatley, *Turning to One Another: Simple Conversations to Restore Hope to the Future,* exp. 2nd ed. (San Francisco: Berrett-Koehler, 2009); quoted in John Paul Lederach, *The Moral Imagination: The Art and Soul of Building Peace* (Oxford: Oxford University Press, 2010), 31.

[14] Miroslav Volf, *Exclusion and Embrace: A Theological Exploration of Identity, Otherness, and Reconciliation* (Nashville, TN: Abingdon Press, 1996), 21.

is alert to "moments pregnant with new life, which rise from what appear to be the barren grounds of destructive violence and relationships." Such a person has "the capacity to imagine something rooted in the challenges of the real world yet capable of giving birth to that which does not yet exist."[15] On that basis he or she is able to make a creative, unique, and often totally unforeseen intervention at just the right moment, thus reconfiguring intergroup relationships so that they become open to the possibility of reconciliation.

Lederach gives the example of two tribes in Ghana who were caught in repeated cycles of violence against each other.[16] The Dagomba tribe has a chieftaincy-based form of leadership and has prospered, while the Konkomba tribe does not have chiefs and has been much less successful. Professional mediators called leaders of the warring tribes to a meeting. A disaster appeared to be on the horizon when the Dagomba chief rose and spoke arrogantly and disparagingly, asking why he should even talk to these low-status people. Then a young Konkomba got up to reply, first calling the chief "Father" and recognizing his authority, then eloquently asking his participation in relieving the Konkomba people's suffering and helping them to fulfill their longing for a better life. The Dagomba chief was so surprised by the respectful outreach that he called the young man "wise," asked for forgiveness, and became open to a long-term process of mediation.

Lederach gives many other examples, each one unique to its particular set of historical contingencies. How does a person become capable of such an act of moral imagination? Lederach writes of how it may require entering into a different relationship to time and space.[17] Everyday life in the Western world is typically structured as a rather frantic effort in the present to make something happen in the short-term future, with little or no consideration of either the deeper past or the long-term future. Place is little more than a backdrop to this frenzy, sloughed off as easily as one can fly from one standard-issue airport to the next. Lederach has found that moral imagination is fostered

---

[15] Lederach, *The Moral Imagination*, 29.
[16] Lederach, *The Moral Imagination*, 7–10.
[17] Lederach, *The Moral Imagination*, chap. 12.

through a way of being in time that holds the deep story of the past as the reservoir of a hoped-for long-term future. Here, place is where our ancestors lived and suffered, and where our descendants will carry on their heritage. This kind of relation to time and space does not work on a schedule but rather is alert to the moment—the time and place—when the past is ready to give birth to a new future.

The person of moral imagination, then, lives in touch with deep communal narratives that bear within them the potential to be "restored" in a way that fosters the community's future life.[18] The connection for us is that the rhythms of the Spirit in the way of emptying and the way of remembering may be a key to developing people of moral imagination. In the way of emptying, one lets go of everything, even down to one's very sense of identity, in self-abandonment to the Spirit. In the way of remembering, a person reaches deep into memory and reconstructs the narratives of the self in view of a new and more life-giving narrative—for Christians, the narrative of the Word. The Spirit's inbreath draws us beyond time into an eternal present; the Spirit's outbreath births us into a refreshed and re-enlivened story. This rhythm fuels the potential for an act of moral imagination.

In his lectures and books on reconciliation Robert Schreiter has described a similar process. The situations that he focuses on are efforts made by individuals and communities to recover from periods of horrifying societal violence. People who are subject to violence, Schreiter writes, are forced to let go of the personal and communal narratives that have provided them with identity and a sense of safety. Oppressors and torturers impose on their victims a "narrative of the lie" that justifies and sanitizes the violence.[19] The end result is often the person's total breakdown into helplessness and loss of self. The only path to recovery, Schreiter writes, is for the person to discover within that place of utmost vulnerability the possibility of an act of "fundamental trust" in a new and life-giving narrative. He continues: "The nucleus of our humanity is restored to us in reestablishing the ability to

---

[18] Lederach, *The Moral Imagination*, 147.

[19] Robert J. Schreiter, *Reconciliation: Mission and Ministry in a Changing Social Order*, The Boston Theological Institute Series 3 (Maryknoll, NY: Orbis Books, 1992), 34–36.

trust. . . . Both preceding that ability to trust and accompanying its unfolding is a reconstruction of memory."[20]

When Schreiter describes how societal violence can break down selfhood, he is describing a violent version of the way of emptying. Obviously, this version is by no means to be desired or recommended, and yet, it happens. Remarkably, it is possible for some of those who pass through the crucible of such extreme suffering to become leaders who can speak and act powerfully out of the new narrative that they have discovered. Schreiter quotes Joe Seramane, a South African who was subjected to imprisonment and torture during the regime of apartheid: "It is through reconciliation that we regain our humanity. To work for reconciliation is to live to show others what their humanity is."[21] Such survivors become, in Lederach's terms, people of moral imagination.

Indeed, while (thankfully) only a minority of human beings undergo such extremes of violence, a much higher percentage experience lesser degrees of pressure from narratives of the lie. Considering the fragmenting pressures described in Chapter 3, we could perhaps even say that culturally sanctioned "narratives of the lie"—consumerism, technologism, narcissistic individualism, to name only a few—have become predominant self-narratives for large numbers of people lacking access to deep ancestral narratives of wisdom and hope. These people, too, have a desperate need to enter into the Spirit's rhythm of emptying and remembering in order to recover the depths of trust and a renewed story that generates commitment to our planetary future. For Christians, the story of Jesus's life, passion, death, and resurrection is the paradigmatic exemplar of a narrative that can provide such grounds for trust and the reconstruction of memory.

The Way of Dialogue

The larger question the book asks is: How may we become persons more capable of catholicity, particularly within the conditions of serious cultural and ecological fragmentation that

---

[20] Schreiter, *Reconciliation*, 37–38.
[21] Quoted in Schreiter, *Reconciliation*, 82.

put such intense pressure on life in the twenty-first century? As is surely evident by now, this is not a self-help book that suggests a quick and easy solution to this problem. Catholicity calls for radical hospitality both to God and to the vast diversity of "others" with whom we are connected by creation's web of differentiated relationality. While affirming the desirability of such a radical level of openness and hospitality, we should never underestimate the struggle, confusion, anxiety, and loss that may have to be undergone in the process of being opened up so deeply.

Some have proposed the model of dialogue as an essential path to the development of more catholic persons and cultures. The ideal of dialogue is a conversation or shared activity in which the participants are truly open to learning from, and being changed by, one another. Tom Murray writes: "Dialogue invokes ideals of equality, participation, freedom, collaboration, responsibility, diversity, creativity and adaptation. . . . [Dialogue] is a metaphor for a respectful and interactive way of *being* with others and with the natural world. To be in dialogue is to listen deeply and to respond with integrity." Dialogue, he notes, can facilitate the movement from more rigid and authoritarian social structures to those which are more responsive and democratic.[22]

Some recent theologies propose that the Trinity reveals an intrinsically dialogical character in God, since the three divine Persons are in a constant dynamic *perichoresis* of mutual indwelling and exchange. Stephen Bevans and Roger Schroeder, for example, write that

> Christian mission is participation in the mission of *God*, and God's being and action are dialogical. God's self-revelation shows a communion in dialogue in which Mystery, "inside out" in the world, is made concrete in Jesus of Nazareth, and God's way of revealing through Spirit and

---

[22] Tom Murray, "Contemplative Dialogue Practices: An Inquiry into Interiority, Shadow Work, and Insight," *Integral Leadership Review* (August–November 2015): 1.

incarnate Word is always one that treats humanity and all of creation with freedom and respect.[23]

Therefore, they propose that "prophetic dialogue" is the best model of Christian mission. Mission is prophetic when it courageously witnesses to the fullness of truth; it is dialogical when it does so humbly, with great sensitivity to the particularity of context and with willingness to grow, change, and adapt on the basis of what is learned within that context.

With this in mind, it is worth repeating here Miroslav Volf's comment on what it means to be catholic: "A catholic personality is a personality enriched by otherness, a personality which is what it is only because multiple others have been reflected in it in a particular way."[24] Volf regards this as an intrinsic dimension of the Spirit's mission. The Spirit invites each one to respectful dialogue with those who are different from oneself—even (or perhaps especially) one's competitors and "enemies"—that will enrich the catholicity of all participants. As Volf states: "The Spirit unlatches the doors of my heart saying: 'You are not only you; others belong to you too.'"[25] Thinking of this in terms of the model of the dialogical self, each engagement in dialogue offers new potential self-positions as well as possibilities for new coalitions of positions. For example, a young and sexually active woman, through dialoguing with an Islamic immigrant woman who wears a hijab, might discover the value of a "modest" position within herself, and a coalition between this and her customary approaches to flirtation might lead to greater subtlety and restraint.

However, Volf identifies the costliness of such hospitality to otherness when he adds: "The distance from my own culture that results from being born by the Spirit creates a fissure in me through which others can come in."[26] While the model of the

---

[23] Stephen B. Bevans and Roger Schroeder, *Constants in Context: A Theology of Mission for Today*, American Society of Missiology Series 30 (Maryknoll, NY: Orbis Books, 2004), 378.

[24] Volf, *Exclusion and Embrace*, 51.

[25] Volf, *Exclusion and Embrace*, 51.

[26] Volf, *Exclusion and Embrace*, 51.

dialogical self regards the self as inherently plural and restless, a strong cultural narrative can provide a sense of integration and "rightness" that lets the fissures inherent in plurality fade into the background. Openness to the Spirit demands that one loosen one's grip on one's inherited cultural narrative, leading to the vulnerability of knowing one is fissured. Thus, when long-held self-positions are challenged, dialogue with truly different others can be deeply disturbing. This may be especially true for those from more traditional cultures, for whom the boundaries of acceptability in the cultural narrative are most firmly held. If the immigrant woman in the example given above is newly arrived from a strict Islamic culture, she may find it very threatening even to hear about different approaches to female sexuality.

For many of us, however, the cultures and ecosystems we inhabit do not suffer from such excessive firmness, but rather from having become so thoroughly fluid and hybrid that the awareness of being fissured is endemic. The opportunity within today's crisis of fragmenting forces is that these acute fissures in the self may become openings for the Spirit's work of engendering hospitality to those who are truly other. Still, this is not a guaranteed outcome. Extreme fluidity of identity can also play out as a superficial and cynical flippancy that does not treat anything or anyone with respect. As Kenneth Allan notes, in postmodernity the self may consist "solely of fragmented, situational images that result in an emotional flatness or depthlessness."[27] While such a style may at first glance seem very open, because it tolerates everything, no matter how outrageous, it is far from being conducive to real dialogue or hospitality.

Entering into the rhythm of the Spirit in the way of emptying and the way of remembering is the prescription for growing in authentic catholicity. It is not a quick fix but rather a lifelong journey with many twists and turns, some of which seem to take us through dark and unnerving landscapes. The way of emptying deconstructs us, unveiling our brokenness, incompleteness, and ultimate vulnerability—and, in the same movement, revealing that these fissures are the very place where the Spirit rushes in to embrace us in tenderest communion. The way of remember-

---

[27] Kenneth Allan, "The Postmodern Self: A Theoretical Consideration," *Quarterly Journal of Ideology* 20, nos. 1&2 (1997): 3.

ing offers the possibility of reconstruction, as our deep stories are loosened from the strictures of the past and give birth to a vision of the future lived as vocation. Following this rhythm over time opens us more and more deeply to hospitality to ourselves, God, and the vast diversity of "others" with whom our lives are interconnected in creation's web of differentiated relationality.

Of particular interest here are the practices that have come to be called contemplative dialogue.[28] There are many different variations on this, but the general pattern is a process in which a group seeks to access together a deep interior contemplative space and then to dialogue toward discovery of the group actions that arise from this collective awareness. Steven Wirth describes contemplative dialogue as consisting of three interrelated practices: contemplative noticing or mindfulness; a nondefended learning stance; and nonviolent engagement. He writes: "At its highest level, Contemplative Dialogue develops a consistent ability to relate with and to the collective mind of a group. . . . This stance provides the commitment to authentic presence that deep group freedom and learning require."[29] This practice, then, enables individuals and groups to grow in their capacity to work collectively to build relationships, solve problems, and enhance the common good.

As Tom Murray explains in considerable detail, contemplative dialogue in any of its forms is likely to awaken both individual and collective "shadows." He defines shadows as "pernicious stuff lodged within the mind/body system that hampers the process of making *connections* between ideas or information that could potentially be related, or has hampered the *perceiving* of something that would otherwise be available to perception."[30] He suggests that such shadows can exist on many levels, including ideologies, cultural prejudices, settled habits, emotional reactions, psychological repression, and existential anxieties. Shadow material has the potential to derail group work, but if a milieu

---

[28] For a survey of these practices, see Murray, "Contemplative Dialogue Practices."

[29] Steven Wirth, *The Path of Contemplative Dialogue: Engaging Collective Awareness* (Georgetown, IN: Centre for Contemplative Dialogue, 2012), 7.

[30] Murray, "Contemplative Dialogue Practices," 14.

of safety can be established where people can work through it together, it is possible for a contemplative dialogue group to reach a level that exhibits an extraordinarily high capacity for catholicity. Murray describes it thus:

> Participants are construct-aware and don't let the limitations of language and concepts constrain them. They know words and concepts are sliding signifiers whose meaning cannot be nailed down precisely—they don't get into arguments about definitions. They look for shared meaning and have moved from "I see it another way" to "what might she mean by that?" and "let's play with that idea." Each thing is taken to be one perspective of many, and it is not assumed that the speaker of an idea is attached to it. Ideas and concepts are at play, not in competition. Participants have . . . a high capacity for uncertainty, unknowing, and paradox.[31]

Exemplars of Catholicity

In conclusion, let us now consider three people whose lives and writings exemplify how the rhythms of the Spirit lead to a way of life notably marked by catholicity.

Etty Hillesum (1914–43)

Etty Hillesum came from an assimilated Dutch Jewish family. Having achieved degrees in law and Slavonic languages while still in her early twenties, this vivacious young woman made her living as a tutor while continuing her studies and carrying on an active social and sexual life. Between March 1941 and October 1942, as the Nazi noose tightened around the Jews of Amsterdam, she kept a detailed journal of her thoughts and activities. The journal was discovered in 1980 and published under the title *An Interrupted Life*. It has subsequently been translated into at least twelve languages, and in some editions a large number of letters she wrote after being deported to the Westerbork transit

---

[31] Murray, "Contemplative Dialogue Practices," 22.

camp have been included as well.[32] Etty died at Auschwitz in November 1943 at the age of twenty-nine.

The fascination of Etty's diaries is that they provide a completely unvarnished view of a young woman undergoing a remarkable process of spiritual growth. There is nothing idealized about this story; Etty writes frankly about her sexual encounters, her menstrual cycles, her family squabbles, her self-doubt and depression, as well as at great length about the mundane activities of daily life and her ever-changing moods. Her complete transparency enables the reader to feel empathy for the lived complexity of her moral choices, even when at times they may offend our own ethical standards. In many ways Etty is far from being a "saint," as we typically imagine them. Yet amid all this froth and mess, we see her being led into the discovery of a spirituality of radical self-giving.

Etty's grim reality is that every few weeks the Nazis impose additional restrictions on the Jews. Gradually, she and her friends realize ever more clearly that the ongoing deportations are actually taking people to death camps. Yet Etty is determined not to hate the Germans; she repeatedly insists on affirming their humanity, even empathizing with the strictures that are preventing them from accessing their more humane potential. Rather than be paralyzed by the ever-increasing oppression, she celebrates her freedom to love simple gifts such as the vastness of the sky, the stark beauty of a winter tree, or the delight of a steaming cup of coffee. Although adhering to no specific religious tradition, she reads Augustine, Paul, and the Gospel of Matthew, and she talks to God with great tenderness. More and more she feels "an overwhelming urge" to kneel down in grateful, reverent prayer.[33]

In October 1942, already in the transit camp (the last step before final deportation to Auschwitz), Etty observed how so many of the women and girls around her wanted above all not to think about their circumstances for fear of losing their minds. She wrote: "I was sometimes filled with an infinite tenderness . . . and I prayed, 'Let me be the thinking heart of these barracks.

---

[32] Etty Hillesum, *An Interrupted Life: The Diaries, 1941–1943; and, Letters from Westerbork*, ed. J. G. Gaarlandt (New York: Henry Holt, 1996).

[33] Hillesum, *An Interrupted Life: The Diaries, 1941–1943*, 105.

And that is what I want to be again. The thinking heart of a whole concentration camp."[34] A few days later, although feeling intensely her own illness and vulnerability, she exclaimed: "Sometimes it bursts into full flame within me, as it has just done again: all the friendship and all the people I have known this past year rise up in overwhelming number and fill me with gratitude. . . . I rejoice and exult time and again, oh God: I am grateful to you for having given me this life."[35] Finally, in the last entry of the diary, she adds: "We should be willing to act as a balm for all wounds."[36]

Etty Hillesum is an exemplar of catholicity because, despite her imperfections and the moral ambiguities she navigates, she manifests a remarkable openness to the rhythms of the Spirit. She is deeply contemplative, repeatedly opening what she calls "the deep well"[37] of her being to the mystery of God. Even when faced with the most horrifying circumstances, she determinedly ponders every event of her life, past and present, in the presence of God in order to bring forth a new story of gratitude, tenderness, and self-giving. She seeks to relate nonviolently and dialogically even with her oppressors, always treating them humanely and with respect. She lives with exquisite sensitivity to the concrete particularity of her environment, and at the same time embraces her shattered world with a "cosmic conscience"[38] that lights it up with a vision of wholeness and hope. Etty was not a Christian, and even her Judaism was more ethnic than religious; but, just as she was—warts and all—she opened her being to a flow of the Spirit that continues to radiate around the world.

Howard Thurman (1899–1981)

Our second exemplar of catholicity and the rhythms of the Spirit is Howard Thurman, an African American who grew up in the

---

[34] Hillesum, *An Interrupted Life*, 225.

[35] Hillesum, *An Interrupted Life*, 229.

[36] Hillesum, *An Interrupted Life*, 231.

[37] Hillesum, *An Interrupted Life*, 44.

[38] Fulvio C. Manara, "Philosophy as a Way of Life in the Works of Etty Hillesum," in *Spirituality in the Writings of Etty Hillesum* (Boston: Brill, 2010), 379–98.

Deep South of the United States during the era when segregation of the races was strictly enforced. He later affirmed that it was from his grandmother, who had been born a slave and was still illiterate, that he truly learned "the genius of the religion of Jesus." As he states, "She moved inside the experience and lived out of that kind of center."[39] Overcoming many obstacles, he graduated from Morehouse College and then from Rochester Theological Seminary. His seminary mentor was so impressed with Thurman's brilliance that he counseled him not to waste it on the "race problem," but instead to address "the timeless issues of the human spirit." Even at this young age Thurman's instinctive response was to know that "a man and his black skin must face the 'timeless issues of the human spirit' together."[40] Indeed, his life's work would demonstrate his keen awareness that attending to the particular and to the universal at the same time is not contradictory, but rather is the only way to authenticity. He writes that the seeker must "know that for all men to be alike is the death of life in man, and yet perceive the harmony that transcends all diversities and in which diversity finds its richness and significance."[41]

Three key experiences that occurred during a Pilgrimage of Friendship to India, Burma, and Ceylon in 1935 powerfully influenced the way this awareness shaped Thurman's life and mission. First, his day-long dialogue with a Hindu professor was a watershed religious experience for him:

That afternoon I had the most primary, naked fusing of total religious experience with another human being of which I have ever been capable. It was as if we had stepped out of social, political, cultural frames of reference, and allowed two human spirits to unite on a ground of reality that

---

[39] Howard Thurman, *Howard Thurman: Essential Writings*, ed. Luther E. Smith, Modern Spiritual Masters (Maryknoll, NY: Orbis Books, 2006), 15.

[40] Howard Thurman, *With Head and Heart: The Autobiography of Howard Thurman* (New York: Harcourt Brace, 1979), 60.

[41] Howard Thurman, *The Search for Common Ground: An Inquiry into the Basis of Man's Experience of Community* (Richmond, IN: Friends United Press, 1986), 6.

was unmarked by separateness and differences. This was a watershed of experience in my life. We had become a part of each other even as we remained essentially individual. I was able to stand secure in my place and enter his place without diminishing myself or threatening him.[42]

A second encounter with far-reaching implications was his meeting and dialogue with Mohandas Gandhi. Gandhi had never before had the opportunity to meet an African American, and he expressed profound interest in learning about the racial struggles in the United States. When Thurman returned to the United States, he went on a speaking tour to present Gandhi's ideas about nonviolence as a spiritual and strategic path toward racial justice. This inspired other African American leaders to visit Gandhi and to embrace the practices of nonviolence within the civil rights movement. Although Thurman himself never became an activist, many leaders of the civil rights movement found in him a mainstay of intellectual and spiritual support.

Thurman's final defining experience came as he stood at the Khyber Pass, looking into Afghanistan. Many of the Asians he had met during the trip had challenged him, asking how he could remain a Christian without betraying people of color. At the Khyber Pass he and his wife, Sue Bailey Thurman, found their life's mission:

All that we had seen and felt in India seemed to be brought miraculously into focus. We saw clearly what we must do somehow when we returned to America. We knew that we must test whether a religious fellowship could be developed in America that was capable of cutting across all racial barriers, with a carry-over into the common life, a fellowship that would alter the behavior patterns of those involved. It became imperative now to find out if experiences of spiritual unity among people could be more compelling than the experiences which divided them.[43]

---

[42] Thurman, *With Head and Heart*, 129.

[43] Howard Thurman, *Footprints of a Dream: The Story of the Church for the Fellowship of All Peoples* (Eugene, OR: Wipf and Stock, 2009), 24.

In 1944, Thurman's vision of spiritual unity overcoming divisions led him to become one of the founders of the Church for the Fellowship of All Peoples, an interracial, intercultural, interdenominational, and interreligious church in San Francisco. At the time, such diversity was audacious and cutting edge, especially because churches were traditionally highly segregated by race. Thurman spent the rest of his life promoting this vision and practice of unity in diversity through his teaching, preaching, and writing.

In view of the themes developed in this book, it is also of note that Thurman had a keen awareness of the pressures toward fragmentation in human selfhood, and of how the wholeness engendered by spiritual experience radiates beyond the individual to the society. He writes: "The real target of evil is to corrupt the spirit of man and to give to his soul the contagion of inner disintegration. When this happens there is nothing left, the very citadel of man is captured and laid waste."[44] Only religious experience, in which a person definitively yields this citadel to God, can heal this fragmentation by touching a person "at his inmost center, at his very core."[45] In Thurman's understanding, then, religious experience sets in motion a process that makes possible the wholeness of the individual and the dialogical harmony of the community.

Pope Francis (1936–)

Our third exemplar of catholicity and the rhythms of the Spirit is Pope Francis. Born in 1936 to Italian immigrants to Argentina, Jorge Mario Bergoglio first planned to study medicine, but in 1958 he decided instead to enter the Jesuits. Shortly after taking final vows in 1973 he was named provincial of the Argentinian Jesuits. Some of the decisions he made during the "Dirty War" (1976–83) were strongly criticized. Bergoglio remained in leadership positions until 1990, while the province grew more divided for and against him. Finally, the Jesuit superior general ordered that he be removed and sent to a small town far from the center

---

[44] Howard Thurman, *Meditations of the Heart* (Boston: Beacon Press, 1999), 110.

[45] Howard Thurman, *Disciplines of the Spirit* (Richmond, IN: Friends United Press, 2003), 121.

of things. This was a time of deep soul-searching for him and seems to have included a way-of-emptying period as he faced much negative feedback and the feeling of being exiled.[46] After that, his predominant themes became mercy, humility, simplicity of life, and solidarity with the poor, although for some time he still embraced quite conservative theological positions. He became a bishop in 1992, a cardinal in 2001, and pope in 2013. As pope, Francis holds the Chair of Peter and is head of the worldwide Roman Catholic Church.

From his first day as pope, Francis has endeared many—while shocking others—with his unconventional gestures, such as living in a residence with other priests rather than in the papal apartments, spontaneously embracing a person with a disfigured face, and inviting homeless men to his birthday lunch. To the despair of theological conservatives, he has given much evidence of having shifted from being the "scourge of Liberation Theology" to being "a Pope for the poor."[47] He provoked both delight and rage when he famously responded to a question about gay priests—speaking to reporters on an overnight flight from Brazil to Rome—by saying, "If someone is gay and he searches for the Lord and has good will, who am I to judge?"[48]

Those who have studied Francis's thought are clear that these are not just the lighthearted gestures of someone who acts or speaks without thinking. He is well known for his commitment to rise early each day to pray and to make all his most important decisions in prayer.[49] In the very first act of his papacy Francis refused the elegant papal vestments, then stepped out on the balcony and said to the gathered crowd: "Let us pray for one another."

Leonard DeLorenzo finds in this inaugural gesture a classic expression of Francis's determination to invite every human being, regardless of status or background, into the mutuality

---

[46] Paul Vallely, *Pope Francis: Untying the Knots: The Struggle for the Soul of Catholicism*, rev. and exp. 2nd ed. (London: Bloomsbury Continuum, 2015), chap. 6.

[47] Vallely, *Pope Francis*, 127.

[48] Quoted widely, including in Eric J. Lyman, "Pope Francis Says He Won't 'Judge' Gay Priests," *USA Today* (July 29, 2013).

[49] Vallely, *Pope Francis*, 121.

of encounter and care for one another.[50] This was even more clearly expressed when, after addressing the US Congress in 2015, Francis said to the crowd gathered outside: "I ask you all please to pray for me. And if there are among you any who do not believe or cannot pray, I ask you to please send good wishes my way." In doing this Francis expresses radical hope that every person—even those without faith or with profound disagreements—can enter this heart-space of encounter and build positive relations on that basis.

For Francis, the chief spiritual challenge of our time is the fragmentation that prevents people from finding a narrative wholeness in either their personal or communal lives. In his 2013 apostolic exhortation, *Evangelii gaudium (The Joy of the Gospel)*, he comments on these threats: "If hearts are shattered into a thousand pieces, it is not easy to create authentic peace in society" (no. 229). He finds in Ignatius's *Spiritual Exercises*, in which memory "unites the fragments of experience with the history of salvation,"[51] a method for bringing seemingly irreconcilable elements (within oneself and within communities) into dynamic unity. Francis's understanding of the wisdom of discernment in the Ignatian *Exercises* is that in abandoning one's will to God, unity can be forged while continuing to affirm diversity fully. Diversity, then, is not just to be tolerated; it is actually essential for a true "union of souls."[52]

The intellectual roots of this attitude lie in Francis's study of Romano Guardini—the subject of his uncompleted doctoral dissertation. For Guardini, oppositions and conflicts are not to be resolved by synthesis but by positive acceptance of the creative tension between the opposing parties. Before becoming

---

[50] Leonard J. DeLorenzo, "The Movement of Intercessory Prayer and the Openness to Encounter," in *Pope Francis and the Event of Encounter*, ed. John C. Cavadini and Donald Wallenfang, Global Perspectives on the New Evangelization 1 (Eugene, OR: Pickwick Publications, 2018), 185–200.

[51] Joseph S. Flipper, "The Time of Encounter in the Political Theology of Pope Francis," in Cavadini and Wallenfang, *Pope Francis and the Event of Encounter*, 214.

[52] Flipper, "The Time of Encounter in the Political Theology of Pope Francis," 215–17.

pope, Bergoglio took this into his own theories of conflict within church and society. As Joseph Flipper notes, "Living within the nexus of tension is the key to his thinking."[53] On this basis Bergoglio distinguishes between "an imperial conception of globalization" that aims at unifying diverse cultures under hegemonic economic and political systems of control, and a "true globalization" that mediates difference by entering into long-term processes of encounter and shared life.[54]

The principle that "unity prevails over conflict" became one of Francis's major themes in *The Joy of the Gospel*, summed up in the statement that "diversity is a beautiful thing when it can constantly enter into a process of reconciliation and seal a sort of cultural covenant resulting in a 'reconciled diversity'" (no. 230). A second principle articulated there is that the whole is greater than its parts. Francis writes: "Here our model is not the sphere, where every point is equidistant from the center, and there are no differences between them. Instead, it is the polyhedron, which reflects the convergence of all its parts, each of which preserves its distinctiveness" (no. 236). Here he almost seems to echo scientist (and Lutheran archbishop) Antje Jackelén's proposal that a "web of differentiated relationality"—which she imaged as a "complex regular polytope" or even a "mandala"—is the best image of relationships that can creatively foster new forms of life.[55] Francis continues with his own pastoral application: "Even people who can be considered dubious because of their errors have something to offer which must not be overlooked" (no. 236).

In *Catholicism*, Richard P. McBrien asserts that, while Roman Catholicism "is *distinctive* in its conviction regarding the fundamental importance of the Petrine ministry to the life and mission of the Church," it is *characterized* "by a *radical openness to all truth and to every authentic value. It is comprehensive and all-embracing* toward the totality of Christian experience

---

[53] Flipper, "The Time of Encounter in the Political Theology of Pope Francis," 212.

[54] Flipper, "The Time of Encounter in the Political Theology of Pope Francis," 213.

[55] Jackelén, "Emergence Everywhere?!"

and tradition."[56] In Pope Francis we see the Petrine ministry joined with a remarkably well-developed theory and practice of catholicity.

There are, of course, many others who could be noted as exemplars of catholicity. Indeed, all those who open themselves to the rhythms of the Spirit are such. If we look around in our neighborhoods and workplaces, we will find them. They are the people who, like Thurman's grandmother, move inside the experience of the rhythms of the Spirit and allow themselves to be breathed into wholeness from that center.

---

[56] Richard P. McBrien, *Catholicism*, completely rev. and updated study ed. (New York: HarperCollins Publishers, 1994), 736, 1190.

Select Bibliography

Balthasar, Hans Urs von. *In the Fullness of Faith: On the Central-ity of the Distinctively Catholic*. San Francisco: Ignatius Press, 1988.

———. "Theology and Sanctity." In *Explorations in Theology I: The Word Made Flesh*, translated by A. V. Littledale and Alexander Dru. San Francisco: Ignatius Press, 1989.

Bateson, Gregory. *Steps to an Ecology of Mind*. Chicago: University of Chicago Press, 2000.

Bauman, Zygmunt. *Liquid Modernity*. Malden, MA: Blackwell, 2000.

Bruner, Jerome S. *Making Stories: Law, Literature, Life*. Cambridge, MA: Harvard University Press, 2003.

Castelo, Daniel. *Pneumatology: A Guide for the Perplexed*. London: Bloomsbury T & T Clark, 2015.

Clayton, Philip. *Mind and Emergence: From Quantum to Consciousness*. Oxford: Oxford University Press, 2008.

Delio, Ilia. *Making All Things New: Catholicity, Cosmology, Consciousness*. Maryknoll, NY: Orbis Books, 2015.

Eakin, Paul John. *Living Autobiographically: How We Create Identity in Narrative*. Ithaca, NY: Cornell University Press, 2008.

Edwards, Denis. *Breath of Life: A Theology of the Creator Spirit*. Maryknoll, NY: Orbis Books, 2004.

Frohlich, Mary. "Critical Interiority." *Spiritus* 7, no. 1 (March 1, 2007): 77–81.

———. "Spiritual Discipline, Discipline of Spirituality: Revisiting Questions of Definition and Method." *Spiritus* 1, no. 1 (March 1, 2001): 65–78.

Gergen, Kenneth J. *The Saturated Self: Dilemmas of Identity in Contemporary Life*. New York: Basic Books, 2000.

Giddens, Anthony. *Modernity and Self-identity: Self and Society in the Late Modern Age*. Stanford, CA: Stanford University Press, 1997.

Gilmore, Leigh. *The Limits of Autobiography: Trauma and Testimony*. Ithaca, NY: Cornell University Press, 2001.

Gregersen, Niels Henrik, ed. *Incarnation: On the Scope and Depth of Christology*. Minneapolis: Fortress Press, 2015.

Herman, Judith Lewis. *Trauma and Recovery*. Rev. ed. New York: Basic Books, 1997.

Hermans, Hubert J. M., and Agnieszka Hermans-Konopka. *Dialogical Self Theory: Positioning and Counter-Positioning in a Globalizing Society*. Cambridge, UK: Cambridge University Press, 2010.

Howells, Edward. *John of the Cross and Teresa of Avila: Mystical Knowing and Selfhood*. New York: Crossroad, 2002.

Hughes, Robert Davis. *Beloved Dust: Tides of the Spirit in the Christian Life*. New York: Continuum, 2008.

Idel, Moshe, and Bernard McGinn, eds. *Mystical Union in Judaism, Christianity, and Islam: An Ecumenical Dialogue*. New York: Continuum, 1996.

LaCugna, Catherine Mowry. *God for Us: The Trinity and Christian Life*. San Francisco: HarperSanFrancisco, 1991.

Lederach, John Paul. *The Moral Imagination: The Art and Soul of Building Peace*. Oxford: Oxford University Press, 2010.

Llinás, Rodolfo R. *I of the Vortex: From Neurons to Self*. A Bradford Book. Cambridge, MA: MIT Press, 2002.

Loder, James E. *The Logic of the Spirit: Human Development in Theological Perspective*. San Francisco: Jossey-Bass Publishers, 1998.

Lubac, Henri de. *Catholicism: Christ and the Common Destiny of Man*. San Francisco: Ignatius Press, 1988.

Lyotard, Jean-François. *The Postmodern Explained: Correspondence 1982–1985*. Minneapolis: University of Minnesota Press, 1993.

Macy, Joanna. *World as Lover, World as Self: Courage for Global Justice and Ecological Renewal*. Berkeley, CA: Parallax Press, 2007.

McFadyen, Alistair I. *The Call to Personhood: A Christian Theory of the Individual in Social Relationships*. Cambridge, UK: Cambridge University Press, 1990.

McGinn, Bernard. "Hidden God and Hidden Self: The Emergence of Apophatic Anthropologies in Christian

Mysticism." In *Histories of the Hidden God: Conceal-ment and Revelation in Western Gnostic, Esoteric, and Mystical Traditions*, edited by April D. DeConick and Grant Adamson, 87–100. New York: Routledge, 2016.

McIntosh, Mark Allen. *Christology from Within: Spirituality and the Incarnation in Hans Urs von Balthasar*. Notre Dame, IN: University of Notre Dame Press, 2000.

McNamara, Patrick. *The Neuroscience of Religious Experience*. Cambridge, UK: Cambridge University Press, 2014.

Mickey, Sam. *On the Verge of a Planetary Civilization: A Phi-losophy of Integral Ecology*. London: Rowman and Littlefield International, 2014.

Moltmann, Jürgen. *The Spirit of Life: A Universal Affirmation*. Minneapolis: Fortress Press, 2001.

Moseley, Romney M. *Becoming a Self before God: Critical Transformations*. Nashville, TN: Abingdon Press, 1991.

Pannenberg, Wolfhart. *Toward a Theology of Nature: Essays on Science and Faith*. Edited by Ted Peters. Louisville, KY: Westminster/John Knox Press, 1993.

Pinnock, Clark H. *Flame of Love: A Theology of Holy Spirit*. Downers Grove, IL: InterVarsity Press, 2015.

Polkinghorne, J. C. "Fields and Theology: A Response to Wolf-hart Pannenberg." *Zygon* 36, no. 4 (December 2001): 795–97.

Rogers, Eugene F. *After the Spirit: A Constructive Pneumatol-ogy from Resources outside the Modern West*. Grand Rapids, MI: Eerdmans, 2005.

Rolnick, Philip A. *Person, Grace, and God*. Grand Rapids, MI: Eerdmans, 2007.

Russell, Heidi Ann. *Quantum Shift: Theological and Pastoral Implications of Contemporary Developments in Science*. Collegeville, MN: Liturgical Press, 2015.

Russell, Robert J., et al., eds. *Neuroscience and the Person: Scien-tific Perspectives on Divine Action*. Berkeley, CA: Center for Theology and the Natural Sciences, 2002.

Sarbin, Theodore R. "The Narrative Quality of Action." *Theo-retical and Philosophical Psychology* 10, no. 2 (1990): 49–65.

Schacter, Daniel L. *Searching for Memory: The Brain, the Mind, and the Past*. New York: Basic Books, 1998.

————, and Elaine Scarry, eds. *Memory, Brain, and Belief.* Cambridge, MA: Harvard University Press, 2001.

Schäfer, Lothar. *Infinite Potential: What Quantum Physics Reveals about How We Should Live.* New York: Deepak Chopra Books, 2013.

Schmitz, Kenneth L. "The Geography of the Human Person." *Communio* 13, no. 1 (1986): 27–48.

Schrag, Calvin O. *The Self after Postmodernity.* New Haven, CT: Yale University Press, 1999.

Schreiter, Robert J. *The New Catholicity: Theology between the Global and the Local.* Faith and Cultures Series. Maryknoll, NY: Orbis Books, 1997.

Taylor, Charles. *A Secular Age.* Cambridge, MA: Harvard University Press, 2007.

Teilhard de Chardin, Pierre. *Christianity and Evolution.* Translated by René Hague. New York: Harcourt, 2002.

Teske, John A. "The Spiritual Limits of Neuropsychological Life." *Zygon* 31, no. 2 (June 1, 1996): 209–34.

Turner, Léon. *Theology, Psychology, and the Plural Self.* Burlington, VT: Ashgate, 2008.

Twenge, Jean M. *Generation Me: Why Today's Young Americans Are More Confident, Assertive, Entitled—and More Miserable Than Ever Before.* Revised and updated. New York: Atria Paperback, 2014.

Van Huyssteen, J. Wentzel, and Erik P. Wiebe, eds. *In Search of Self: Interdisciplinary Perspectives on Personhood.* Grand Rapids, MI: Eerdmans, 2011.

Volf, Miroslav. *Exclusion and Embrace: A Theological Exploration of Identity, Otherness, and Reconciliation.* Nashville, TN: Abingdon Press, 1996.

Welker, Michael. *God the Spirit.* Translated by John F. Hoffmeyer. Minneapolis: Fortress Press, 1994.

Wildman, Wesley J. *Religious and Spiritual Experiences.* Cambridge, UK: Cambridge University Press, 2011.

Wirth, Steven. *The Path of Contemplative Dialogue: Engaging Collective Awareness.* Georgetown, IN: Centre for Contemplative Dialogue, 2012.

Zizioulas, John. *Communion and Otherness: Further Studies in Personhood and the Church.* Edited by Paul McPartlan. London: T & T Clark, 2006.

Index

An eye-opening, tender account of how women in the Islamic community have experienced shame and abuse in their suffering instead of acceptance and compassion. Riveting, deeply moving, beautifully eloquent—I could not put this book down. *Covered Glory* brings a message of hope and redemption to Muslim women who long for deliverance, reminding us all of the freedom and dignity found in the relentless love of Christ.

Vaneetha Rendall Risner, author of *The Scars That Have Shaped Me*

Covered Glory provides a clear, compelling explanation of God's honor for the shamed. This book is a treasure chest of ah-ha moments, biblical insights, and inspiring stories. For anyone ministering among Muslim women, Audrey unlocks the cultural forces that so often define life.

Jayson Georges, author of *The 3D Gospel*

Shame is not a burden borne only by women or Muslims. Shame is central to the curse and affects us all. The gospel gives us power over fear and honor to cover shame. Through story, honest testimony, and loving insight, Audrey Frank magnifies Jesus—our shame swallower—and in doing so helps us all to overcome the crippling weight of shame to stand our sacred ground.

Dick Brogden, author of *Live Dead Joy*

Covered Glory by Audrey Frank shows how God transforms shame into honor and creates our soul's poetry.

DiAnn Mills, author of *Fatal Strike*

This moving book is a refreshing description of the gospel and a must-read for anyone working with Muslims.

Roland Muller, author of *Honor and Shame*

Audrey Frank's book is a glorious liberation for the hidden heart. No longer invisible, we are seen; no longer exposed, we are safe. A critical resource for the Western church as we welcome the Muslim world into our neighborhoods.

Jami L. Staples, founder of The Truth Collective

In *Covered Glory*, Audrey Frank does a masterful job of taking us inside the Muslim world and the honor-shame worldview. Through true stories of Muslim women, personal testimony, and solid exposition of Scripture, she uncovers the huge burden of guilt, shame, and fear so many women deal with. She then weaves through this reality the Good News of the gospel to show us the One True God who sees us, knows us, and loves. This is a great book of God's grace that deserves to read by all.

Pastor R. Johns, Jr., The Heights Church

Audrey shares not only from a wealth of experience in Muslim contexts but from a place of deep, personal experience. *Covered Glory* is a welcome contribution to the growing awareness about the topic of honor and shame. Audrey takes a topic that is told in stories a world away and makes it accessible and relatable to the Bible. This book will not only help people seeking to understand their Muslim friends but also those seeking to understand the growing phenomenon of honor and shame in Western cultures.

Dr Brian Hébert, editor of The Diaspora Art and Culture Project

In *Covered Glory*, Audrey Frank masterfully weaves biblical truths with riveting true-life stories to provide understanding, perspective, and practical help that we and our Muslim friends all might live free from the shackles of shame.

Carrie Gaul, Liaison for International Outreach, Revive Our Hearts

Covered Glory will equip readers to overcome the bondage of shame. Audrey shares real stories (including her own!) of women who have experienced restoration by encountering a glory that was once covered to them. Audrey writes with knowledge, wisdom, experience, and authority. I thank God for entrusting her with such an excellent text.

Jairo de Oliveira, author of Where There Is Now a Church

Audrey Frank is a storyteller theologian. In *Covered Glory* she leads with vivid stories from her years of work in the Muslim world and from her own childhood. Through these stories Audrey carefully unravels for the reader the inner workings of an honor-shame culture. Not satisfied to simply explain this essential Islamic worldview to Westerners, she also ushers us into an ancient and established paradigm for Redemption. As we begin to see clearly through this new lens we find the dynamic of honor and shame not only in the moving stories of Audrey's neighbors, patients, and friends, but in the Christian scriptures and even in our own lives.

Audrey Frank transports us into the world of our Muslim sisters. But as she does so, she also uncovers our own struggle with shame here in the West. Her transparency and wisdom shine through as every word points to the love and grace of our heavenly Father. This is a book of reconciliation—between worlds, between perceptions, and especially between God and His precious daughters.

"Shame on you" are common words across the Muslim world. *Covered Glory* addresses the issue of shame and honor through a realistic perspective, revealing how the good news of Jesus sets people free. This book is a must-read to all who serve among Muslims.

Audrey Frank tells fascinating stories with vulnerability, love, and wisdom. The stories come from her years of experience living in the Muslim world. Audrey also unpacks numerous passages of Scripture—bringing to the surface the Bible's own honor-shame dynamics, and then applying that wisdom to real-life situations. The reader is personally enriched and well-instructed about ministry among women in the Muslim world. *Covered Glory* is a wonderful contribution to the literature about honor-shame and Christian missions. Any follower of Jesus who is serving and blessing Muslims will benefit greatly.

Audrey Frank gives us a personal and practical look at the manifold ways that honor and shame shape the human experience. She intertwines narrative with lucid exposition. *Covered Glory* opens our eyes to discover how intimately acquainted we all are with shame, which steals our sense of worth. All the while, Audrey directs our attention to "the *God of Instead*, He who gives beauty instead of ashes, gladness instead of mourning, and praise instead of despair." For this reason, I am grateful and enthusiastically recommend this book.

Covered Glory

Audrey Frank

HARVEST HOUSE PUBLISHERS
EUGENE, OREGON

Cover design by Studio Gearbox

Cover photo © Alexander Grabchilev / Stocksy

Published with the assistance of David Van Diest from the Van Diest Literary Agency, 34947 SE Brooks Rd., Boring, OR 97009.

All the incidents described in this book are true. Names, circumstances, descriptions, and details have been changed to render individuals unidentifiable.

Covered Glory
Copyright © 2019 by Audrey Frank
Published by Harvest House Publishers
Eugene, Oregon 97408
www.harvesthousepublishers.com

ISBN 978-0-7369-7548-3 (Trade)
ISBN 978-0-7369-7549-0 (eBook)

Library of Congress Cataloging-in-Publication Data

Names: Frank, Audrey, 1971- author.
Title: Covered glory / Audrey Frank.
Description: Eugene : Harvest House Publishers, 2019. | Includes
    bibliographical references and index.
Identifiers: LCCN 2019004512 (print) | LCCN 2019011434 (ebook) | ISBN
    9780736975490 (ebook) | ISBN 9780736975483 (pbk.)
Subjects: LCSH: Missions to Muslims. | Christianity and other
    religions--Islam. | Islam--Relations--Christianity. | Identity
    (Psychology)--Religious aspects--Christianity. | Shame--Religious aspects.
    | Christian converts from Islam. | Women--Religious life.
Classification: LCC BV2625 (ebook) | LCC BV2625 .F73 2019 (print) | DDC
    261.2/7--dc23
LC record available at https://lccn.loc.gov/2019004512

Printed in the United States of America

19 20 21 22 23 24 25 26 27 / VP-SK / 10 9 8 7 6 5 4 3 2 1

This book is dedicated to all who have
been eclipsed by shame,
hidden beneath its smothering darkness.
May you find courage to believe what is really true about you.
You are valued beyond measure,
lovingly formed by a Creator God
who made you to know His love and
thrive in relationship with Him.
You matter. You are seen. You are known.
And you are loved—an insider, forever.
To those whose true stories are told within these pages,
and to the God who rescued them from shame,
I thank you from my heart for showing me the way.

He reached down from on high and took hold of me;
he drew me out of deep waters. He rescued me from my
powerful enemy, from my foes, who were too strong for
me. They confronted me in the day of my disaster, but the
Lord was my support. He brought me out into a spacious
place; he rescued me because he delighted in me.

PSALM 18:16-19

Contents

Foreword

NIK AND RUTH RIPKEN

Names are important. As first-time parents, we sat in our bed with baby-name books spread out across the blanket. Pages were tagged and corners folded marking the places we'd highlighted names that we liked. We investigated the meaning of each name. We tried them out for how they rang together: first name, middle name next to Ripken. We imagined a little boy or girl living his or her life with that name. We looked at how the initials would appear. Just as we settled on a name, we changed our minds. This precious child who would join our family deserved a perfect name.

Overseas, in cultures so different from ours, names are much more important than we had ever imagined. After two fruitful years in Malawi with continuous bouts of malaria, we had to move south among the Xhosa-speaking people. There, in South Africa, a third boy would be added to our family. Our influential Xhosa friends asked for the honor of naming our son in their traditional way. Among their families, when the first child is to be born, the parents of the husband live with the family for approximately two weeks, studying the home and naming the child in accordance with what they witness inside the family. Therefore, children will carry names that mirror what is found inside your home. Children could be named Peace, Joy, or Love. They could also receive more negative names descriptive of meanness, hatred, or infidelity. Our friends, representing Nik's parents, studied our home.

You can imagine that there were tense moments as we tried to be on our best behavior! Our third son now proudly bears the Xhosa name Siyabulela, which means "We are thankful to God." His Xhosa nickname is "Sabu."

Later, living in the Muslim world, a major conversation starter was discovering a person's name and its meaning. Many Muslims place great seriousness on baby naming, believing a name can define and impact the child directly. In many parts of the Muslim world, the child does not receive a name until 40 days after birth at a special ceremony to mark the occasion. The baby's name becomes part of the passed-on, generational genealogy. Many Muslims can recall the entire history of their people, wrapped around the names of their ancestors. Most Somali families can recite 40 generations of names. One man, from a Hindu background in India, could recite 77 generations of names!

Names are important.

Our interactions with Muslim women have revealed to us the depth of shame carried simply due to female gender. A specific name can intensify the burden of guilt one must endure just by being born female. In public, most women in Central Asia will only hear their names spoken out loud by female friends. Her husband will never speak her name in public, and his brothers will never know her name, nor see her face uncovered. When terrible shame is experienced by an extended family due to the actions of a young woman, resulting in an honor killing, her name will never be spoken again. She is taught to honor, respect, and obey without question the male members of her family. She is never to do anything that would dishonor her male family members. Her brothers learn to shadow her every movement to assure that dishonor will not enter the family through this female. The honor of the group, the family, is more important than any one part. Especially if that part is female.

Culture applies labels decreasing a woman's worth, causing her to struggle with who she is, almost from birth. Life forces on women a heaviness, a burden that weighs them down. Ruth has witnessed that it matters little where women live, nor the education they attain; the shame and guilt of abusive names pull women down into a pit that is hard to escape. Ruth observes, "No matter how we hide the pain, guilt, and shame, the 'sin' of being born female is an everyday stain on our self-image." Such a corrupted view of woman's nature follows her into eternity. Paradise itself is off-limits to most Muslim women.

Then the Savior arrives in those cultures, through women witnessing to women. It is when their stories intersect with the gospel of Jesus that the sin and societal burdens holding them captive are transformed and released. Author Audrey Frank has done a masterful job of illustrating the realities of how women (and men!) are held hostage by names given us by circumstances, society, cultures, and families. She bravely weaves her own story into this book to show us how Jesus can bring wholeness, cleansing, and a new life. The arrival of *Covered Glory* is timely, as the church seeks to make Christ known especially among Muslim women who have never known hope beyond the diminished life they are currently experiencing.

Western women often struggle for their civil rights, such as the right to equal pay and equality in the job arena. Can Western women, whose struggle is for civil rights, fully understand what it is to not have the right to be fully human just because one was born female? Globally, it is nigh impossible for women to have the right to be human, equal to a man. Through what avenues can they express their desire to be human, full partners in their homes, extended families, and in the public arena? Jesus makes Himself and His salvation equally accessible to women both inside their homes and inside the marketplace of life. He truly "sees" the woman at the well and cares enough to ask, "Woman, where is your husband?" (John 4). He allows Himself to be touched and recognizes in public the value of a forgotten woman with her issue of blood by asking, "Who touched me?" (Matthew 9). He rescues and then asks the adulterous woman, "Woman, where are your accusers?" (John 8). He asks us, "What is holding you captive?" Jesus recognizes that women matter. He notices them. Loves them. Died for them. He is the God of both Adam and Eve!

Audrey reminds us of how, in the words of the psalmist, God knows our names. Before we were born from the womb of a woman, He knew us. Should we assume that Western culture is inherently good and all others inherently bad? Is it simply a benefit of one's Western passport or the location of our birth that we can receive the message of Christ?

Cultures and worldviews clash. Jesus finds ways to impact all cultures as He blends our stories with His. He sends us to listen, to listen to women's stories from all cultural backgrounds. As spiritual midwives we can help blend their stories, however corrupted from creation's intent, into encounters with Christ. God is sending countless Muslim women dreams and visions that cause them to wonder and ask if there is hope in this world or eternity. A huge challenge faces women who have found love, acceptance, and worth through Jesus. He has healed us and made us whole. Are we keeping Jesus to our Western selves? How and where can these women intersect with us and His story?

Audrey bravely places her life and her story where she can continue to rub against women of the world: the hurting, the outcast, the burdened, and the captive. Within these pages, Audrey illustrates faithfulness in obeying Jesus' command to cross the street and the oceans to share God's grace. Nothing less will bring healing, bind up the broken, and give hope to the hopeless. As you read her book you will find amazing stories that will confront your culture and worldview. Audrey beautifully weaves God's story with the stories of those with whom she has lived, served, and loved. She continues to bring hope to cultures where shame is written across the lives of women like a giant Scarlet Letter, labeling them unclean and unworthy.

God knows our names. Whose name do you know? For whom do you cry out to God?

Reading *Covered Glory* can make us furious with the realities that women around the globe endure. We can choose to ignore what we read and carry on with our daily routines. We can spend time talking about those horrible realities, never confronting the ways that we, ourselves, are held captive. We can promise to pray for "those people, those women." But *Covered Glory* all but demands a response. We must embrace, with action, that which we have read. We are commanded by Jesus to help women (and men) around us and around the globe. The shame related to one's name can be changed by a Father God who is seeking us, calling each by name. God takes the shame, hurts, and pains which this world inflicts on us and uses every experience to help us identify with others. He will not waste any part of our story but will use it to change lives.

Many women around the world know what it is like to experience crucifixion. The psalmist writes that "tears last for a night, but joy comes with the morning" (Psalm 30:1-12). It is time for the resurrection.

Nik and Ruth Ripken
March 28, 2019

Nik is the author of *The Insanity of God*. He and Ruth are leading experts on the persecuted church in Muslim contexts, having served cross-culturally for more than 25 years and conducted research on the persecuted church and Muslim Background Believers in approximately 60 countries.

Glossary of Terms

abaya: a full-length, robe-like outer garment worn by some Muslim women

'ayin: spring, well of water; colloquially, it can mean one's family of origin in some dialects

Al-Wadud: one of the ninety-nine names of God in Islam, meaning the Loving, the Kind One

burqa: the most concealing of all Islamic veils, a one-piece veil that covers the body and the face, sometimes leaving a mesh screen to see through.

bqiti fia: a colloquial Arabic expression of sympathy meaning, "I feel your pain; I understand what you are going through"

daw': light, typically man-made or artificial

ghairat: (Pashto, not Arabic), usually translated as "honor" in English, describing one's position of honor, a code of integrity, dignity, and pride.

Hadith (pl. *ahadith*): traditions relating what was said or done by Muhammad or his companions, authenticated by a chain of oral transmitters

Hajar: the Arabic name for the biblical Hagar, the mother of Ishmael

hajj: annual pilgrimage to Mecca, culminating in the feast of sacrifice

haram: forbidden

hijab: a head covering worn in public by some Muslim women

hijrah: migration, particularly of early Muslims from Mecca to Medina in AD 622

hubb: love and affection

Injil: the Arabic name of the Gospel of Jesus, which Christians call the New Testament

kufi: a brimless, round cap worn by Muslim men

lesso: a vast, sheet-like cloth worn over skirts by women in some parts of Africa

Masihi (fem. *Masihia*; pl. *Masihin*): Christian

melhfa: a voluminous rectangular cloth worn by Muslim women in some parts of the world; part is wrapped around the body forming a dress and part is placed over the head and shoulders.

mut'a: a private and verbal temporary marriage contract for the purpose of pleasure

nawafil: optional prayers believed to confer extra benefit on the person performing them

niqab: a veil worn by some Muslim women that covers the lower face, allowing only the eyes to be visible

nour: light that is natural or created by God, not by humans

qiblah: direction of Muslim prayer (toward Mecca)

Qur'an: the holy book of Islam

sabaya: young women captured in war by the enemy; in recent times this has come to mean young women captured and forced to become sex slaves by Islamic extremists

salah (*salat* in conjoined form): formal prayer

salat-al-maghrib: sunset time of prayer

saum: fasting

scimitar: a short sword with a curved blade

shahada: the Muslim profession of faith

souq: marketplace

tabib (fem. *tabiba*): a doctor

wudd: love, affection demonstrated by action

zakat: alms-giving, charity

Your Story, Her Story

Instead of your shame you will receive a double
portion, and instead of disgrace you will rejoice in your
inheritance. And so you will inherit a double portion
in your land, and everlasting joy will be yours.

ISAIAH 61:7

It has been said that shame is put upon one by another. No one voluntarily takes it up and wears it proudly. Rather, like a heavy wool shroud saturated with the weight of humiliation and fear, it forces its wearer into hiding. The one cloaked in shame loses her voice…for a time. Shame is not unique to least-developed countries, the seemingly forsaken places. It is not merely the plight of women behind veils, young girls trafficked across borders. Shame is lurking in every culture and every land. Perhaps shame lurks in your own story too.

This book seeks to give a voice to the voiceless. In its pages you will observe firsthand the magnificent work of the *God of Instead*, He who gives beauty instead of ashes, gladness instead of mourning, and praise instead of despair. The Savior is moving in the world today, preaching good news to the poor, binding up the brokenhearted, and proclaiming freedom for the captives. He releases those imprisoned by shame, bestowing on them the favor of the Lord (Isaiah 61). This is the hope that beckons all who come to Jesus Christ.

Hope calls us forth from the darkness, singing songs of deliverance with a clear, resonant voice, promising an inheritance of joy. In these pages, may you find your own voice rising with the voices of women around the Muslim world who have been called out of shame and ushered forth into honor and hope, freedom and deliverance. May you discover that both your voice and their voices share the same cry for honor restored. We are much more alike than we realize.

I learned about our similarities firsthand. I could not have imagined as a child that my story was preparing me for the stories of the women in this book. I had no idea I was part of a greater, silent group of women who are loved and pursued by the same Rescuer, Jesus Christ. Now as I lay my pain, my healing, and my joy down alongside the Muslim women in my life, I can see so clearly that my story and theirs are part of the greater story of what God is doing in the world today. My own pain has become deep joy as I have sat across from women around the world, watching the light burst forth in their eyes as they realize for the first time that Jesus values them, honors them, and completes them.

As a young American Christian girl, I just wanted to be good. I listened to my parents and my pastor, and I went to church on Sunday. I loved God and tried very hard to be a good Christian. But in the privacy of my home, things were terribly wrong. Those who should have loved and protected me abused me instead. Shame suffocated me and choked my dreams. God did not seem to be answering my prayers. Why did God not rescue me? My confusion grew as the despair of my heart deepened.

One rainy afternoon when I was 13 years old I decided it must end. Trembling with fear, my eyes tightly shut, I wanted to die. Life had become too unbearable, the shame of abuse too heavy to endure. I could see no other way to freedom than death. With all my might, I cried out to God to take my life. I knew He had the power to do it. And why shouldn't He? My life was of no value.

Suddenly the door to my room opened and my eyes grew wide with alarm. Standing in my doorway was Jesus, His hand outstretched. *I am the only way out of this. Follow Me.* An unexpected, shocking peace filled my heart as I tried to comprehend what I was seeing and hearing. *Yes! Yes, I will follow You!* The answer of my soul rose like a chorus of hope, its crescendo deafening the fear that had gripped me only moments before.

On that day, I began the long journey out of shame. I realized my God knew me. He knew me and cared enough to come to me in the place of my shame and confinement and rescue me. This was the moment the chrysalis of my old life cracked open, freeing me to fly into hope. I believed Jesus's words that afternoon, and I began following Him out of shame and into honor, restoration, and freedom. I am still making that journey.

I thought my experience was unique. I had no idea that in the Muslim world, girls like me were also encountering Jesus in visions and dreams and choosing to believe His life-giving words. I did not realize how much I was like them, trying to be good, following the religious rules of my parents, trying to win God's favor but fearing I never could.

As an adult, my journey with the Savior took me to the other side of the world, where I shared the love of Christ with all who would listen. One night in the inky darkness, a Muslim woman came to my door and quietly knocked. Her little daughter had fallen into the fire and was seriously burned. I brought them into my small front room and by the light of a kerosene lantern began to tend the little girl's wounds. As I gently applied medicine to the burns, I explained that I was doing this in the name of Jesus, the Messiah. I told the young mother that Jesus had been wounded for us, that He had taken our shame and fear away and given us honor and freedom instead. I was really sharing my own story, the story Jesus had written in my life as I had trusted His promises.

With a gasp, the woman exclaimed, "So His name is Jesus! He said you would come one day and tell me His name. *I have been waiting.*" The joy in her eyes lit the dark room even as tears streamed forth, sparkling in the lamplight. I was flooded with confusion. She had been waiting for me? Her incredible story came tumbling out.

As a young girl, she had been quiet and shy. Her family was too poor to send her to school, and she never learned to read. Islam and animism blended together into Folk Islam, coloring her secluded life with fear and superstition.[1] As a young man her father had accepted the teachings of a Muslim missionary who came through the village. He repeated the *shahada*, or Muslim profession of faith, and donned the traditional brimless cap and tunic. Nonetheless, he continued to rely upon the beliefs of his ancestors, seeking power over the spirit world through appeasement. His children always wore charms to ward off sickness, and when the crops failed, he visited the local witch doctor to discover what he must do to make the spirits happy so they would bless his crops with rain and harvest.

His oldest daughter's days consisted of caring for her younger siblings and doing chores on her family's little plot of land. One day, as she hand-plowed the garden, her father came to her and announced she would soon be married. The man who was to be her husband was more than 30 years her senior, and her father was in debt to him. Her betrothed was a powerful witch doctor, famous for his strong and effective curses. Her father had sought his help for retribution against neighbors who had stubbornly encroached on the boundaries of his fields. The curse had apparently worked, and the neighbor's oldest son had died. Now she would be the payment that would settle her father's debt. She was 14 years old.

One night shortly after her marriage, the girl-bride had a dream. Her eyes danced as she explained to me, "A man dressed in light came to me and said, 'I am the Way, the Truth, and the Life. Follow Me.'² He showed me the wounds on His hands and feet, but they were healed. He told me that He is God and promised to rescue me. He said one day someone would come and tell me His name. I have been patiently waiting for you. Now I know His name! *Jesus! Jesus!*"

I sat in silent astonishment. I had gone to seminary, studied Islam and its holy book, the Qur'an, and learned the local language. I had tried my best to adapt to the culture so the gospel would be welcome. But no training could have prepared me for the shock I was feeling in that moment as I realized the exquisite resemblance between this Muslim woman's story and my own. And to think that God allowed *me* to be the one to tell her His name, when He could have chosen any other means to do so! Her story and mine were eternally, inextricably bound together in His bigger story. We had no doubt as we sat there in silent communion that we were known and loved by the Messiah.

A quiet voice said to my heart, *She knows what the pit looks like. She lived there too. And I came to rescue her like I rescued you. She mattered that much to Me.* As a young girl, I was exploited by sinful people, and shame became my master. On that dark night in the flickering light of a kerosene lantern, a woman sat beside me who had also been bound by shame from girlhood. Her childhood cut short, she had become enslaved to another person's sin. And Jesus came to her and promised her hope like He had to me. As I listened to her story, I was ushered into a sisterhood of common experience, common suffering, and common need for a Savior. Jesus had rescued us both from shame.

Perhaps you do not identify with shame. Maybe your story seems far from the experience of the Muslim woman you see on the news, weeping alongside the rubble that was once her home before a bomb blast tore it apart. You want to understand and help, but her world seems beyond your reach.

Do you stand like an explorer on the edge of a great chasm, wondering if it is even possible for you to cross the deep divide that appears to exist between you and the veiled woman you see in the grocery store? As she ushers her children down the street in your city, do you wonder inside if she worries about them like you do your own?

Does the Muslim girl next to you on the bus have dreams like yours? Is she an enemy? Can she see that you are afraid of her? Have you ever wondered if she is afraid of you?

What makes her feel honored? For that matter, what is honor in the first place? What is the difference between honor in your culture and honor in the Islamic culture? What does the Bible say about honor and its role in the restoration of women? How can you practically cross the chasm and build a sincere, authentic relationship with her? How can you overcome your feelings of fear and mistrust?

This book seeks to answer these questions and many more as we explore the Islamic worldview of honor and shame and their vital functions in our perceptions of Muslim women. An understanding of the honor and shame worldview will open doors to friendship and respect. Through its lens, you will become a more effective communicator of the gospel of Christ.

There is a Rescuer who knows each person by name, a Savior who sees each one. His name is Jesus, and He is moving and working in cultures around the world today. God has been restoring the honor of people throughout history. Jesus Christ, the Word of God incarnate, stripped shame of its power and secured our honor forever.

Our journey with Christ may be part of someone else's story. The challenges we have faced, the unique struggles and joys, the private triumphs and the cries of our hearts have all prepared us to come alongside Muslim women and live life with them. We have been equipped to share our common need for a Savior and the faithfulness of the One who rescues women from shame.

Nothing, in fact, separates us from our Muslim neighbors except for our experience of the redeeming power of Jesus Christ. We are not as different as we may think from the women we see behind the veil at the department store, at the soccer field, or on college campuses. Our needs and theirs are the same. Our solution and theirs are the same. The first step toward compassion, toward true comfort, is the realization of how much we are alike.

We serve a God who sees us. He sees every woman. He is the God who saw me, and the God who saw my Muslim friend. He came *Himself* to rescue each of us from shame, because we matter that much to Him.

Our desperation, our life's challenges, our dreams, and our hopes are exquisitely similar to those of Muslim women around the world. And our need for a Savior to rescue us from shame is identical. What is *not* identical, however, is how you both view the world. An understanding of her worldview will aid you greatly in sharing the love of the Messiah with her.

In the pages of this book, you will begin to learn exactly how to do that. You will hear stories of Muslim women from far and near, chronicles of their exceptional journeys from shame to honor. You will learn more about the predominant Islamic worldview of honor and shame and how it specifically impacts women. You will acquire tools to help you explain to your Muslim friend the way out of shame by using examples of honor from Scripture. Most of all, as your stories intertwine, you will be disarmed by the overwhelming love Jesus has for both of you.

❧ FOR FURTHER STUDY ❧

This book seeks to ignite the shame conversation by allowing readers to peer into gripping, true accounts of brave women across the globe who have taken the daunting journey from shame to honor in Christ. Some women in these pages are still on the journey. Others have fully embraced the honor Jesus gives and become His followers.

Where are you in the journey from shame to honor? The study questions at the end of each chapter are an opportunity for you to deepen your understanding of what the Bible has to say about shame as you examine your own position before God. For all who are hiding, may you hear His voice calling you by name, inviting you to become an insider, forever.

Part One

Honor
Understood

Identity Theft

All day long I feel humiliated and am
overwhelmed with shame.

PSALM 44:15 NET

SHAME: A FEELING

On a small, rural American community, a teenage girl quietly climbed through her bedroom window and leaped to the ground, running to the designated meeting spot. Hidden around a curve in the narrow road, the getaway car waited, its lights turned off in the darkness. A shadowy figure stood by the open trunk. The girl scrambled inside, her small bag landing with a thump over her shoulder. The door slammed shut and she lay in the blackness, trembling as the engine started and the car began its descent down the steep mountain. In this place where no light shone, a second life was hidden. The young runaway carried a tiny baby in her womb, unseen, unplanned, and unwanted.

A suffocating, heavy-as-lead, immobilizing feeling accompanied the inky darkness on that unforgettable night as the 16-year-old escaped in the trunk of a car. It was the feeling of shame, and it would not only guide this mother-to-be's choices but would define her baby's life. This powerful feeling would cause deep agony, painful rejection, and even attempted suicide. But, in the glorious end, it would eventually lead its bearers to find God.

SHAME: A POSITION

One burning-hot day many years later on the other side of the world, a young Muslim woman groaned with the pains of labor. She crouched in the door of her rough-hewn stone house, a silent scream welling up in her chest. The baby would not wait for the midwife. Her nine-year-old sister frantically gathered linens, eyes wide with alarm as she shouted for help. In a distant field, an old woman heard the screams, dropped her wood bundle, and ran toward the house to help.

A newborn's cry pierced the bright afternoon sky as the exhausted mother collapsed on the floor. Then suddenly the room fell silent as everyone stared at the infant boy still kicking in his newborn warmth. His face was horribly disfigured, marred by a cleft lip and palate. The villagers acted swiftly, following an unwritten set of rules. The new mother, father, and baby were ushered away under cover of darkness that same night, never to be seen in the village again. Their names were not spoken from that day forward.

That small family lost their position of belonging, or honor, on that fateful day. According to the beliefs of their culture, the birth of a child with a disability brought shame on their family, their village, and their tribe. The little family found themselves in a new social category that would define the rest of their lives. They were in a position of shame. This undesirable status would plunge them into poverty, addiction, and prostitution. But in the magnificent end, it would lead them to find the God who delivers from all shame.

SHAME: AN IDENTITY CRISIS

The experience of shame is much more than a devastating emotion or being ostracized by a group. In roughly one-third of the world, the part sometimes referred to as the "Western World," people tend to reduce shame to just one more negative emotion, a feeling they would prefer to avoid. In the other two-thirds of the world, also called the "Majority World," its eradication is pursued with vengeance.

In Western cultures, people often talk about overcoming *feelings* of shame. Shame is undesirable, to be avoided. It is a verdict, decided by uncompassionate people who pass judgment on others, sometimes without even knowing them personally. Twenty years after her infamous affair with Bill Clinton, Monica Lewinsky said, "Shame sticks to you like tar," describing her humiliating experience as being "like [having] every layer of my skin and my identity… ripped off."[1] Shame changed Monica Lewinsky's identity. She who once was considered *good* became a symbol of *bad*.

Though the affair was consensual, Lewinsky bore the greater burden of shame. Enduring intense public scrutiny, Monica Lewinsky became a household name. Bill Clinton, on the other hand, went on to finish his second term as president of the United States and left the White House with strong public approval ratings. Monica was not allowed the privilege of public forgiveness and approval. Instead, she was further ostracized and mocked. At times she considered ending her life.

In the two decades since the famous Starr investigation into the relationship, Monica has been bravely taking one step at a time toward healing and rebuilding her life. Today she is an inspiring champion for others suffering from shame. She has learned that shame does not have to dictate the end of her story.[2] Monica Lewinsky has sadly been forced to work through her shame in front of a world audience. For many Westerners, however, shame is something secret and hidden, dealt with on a very private level, if at all.

In Western culture, shame typically focuses on the individual. People are responsible for themselves. Honor or shame directly affect the person, not necessarily the group. As a result, there are resources for the individual that make shame recovery more possible. Self-help books, counseling, and support groups are available. Lewinsky was ostracized and removed from the political arena where she once had the potential to expand her career and position in that group. However, she has been able to rebuild and repurpose her life despite what happened to her 20 years ago.

In the majority world, where belonging to the group is more important than individual uniqueness, honor and shame are actual positions in society. Those who follow all the rules of such a collectivist community maintain positions of honor, or belonging, in the group. In collectivist cultures, the group's health matters more than that of any independent person. A focus on what is best for the individual is often viewed as strange or greedy to those peering in through an honor-shame worldview.

To remove shame from the group, the one shamed in that society may essentially disappear, never to reemerge. The 14-year-old village girl who obediently marries a man much older than her and bears him a son the following year holds a secure place of honor in her family and community. The 10-year-old boy who fasts during the Islamic holy month of Ramadan brings honor to his family and is deemed a faithful son who will one day grow up to be an honorable man. But those who break the rules, who do something separate or different, bring shame upon themselves, their families, and their communities. The girl who refuses a customary arranged marriage because she loves another is forced to flee from her family for fear of death. The woman who was wearing Western clothing instead of a burqa when she was sexually assaulted on the bus is blamed for the perpetrator's actions and later beaten by her mother for shaming the family.[3]

Honor is lost, and shame is the consequence. Sometimes the shift from honor to shame happens through no fault of one's own, as in the case of the young mother who gave birth to a child with a disability in a culture where deformity is deemed shameful and who was forced to move away from her village. Whether someone's deed is intentional or not, the one who diverts from the prescribed route of honorable behavior is forced into a position of shame.

Shame changes one's very identity. The one who once was *accepted* is now *rejected*. The *insider* is now an *outsider*. Those operating from a Western worldview usually seek to avoid shame at all costs because of the discomfort and destruction it brings to one's self-esteem. Many people from an honor-shame worldview, on the other hand, seek to avoid shame at all costs because it casts one outside of society and brings dishonor to the family, the tribe, and the nation. An encounter with shame, no matter the individual's culture or worldview of origin, impacts what that person believes about him- or herself.

Shame whispers its ancient lie: You are without value. You are rejected. You are dirty. You are bad. Some linguists suggest that our English word *shame* derived from a term meaning to "cover one's self."[4] Shame covers the truth about its bearer. Her value is no longer visible to her. Instead, she is covered in a lie about who she is.

SHAME'S BEGINNING

> God created humankind in his own image, in the image of God he created them, male and female he created them (Genesis 1:27 NET).

> Adam and his wife were both naked, and they felt no shame (Genesis 2:25).

There was a time when man and woman knew exactly who they were. They did not doubt, they were not confused, and they did not engage in comparison. Humanity was not on a quest for affirmation, for it needed none. Man and woman, created in God's image, walked with God and rested, satisfied in the deep assurance of their value. Shame did not exist. Their nakedness symbolized only their complete acceptance by God and each other.

This is the earliest picture of honor, the opposite of shame. Honor is essential to both relationship and belonging. Honor is unquestioned value. Honor is reciprocal. It is given and returned. Honor nurtures a sense of belonging, creating and facilitating deep, meaningful relationships. This is the rich and fulfilling environment into which man and woman were created, invited, and included in the circle of fellowship with God and each other. Honor was God's intention for humankind.

But when the first lie was whispered to the first woman, the honor of humanity was questioned.

> Now the serpent was more crafty than any of the wild animals the LORD God had made. He said to the woman, "Did God really say, 'You must not eat from any tree in the garden?'" (Genesis 3:1).

Man and woman began to scrutinize themselves. God's enemy challenged the very source of humanity's value. The serpent questioned the character of God and cast doubt on His character. "'You will not certainly die,' the serpent said to the woman. 'For God knows that when you eat from it your eyes will be opened, and you will be like God, knowing good and evil'" (Genesis 3:4-5). *You will be like God.* Man and woman were already complete, lacking nothing. Made in His image, they walked beside Him in fellowship and had all they needed for life. This was the essence of their identity. The lie hidden in the temptation was this: *You are not complete. He is actually against you. You are missing out. God cannot be trusted.*

When the man and the woman believed that lie, shame crept into the soul of humanity and began its insidious work of identity theft. Stealing woman's and man's identities, shame demanded they take their eyes off God and begin the long examination of themselves that would stretch through the ages, spreading its insecurity throughout all generations. Shame drew man and woman out of sacred fellowship and identification with God. They experienced the anguish of separation from the source of their identity. They found themselves outsiders in a lonely place. Many of their descendants would turn against God and each other.

Shame is a feeling of agonizing loneliness, a state of not belonging. Shame ostracizes its bearer and forces him away from relationship. He must rely upon himself. This leads to radical individualism and an impaired ability to form healthy relationships with others or with God. The one covered in shame has forgotten her created identity, the right given to her by the One who lovingly made her and instilled her with value. She has forgotten that she is made in the image of God, priceless and cherished. Shame has stolen her identity.

❧ FOR FURTHER STUDY ❧

1. Psalm 139 is a beautiful example of the intended relationship of belonging between God and people. Verse 1 reads, "You have searched me, LORD, and you know me." The Hebrew word here for "know" is *yada'*, and one primary element of its rich meaning is to understand. A crucial element of any trusting relationship is understanding. God demonstrates our belonging to Him, and His belonging to us, through this intimate term in the very first verse of Psalm 139. He understands you and me better than we understand ourselves. Read the psalm and underline each word or phrase that illustrates God's intimate knowledge of us.

2. Reading this psalm may be new or painful for some. Perhaps you have never felt known by God, or you may have been hurt by those who claimed to understand you and now you do not trust God or people. Read the psalm once more and ask God to show you today that He indeed knows you and loves you. Find a follower of Christ you can trust and ask her or him to pray with you for increased hope and healing.

2

The Cart Puller's Son

As it is written: "See, I lay in Zion a stone that causes people to stumble and a rock that makes them fall, and the one who believes in him will never be put to shame."

ROMANS 9:33

he American baby once hidden in the darkness of a runaway's womb grew into a teenager. Surrounded by lies, she came to believe she was inherently bad. The girl did not recognize this chief signature of shame: the belief that *I am bad.* She believed it was the truth about herself.

One day, in desperation, she sought to end her life. She had been extremely careful in her planning, ensuring that no one would be home that afternoon. As she lay on the bathroom floor, fiercely gripping the bottle of drugs that she believed held the key to escape, she heard a voice calling her name. *Who could it possibly be?* The door opened, and the face of the local pastor peered anxiously inside. "I knew I was supposed to come by your house today! When I saw the front door ajar, I sensed something was wrong and came inside," he exclaimed.

Front door ajar? She felt sure she had locked it. With strong arms her rescuer scooped the girl up and led her to safety, to *life.* The minister and his wife showed the girl empathy and compassion. They loved her exactly as they found her. She never had to perform for them.

But deep in her heart, empathy and compassion were not enough. They could not close the jagged wound in her identity. "Where were

You, God?" her soul cried in the dark to a heaven that seemed silent. *"Where were You* when shame was laid over me like a burial shroud?" A long year of sleepless nights passed as she wrestled with God. Then one humid, summer night, she sat under the stars and listened to a preacher. He was telling the story of a little girl who was unwanted, abused, and discarded. The similarities to her own story were breathtakingly cruel.

With eyes sparking like fireworks he demanded, "Where were You, God, when shame violated this little one of Yours?" The question was the same challenge she had been screaming to God in the most private place of her heart. The young woman bade her heart to be still as she waited for the man of God to continue his mesmerizing story. "Where were You, God?" he shouted once again.

The silence stretched long to make room for the answer. With a booming voice, the preacher described how Jesus answered his question. "'I was here,' cried the Savior. Suspended in agony on the cross, arms outstretched toward the shame-bringers, He declared with ragged breath, 'Father, forgive them.'"

With the preacher's words, the girl who was once a baby hidden in the trunk of a car was concealed no longer. Her hiding place was ripped open, and she sat naked and exposed. The final barrier between her and God hung in the air like a fragile bubble about to burst. She saw Jesus hanging there, saying those irrevocable words. She *heard* Him. And He looked right into her soul.

She finally had her answer. Where was God? He was dying for that shame as it suffocated her and stole her identity. He was giving His life to defeat it, securing her value forever. Now she had a new question to ponder. *What love is this?*

I was the American teenager sitting in the outdoor chapel that night. My question, "Where were You, God?" had been answered, and its shackles clattered to the famine-cracked ground of my heart. Life changed for me. I committed myself to the One who had given Himself to remove my shame. It was the least I could do for such a Savior.

As an adult, my journey of love took me across the sea, to live and serve in a culture completely different from my own. I was a member of a medical team that repaired cleft lips and palates free of charge. My job was to care for patients from beginning to end, remaining by their sides before, during, and after surgery. As a speech-language pathologist, I consulted with surgeons to decide what type of surgery would most benefit feeding and speech in the months following the procedure. I loved watching the transformation from defect to wholeness, shame to honor.

I sought out the shamed and gently showed them their value. One evening my husband and I knelt in prayer together on the cold tile floor of our crumbling house. We had settled in an ancient Arab city where donkeys still carried heavy loads down winding cobbled streets. That night my husband and I prayed for the hidden ones, the children born with facial deformities, concealed in the labyrinth of the city from the prying eyes of those who would cast them out in disgrace. The next morning would mark the first of a ten-day project in the city to do as many surgeries as possible. "Show them to us, Lord. Bring them out of hiding so that we may help them," we prayed.

On the other side of the city, a Muslim woman sat on the soft cushion that served as both couch and bed in the tiny room in which she and her husband and children lived. In her hands, Nida held a crinkled piece of paper, its edges worn and faded. She had carried the flyer in her pocket for several weeks now, pulling it out occasionally to marvel and daydream. In the center was a picture of a little boy, his face wide with a happy smile. It was a grin much like their little son's, whose expression of happiness was grossly disfigured by a gap stretching from the middle of his upper lip through the roof of his mouth. Below, in printed words she could not read, was information. But about what, exactly? The paper had been tacked to a wall outside the clinic and she had stolen it, hoping no one saw her tuck it inside her skirt. She showed it to her husband, and their curiosity grew.

They had been in the bustling city for almost two years. Her husband found work as a cart puller, and she had borne another son. The new baby's lips were smooth as silk, and he nursed effortlessly at her breast. The little one had been deemed worthy of the name of Islam's honored prophet, a name usually given to the firstborn son. His would be a life of honor, unlike their first son, whose birth defect had ushered their family into exile.

The paper she held in her hand must mean something, she thought. She cried out in the only way she knew, using familiar Islamic words of supplication. "God, please help my son. Have mercy on him and on us," she prayed. Her husband was dozing, exhausted from his day's work. The children cried for food and duty dragged her out of her reverie, back into the reality of her hard life.

The next afternoon, as my husband walked home from the market, he took a wrong turn by mistake and found himself in an unfamiliar neighborhood. As he turned to retrace his steps, a woman emerged from the narrow space between two overhanging walls. On her back, tucked snugly into a thick cloth, she carried a small child. He slept soundly, his mouth agape, unaware of the bump-bump of his mother's footsteps over the uneven stones, oblivious to the man who stood in the shadows astonished, staring at the child's bilateral cleft lip and palate.

Surely You are a great God who hears our prayers, my husband declared silently, his heart pounding. Within moments the mother and child reached the busy part of the market district, a place familiar to my husband, who followed a careful and respectful distance behind. As they passed a friend's small shop, he ducked quickly inside and asked for help approaching the mother in a way that would not frighten her. The merchant and other friends were glad to assist and within minutes made the introduction.

Such a delicate conversation could not be had in a public place. The mother did what her family's position of shame dictated: She invited the American man to leave the crowds and follow her to the privacy of her home where her husband waited for his daily afternoon coffee. They could speak about the boy's disability there with her husband present, away from the street gossip.

The sound of children crying punctuated the air as they drew near her street. The secluded neighborhood was infused with the stale smell that settles in the corners of neglected places. Ducking beneath a low arch, the unlikely trio came to a narrow door hanging from hinges lacquered by decades of cheap brown paint. "Excuse me, sir. I'll be right back," the young woman said softly to her guest, avoiding his eyes as she disappeared inside. From within, a harsh male voice mingled with her hushed tones before the door quickly opened again. "Please come in. You are welcome here," she beckoned.

Ushered into the humble home the mother shared with her husband, children, and other outcasts, my husband found himself surrounded by a dozen curious eyes. Word of his mysterious visit had spread quickly. People crowded around in the small courtyard, its broken mosaic walls and crumbling fountain providing a glimpse of former grandeur. It was now inhabited by those who had no other place to go.

My husband decided to explain himself without further delay. Swallowing hard and sending up a quick prayer for favor, he invited the family to bring their son to the hospital for help. The young mother froze for a moment and her eyes welled with tears. Reaching into her pocket, she removed the treasured piece of paper and showed it to him. "I cannot read," the mother quietly murmured. "Can you tell us what this says?"

My husband's hands trembled. The precious paper he held was a flyer advertising the same surgery project he was inviting her to the next morning! He read it slowly to the growing crowd.

Eyes that had stared with curiosity moments before grew wide with amazement and disbelief. The American's visit was no mere coincidence. A miracle had just occurred, and it rendered every witness speechless. Breaking the silence like a thunderbolt of praise, the mother cried, "God sees me and He sees my son!"

❧

Indeed, God does see the shamed. He not only sees them but He pursues them in their hidden places with the singular purpose of rescuing and restoring them. He saw me, the little American girl concealed in a life of disgrace and abuse. He saw my friend Nida, the Muslim mother who, through no fault of her own, bore a child with a disability and consequently lost her position in her family. And in His joyful, mysterious will, God wove our stories together so that we might never doubt His great love for us again.

The unseen are seen by God. The hidden are found. The shamed are rescued, and treasures covered in darkness are brought into the glorious light of His liberating love. Instead of shame, honor is their portion and inheritance. Over the years to come, Nida's son would not only receive surgery to repair his cleft lip and palate, but he and his parents would also receive the good news that there is a Messiah who removes shame.

This chapter has told a tale of two different cultures, two distinct worldviews. Nevertheless, it illuminates one universal experience of shame and restoration through Jesus Christ. The American baby who began life under the cover of shame was rescued and her identity as one valued and honored was restored. The small family whose baby was born with a deformity, who as a result were rejected and disgraced by their village, were rescued in the end, their true identity of value and honor revealed.

The One who died on the cross redeemed every man and woman from shame. That is exactly where He was when their identity was stolen. He was purchasing it back with His own life. This is the power of the Messiah who removes shame and restores honor.

❧ FOR FURTHER STUDY ❧

1. Read Hebrews 12:2. We see here that Jesus carried humanity's shame upon the cross and abolished its power forever. But for those bent and broken under shame's crushing weight, this can be hard to believe. Do you believe God has abolished the power of the shame you carry?

2. Read Isaiah 54:17 and answer the following questions.
   - What is the promised heritage of the servants of the Lord in this passage?
   - How can this promise be applied against the weapon of shame?

3. Read Isaiah 61:7-8 and answer the following questions.
   - What do God's people receive instead of shame?
   - How long does this gift last? Underline the "instead" phrases in this passage.
   - What does verse 8 say that God loves? Why is this important?

My Father's Name

I summon you by name and bestow
on you a title of honor.

ISAIAH 45:4

One afternoon over hot spicy tea, my friend Amal and I looked through my wedding album and chatted about our differing traditions. Suddenly she looked up at me and asked bluntly, "Why do you and your husband have the same last name? Do Christians marry their brothers? You and your husband look alike. This is *haram* (forbidden) in our culture."

I was still not used to the misperceptions my Muslim friends often had about me as a Western Christian and, laughing, I shook my head and explained. "Are you kidding? It's *haram* in my culture too! I would never marry my brother, even if I had one, which I don't. For us, when a woman gets married, she traditionally takes her husband's family name. She may choose to keep her own name or combine the two, but typically she takes her husband's last name when they are married."

Her eyes grew big as she scolded me. "Shame on you! You should never give away your father's name. How will you know who you are or where you come from?"

How will you know who you are or where you come from? Amal's question exposed the foundation of honor. Knowing who we are and where we come from is the core of personal identity. This knowledge leads either to honor or to shame, particularly for those from that worldview.

In patriarchal societies like Amal's, honor is traced back through the generations, and the fathers in particular. In Western culture, family-ascribed honor is becoming an antiquated idea, cast aside and nearly forgotten. I envied Amal's confident, secure knowledge of who her father was, who she was as his daughter. I never knew my father and had struggled with shame my whole life. I knew my Father God loved me, and as I learned who He was, I learned more of who I was. But the ache of not having that legacy from an earthly father still bothered me at times. When I thought deeply about Amal's question, I could only conclude that there is a higher source of honor, an ultimate genesis of every person's identity, a transcendent belonging that bonds humanity together and instills it with value. It was for this original honor I began to search.

As I continued to study and explore the subject of honor, I began praying earnestly about writing this book. Over the years, as I came to know and love countless Muslim women, the issue of honor and shame became paramount in my thinking and understanding of their journeys. It was always there, in every story. One evening before a women's training conference, I knelt with a friend and asked God, "If You want me to write about this, please confirm it to me. Make it undeniably clear to me."

The next morning after I finished teaching a session on honor and shame at the conference, a young woman from the Muslim world approached me, tears glistening in her eyes. "I never understood my worldview until you explained it to me today. Have you written a book about this?" I learned she had quietly been following Jesus for almost a year. Her search for honor in the Qur'an had been discouraging and confusing. Faithfully poring over Islam's holy book to prove a case for the honor of women, she had instead discovered a case against it. This bitter disappointment led her to examine women in the Bible and their interactions with God. The honor offered to women by Christ had persuaded her to follow Him and never look back. Now here she stood before me, asking to be taught more.

That conversation haunted me. A woman who had grown up in an honor-shame culture did not understand it herself? Intuitively, she clearly grasped the absence of honor in her life. This intuition, this drive, this God-created need in her compelled her to search for it. But she needed help to understand honor and its implications for her own identity and her own relationship with God.

As I thought about this more and began to engage the subject intentionally with women in my travels, in the states and abroad, I discovered that this young Muslim-background follower of Christ was not alone in her vague understanding of the concept of honor. Many women are aware of its absence, long for its presence, and are confused about what it actually *is*. The question women of all ethnicities and walks of life ask me again and again is, "What is honor, exactly?"

TRUE HONOR

What is honor? Is it a vague and noble idea from the past? Today's world events are forcing us to reconsider this dusty, seldom-used concept. It seems cultures from an honor-shame worldview are encroaching on freedom everywhere with their pursuit of honor. Suicide bombings claim the lives of innocent civilians; so-called honor killings continue to send shock waves across the media. But, we ask, how is killing innocent people honorable? How does such senselessness bring honor? We walk away confused, in anguish, more repelled than enlightened.

Ask ten people what honor is and you will get ten different answers. For some, the word *honor* suggests ideas like honesty, respect, or reliability. For others, honor is the use of certain social niceties like "please" and "thank you." For most Muslims, honor is an actual position in society. It is attached to a group, not an individual. Honor must be protected at all costs or one loses one's standing in the community.

But beneath it all, behind the different cultural and individual interpretations of honor, there must be an origin, an absolute truth. What is the genesis, the standard, from which honor as we now know it has issued?

This quest takes us to God's Word, the Bible, to give us the measuring stick for what true honor is. For God is the author and finisher of our faith (Hebrews 2:2), and He has created and crafted all original thought and truth (Psalm 111:10; John 16:13). Many counterfeits of

His work exist, and they confuse us and leave us angry and depressed. Humanity hungers for the satisfaction of true love, true justice, and true righteousness. When we encounter the toxic pretense of selfishness masquerading as love, corruption posing as justice, and hatred pretending to be righteousness, we are angry. The resulting lack of fulfillment becomes a catalyst for discouragement and depression. Hearts originally created to be nourished by God's truth are instead starved and deprived, leading to dysfunctional individuals, families, and communities. This is surely the case as we consider the many conflicting concepts of honor today. To understand the counterfeits we see, we must study the original.

> I summon you *by name* and bestow on you a *title of honor*, though you do not acknowledge me (Isaiah 45:4, emphasis added).

In the above verse, the Lord is speaking to Cyrus, whom He had called His "anointed" (verse 1). God knew Cyrus *by name*. He knew exactly who Cyrus was and who he was to become. Cyrus of Isaiah 45:4 was the Medo-Persian king who would one day conquer Babylon (539 BC) and allow the Jewish exiles to return to Jerusalem.[1] The prophet Isaiah predicted this 150 years before Cyrus was born.

As a Mede, Cyrus would not grow up personally knowing the God of Israel. He would instead worship idols.[2] Did he ever suspect that he was set apart by a God who knew him long before he was born? We know that he increased in power and man-given honor, to the point of such might that he successfully attacked and conquered the empire of Babylon alongside his uncle, the Persian king Darius (see Daniel 5). In quiet moments, when that great warrior removed his armor and laid down his sword, did he ever sense he was created for a higher honor, one that would glorify God and aid in the victory of a kingdom not of this world?

I find it fascinating that God chose a man of renowned worldly valor to display His greater glory. As mighty as Cyrus was, he would take on a new name, given by God Himself, and his former honor would be swallowed up in the unsurpassable glory of the Lord. Isaiah refers to Cyrus as God's shepherd (44:28) and the Lord's anointed (45:1). God bestowed on Cyrus a *title of honor*, also translated *surname*.[3]

The honor and legacy of the One giving that surname is described in God's address to Isaiah (45:5-6):

> I am the LORD, and there is no other; apart from me there is no God. I will strengthen you, though you have not acknowledged me, so that from the rising of the sun to the place of its setting people may know there is none besides me. I am the LORD, and there is no other.

The Lord's declaration in verses 5 and 6 was both personal and public. Personal, in that it spoke in quiet tones to Cyrus himself that the Lord was the only true God. Public, in that through Cyrus, the world would know there is no God apart from Jehovah. This is so often how the Lord interacts with us. He knows us by name, personally, intimately. He displays His faithfulness to us so that we may first know for ourselves that we are valued, that He has known us since before we were born, and that He is the only true God. Then He surnames us, making us part of His family, giving us a title of honor so that we may display His honor to the world. The duality of the personal and public declaration of God's honor in this passage is a beautiful picture of how original honor, that which comes from the one true God, addresses worldviews of both individualist and collectivist cultures. God offers unfading honor to both the person and the community through the Savior.

Cyrus pointed toward the Messiah who would one day come to set the captives free. The great Cyrus became the anointed shepherd. He is remembered by the honorable name given him by the Lord.

THE HONOR OF A NAME

Honor is all about a name. For Amal, who viewed the matter through her cultural lenses of honor and shame, the common Western practice of laying aside our father's name for our husband's signified laying aside the most important thing about us: our identity. Because in honor-shame cultures, honor is an actual position in society, and one's name is the most obvious identity marker by which society can assess one's position. Names carry honor or shame. People stand in positions of honor or shame based upon the reputation of their family names.

Jayson Georges, in *Ministering in Honor-Shame Cultures*, tells the story of one Middle Eastern man who, after becoming a follower of Christ, immediately began memorizing the genealogy recorded in Matthew 1:1-18. For this man, who had been shaped by an honor-shame culture, knowing his spiritual lineage was paramount to his new identity.[4]

If we think back, we might remember that our own Western culture once held similar values and consequent practices. Malcolm Gladwell, in his book *Outliers*, devotes an entire chapter to the subject of what he and sociologists call a "culture of honor" in the Appalachian mountains of the United States. The culture of honor, Gladwell purports, still exists today in the United States. In examining historical patterns of criminality centered around defending one's family in that region of the United States, he explains, "The so-called American backcountry states—from the Pennsylvania border south and west through Virginia and West Virginia, Kentucky and Tennessee, North Carolina and South Carolina, and the northern end of Alabama and Georgia—were settled overwhelmingly by immigrants from one of the world's most ferocious cultures of honor."[5]

My own beloved late father-in-law, born in a pocket of the United States still deeply engaged in honor culture practices, regularly bought jewelry for his wife and daughters from a small-town jeweler that had been owned and operated by the same family for more than four generations, spanning over 120 years. My husband and sons continue to do business there today, even though it requires a considerable drive to another town. The value of a family name and the honor it represents remain a guiding principle for many consumers in Western cultures today.

Although the West is largely individualistic, a perspective that places emphasis of the individual above the group, an honorable family name is not completely out of vogue.

Summoned by Name

The first element of original honor is that we are *summoned by name* by the Creator God who made us. No matter where we live, in what culture we grew up, or what our worldview is, the honor God designed always begins at the same place. We are summoned by name and accepted exactly as we are. God knows us by the name we bear right now, whether it is honorable or shameful by human standards. He knows all about us and calls us anyway, for He sees who we can be, not who we might falsely believe ourselves to be. That is true for the Muslim woman who practices magic to try to get her husband to love her, and it is true for the Western woman who is a single parent trying to raise her children alone. Wherever we are, we are fully known. And the One who loves us calls us by name and desires to restore honor to us.

Given a New Name

In Arabic, the word *'ayin* can mean spring or a well of water.[6] In some Arabic-speaking cultures, it is used colloquially to mean the spring or well from which a person comes. In other words, it references his family of origin. A pure and clean well is vital to life and health. This metaphor vividly illustrates the importance of an honorable family name in honor-shame cultures. A Muslim woman's badge of honor is her father's name. It reflects her value, her purity, her worth, and her dependability. Culturally speaking, she does not stand alone; she is backed by the strength and valor of a righteous and honorable father. His behavior within the four walls of her home might not seem honorable to a Westerner peering in, or even to his daughter who suffers abuse at his hand. Despite that, as a man and the leader of the household, he possesses positional honor within the Islamic worldview that transcends his personal behavior.

Not only does our heavenly Father know our names, He bestows upon us a new name, His own family name. He confers on us a title of honor. We are given an honorable identity. He has imputed to us the honor that is His very own. Before we acknowledge Him, He has already begun His pursuit of us, calling us by name, to bestow upon us His own name. We become His, and like my friend Amal, we can wear the name of our father with great pride. By this honorable name we are given a status of honor, value, and strength. We are loved. Our position is secure.

I know Muslim-background women whose fathers were loving and kind. I know others who were deeply harmed by their fathers. For some, the discovery of the Father heart of God in the Bible transformed their wounds and became the signature of their healing journey.

Glorifying God's Name

Third, and perhaps most astonishing of all, He extends the honor of receiving a new name to every person through His Son, Jesus Christ, regardless of our own merit. But this raises the question: Why would God give us an honorable name—His own name—even though we have not acknowledged Him? The answer to this question reveals the deepest purpose of honor. "I will strengthen you, though you have not acknowledged me, so that from the rising of the sun to the place of its setting people may know there is none besides me. I am the LORD, and there is no other" (Isaiah 45:5-6). The purpose of honor is so that the Lord can be known throughout the earth. We carry His name so the world can know He is the Lord and there is no other. We, His name-bearers, reflect His honor to the world.

The concept of honor is an innate part of the Christian's identity, though it is little understood by many in the West today. Genuine, God-given honor brings life and restoration, purpose and identity to its bearer. Honor is the exchange of our shameful identity for an entirely new and clean one, the surname of the God of heaven and earth. We exchange our weakness for the totality of His strength, and we bear His name to an estranged humanity. Honor always lifts its bearer up from a place of denigration to a place of worth.

Amal was right in a way. If we do not know our father's name, how will we know who we are or where we come from? Women across the Muslim world are waiting to know the Father God who calls them by name, offering them honor in place of shame. The honor Amal longed for originates in God, was fulfilled in Jesus Christ, and is intended for every person.

⚙ FOR FURTHER STUDY ⚙

1. Read Isaiah 61:7 again. In this passage we are promised that God will remove our shame and, in its place, we will receive an honorable inheritance from our heavenly Father. Identify three characteristics of the inheritance we receive as part of God's family.

2. The Qur'an (the Muslim holy book) directs that sons receive an inheritance equivalent to that of two daughters,[7] meaning males receive twice as much as females. Compare the following portion promised to women in the Qur'an with the inheritance the Lord promises to all His followers, including women, in Isaiah 61:7.

   > Allah charges you in regard with your children: a son's share is equal to the share of two daughters; if the [children] are [only] daughters and two or more, their share is two thirds of the legacy, and if there is only one daughter, her share is half [of the legacy]; and each of the parents inherit one-sixth of the legacy if the deceased had children, and if the deceased had no children and the parents are the only heirs, the mother inherits one-third; if the deceased had brothers, the mother inherits one-sixth; [all this is] after executing the will and settling the debts of the deceased. You do not know which of your parents and children benefit you the most. This is Allah's injunction; surely Allah is All-knowing, All-wise (Surah Nisa' 4:11).

   > Instead of your shame you will receive a double portion, and instead of disgrace you will rejoice in your inheritance. And so you will inherit a double portion in your land, and everlasting joy will be yours (Isaiah 61:7).

3. What does Isaiah 61:7 demonstrate about the value of men

and women to God? Are they equally valuable to Him and equally worthy of inheritance?

4. How could Isaiah 61:7 be used to open a conversation to the gospel around the topic of inheritance with Muslim women?

Burn Away the Shame

Now Sarai, Abram's wife, had borne him no children. But
she had an Egyptian slave named Hagar; so she said to
Abram, "The Lord has kept me from having children. Go,
sleep with my slave; perhaps I can build a family through her."
Abram agreed to what Sarai said. So after Abram had been
living in Canaan ten years, Sarai his wife took her Egyptian
slave Hagar and gave her to her husband to be his wife.

GENESIS 16:1-3

COUNTERFEIT HONOR

I met Hamida on a gray afternoon among throngs of people crowding around a chain-link fence. They had journeyed from near and far by car, bus, train, or on foot. Now they waited and hoped to receive life-changing surgeries at our temporary hospital project. Hamida stood regal and unmoving in the midst of this sea of anxiety. The bright orange *melhfa* she wore swirled and enveloped her in the color of sunset, partially concealing her face from view. When she sat across from me two hours later, I understood why. Women from her area did not typically cover their faces with the large rectangular cloth that served as part dress and part head covering, but today Hamida's melhfa served as her hiding place.

The left side of Hamida's face was completely disfigured by an ugly scar that dripped cruelly down her neck. When I asked her about it, she whispered, "My mother-in-law did it with boiling oil." I pressed her further for the reason. Looking down at her henna-dipped fingernails, she answered, "She said I deserved it. To burn away the shame I brought to her family. I cannot get pregnant." Hamida refused to elaborate further, but quickly added, "I walked many miles so you can help me." I wondered if her family knew she had come. I doubted it. The shame of barrenness she carried could never be burned away with her mother-in-law's horrible act of counterfeit honor.

Hamida had grown up believing that a woman's value was dependent upon having a child. In her culture, having children brought honor to the family, particularly if those children were boys. Because Hamida could not get pregnant, she believed she had no value. When her mother-in-law punished her with boiling oil, seeking to remove the shame Hamida had brought to the family, Hamida believed she deserved it.

We grow up looking around us to learn what is true about us. We listen to what is spoken to us to form an intricate belief system of who we are. Therefore, the belief of countless women about who they are is based on lies. God never intended this counterfeit.

But since the first, tantalizing, beautiful, tempting lie was whispered to the first woman and man, the counterfeit grew to such prominence that entire cultures have based their belief systems, and therefore the treatment of their women, on lies. The truth about female creatures is that they were made in God's image and given equal value to males. But this truth has become obscure in some cultures. Distorted truth makes reality unbearable for many women.

THE BURDEN BEARERS

Corruption always begins with a lie. Honor has been corrupted and distorted, and women are most often its burden bearers. Instead of bearing the identity of one loved by God, cherished and accepted, women like Hamida shrink back into the shadows of shame, hidden and exploited. The truth that they are known and valued by God is concealed by the lie that God is a harsh and distant judge, condemning them to a position of lesser worth than their male counterparts.

Such women bear the burden of accomplishing their own honor and salvation, with no guarantee of success. A Muslim woman can pray five times a day her entire adult life, give alms to the poor, bear strong sons for her husband, fast during Ramadan, and make the *hajj*, or pilgrimage, to the holy city of Mecca, yet still not be sure of God's forgiveness.[1] In the *hadith*, a collection of sayings traditionally attributed to Muhammad, the prophet of Islam said, "I looked at Paradise and found poor people forming the majority of its inhabitants; and I looked at Hell and saw that the majority of its inhabitants were women."[2] Such a deprecating statement by the prophet himself leaves many Muslim women silently despairing, longing for a different existence. God seems a harsh and distant judge, and they often feel far below His notice or approval. Their shoulders stoop lower and lower beneath the burden of corrupted honor.

IDENTIFYING COUNTERFEIT HONOR

Understanding the origin and purpose of true biblical honor gives us a standard by which to recognize and expose counterfeit honor. As we saw in the last chapter, original honor involves three key elements: We are known by name *by God Himself*; we are given value *by God Himself*; and this knowing, this value, is extended to every person regardless of merit. It cannot be earned. It was only accomplished through the sacrifice of God Himself through His own appointed means, God the Redeemer, Jesus Christ.

True honor is antithetical to the idea that rules and right behavior assure acceptance by a higher power. The religion of Islam dictates rules and behavior as a means to God's favor. Follow the rules and gain acceptance. Break the rules and you are rejected. Counterfeit honor demands careful adherence to laws made by man. True honor invites relationship with a God who comes near and whispers our name, bestowing us with unmerited worth simply because He loves us. Counterfeit honor breeds either self-righteous pride or hopeless despair, according to one's performance. True honor fills the heart with relief and wonder, healing our brokenness and setting us truly free. We are accepted. We are loved. We are known. This is the gift of original honor.

Counterfeit honor separates and condemns. It has been suggested by Jayson Georges that counterfeit honor, or "bad honor," occurs when people are given respect for the wrong reasons.[3] They demand it by robbing others of dignity, and it always comes at the expense of other people. Counterfeit honor is temporary, destructive, and contradicts God's purposes.

The Bible describes counterfeit honor as pride or idolatry that inevitably ends in shame. *Pride* is the term used when honor is ascribed to one's self, as in the instance of King Uzziah in 2 Chronicles 26:16: "After Uzziah became powerful, his pride led to his downfall. He was unfaithful to the LORD his God, and entered the temple of the LORD to burn incense on the altar of incense." Uzziah believed himself to be honored, or above, the regulations given to Moses in Exodus 30 that dictated only the anointed priest could enter the temple of the Lord to burn incense at the altar of incense. This self-focused honor led to Uzziah's demise.

Idolatry, another form of imitation honor, is worship given to others. The first and second commandments in Exodus 20:3-4 clearly forbade God's people from worshipping anyone other than the Lord. Yet repeatedly the Israelites worshipped other gods and followed the practices of the surrounding nations, resulting in exile and separation from God's presence (2 Kings 17:6-20). The evidence of false honor is destruction and distance from God. Personal identity, personal worth, rights, safety, health, and life—all are victims of the destruction counterfeit honor produces. This is in direct contrast to the new identity, value, justice, safety, and security true honor brings.

Much of the violence from the Muslim world that we observe in the media is a result of counterfeit honor. This fraudulent imitation goes hidden and unseen by us in the lives of many Muslim women. Like any false promise, it leads to the opposite of its purported hope. Counterfeit honor, ironically, leads directly to shame.

God's Intention

Hamida's shame resulted from this false honor. But it did not start with Hamida. Her mother-in-law and the women before her believed the lie that a woman is only valuable if she can bear a child, particularly a son. They believed that honor could be restored through their own actions, however horrific and inhumane. In their worldview, the weight of honor rested entirely upon them. This is a burden no woman was created to carry.

This belief system is completely counter to the gospel message and God's original intention. The truth is that no one, woman or man, can restore honor to fallen humanity. Such restoration requires the authority and power of a name higher than any other name and the exercise of sovereignty that overrides all earthly authority. This sovereignty is found in Christ, in the name of the God of the universe who bestows His very own honorable name upon His children through His grace.

Counterfeit honor first emerged in the Garden of Eden. God's enemy sought honor and exaltation for himself above the Creator. With enticing words, he persuaded the first man and woman to seek honor for themselves over God. He convinced them to reject God's way and choose their own. They did not know this devastating choice would constrain all of humanity within the bonds of deception. The construction of the false honor idol began with that first fateful bite of mistrust in a loving God. With this ruinous decision came an inheritance of counterfeit honor that has been passed down through every generation of humanity since. As a result, Adam and Eve hid, becoming the first humans to experience shame (see Genesis 3:8).

Counterfeit honor leads to more shame and destruction, resulting in greater distance from God. True honor releases people from shame. It heals and restores the wounded. God's honor draws us nearer to Him. It pursues us and draws us into relationship with God. Authentic honor is imputed by God to those who follow His Son, Jesus. It rebuilds broken hearts and shattered lives. It preserves and protects God's people.

Honor is expressed in diverse and complex ways across world cultures. But honor originates with the author and finisher of our faith, the God who calls us by name and bestows on us His own name, making us part of His family. This is our starting point for understanding exactly what honor is and what it is not.

❧ FOR FURTHER STUDY ❧

1. Genuine, God-given honor brings life and restoration, purpose, and identity to its bearer. True honor's purpose is to bring glory to God. Counterfeit honor, on the other hand, is temporary and leads to more shame, more destruction, and greater distance from God. It exploits others for the wrong reasons and is contrary to God's purposes. With this contrast in mind, read the following passages from the book of Esther and consider the questions that follow.

2. Read Esther 1:4-19. The king demanded that Queen Vashti honor him by parading her beauty before him and his men at a drunken banquet. It was against the custom of the Persians for women to appear in public, therefore King Xerxes was actually dishonoring the queen by asking her to do this. In response, she refused.

   • Was the king practicing true honor or counterfeit honor?

   • What was the result?

3. Read Esther 4:11; 5:1-3; 7:3-10. Verse 11 informs us that according to Persian court customs of the time, Esther's approach to the king's presence without a summons was highly dishonorable, punishable by death.

   • Although Esther risked her life to dishonor the king this way, how was she actually demonstrating true honor?

   • What was the result?

I Never Knew
I Could Be Clean

The teachers of the law and the Pharisees brought in a
woman caught in adultery. They made her stand before
the group and said to Jesus, "Teacher, this woman was
caught in the act of adultery. In the Law Moses commanded
us to stone such women. Now what do you say?"

JOHN 8:3-5

Babies were snugly tucked into colorful slings on their backs as the women gracefully balanced handwoven baskets with food and cookware atop their heads. They had walked for days to hear the Christian teach from the Bible. Under sprawling acacia trees, they sat and settled on the dusty African ground, leaning in to hear the words of life.

Hours later, as the sun began its quiet descent toward late afternoon, the drums and singing began. With simple words and exquisite harmonies, the worshippers poured out praise to the Messiah. The celebration was rare and priceless.

Afterward, as nightfall settled over the landscape, the fire burned low, its embers glowing a soft orange under the starry sky. Soft rustling and murmurs could be heard as women settled down for sleep on their thin *lessos*, the vast sheet-like cloths they wore over their skirts.

A wizened old lady slowly made her way to the teacher still sitting by the fire. "Thank you." Her words were quiet, barely above a whisper.

The teacher waited. The old lady's face, already lined with years of hard work, labored to form more words. "I always knew I could be forgiven. But I never knew I could be *clean*." Her eyes shone with a new light, the light of revelation and freedom.

Sin has soiled the soul of mankind since the first dirty lie in Eden. It flung its filth on the clean, pure soul of man and woman and stole their sense of value. Man and woman would never again, on their own, be able to make their hearts completely clean. Honor matters because everyone, deep inside, needs to know he or she can be made clean.

Behind the drama of humankind's downfall was One who preserved the value of life. He never forgot. With His own life, God protected the value of the life He had created. He rose that moment and began His longest journey: the quest to restore worth to the human soul, to make hearts *clean again*. *Clean* is merely a common word for holy. The holy Creator God chased after mankind. His heart was consumed with purpose and longing to make them holy again so that they might be reunited with Him.

The honor God gives is paramount because it promises restored relationship with Him. The universal human desire to have a heart clean, restored, and holy can help us understand the compulsion that drives entire cultures to see the world through the lenses of honor and shame.

Honor goes by many ordinary names: *clean, accepted, loved, good.* And around the world, humankind made in God's image longs to be called by those honorable names. A little girl who feels alone in a prison of abuse, as I once was, longs to be *loved*. The young woman trafficked for her body wonders if she will ever be *clean* again. The man who wrestles with his addiction to pornography wonders if he can ever be the *good* husband and father he wants to be.

The alcoholic fights with all his might to be *clean*, knowing down deep that his problem is more than liquor. The young jihadist straps a bomb to his chest, hoping with all his might that with his sacrifice Allah will finally call him *accepted*. The Muslim woman in the workplace, marching for her rights, cries for *acceptance* and *value*. The desire for honor is a cry for all of these things, and it rises from the depths of the human soul. This is why honor matters.

THE UNIVERSAL EXPERIENCE OF SHAME

We have all been touched by what Werner Mischke calls "the shadow of shame,"[1] regardless of our gender, geography, or ethnicity. Shame is a universal experience. Shame steals our sense of value. It silences our hope. Shame stalks us throughout our lives like a stealthy predator seeking to rob us of joy. Shame was never our intended inheritance. We were created for honor, created to bear the name of the holy God who intentionally infused us with value and purpose. As long as we live in the shadow of shame, we are spiritually and emotionally debilitated, incapable of freely running the path intended for us.

That was certainly true for me, at least in the early years of my life. Born outside of marriage to a teenage runaway, I lived life outside the honor code from the beginning. Honor is a position in society, a place of acceptance within a societal group such as a family, team, or tribe. An illegitimate child who reminded my family of their disgrace, I was born into a position of shame. Reminded regularly that I was different, bad, and unacceptable, I grew up not merely questioning my value but believing I had none. It was in the pages of my childhood Bible, given to me by my great-grandmother when I was seven years old, that I read about honor for the first time. Hidden away in my bedroom, I would pore over the Old and New Testament stories of people for whom God had fought. They were people He had rescued and given new names and new joy. I was smitten with this love story of honor. Over the years it became my own story. Shame was replaced with honor, won for me by a God who fights for the broken.

Years later I met Nida, who intimately understood what it was like to have shame put upon her by circumstances beyond her control. In the years after her family's providential meeting with my husband, her son underwent three different cleft lip and palate surgeries. I celebrated with her as other babies were born, each perfectly formed. Her little family grew, and so did her hunger to know Christ.

Regardless, shame still cast its shadow on Nida's family even as their circumstances improved. The only work her husband could find was to push carts full of heavy loads across the uneven cobbled streets. He began to grow angry and resentful and blamed Nida for their harsh circumstances. It was her fault, he regularly reminded her, that their firstborn son was born deformed. Nida was to blame for their expulsion from the family and the village. Nida was blamed for the family's position of shame.

Her husband's beatings became so violent that one afternoon his blows knocked her front tooth out. She lay on the floor, wishing for a final strike that would take her out of this life. Her beautiful baby girl crawled toward her, crying and seeking the comfort of her breast, while her two small boys cowered fearfully in a corner. Nida's husband stormed out of their small one-room dwelling, slamming the door fiercely behind him.

Several hours later, he returned drunk and boisterous. Allowing the full fury of his rage to blow, he forced Nida out into the dark loneliness of the night, slamming the door behind her. Nida crumpled into a heap in a cobbled alcove, shame whispering to her soul that she had no value.

I passed her on the street one day, not far from my house. I had been searching for her for months. She had disappeared from my life without a trace. But on this bright day, there she was, and our eyes met as we crossed paths on a busy street. We were near my neighborhood, so I invited her to come home with me for tea. She accepted my invitation with one little son tagging behind and another in her arms.

Nida was stripped of pride and had nothing to gain or lose that day. She was raw and real, honest and humble, broken and truly poor in spirit. Devoid of self-pity, she sat before me, an exposed soul. I searched her eyes in vain for the self-dignity and pride I had once seen sparking in her like electricity. I saw nothing in her this day but brokenness, and it alarmed me. I leaned close and asked gently, "What has happened to you, Nida?"

She looked at me resigned, all the fight in her gone, and replied wearily, "I have nothing to hide now. I will tell you everything."

Tears streamed down her face as she explained to me her disappearance from my life. After her husband chased her out of the small room they shared for shelter, she fled to her father's home. He refused to give her refuge, blaming her for not pleasing her husband. She had to find work, and the only work she could find was prostitution. When her husband learned of her employment, he allowed her to see her children again if she would give him her income.

"Now I have no one," she said. "I wait on God." I sat there and grieved with her for a long time, neither of us speaking. It's okay to do that. To be so grieved by your friend's grief that you sit in silence with her for a while. After the silence, as we wiped our tears, I shared with her the story from John 8 of the *Injil* (New Testament) about the woman caught in adultery. Her eyes grew large as I related Jesus's bold challenge to the men to throw the first stone. I watched Nida carefully as a light leapt forth in her eyes. She said to me, "I need you to read the whole story out of the *Injil* itself. I need to memorize this!" Up until that moment I had been telling the story. Nida wanted to hear the official version to make sure it was really true.

I retrieved my *Injil* from the high shelf in our dining room. According to cultural practice, the Word of God was given the highest place in the room, positioned carefully upon an ornately decorated wooden stand. I held the holy book in my hands and read the story of John 8 aloud. As I spoke, the despair in Nida's eyes transformed to hope. Nida saw herself in the story. Ashamed and accused, cast in the dust. Made clean again, forgiven, honored. She ran to Jesus that afternoon and worshipped Him, giving her life to Him fully, while tears of joy dropped down her face like rain. I was disarmed by the simplicity of her acceptance. I expected more of a fight. After all, I had known her for a long time and had been sharing truth with her with no apparent results. But today was different. She had been completely broken since I had seen her last. "I want to follow Him, because He knows me," she declared, right there in my little sunroom, sitting on a hard, wooden chair while the sun streamed over us like joy beams.

Nida did become a follower of Jesus that day, and she took the good news of His salvation back to her community. Today Nida lives outside the city gates, in a crumbling area of town designated for garbage and "unclean" women and children. Nida is sharing her story of honor and shame with her neighbors. She has memorized several books of the Bible. In that place, she has brought God's burden bearer, Jesus Christ, who suffered outside the gates for every man and woman. Her children are growing up to know Jesus from a young age. They will not need someone else to tell them about Him. Their mother did. All because she identified with this woman whom Jesus did not condemn to a life of shame but set free instead.

Nida's story reminds us of another One who went outside the gates, experiencing the shame of expulsion and rejection so that all who know shame might be redeemed.

> The high priest carries the blood of animals into the Most Holy Place as a sin offering, but the bodies are burned outside the camp. And so Jesus also suffered outside the city gate to make the people holy through his own blood. Let us, then, go to him outside the camp, bearing the disgrace he bore (Hebrews 13:11-13).

Our God and Redeemer understands the universal human experience of shame. He not only understands it—He has abolished it. Many women today from every people group harbor the belief that they are dirty, unworthy, and deserving of rejection. Jesus pursues them to the depths of their darkness and shame. No place is beyond the reach of His relentless love. The ground of shame's prison quakes with the thundering of His approach. Freedom and honor are His mission, and all who will be found by Him will be saved.

A PAGEANT OF HONOR

The importance and purpose of honor is perhaps most elaborately illustrated in the Old Testament book of Isaiah, chapter 61. It reads like a magnificent pageant, with the sovereign God Himself walking among a fragmented and suffering humanity, restoring the shamed and bestowing them with approval and favor.

The Spirit of the Sovereign LORD is on me, because the
LORD has anointed me to proclaim good news to the poor.
He has sent me to bind up the brokenhearted, to proclaim
freedom for the captives and release from darkness for the
prisoners, to proclaim the year of the LORD's favor and the
day of vengeance of our God, to comfort all who mourn,
and provide for those who grieve in Zion—to bestow on
them a crown of beauty instead of ashes, the oil of joy
instead of mourning, and a garment of praise instead of a
spirit of despair. They will be called oaks of righteousness,
a planting of the LORD for the display of his splendor...
Instead of your shame you will receive a double portion,
and instead of disgrace you will rejoice in your inheritance.
And so you will inherit a double portion in your land, and
everlasting joy will be yours (Isaiah 61:1-3,7).

The Redeemer of Isaiah 61 comes to proclaim the good news of
honor. He demonstrates the ministry of honor as He kneels by the
brokenhearted, tenderly binding up their wounds. We can hear honor
in His cry of freedom to the captives who are lying shackled and
chained. He gently leads those hiding in the darkness of disgrace into
the light of truth and whispers worth into their souls. He rises with
a mighty shout to proclaim the year of the Lord's favor and the day
of His vengeance, for with honor comes vengeance. God is the great
Avenger, the One who justly punishes those who have harmed His
children. Honor exposes injustice and vanquishes the power of shame.
Honor returns to the shamed what is rightfully hers. The God of Isaiah
61 is a tender, healing warrior, fighting to restore honor to His broken
people. Honor rebuilds, restores, and renews the human soul.

❧ FOR FURTHER STUDY ❧

1. In this chapter we learned that *holy* is another word for clean. Sin has soiled human hearts, and men and women cannot make their souls clean or holy again on their own. God sent His Son, Jesus, to restore relationship between God and humanity. Jesus reinstated genuine honor by taking upon Himself the shame of mankind. With this in mind, read the following passage and reflect on how Jesus accomplished this.

2. Read John 12:12-13. Here we see another pageant of honor as Jesus enters Jerusalem.

   - What are the elements of honor in this scene?
   - How is honor demonstrated and to whom?

3. Expecting the Messiah to be an earthly king, the people cast their garments and palm branches to exalt Christ and usher Him into a human kingdom.

   - How was God's plan different from human expectation?
   - How is the human concept of honor different from God's?

4. Read John 12:14 and answer the following questions:

   - In what posture does Christ put Himself to receive the honor being paid Him?
   - How was this different from the way an earthly king would enter a city?

5. In the culture of Jerusalem both then and now, donkeys are regarded as dirty work animals. The word *donkey* is a word used to insult others. How might Jesus's entrance on a donkey have challenged the view of shame and honor by the people of that time and culture?

6

We Wanted to Matter to God

> You know that it was not with perishable things such as silver or gold that you were redeemed...but with the precious blood of Christ, a lamb without blemish or defect.

1 PETER 1:18-19

I couldn't understand why the more we talked about Jesus, the more outwardly pious my friend Imani became. When I first met her, she rarely bothered to cover her hair with a headscarf. She wore shirts not long enough to conceal her hips, and she didn't seem to care about her evening prayers. Her mother, on the other hand, adhered to strict rules about attire and was never seen in public without her full *hijab*, allowing only her eyes to peek out. The *hijab*, a head covering worn in public by some Muslim women, seemed to hold no appeal for Imani. As a young college student, Imani did what she wanted to do, following the fashionable trends trickling in from Europe.

Imani was downright excited about Jesus. She wanted to learn everything I could tell her about Him. Peppering me with questions, her eyes sparkled with zeal and curiosity. "No one has ever told me these things before! I did not know how powerful He was!" she would exclaim as we wound our way down the cobbled, narrow streets of the old city.

The more we talked about the Messiah, the more Imani changed,

9

at least on the outside. She suddenly began wearing a headscarf. I had learned that I could determine how religiously conservative a friend was in that particular culture by the way she wore her headscarf. From what I could tell, the tighter the scarf, the more devout the girl. At least, that is how it seemed in public. Imani bought a special headband to wear under her scarf to make sure no unruly hair escaped. The scarf fit as tightly as possible. She was making a public statement of her serious devotion to God.

While we had once met for afternoon walks in the park wearing casual but conservative clothes, now Imani arrived in her full hijab. And we never met during prayer time because the new Imani now prayed faithfully all five prescribed prayer times daily. When we did meet, the discussions about Jesus grew, and we began to read the Bible together.

I was confused. Why was my friend becoming more Muslim the more she learned about Jesus? It took me a long time to realize we were experiencing conflicting beliefs of how one attained honor before God. Honor looked one way in her life, another in mine.

ASCRIBED HONOR AND ACHIEVED HONOR

Social anthropologists suggest there are many "honors" in the world. Across world cultures, honor is understood and expressed in many different ways. However, the two universal ways honor is received or bestowed can be explained as ascribed honor and achieved honor.[1] The two paradigms provide a helpful framework through which we can begin to recognize and understand honor. No matter the varying definitions of honor around the world, humanity approaches honor through these two basic avenues, though at any given time in history, one might be more prominent than another in a culture, particularly in that culture's approach to God.

As a follower of Christ, I believe my value to God comes from outside myself. By declaring me valuable, my Savior Jesus did for me what I could not do for myself. Not only did He confirm that I matter, He redeemed me and sealed my worth with His shed blood on the cross. When I placed my trust in Him, He purged my heart of sin and made me a new creation. His actions, His efforts, and His obedience established my honor before God. I bear His name now and I belong to His family. Nothing can separate me from His love.

As a Muslim, my friend Imani, however, believed that she had to work hard to win the approval of God. Her honor and value to Him had to be earned by her own actions, efforts, and obedience. Worth before God depended on her behavior. The more she heard about Jesus, the more she wanted His acceptance. So she behaved in the only way she knew how to: in accordance with her own set of religious rules, which dictated how to get God's approval. She dressed carefully to demonstrate her chastity and faithfulness. She prayed more. The rules of Islam became her roadmap to honor. For her, value to God had to be earned. For me, it could never be earned by my own actions. Rules had been abolished by Jesus's sacrifice.

We did not know it, but we were exemplifying the two primary human approaches to honor: ascribed honor and achieved honor. Ascribed honor is honor received through no action of one's own. It can come through one's bloodline, family, or birth order. Ascribed honor can also be determined by the amount of wealth, land, or power one's family has.

Achieved honor, on the other hand, can be earned. The United States of America has been built largely on this glittering possibility. Men of no position back in their native countries could come to America and work their way to positions of achieved honor. Such an opportunity was not available to them at home in cultures where one's ascribed honor, or that into which one was born, dictated one's path in life.

When I became a follower of Jesus, I understood that through Christ, honor and worth had been ascribed to me in the eyes of God. Jesus accomplished that, not me. I further understood that I could not accomplish it on my own because I am an imperfect human who falls short of the holiness of God. In my lack, God provided a perfect Savior to stand in my place. When I accepted God's given sacrifice of Jesus Christ for my own shame and sin, I gained a position of belonging in the family of God and a guaranteed place in heaven one day. Not only that, I entered into an intimate relationship with God and began to experience His great love for me. I was ascribed with the honor of belonging to God like a child belongs to his or her father.

As a Muslim, Imani believed that her honor and worth before God depended on her own ability to achieve it by following all the rules of Islam. In order to gain God's approval and live a good and responsible life, Muslims are exhorted to satisfy the five pillars of Islam: shahada (faith), salat (prayer), zakat (charity), saum (fasting), and hajj (pilgrimage to the Islamic holy city of Mecca). Beyond those five global admonitions, Imani's culture has an abundance of religious rules pertaining specifically to women. Outward appearance, such as wearing the *hijab*, is only one of the ways women demonstrate their faithfulness. For even the most devout woman, though, heaven is never guaranteed. After all their efforts to please God, many Muslim women report that they still feel He is distant and does not really know them. They are trapped in the belief that they must achieve honor before God through their own behavior.

THE HUMAN APPROACH TO HONOR

A person's worth in the eyes of her community is determined by a number of different cultural rules. Some people believe that honor starts on the inside, a feeling that grows until it leads to behavior that can be observed by the community on the outside. An example would be Mother Teresa. As a young girl, she was drawn to serve the poor. Her honorable desires led to honorable behavior that has been recognized by the world.

Others, such as some Bantu tribes of Sub-Saharan Africa, see honor as an opinion the community has about a person, which is then projected onto that individual. An example of this would be the head male in a Bantu village. When the crops fail, the villagers expect him to provide goats to appease the spirits and restore harmony. As the eldest leader of the group, he is socially and culturally responsible to be generous because of his position as most the honored (wealthy, oldest, wisest) leader.

It should be mentioned that these examples are but two of the many ways humanity pursues worth, but they merit examination in our discussion of ascribed honor versus achieved honor. The first illustration begins with the individual and is eventually recognized (ascribed) by the community. The other begins with the community and is accomplished (achieved) by the individual. Each of these approaches to honor is incomplete because each begins and ends in human wisdom.

An approach to honor founded on human understanding alone is ultimately flawed. First of all, human wisdom cannot fully comprehend the value of a person. We simply do not understand how important, how treasured, we are to God. If we totally understood our worth to God, we would never seek it from others. We long to know we *matter*.

Although they walked with Him and talked with Him, even Adam and Eve did not realize how much they mattered to God. If they had, surely they never would have so easily discarded their relationship with the one who knew and loved them completely. As a result of that critical choice, they unknowingly sent themselves and all the generations after them on the breakneck pursuit of value apart from God. The problem is, no honor that depends on the opinion or behavior of other people is ever enough. Adam's sons and daughters still hungrily seek approval from a source than cannot fully satisfy. Apart from God, they will never find the fulfillment for which they long. Honor based in human knowledge and opinion can never adequately satisfy.

Like patches of blue sky on an overcast day, we do sometimes get glimpses of the love for which we were created. Those who love and affirm us give us a peek into the deep, immovable worth we have in God's eyes. In return, we honor those we love the best we can, but even then, we do not do it perfectly. If we do not comprehend how dear even our dearest loved one is to God, how can we possibly bestow lasting honor on one another?

Life is at stake in this honor pursuit. We are not just talking about encouragement, respect, and admiration. The honor God gives has eternal significance. And this is the honor we have been given a right to through Jesus. No human being can ever fully comprehend the value of a person to his or her Creator, nor can one fully save the life of another. The psalmist declares in Psalm 49:7-9, "No one can redeem the life of another or give to God a ransom for them—the ransom of a life is costly, no payment is ever enough—so that they should live on forever and not see decay." Thus, the second primary flaw in human honor methods: Value is crucial to redemption. Why redeem something with no value?

Thanks be to God, we are not relegated to worthlessness. He has counted every person precious and unique. Because of His immeasurable love for us, God sent the Redeemer, Jesus Christ, to restore our relationship with Him forever. First Timothy 2:5-6 declares, "There is one God and one intermediary between God and mankind, the man Christ Jesus, who gave himself as a ransom for all people. This has now been witnessed to at the proper time." *This* approach to honor is complete, for it originates in the will of God and finds its fulfillment in the work of Jesus Christ.

We've already established the origin of honor. True honor originates in the One who created every man and woman. God knows each of us by name and has ascribed to every person intrinsic value. Through His Son, Jesus Christ, God made a way for every person to know who he or she is and what his or her value is to God. He bestows upon His children His own name, a title of honor. In response to this beautiful gift, followers of Christ return honor to God in the form of worship and honorable deeds done in His name. The reciprocity of the God-humanity relationship is a cycle of giving and receiving honor, growing in relationship. This is what honor looks like in its complete and perfect form.

The Ascribed Honor of Jesus

Jesus demonstrated both ascribed and achieved honor. His ascribed honor is outlined for us in the first chapter of the gospel of Matthew. This grand list evidencing Jesus's right to be the Savior of humanity begins with the words, "This is the genealogy of Jesus the Messiah the son of David, the son of Abraham" (1:1). Matthew begins with Jesus's position of honor as the Messiah and then lays out His genealogical credentials that made His position honorable. Abraham was the father of the nation of Israel, which, 14 generations later, led to the great king David. Every Jewish person reading Matthew's recorded genealogy would know the Old Testament prophecies foretelling the Messiah who would come from the lineage of Abraham and David (2 Samuel 7:12-13; Psalm 89:35-37).

Jesus's bloodline was impeccable. In an ironic twist, even women considered shamed in the honor-shame worldview of the time featured in Jesus's ancestry. Infamous outsiders in Jesus's lineage include Tamar, who scandalously stood up for her own rights against her father-in-law; Rahab, the risk-taking prostitute of Jericho who hid the Israelite spies sent to survey the city; Ruth, a humble Moabitess with a tenacious work ethic; Bathsheba, the married object of King David's romantic obsession; and Mary, pregnant out of wedlock. *Impeccable* in God's sight, evidently, is measured by faith, not social standing.

I once heard the story of a Muslim man from the United Arab Emirates who read this passage in Matthew. He could not believe his eyes. Right here was evidence of Jesus's right to be the Savior! Tracing back further than any prophet ever had, the lineage of Jesus made an undeniable case for the veracity of His claims. The Muslim man was convinced. He began to follow this Messiah whose genealogical record was inarguable. In the culture of the United Arab Emirates, pedigree is imperative to one's position of honor and validity.

Jesus demonstrates ascribed honor, a position given Him by His Father in heaven. In the culture to which Jesus came, honor and shame permeated the predominant worldview. God, of course, understood this and affirmed His Son's ascribed honor publicly, demonstrating Jesus's position in Luke 3:21-22: "When all the people were being baptized, Jesus was baptized too. And as he was praying, heaven was opened and the Holy Spirit descended on him in bodily form like a dove. And a voice came from heaven: 'You are my Son, whom I love; with you I am well pleased.'" Shame stood in the shadows of the riverbank that day, its accusing voice silenced by the God of heaven and earth. The one born to a virgin, the son of a humble carpenter, had been publicly ascribed the honor of sonship by God Himself. Jesus's identity has not changed; humanity's revelation of who He truly is has just irreversibly shifted.

Luke continues in verse 23, "Now Jesus himself was about thirty years old when he began his ministry. He was the son, *so it was thought*, of Joseph" (emphasis added). This statement of supposition opens Luke's record of Jesus's complete genealogy tracing all the way back to Adam, "the son of God," in verse 38. The Son with whom "I am well pleased" is descended from the first son of God made in God's image (Genesis 1:27). Jesus, the Son of God, would later declare, "I am the Alpha and the Omega, the First and the Last, the Beginning and the End" (Revelation 22:13). Jesus bears the name above all names, and His position of ascribed honor as the Son of God sets Him apart from every other prophet in history.

Muslims believe that *Isa Bin Maryam* (Jesus, the son of Mary) was a mere prophet. He is revered in Islam, alongside Moses and David. The Qur'an says that Jesus is the Christ; that His mother, Mary, was a virgin; that He was a prophet, pure and sinless; and that He would be born, die, and rise from the dead.[2] However, for the majority of Muslims, the claim that Jesus was the Son of God is offensive. Many Muslim scholars teach that the Christian Trinity consists of Mary, the mother; God, the Father; and Jesus, the Son. The implication is that Jesus was the result of a sexual union between God and Mary. When encountering this misconception, Christians can strongly agree with Muslims that this indeed would be blasphemy, never permitted by God.[3] Jesus's ascribed honor as the Son of God could only come through a miraculous conception and virgin birth.

The Achieved Honor of Jesus

Not only did Jesus display ascribed honor, He also illustrated achieved honor. God Himself, in the person of Jesus Christ, entered into humanity's worldview by subjecting Himself to the dictates of human culture and made choices that, in the eyes of heaven and earth, earned (achieved) Him eternal honor. Although God was the Creator and embodiment of ascribed honor, He humbled Himself by becoming man. Philippians 2:6-11 explains to us the extraordinary and astounding attitude of Jesus Christ:

Who, being in very nature God, did not consider equality with God something to be used to his own advantage; rather, he made himself nothing by taking the very nature of a servant, being made in human likeness. And being found in appearance as a man, he humbled himself by becoming obedient to death—even death on a cross! Therefore God exalted him to the highest place and gave him the name that is above every name, that at the name of Jesus every knee should bow, in heaven and on earth and under the earth, and every tongue acknowledge that Jesus Christ is Lord, to the glory of God the Father.

What God is this, who would lay aside His ascribed honor, His pedigree, to labor alongside humanity and earn honor that was already His? This is the God who made you and made me. He is the one who chose to lay aside His glory to heal us, so that we might know true value and honor. We are known by name, by God Himself, and He has given us immeasurable, priceless worth. You and I matter to God.

His mission among humanity is outlined in the beautiful honor litany of Isaiah 61, further illustrating the Savior's interwoven beauty of ascribed and achieved honor:

The Spirit of the Sovereign LORD is on me, because the LORD has anointed me to proclaim good news to the poor [i.e., the Messiah's ascribed honor]. He has sent me to bind up the brokenhearted, to proclaim freedom for the captives and release from darkness for the prisoners, to proclaim the year of the LORD's favor and the day of vengeance of our God, to comfort all who mourn, and provide for those who grieve in Zion—to bestow on them a crown of beauty instead of ashes, the oil of joy instead of mourning, and a garment of praise instead of a spirit of despair [i.e., the Messiah's achieved honor]. They will be called oaks of righteousness, a planting of the LORD for the display of his splendor [i.e., our ascribed honor as a result of the Savior's obedience] (verses 1-3).

Isaiah goes on to describe the result of Jesus's work of honor: the removal of shame and disgrace from you and me.

> Instead of your shame you will receive a double portion,
> and instead of disgrace you will rejoice in your inheritance.
> And so you will inherit a double portion in your land, and
> everlasting joy will be yours (verse 7).

ACHIEVED HONOR AS AN EXPRESSION OF WORSHIP

Once we realize we have been *ascribed* honor through the precious gift of Jesus, honor behavior flows from us as an act of worship. Our inheritance is no longer disgrace. The overflow of this double-portioned reality is everlasting joy. We ironically begin to *achieve* honor here on earth as we imitate our Messiah by loving and serving others. But the beauty and the mystery of the matter is this: Our motivation is no longer human applause and social status. Our desire is to bring honor to the Savior who first honored us. We see here, therefore, that honor is the heart of our relationship with Him. God ascribed honor to us, we return honor to Him, and the cycle continues, all the while growing in our knowledge of and companionship with each other.

Within the human honor paradigm often lies a kernel of selfish desire for public adulation and accolades. But after the human heart has been completely won by the immeasurable love of Christ, secure in its value to Him, no human admiration or award can match the love of Jesus. Our hearts overflow with honorable deeds, giving us a platform to declare the glory of our great Father God whose honorable name we bear.

Honor leads to relationship with God and each other. As we grow in our understanding of how much God loves us, we are compelled to reciprocate that love. What once may have been merely a set of moral rules to live by becomes a living interaction between two beings, God and human, who know and love one another. Grasping God's love for us compels us to see others as also loved and valued by Him. Our perspective changes, and we begin to love others better. We see what we could not see before: We see value in one another, regardless of our outward appearances and behaviors.

Honor leads to worship. When I first began to intentionally study honor and shame, I saw it as a strategy to better understand the ones I loved from an honor-shame worldview and a way to start the gospel conversation more effectively with them. However, as I deeply examined the Bible, searching for honor, I was overcome by the glory and beauty of God. Many times I sat bent over my keyboard, weeping through the writing of these chapters as I stopped to worship the God I was coming to know through the lenses of honor and shame. My original posture as a strategist and missiologist was replaced with arms aloft in worship, in awe of the God who removes our shame, bestowing honor instead. The story of honor and shame became my own. This epic story belongs to every person, and the result of its revelation is an overwhelming desire to worship.

Honor might be the lynchpin of understanding our importance to the One who created us. The position of humanity designated by its Creator is one of perfect love. We are perfectly loved so that we may in turn perfectly love. That position cannot be achieved if we fail to realize we have been given honor by God. We *do* matter.

TWO PATHS, ONE PURSUIT

Imani and I were conceptualizing and therefore approaching our worth to God in two different ways. She was working hard to earn it while striving to achieve it. I had accepted that my value to God had been ascribed to me, earned by Jesus Christ and given to me, regardless of my flaws. While Imani was seeking perfect behavior to gain acceptance by God, I had abandoned my pursuit of perfectionism and fallen upon God's perfect sacrifice in my place. We were demonstrating what the seeking of honor looks like in its two most basic forms. Though we were running along two different paths, we were in pursuit of the same goal. We wanted to matter to God.

My experience with Imani opened my eyes to the longing in all of our hearts, regardless of worldview, to be accepted by God and to our innate tendency to perform in order to gain that acceptance.

Not so long ago, I was like Imani in many ways. I longed for nothing more than to be devout and loved by God. So I set my mind to work at it day and night. Thus began my long journey into perfectionism, performance, and exhaustion. I was one of many in the long parade of weary Christians who march on endlessly through the days, desperate to gain God's approval. How blessed is the relief when collapse finally comes! For it does come to all who strive to earn what Jesus already established for each of us through His death and resurrection. We are loved—and we have been since the beginning. Our value to God has never faded, although our belief in that truth has been assaulted and battered by suffering and shame. Jesus draws near to each of us, no matter our worldview, and invites us to experience honor in its complete and perfect form: relationship with God Himself.

Many Christians today believe in Jesus Christ, yet they trudge the interminable daily trek of trying to earn honor that the Savior has already attained for them. The problem for me was that, although I had placed my belief in Jesus Christ, I continued to also believe many conflicting voices who declared to me my worth—or lack of worth, which led me to work tirelessly to please God. I straddled two approaches uncomfortably: achieved and ascribed honor.

I craved the honor that was noticed and applauded by the world. I labored to be honorable in word and deed. With each accomplishment, I grew further from the quiet, unseen, seldom-awarded honor Christ had achieved for me and the ascribed honor He paid for with His life. For me, the change came when I found human honor to be a cruel and fickle lover. Its appetite was endless. When I did manage to gain respect and admiration, the satisfaction was fleeting. Conversely, when human praise evaded me despite my best performance, I was crushed and determined to try even harder. The push and pull of my honor quest left me bone-weary and disillusioned.

Exhausted by my pursuit of honor, I knew there had to be something steadfast, immoveable, and true that never changed according to my performance. The discovery and acceptance that, as the song goes, "Jesus paid it all," was a relief that transformed my life. As I grew used to this new way of understanding my value to God, the freedom in my life to love others and be myself increased.

The honor humanity offers, no matter its form, cannot set our hearts eternally free. The Savior, Jesus Christ, who has been *ascribed honor* by the Father, has also *achieved honor* for every person through His death and resurrection. This is what honor truly looks like. Those who are willing to peer into its depths will be liberated to love themselves and others across every cultural boundary.

❧ FOR FURTHER STUDY ❧

1. In this chapter we examined both the *ascribed* and *achieved* honor of Jesus. Ascribed honor is honor received through no action of one's own. Achieved honor, on the other hand, can be earned. Why is it important for the Savior of humanity to have both?

2. Paul, the great Christian missionary, had more reason than any to boast about his achieved honor. Read Philippians 3:3-11 and answer the following question:

   - What compelled Paul to exchange his worldly honor, that which he had earned himself, for ascribed honor accomplished and given by Christ? Compare his former, achieved honor with his ascribed honor as described in this passage.

3. Why can't achieved honor, that which a person tries to earn through following religious rules and being "good," gain him or her entrance to heaven?

Shame on You

Abraham said to God, "If only Ishmael might live under your blessing!" Then God said..."And as for Ishmael, I have heard you: I will surely bless him; I will make him fruitful and will greatly increase his numbers. He will be the father of twelve rulers, and I will make him into a great nation. But my covenant I will establish with Isaac, whom Sarah will bear to you by this time next year."

GENESIS 17:18-21

Zaynab tells the story of the day she learned the ultimate price she would pay if she ever brought shame upon her family. Zaynab was a good Muslim girl from a loving family. Their community respected her father as a righteous and honorable man. Zaynab's father adored her and frequently gave her presents of jewelry and sweets.

One year Zaynab's family made the long journey to the holy city of Mecca, fulfilling the fifth pillar of Islam, hajj. As they wound their way through the throngs of pilgrims, they heard the sound of angry shouting up ahead. Zaynab's father stretched his neck high to peer into the square and taking Zaynab's hand tightly, pulled her quickly to the edge of the pulsing crowd of onlookers. There in the center was a girl in full hijab, kneeling before several men. One man held a scimitar, a sharp, curved sword, high in the air. In a loud and commanding voice, another announced to the crowd the girl's crime: She had walked home alone with a boy. Her sentence was death by beheading.

Zaynab struggled to turn away from the unbelievable scene and loosen her hand from her father's fierce grip. "Stay here and watch," he commanded her. "Today you will learn a lesson. This could happen to you, too, if you bring shame on our family." Zaynab watched in fear, tears streaming down her face, as the blood flowed onto the street from the dead girl who had shamed her family.

"Honor killings" such as the one Zaynab and her father witnessed have gotten much attention in recent years. We conclude from these gruesome scenes that all Muslims are violent. We all have a worldview, a unique set of perceptions about the world. Through this set of perceptions, we judge the world and live our lives. Our worldview is the framework through which we define and respond to injustice, determine right and wrong, and build families, communities, and nations.

THE BEGINNING OF WORLDVIEW

Sometimes our actions throw us into irreversible consequences. This is where Adam and Eve found themselves. They had never before experienced shame or separation from God. In a wild rush of never-before-felt emotion, we see them frantically trying to cope with what had happened as a result of their sin. Like children who panic after doing something their parents clearly prohibited, they tried to find a way out of trouble. "Then the eyes of both of them were opened, and they realized they were naked; so they sewed fig leaves together and made coverings for themselves" (Genesis 3:7).

Here we witness the first cover-up, the beginning of a phenomenon that would continue for all generations to come. God created Adam and Eve with the ability to know the difference between right and wrong. They knew they had done wrong. They reacted with humankind's first basic emotional response to sin: guilt. Guilt makes us try to cover up wrong and then hunker down, hoping no one will find out: "Then the man and his wife heard the sound of the LORD God as he was walking in the garden in the cool of the day, and they hid from the LORD God among the trees of the garden. But the LORD God called to the man, 'Where are you?'" (Genesis 3:8-9).

The second emotional reaction to sin was shame. Shame forces its bearer into hiding, believing that he or she can never face others again. In the story of Eden, God was on His way to find the man and the woman. They heard His footsteps. But the last thing they wanted at that moment was to face God. Nothing was familiar anymore, and they were not sure what God would do to them. Would the One who lovingly formed them, who walked and talked with them every day, now kill them?

In hiding, we forget the character of God. Shame drowns out the truth that He loves us and wants nothing more than relationship with us. Hearing God's voice calling out to them, Adam and Eve cowered in the shadows and changed the course of humanity. Man and woman have been hiding from God and one another ever since. Shame has penetrated humanity's relationship with God and with one another, and we have become lonely in our pain. In our shame we begin to question if His intentions toward us are for good or evil.

In the shadows of the hiding place, a third emotion wrapped its icy fingers around the hearts of Adam and Eve: "[Adam] answered, 'I heard you in the garden, and I was afraid because I was naked; so I hid'" (Genesis 3:10). Fear entered gleefully, immobilizing them with its evil power, defaming the One who loved them most. Adam and Eve were now afraid of God, the Creator whose fellowship and love they had enjoyed openly and freely.

Guilt, shame, and fear—the basic emotional responses we see demonstrated in the Garden of Eden—have become the primary building blocks of worldview as it emerges in cultures across the world today. Every culture contains elements of all three, but many cultures are characterized by one dominant emotional response at any particular time in history.

Guilt

In Western cultures, innocence or guilt is the yardstick typically used to measure behavior and beliefs. Conduct is judged based on right versus wrong. Westerners talk about things being "right for me" or "not right for me." Social issues are debated on the basis of their perceived rightness or wrongness. Almost every major issue in American and European countries is centered upon deciding whether something is right or wrong or whether someone is innocent or guilty. It is right to recycle. It is wrong to litter. It is right to give. It is wrong to steal. Political candidates are examined based upon whether their beliefs and policies are seen as right or wrong. The justice system of the West is built around the judgments of innocence and guilt, or right and wrong.

This is what Roland Muller calls a predominantly "guilt-based culture."[1] Accordingly, the Western approach to the gospel is also primarily guilt-based, meaning emphasis is placed on one's guilt before God and the need for a Savior. This is not wrong. It is, however, incomplete.

Fear

I once lived in a small East African village. Our village elder was highly respected for the large number of goats and sheep he owned. It took several young boys to herd the animals every day across the rolling hills. One day the elder's aging mother became sick. She was seriously ill, so the people called upon the witch doctor.

Over the course of two weeks, more than half the elder's livestock were slaughtered. After consulting the spirits, the witch doctor had determined the village ancestors were angry with the elder for planting a new kind of bean that year along with the typical corn. Thus, they had brought this sickness upon his mother. To appease their anger, the spirits now demanded the sacrifice of many animals. I am sorry to say that the elderly woman died at the end of those two weeks of long nights, animal sacrifices, and frantic singing to the spirits.

My neighbors in that village were driven by fear, and it dominated their worldview. They practice what is called *animism*, or worship and appeasement of the spirit world. They believe that gods and spirits exist in the universe, and they must live peaceably with those unseen authorities by appeasing them.[2] In such cultures, fear is the primary building block of their worldview.

Power is an important concept in fear-based cultures. Animists believe they are at the mercy of spirits who can be easily offended, bringing punishment down on individuals and whole communities. When something bad happens, the assumption in fear-based cultures is that the spirits have been angered. Spiritual power has been knocked out of balance and must be restored or punishment will result. The fear of punishment can only be relieved by appeasing the offended spirit or calling out to a greater spiritual power. If it is believed that a spirit has been offended, as in the case of the village grandmother, great effort will be made to please the spirits and restore peace to the community.

Shame

Many cultures around the world, especially in the Middle East and Asia, exhibit a predominantly shame-based worldview. The honor-shame worldview features strongly in *collectivist societies*, those that make decisions based on how they impact the group to which one belongs. Within these cultures, honor is an actual position in society. Shame robs one of that position, moving him or her outside the group. Isolation and separation are seen as highly undesirable. Avoiding shame is of utmost importance.

Westerners are often confused by this perspective. Individualist societies emphasize independence and original thoughts and ideas. Decisions that appear to deny the individual his or her uniqueness seem oppressive or unjust through the eyes of the Western worldview. To one with an honor-shame worldview, however, the group is always more important than one's own rights.

A basic understanding of worldview prepares us to examine honor and shame in Islamic cultures more objectively. However, I must qualify this. The more I learn about how my Muslim friends view honor and shame, the more I realize all I have yet to learn. This book is only a glimpse into an intricate and complex way of viewing and making sense of the world. Worldviews are cultivated over centuries. No one book can thoroughly explain all their nuances. Even a small amount of understanding of the honor-shame worldview, however, can produce a tremendous result as we seek to build authentic relationships between cultures. For a more thorough examination of the three worldviews presented in this chapter, see the appendix for recommended resources.

NOT A CULTURE OF VIOLENCE

We were not often out at night in the marketplace of the old Arab city. On this particular evening, a visit with friends had gone later than expected and we found ourselves navigating the twists and turns of the narrow streets with our sleepy children in tow. The air pulsed with sound. The meat seller's rap-shouting declaring his discounted last cuts of meat to the crowds thumped like a bass drum. The silversmiths' tap-tap-tapping as they hammered their fine chisels into soft silver, creating intricate geometrical patterns, danced in the background. Underneath it all was the buzz of a thousand conversations as families like ours took in the cacophony of sights and sounds of the night souq, the busy market that sold everything one could possibly need.

Suddenly and without warning, the masses stopped in their tracks, jamming the passageway. A different feeling immediately filled the thick air: panic and fear. Mothers ran with their babies; fathers scooped up little children and ducked into alcoves. We huddled along the wall to avoid being crushed. Two men were fighting in the middle of the street, the glint of their curved knives flashing in the lamplights. Snatches of angry words reached our ears, words like "shame," "kill," and "God forbid." We had stumbled upon a battle for honor. The bazaar that had only moments before resounded with family laughter now emptied out, replaced by the sounds of an age-old effort to vanquish shame.

No society, in the hearts of its men and women, likes violence. Confrontation, rejection, and death are undesirable in every culture. Civilizations create intricate systems to avoid reaching the point of violence. Violence is a last resort. This is true in Western cultures and this is true in Islamic cultures. If we take pause and lay aside our presuppositions for a moment, we observe several other, nonviolent ways Muslims attempt to deal with shame.

Avoidance

Let's go back to Zaynab and her father for a moment. A Western, innocence-guilt worldview responds to their experience indignantly, deeming her father wrong to have forced Zaynab to witness the beheading of a girl who had done nothing criminal. From a Muslim perspective, what he did demonstrated the first and mildest form of handling shame: *avoiding it altogether*.

By imposing on his daughter the unforgettable scene, he was seeking to avoid the same thing happening in his own family. Through his worldview of honor and shame, he believed he was showing love to his daughter by warning her. He was saving her from the same fate, from a life of shame and possibly even death. Furthermore, he was saving his family from the same fate, that of losing their position in society through shame. Someone with an honor-shame worldview is always thinking about behavior within the context of the group, not the individual. They are constantly thinking about how to avoid shame.

A colleague shared with me a story that illustrates distinctly the desire to avoid shame. Paul's friend, Rashaad, asked him where to invest one hundred thousand dollars he had inherited. Paul worked out a plan with him to open a Western-style butcher shop with steaks, roasts, and other cuts that Westerners and people who had lived in the West were looking for but could not find. Together they worked out how Rashaad's cuts could be transported and sold in stores all across the city. The plan appeared to be pleasing and acceptable to Rashaad, who committed many hours to developing it with Paul. But, in the end, Rashaad chose to buy an olive grove instead. Paul was bewildered.

When asked why, Rashaad said that if the olive crop were to fail, it would be because all the olive groves in the country had failed, and no shame would be attached to his family. But if he invested in the butcher shop and it failed, he alone would bear the shame. Rashaad chose the mildest form of handling shame: avoiding it altogether.

This concept can be confusing and frustrating to Westerners, especially those working with men and women from honor-shame cultures in business or other cooperative endeavors. This story, along with that of Zaynab's father, demonstrates how deeply honor and shame affect men as well as women. They fear failure and the consequent shame it brings. As a friend of mine says, this is why men from Islamic cultures tend not to be adventurers and entrepreneurs. They are consumed with avoiding shame. Perhaps it occupies their minds as much as it does those of women, although they bear it differently.

Covering

An adage in our family goes like this: Hospitality means that you treat friends like family and family like friends. We did not create the expression, but we have often quoted it with a smile. Our house is usually full of family and friends, and our hearts are set on making all of them feel at home and accepted.

One day that attitude backfired, and the results were perplexing and discouraging. I had left my camera on the counter in our kitchen during a gathering of the underground church that met in our home each week. We did not really meet "underground," but the term had come to describe church gatherings that happened in secret during times of persecution or in places where Christian worship was illegal. This particular day we were having a celebration, and the people who filled our home were friends. Furthermore, they were followers of Christ, former Muslims who had made the courageous and sincere decision to disobey their government, leave Islam, and become *Masihin*, or Christians. The only recourse was to gather behind closed doors with other Jesus followers. Today we were rejoicing with a new couple who had recently gotten married.

Slipping into the kitchen to check the teakettle, I put the camera on the counter and promptly forgot about it in the hustle of preparations. Pictures had already been taken, and I didn't need it again right away.

A couple of hours after the guests had left, I remembered the camera and went into the kitchen to retrieve it. It was not on the wooden cabinet where I had left it. Assuming my husband had put it away, I asked him about it. Nope, he had not seen it. My sons were too small at the time to reach the cabinet, so I knew they hadn't played with it. I went down the mental list of possibilities, eliminating each one.

Surely it couldn't have been stolen by one of our guests! I thought to myself incredulously. We were a close, trusted group. My husband and I had always done right by these people, generously giving ourselves, our home, and our time. It would not make sense, would not be right for them to respond to our generosity by stealing from us. I was simmering in my innocence-guilt worldview, trying to make sense of the situation. After lengthy conversations and analysis of the afternoon's events, my husband and I realized it could have been only one person. As reality dawned on us, discouragement and disappointment weighed heavy on our hearts.

The next week the person we suspected appeared in all new trendy clothes and shoes, having evidently been on an uncharacteristic shopping spree. Surely not! we thought. Later that week we received confirmation from another person that the culprit was, indeed, who we thought. *How on earth do we confront this?* we wondered.

We decided to talk to the pastor about it. Many of the church members were also his family members, so we assumed he would understand how to sensitively approach the situation. In our naive understanding of honor and shame cultures, we thought we were preserving the thief's honor by bringing in a mediator from the same family and pursuing a logical solution.

Imagine our shock when the pastor made up a cover story! Instead of confronting the thief for us and seeking reconciliation and justice, he covered the crime and made it clear the conversation would gain no more traction. My husband and I did not understand it at the time, but the pastor was illustrating another stage of handling shame: *covering*. He was a follower of Christ, but that had not converted his worldview to a Western one. Nor should it. Too often, cross-cultural Christians confuse worldview with righteousness. From our Western, right-versus-wrong worldview, sin is to be confronted. From our pastor friend's perspective, shame is to be avoided, and if that is not possible, it must be covered.

I realize now, with the clarity of retrospect, what was at stake for him: loss of position in the small community of believers and loss of a safe location to meet for worship. In his position as an elder leader, he had a cultural responsibility to protect the women in his family. He did this by covering the shame one family member brought by stealing from us. His eyes admitted her crime even as his words covered her shame. If shame cannot be avoided, it will be covered in Islamic societies, if at all possible. We did not have the experience and worldview understanding to see his struggle as noble at the time. I wish we had. His behavior looked like dishonesty to us, and we were incensed.

It took us a long time to work through our confusion and disappointment. That was time we could have spent growing in relationship, discipleship, and worship.

Denial

I was so full I could not even sit upright. Leaning back gratefully on the luxurious couch behind me, I caught my friend Nour's twinkling eyes. "Eat more! More is coming! You can't stop yet!" About that same moment her aunt Atiya walked in, bearing a heavy clay dish piled high with steaming rice and lamb. Placing it deftly in the center of the table, she quickly tucked her head down and left the room as quietly as she had come.

"Thank you, Atiya!" I called after her. She did not respond.

"She isn't here," said Nour.

I was confused. I thought she meant that Atiya had left the house.

"Where did she go? Surely not for more food!" I said with a laugh.

"She's in the kitchen, her place," replied Nour nonchalantly.

"Oh. I thought you said she isn't here."

"She's not. It's an expression," explained Nour, not really explaining at all.

I rolled my eyes on the inside. *Not, "it's an expression" again,* I thought to myself. I hated when my friends said that in response to my misunderstandings in Arabic. Just when I thought I was making progress with the language, I would run into an obscure expression that seemed impossible to understand. Nour must have noticed my dismay and was feeling unusually generous that day. "Okay. I'll explain it to you. She isn't married anymore, so she isn't here." This seemed to Nour to be a satisfactory explanation.

I was too mortified to probe for a deeper explanation. I loved Atiya and I was expected to eat her delicious food, but she wasn't allowed to receive my gratitude for it. She wasn't allowed to exist, except to make the food appear and the dirty dishes to disappear. A heaviness settled around my heart and I lost my appetite.

I felt lied to. But after deeper consideration, I perceived that Nour's insistence Atiya was not there, when she actually was, was *not* a lie in my friend's mind. But the reason why she would say that was obscure to me. Later I asked another friend about the expression. She explained to me that when a woman is sent away by her husband, back to her father's home, she brings shame on her father's house. The way that shame is handled is by denying her existence. Such a woman will often accept the arrangement in exchange for her life, room, and board. Nour didn't consider her attitude toward Atiya to be wrong. She did not lie to me, according to her worldview. I don't really think she evaluated it closely. She was merely doing what women in her culture had done for centuries to cope with shame: She was denying its existence.

A Last Resort

We have taken a closer look at three unofficial but clearly observable ways Islamic cultures handle shame. These three strategies can be seen across North Africa and the Middle East, from the arid plains of the Fertile Crescent that stretch from Egypt to Iraq and even in the nomadic sands of the Sahara. In the wake of the greatest refugee crisis in history, they can be witnessed in Western nations today as well. What has received the most modern attention, however, is not these milder methods to restore honor, but rather the last resort, the kind of violence Zaynab and her father witnessed in the beginning of our chapter.

When avoiding, covering, and denying have failed, all that is left is purging. Purging is the last resort in an effort to deal with shame. It might manifest in the form of expulsion from the family or tribe. Purging may be like Hamida's story in chapter 4, whose mother-in-law threw boiling oil on her to supposedly remove the shame her barrenness had brought on the woman's family. Ultimately, purging can take the form of death.

A STRUGGLE AGAINST SIN

The struggle in honor-shame cultures to restore honor is, at its heart, the age-old struggle against sin. Avoiding shame or managing it is a way of life, an effort to cope with sin. But these carefully constructed methods will never work, for they have no power to remove sin from human hearts. This is where the gospel so beautifully responds to the shame battle. Jesus knew we cannot avoid the shame. So He embraced it head-on, endured it, despised it, and ultimately defeated it. This is beautifully illustrated in Hebrews:

> ...fixing our eyes on Jesus, the author and perfecter of faith, who for the joy set before Him endured the cross, despising the shame, and has sat down at the right hand of the throne of God (12:2 NASB).

The human attempt to manage shame through covering or purging is a mutation of the salvific covering and purging of sin and shame done by God Himself. The problem with these impaired human methods is that all have fallen short of the glory of God. We are disqualified deliverers.

> For all have sinned and fall short of the glory of God (Romans 3:23).

We have been sentenced to separation from God, and no one but Jesus Christ can bring us back into relationship with God. Romans 3:23 balances both *sin* and *shame* (falling short of God's glory) as obstacles we all face in life's most crucial dilemma. No amount of covering or seeking to purge my or another's shame will suffice. There must be divine intervention by One completely holy (clean, without shame) and innocent (without guilt). That one is the Messiah, Jesus.

THE GREAT COVERER

Throughout the story of God's great love for humanity, we see Him covering our shame. It began with the first blood ever shed. In Genesis 3:21, animals were slaughtered so shame could be covered and skins made for Adam and Eve to wear. This first blood sacrifice to cover man and woman's shame foreshadowed the blood Jesus would one day shed to cover the shame of humanity forever.[3]

In Ruth 3, we see another powerful example of covering. Ruth had originally married Mahlon, son of Elimelech and Naomi. Mahlon and his family were Israelites from Judah. After the deaths of both her father-in-law and Mahlon, Ruth moved to Bethlehem with her mother-in-law, Naomi. According to Levitical law, if a woman's husband died and she was left childless, her husband's closest male relative was required to marry her so an heir could be born to carry on the name of the dead man. This relative was known as a "kinsman redeemer."[4] Upon her mother-in-law's instruction, Ruth approached her kinsman redeemer, Boaz, after he lay down at the end of a long day of threshing barley. Lying at his feet, Ruth asked Boaz to cover her with his cloak (Ruth 3:9). Her request for covering was symbolic for seeking protection. Ruth was essentially asking her kinsman redeemer to grant her protection by marrying her and fulfilling his requirement to help her have an heir to carry on her late husband's name. As a foreigner and childless widow, Ruth was an outsider. Others still saw her as the Moabitess, even though she had come back to Bethlehem with Naomi (Ruth 2:6). Boaz, when he first saw her, assumed she was a slave (verse 5). Without children, even the position of honor she once gained as wife of Mahlon would be forgotten.

If we consider the situation through the eyes of the honor-shame worldview, we can see that as an outsider Ruth likely suffered shame, the common verdict for anyone not belonging to the group. But this was not to be Ruth's final story. In a dazzling preview of Christ's mercy, Boaz granted her request for covering and bestowed Ruth with the honor she sought.

Like the literal covering of Adam and Eve, Boaz's covering of Ruth powerfully illustrates the coming of another kinsman redeemer, the Messiah, "born of a woman, born under the law, to redeem those under the law, that we might receive adoption to sonship" (Galatians 4:4-5). Jesus would redeem us by becoming a curse for us (Galatians 3:13-14). He allowed *Himself* to be covered in *our* sin and shame. This is the climax of divine reversal, the holy putting on the unholy so that the unholy might be made holy. He covered His glory so that we might stand uncovered and clean before God.

Second Corinthians 3:18 states beautifully: "We all, who with unveiled faces contemplate the Lord's glory, are being transformed into his image with ever-increasing glory, which comes from the Lord, who is the Spirit." The covered glory of Jesus Christ on the cross has made it possible for us to stand before our Lord, unveiled and reflecting His glory like a pure, beaming bride on her wedding day gazing into the face of her beloved.

Death on a cross was the most shameful form of Roman execution. A man called Rabbi and Lord by His followers, stripped naked and nailed to rough-hewn beams of wood for all to mock, would have from any cultural perspective been horrifically shameful. This is the very reason Muslims argue that if Jesus had indeed been God incarnate, He never would have allowed such humiliation of Himself. But therein lies the wisdom of God that makes foolish the wisdom of man: "For the message of the cross is foolishness to those who are perishing, but to us who are being saved it is the power of God" (1 Corinthians 1:18). Precisely *because* Jesus ultimately covered your shame and mine when He hung naked and exposed on a cross, we can come out of the shadows and live. Shame has been abolished. No manmade method can accomplish this. God, through Jesus Christ, did all of these things, once and for all.

> But God chose the foolish things of the world to shame the wise; God chose the weak things of the world to shame the strong. God chose the lowly things of this world and the despised things—and the things that are not—to nullify the things that are, so that no one may boast before him. It is because of him that you are in Christ Jesus, who has become for us wisdom from God—that is, our righteousness, holiness and redemption (1 Corinthians 1:27-30).

The hollow pride and knowledge of man has been nullified by the One who became for us the very wisdom of God. The Great Coverer, Jesus the Messiah, paid the price for our honor, and we have been redeemed.

THE FINAL PURGE

The last resort, the ultimate sacrifice required to remove our shame, was indeed violent. It involved the death of God Himself, in our stead. The purging of shame came at great cost, not to us, as the honor-shame worldview misguidedly believes, but to God Himself. The next time you see news of an honor killing, cry out to God for the eyes of the Muslim world to be opened to the last resort accomplished for them on Calvary. Shame has been purged for them once and for all. Ask God to help them find the restoration they seek through His Son, Jesus Christ. And if you are carrying shame, avoiding it, covering it, denying it, or considering extreme measures to purge it from your life, may your eyes be opened to the beckoning arms of Christ, who is waiting to take it from you permanently and help you overcome its damaging effects in your life.

THE STRUGGLE IS OVER

The Muslim's struggle to overcome shame is at the heart a human struggle for redemption. The good news of the gospel is that not only are the fearful delivered and the guilty forgiven, but the shamed are given honor. The Messiah has covered Himself in our shame and sin so we no longer have to use man-made methods to handle our brokenness. He has purged once and for all the shame that separated us from God. We do not have to shed blood and commit acts of violence to end the shame. Through faith in the Messiah Jesus, we can stand honored and forgiven before God again.

❧ FOR FURTHER STUDY ❧

1. Read again the account of Adam and Eve's separation from God in Genesis 3:6-10. Underline the words that indicate guilt, shame, and fear.

2. How have you responded to your separation from God? Do you cover up? How are you hiding from Him? Are you afraid of God, and if so, why?

3. Take time to get alone with God and think about your position with Him. Listen for His voice calling you. He is calling you now, just like He did Adam and Eve, asking, "Where are you?" Respond to His call today and let Him restore you. Write a simple prayer below inviting Him to draw near.

The Burden Bearers

Because the Sovereign LORD helps me, I will not
be disgraced. Therefore have I set my face like
flint, and I know I will not be put to shame.

ISAIAH 50:7

Some people come into your life and change it forever. This is what happened to me after I was introduced to Saadiya. The first day I met her, I had no idea the secrets she carried. I could not then imagine the joys and sorrows we would one day share or how close we would become. That first afternoon, as she stood in my living room, her eyes shyly cast down at the mosaic tile floor, I could not yet perceive the treasure she was. But God knew. He had always known. In His great love, He drew her out of shame and showed her how much He loved her.

When I met Saadiya, she was a single mother living in her father's home. I learned later that one of the most shameful experiences a Muslim woman in Saadiya's culture can go through is to be rejected by her husband and sent back to her father's house. The reason for the rejection is not as important as the shame it brings, and the woman bears the responsibility. Such rejection by her husband not only dishonors the woman and her children, it also dishonors her father and her extended family. In many cases, families refuse to allow daughters in these circumstances to reenter their homes.

Saadiya had been young and hopeful once. After completing her education, she secured a respectable position as a bank clerk. She met her husband, and both families agreed the match was strong. The couple was soon married. Saadiya bore two sons, and her position of honor in the family grew. She was doing everything a woman should do to maintain honor in the group according to the conventions of her culture and religion.

Her husband was good to her in the beginning. But shortly after the birth of their second son, he began to drink excessively and abuse Saadiya. The beatings grew more violent, and one day in a rage he grabbed iron rods and tried to blind her. He nearly succeeded. She lost the majority of her sight, severely impairing her ability to do many of the things necessary to keep a house and raise two busy little boys. Shortly after, her husband forced her out of the house with the children.

With nowhere else to go, Saadiya fled to her father's home for refuge. Her elderly, widowed father and disabled brother allowed her to live in their house in exchange for her servanthood. She was relegated to being a slave in her childhood home. Sisters and nieces were not allowed to mention her name or include her in the family circle. Quietly, humbly, she accepted this position of shame.

A few years later, Saadiya gained outside work as a housekeeper. The school fees for her sons were increasing, and she had to find a way to support them. Her father was growing older and more dependent upon her, and her brother's health was declining. Her work as a housekeeper provided just enough for them to get by. But when her husband heard she was working, he appeared demanding money. Although he had taken other wives after expelling Saadiya, he now visited her again, demanding the privileges of a husband in secret. Her shame grew worse. She felt dirty and trapped.

I met her during this time. In the beginning she never spoke of what she suffered, carrying it secretly in her soul like a deserved life sentence. In time, her family and friends began to speak to me about it in hushed whispers. As our relationship grew, Saadiya confided in me and I confided in her. We became like sisters, sharing comfort and sorrow, joy and pain. Saadiya sat with me me during some of the most difficult moments of my life, and I poured endless cups of hot tea as she unburdened her heart to me. We celebrated life together, and I learned from her exquisite humility how to suffer gracefully. Saadiya taught me that no matter where we come from, our hearts are all crafted alike to swell with the changing tides of joy and sorrow. As we lay our delights and our longings down alongside each other's, we experienced the grace and power of God in a mighty way. His love for us did not need explanation in that fragile and brave space.

Eventually Saadiya decided to seek a divorce. This bold move would place her in an all-male court, and the laws of her country state that a woman's testimony is worth only half that of her husband. She would have to testify convincingly to the judge that the abuse she had undergone was just cause for divorce.

Saadiya came to my house on her way to court, breathless and courageous, but also fearful. As my friend looked to me for strength, I took her to the only place I knew to go in such moments. I took her to my Father God and His words. They would tell her what was true about her, no matter what any court decided. We read together these gracious words in Isaiah 54:4-6:

> Do not be afraid; you will not be put to shame. Do not fear disgrace; you will not be humiliated. You will forget the shame of your youth and remember no more the reproach of your widowhood. For your Maker is your husband— the LORD Almighty is his name—the Holy One of Israel is your Redeemer; he is called the God of all the earth. The LORD will call you back as if you were a wife deserted and distressed in spirit—a wife who married young, only to be rejected," says your God.

The words actually shocked me. I could not believe their precise relevance to my friend's situation. As we read the passage together, we both cried. The intimate words were like deep, healing medicine going to the inmost parts of her soul and mine. They showed her, a Muslim woman who had been taught that God was distant and menacing, that she was known by God. They posed the question to me, a Christian woman who trusts that God loves her but often doubts her value: *Do you believe I know you this well?* We both understood in that moment that God loves women everywhere and profoundly understands the issues they face. As we gazed upon His truth together, we received what each of us needed from God. We stood side by side, recipients of His grace and mercy.

I prayed for Saadiya that God would stand with her like a husband in court that afternoon. I boldly asked Him to let her feel His presence in such a powerful way that she knew without doubt that she was not alone. Hers was a complete testimony, with God standing protectively, defensively with her before the judge. I asked Jesus to show her that He is her Redeemer.

The next morning she came running to my house, her face beaming. "He was standing right here!" she exclaimed, patting her right shoulder. "Right *here*! I *knew* God was with me. I was not afraid at all. I did not cry."

The judge granted her freedom from her husband without argument. We danced in circles around my kitchen while the kettle boiled, singing along with us as we praised God. Saadiya encountered our living God through His living Word that day, and so did I. She is now beginning to understand that He loves her and has come to remove her shame.

A PRECARIOUS POSITION

In many parts of the world, especially fundamentalist Islamic societies, honor has been corrupted and distorted. Women are most often its burden bearers in Islamic societies. Instead of bearing the identity of one loved by God, cherished and accepted, women shrink back into the shadows of shame, hidden and exploited. The truth that they are known and valued by God is concealed by the lie that God is a harsh and distant judge, condemning them to a position of lesser worth than their male counterparts.

The responsibility to maintain honor within one's group is a precarious position for women like Saadiya. Circumstances beyond their control can jeopardize family honor, and they are often held accountable for it. For example, the woman who is infertile brings shame to her husband and herself.

In some cultures the language reflects this positional honor or shame—married women who have not borne children are called "little girls," and those who have become mothers are called "women."[1] In many instances, an additional wife is taken with the hope that she will bear children, relegating the first wife to other household duties.

I did not understand the burden women in honor-shame cultures carried when I first began living among them more than 20 years ago. My husband and I had been married three years when we arrived in the remote, dusty village that would be our home for the next two years. We had no children, but our hearts were hopeful and expectant that they would come in due course.

As I learned the language, I began to understand that I was being mocked by the women and children in the village. Neighbor women on their way to the village well would grin bright, toothy smiles behind their hands as they called me "little girl." I thought naively at first it was because I wore my hair in a ponytail with a ribbon. Little did I know it had nothing to do with my hairstyle but everything to do with the fact that I did not have any children. Three years of marriage with no children was a clear conclusion in their culture: I was barren, and my husband needed to do something about it to preserve his honor.

One afternoon as I worked inside our house, a dignified village elder arrived at our door. My husband greeted him and, as was the custom, walked outside with him to talk. After the traditional polite greetings, the old man got down to the real business and purpose of his visit.

"I can see that your wife is a good housewife. I see your laundry hanging out each day, and your front step is clean," he began. My husband nodded and thanked him, expectantly waiting for more. "She is a good housewife," the elder repeated, emphasizing house. "But you have no children." He paused here to hang his head and click sympathetically. "I have a young daughter who is healthy and can give you many children. She is old enough to be married," he continued.

Inside my house, I gasped. By this point I was peeking through the shutters and unabashedly eavesdropping. My Western mind was not used to such a casual conversation about my functions as a wife. I wondered what my husband would say. After a long pause, he replied, "Sir, as a Christian man, I take only one wife."

"But what about your family name?" the elder said. "Who will remember you? You need children to be remembered, to work for you and care for you when you are old. My daughter will give you children, and your first wife can still be in charge of your household."

He waited for my husband to process this before continuing. My husband, on the other hand, was trying to think of how to respectfully bridge the cultural divide and respond in a way that did not insult this respected village elder.

"How many cows did you pay for your wife?" the old man asked.

Here was my husband's opportunity to honorably decline the offer of an additional, "childbearing" wife. "Sir, I am still paying for her," he replied.

The dignified gentleman's eyes grew big with understanding as he exclaimed, sighing with sympathy, "Ohhh! I understand you now."

They continued to talk awhile longer after that, about such things as the crops and the hope for rain. But the subject of my husband's honor in relation to my fertility was not mentioned again. The matter had been closed. My husband obviously could not afford to purchase another wife, regardless of his religious beliefs.

For the two years we lived in that particular village, I never did have a child. We suffered two miscarriages, but it was not until after we moved away that our first son was born. On a regular basis, at night after the village had gone to sleep, women would come to my door shrouded in darkness and visit me. Sitting beside me on the wooden slab that served as our couch, they would pat my leg and lean in close, murmuring, "I understand. I am barren too. We are sisters." Unwittingly I had entered into a sisterhood of burden bearers. Through their eyes, I began to understand only a little the precarious position of women facing circumstances beyond their control, but who nevertheless were responsible for bearing the burden of honor and shame.

DIFFERENT ROLES, SAME NEED

Within the honor-shame system, women and men perform different roles. Women are responsible for training children about what is shameful and how to avoid shame. This is one reason why some Muslim women appear to be promoting the very things Westerners consider oppressive to them, such as the *hijab*, or the extreme and disturbing example of female circumcision, also known as female genital mutilation (FGM).[2]

FGM, which is traditionally thought to reduce a woman's libido, is one way communities seek to ensure marital fidelity. The practice is a social norm in many cultures and is associated with ideas about femininity, including the notion that removal of such organs makes a girl more beautiful and clean, thus increasing her marriageability.[3] As girls, females are taught that they are responsible for the sexual temptations of men. It is shameful to reveal too much skin, for it tempts men, so they must cover themselves. It is shameful to enjoy intercourse, so the organ of enjoyment must be removed. Women teach their daughters what they have been taught: Avoid shame at all costs. This perpetuation of shame instruction can cause females to feel the emotional impact of shame more than men.

Men have an important role in honor-shame training as well. As children grow into preteens and early teenagers, it is the responsibility of men to train them in what is honorable. Women have done their jobs of training in early childhood about what is shameful. Now men continue the training by teaching older children, both boys and girls, what is honorable and how to maintain the honor position.

This is one reason we hear of brothers participating in honor killings after a sister has shamed the family, as in the horrifying case of one brother who shot his sister after she married a non-Muslim.[4] The man who committed this act of violent shame purging is now all alone in prison, his honor stripped rather than restored, as he had hoped and intended.

Stories like these draw an alarming picture of inequality between men and women. As we probe these terrible realities and the impact of honor and shame on Muslim women, we will be tempted to vilify all Muslim men.

Muslim women and Muslim men perform different roles in the

honor-shame paradigm. However, their need for the honor-establish-
ing, shame-abolishing gospel of Jesus Christ is identical. Both stand
equally loved and valued by God; both stand equally in need of a Savior. We must keep this vital truth in mind as we examine honor and
shame in a book intended for a largely female audience. Men, too, feel
the impact of shame acutely. The gospel that removes shame is their
gospel too. We are all deeply loved and pursued by our Redeemer, no
matter our interpretation of the world around us and the means by
which we pursue value.

In our human attempt to bring order to our societies that are fragmented by sin, we create cultural systems. These systems are broken
and imperfect. The honor-shame worldview is but one such attempt
to make a right path through the wrongness. Like every worldview, it
is incomplete. But the good news is that there is One who makes all
things complete, has finished the task for us, and invites us to lay our
systems at His feet and follow Him as He leads us in a right way.[5] His
name is Jesus, and He is the ultimate honor bearer for women from
every worldview.

❧ FOR FURTHER STUDY ❧

1. Jesus honored both men and women during His time on earth, and He continues to honor them today. His interactions with both illustrated their equal value and worth in God's eyes. However, His respect and inclusion of women in His ministry was countercultural and controversial at that time. Women were the primary bearers of shame in the culture of Jesus's day, and He understood and addressed this. Read the following New Testament passages and identify in each account the shame the woman carried and how Jesus removed it, giving honor instead.

2. Read Matthew 28:1-10.

   • What shame did the women carry? Hint: In the cultural context of the day, who were the primary authorities and trusted news bearers, women or men?

   • How did Jesus honor the women?

3. Read Luke 13:10-17.

   • What shame did the woman bear?

   • How long had she been unable to stand up straight?

   • Why was the male synagogue ruler indignant?

   • How did Jesus honor the woman?

   • How did Jesus expose shame and restore honor when He responded to the synagogue ruler?

   • Note in 13:17 the responses of the people present. Who was humiliated in the end, and why? Who was delighted, and why?

4. Read Matthew 26:6-13.

   • What shame did the men in Simon's house put upon the woman with the alabaster jar?

   • How did Jesus remove her shame and give her honor instead?

Part Two

Honor
Restored

9

No Longer
Miss the Mark

Return to your fortress, you prisoners of hope; even now
I announce that I will restore twice as much to you.

ZECHARIAH 9:12

One gray afternoon, in a village called Lovely, a woman encountered Jesus the Restorer. Known in Hebrew as Nain, the village was beautifully tucked at the base of a steep mountain. Such a setting was worthy of the name Lovely.

There was nothing lovely about the little town, however, in this woman's mind on this particular day. Her only son was now dead and she was already a widow. Her world had come crashing down around her. No place, no matter its beauty, could restore what her heart had lost. Everything was desolate. The honor she had once known as a wife was a distant memory. The esteem she carried in her community as the mother of a son was now covered in a death shroud, carried to the burial grounds outside the town gate. And what of her future? How long before she followed her husband and son beyond the gate? Disbelief and shock masked her face as she put one heavy foot in front of the other along the narrow mountain road, weeping her way through the nightmare.

Soon afterward, Jesus went to a town called Nain, and his disciples and a large crowd went along with him. As he approached the town gate, a dead person was being carried out—the only son of his mother, and she was a widow. And a large crowd from the town was with her. When the Lord saw her, his heart went out to her and he said, "Don't cry." Then he went up and touched the bier they were carrying him on, and the bearers stood still. He said, "Young man, I say to you, get up!" The dead man sat up and began to talk, and Jesus gave him back to his mother (Luke 7:11-14).

What she did not know, what she could not perceive in her state of shock and grief, was that even before the death wail rose from her throat, help was on its way. God Himself was making His way toward her. He who was anointed to preach the good news to the poor would declare news to her that was beyond her wildest imaginings. He who was sent to bind up the brokenhearted, to comfort those who mourn, was at that very moment drawing near to the sorrowful death march. This woman in the city of Lovely would, in mere moments, meet the Savior face-to-face. The day she thought would destroy her future would secure it instead.

In Luke 7:12 we read, "A dead person was being carried out—the *only* son of his mother" (emphasis added). The Greek word here for "only," *monogenēs*, is also used in the Gospel of John to describe Jesus's relationship to God the Father.[1] John, the beloved disciple, used this particular word to illustrate Jesus's complete uniqueness. The word *monogenēs* means one and only, unique. Never before and never again would there be one like Jesus.

Monogenēs is again used in Hebrews 11:17 to describe Isaac during the agonizing obedience of Abraham's willingness to sacrifice his promised son. This highly personal term gives us insight into the deep love God the Father has for His only Son, Jesus Christ. By the same token, it also gives us a deeper understanding of the profound pain God the Father felt when that one-of-a-kind Son, precious and beloved, gave His life to save ours.

This same word, *monogenēs*, is used here in the story of the unnamed widow. A woman who, according to her honor-shame culture, had been stripped of honor and was bereft and desolate. This impactful word is used to describe the son who had died: "As he approached the town gate, a dead person was being carried out—the *monogenēs* [unique, only one of his family] son of his mother, and she was a widow" (Luke 7:12). Then we are told, "When the Lord saw her, his heart went out to her and he said, 'Don't cry'" (verse 13). Such a command on its own might seem cold-hearted. But this was the Lord speaking, the one who would later conquer death on the cross. And this same Lord's "heart went out" to a mourning mother.

I came to better understand this concept in an honor-shame context one day when I, too, was paralyzed by grief. We had lost a child late in pregnancy, and I shut myself in my room for many days. When my dear friend Sana learned of our loss, she came immediately to me and said, "*Bqiti fia, khati. Bqiti fia.*" She mourned with me, for she, too, had known the loss of a child. The Arabic language is poignant and lyrical, much like Hebrew. *Bqiti fi*a means "You stayed within me. Your sorrow and pain lodged itself within me, for it is my pain too." These beautiful words are a deeply personal expression of compassion and empathy and feel like balm to the soul.

I believe that day in the village called Lovely, the pain of a widow lodged itself within the heart of the Savior. It was His pain too. Fully man and fully God, He understood firsthand what that woman felt. He knew the hard obedience that lay before Him as the Son, and He knew the pain it would cause the Father to accomplish eternal restoration for humankind. The Lord understood love and loss. He had the power to comfort and restore the widow of Nain. And that is exactly what He did. The place called Lovely became truly lovely on that afternoon long ago, when a little-known woman, devastated and hopeless, encountered Jesus the Restorer. The crown of beauty, the oil of gladness, and the garment of praise Jesus gave her that day are ours as well. Jesus is a restorer of women's dignity.

GOD'S BURDEN BEARER

Jesus was born into an honor-shame culture. He grew up in an environment preoccupied with honor and shame. Within that context His life and encounters with men and women take on a deeper layer of meaning than most Westerners have ever considered in Sunday school class. His birth itself challenged the conventions of His culture's worldview. From Jesus's conception in the womb of a virgin, God addressed the issue that was foremost on everyone's minds: how to avoid shame.

At the time of Mary's divine visitation, every young Jewish man expected his betrothed to be a virgin. He also anticipated that their union would quickly produce a child. A son to carry on his father's honorable name would be most welcome. Firstborn sons were held in the highest esteem and given authority over younger siblings. Jesus's conception and birth broke all the honor rules of the day. If not for the appearance of the angel of the Lord declaring to Joseph that "what is conceived in her is from the Holy Spirit" (Matthew 1:20), the righteous Israelite never would have taken Mary home as his wife. His assumption through his honor-shame worldview was that Mary was disgraced and unclean because she was pregnant out of wedlock.

Like many men from that worldview still are today, Joseph was preoccupied with avoiding shame, both for himself and Mary. Without God's intervention, Joseph would have followed the dictates of his culture, avoiding shame by divorcing her quietly (Matthew 1:19). As it happened, Joseph married a virgin and gained a son who would carry on His heavenly Father's name for eternity.

The Jewish people were also intimately familiar with the concept of burden bearing in relationship to sin and shame. Old Testament law taught them the necessity of a burden bearer, a sacrificial animal that would serve as a substitute for the people, bearing the penalty of their sin. In Hebrew, this was called an *azazel*. In modern English, we translate it "scapegoat." Azazel literally meant "goat of removal."[2] According to *Easton's Bible Dictionary*, the form of this word signifies the total separation of sin from the people: It was wholly carried away.[3] The visible demonstration of the scapegoat being sent into the wilderness, outside the camp, emphasized the validity of the transaction.

On the Day of Atonement, the most holy day of worship in the Hebrew calendar, the high priest performed two vital ceremonies, involving two goats: One would perish and one would live (Leviticus 16:7-10). The purpose was also twofold: to make the people clean before the Lord and to remove their sins. The first goat was sacrificial; the second was the scapegoat.

First, the high priest killed the sacrificial goat, taking its blood into the center of the most holy place in the tabernacle. There the blood was sprinkled on the altar, symbolically cleansing God's people, the high priest, and the sanctuary. After that, the high priest placed his hands on the head of the scapegoat and confessed the sins of Israel, symbolically transferring those sins to the living animal. The scapegoat was then taken deep into the wilderness, far outside the camp or city, and released, as an illustration of the people's sin and shame literally being carried away.

This elaborate Levitical ceremony served the purpose of making God's people clean before Him. In chapter 3, we discussed that *clean* is one of the many synonyms for "honored." *Dirty* is another word for ashamed or sinful. God provided a way to become clean again for His people who had been dishonored and dirtied by sin and shame. The process involved sacrifice and burden bearing.

Jesus embodied both the sacrificial animal and the scapegoat. Through His blood He provided atonement or cleansing from sin for every person. As a result, we can now enter the most holy place and we are eternally redeemed (Hebrews 9:11-12). Christ was crucified outside the walls of the city, His death a spectacle of shame in the culture of His time. Like the scapegoat, His death is a visible demonstration of the complete removal of our sin and shame.

God is patient. He sent His Son, Jesus, to be both the sacrifice that would make us eternally clean before God and the scapegoat who would bear our shame and sin upon Himself, away from us forever. This is God's provision and the only way of redemption for every person.

> Come to me, all you who are weary and heavy laden, and I will give you rest. Take my yoke upon you and learn from me, for I am gentle and humble in heart, and you will find rest for your souls. For my yoke is easy and my burden is light (Matthew 11:28-30).

Pray that Muslims around the world will hear this gentle invitation and lay their burdens at the feet of God's burden bearer, Jesus Christ. May they exchange the yoke of religious rules for the rest He offers. He has already taken the disgrace far from us, making a way for us to stand clean before God for eternity.

GOD'S CHOSEN LIBERATOR

Jesus was fully aware of the burdens women carried in their efforts to avoid shame and maintain honor, and He addressed them with truth, compassion, and mercy. In His time here on earth, Jesus was deliberate and intentional in His interactions with women. He was making a statement about freedom and equality. He was also leaving for us a carefully drawn map that we might be able to navigate the very character of God regarding the issue of women in society.

Jesus was a liberator of women, and He remains so today. The Lord's emancipation of the oppressed and overpowered is beautifully described in Psalm 18.

> He reached down from on high and took hold of me; he drew me out of deep waters. He rescued me from my powerful enemy, from my foes, who were too strong for me. They confronted me in the day of my disaster, but the LORD was my support. He brought me out into a spacious place; he rescued me because he delighted in me (verses 16-19).

The well-known story of the adulterous woman in John 8:3-11 is one such occasion where a woman found herself in deep waters, confronted and condemned. Found with a man who was not her husband, she had been violently dragged by the religious leaders to the public square. We learn that she had been caught in the act of adultery, which, according to the law of that time, placed her in a clear position of shame and an expected death sentence.

Thrown to the ground by her accusers, she was filthy, humiliated, and completely exposed. More exposed, in fact, than even she realized. For the man in front of whom they had forced her was God Himself. Standing before her was a man who would within a short time bear her shame and sin on the cross. Of course, no one had any idea.

We have commonly read this story with an emphasis on the hypocrisy of the religious leaders of the day. Now when I read it, I see a story of shame exposed and its bearer redeemed. Intending to trap Him, the teachers of the law and Pharisees brought what they considered a clear case of legal and moral wrongdoing before Jesus. Religious law of the day demanded indictment of one caught in adultery. Had they known that the One they asked to judge was *the* Judge, the Rescuer, the Lord spoken of in Psalm 18 above, which they all surely knew by heart, they would have trembled in fear and shame and joined the condemned woman on the ground in humiliation and repentance.

But they did not. They were operating within their broken system of rules, distorted by humankind.

> [They] said to Jesus, "Teacher, this woman was caught in the act of adultery. In the Law Moses commanded us to stone such women. Now what do you say?" They were using this question as a trap, in order to have a basis for accusing him. But Jesus bent down and started to write on the ground with his finger. When they kept on questioning him, he straightened up and said to them, "Let any one of you who is without sin be the first to throw a stone at her." Again he stooped down and wrote on the ground. At this, those who heard began to go away one at a time, the older ones first, until only Jesus was left, with the woman still standing there (John 8:4-9).

"If any of you is without sin…" Only one in the temple courts that day stood sinless, and it was the Savior Himself. The manner in which Jesus confronted them spoke of their equality before God. Accuser and accused, the men and the woman, condemned. Accuser and accused, the men and the woman, in need of a Messiah to save them. None of them able to redeem themselves by their good works.

The air, which moments before quivered with anger and rage, grew still and silent as those religious men let Jesus's words sink in. Starting with the oldest and wisest, they responded with honesty. They could not deny their own shame. So they left the scene, carrying their burdens with them, away from the One who could have released their souls' struggle against sin.

The condemned woman's encounter with Jesus draws a poignant picture of how He deals with our shame. Among its other lies, shame tells us that because we bear it, we are less valuable than others. This belief has led many to despair of life itself. I wonder how the woman felt as she watched the men leave. Was she in despair, expecting death at the hands of the remaining man before her? She must have been astonished and bewildered as her accusers crept away one by one, leaving her crouching there, dirty before Jesus. If this man had the humble audacity to confront her critics, *what else might He do?* She was riveted in place by a rare mix of shame and curiosity, despair and hope. I wonder what went through her mind.

> "Woman, where are they? Has no one condemned you?"
> "No one, sir," she said. "Then neither do I condemn you," Jesus declared. "Go now and leave your life of sin" (John 8:10-11).

"Leave your life of sin." The Greek says it this way: "Go now and *mēketi*[4] (no longer) *hamartane*[5] (miss the mark in your relationship to God)."

The woman thrown at Jesus's feet lived in a culture where righteousness was determined by how well one followed religious rules. This was no easy feat for any person. In the years since the Ten Commandments were given to Moses, Jewish leaders had added many additional, tedious rules. For example, the fourth commandment was to "Remember the Sabbath day by keeping it holy" (Exodus 20:8). Essentially this meant Jews were not to work on the Sabbath. The Pharisees added 39 separate categories to define *work*, and within each were subcategories.[6] One's standing before God depended on adherence to the rules.

Similarly in Islam, righteousness, or acceptance, before God depends on how well one follows the rules. If good behaviors outweigh bad, the Muslim *may* attain God's approval. Like the accused Jewish woman in John 8, many Muslim women today live their lives wondering if they can ever hit the mark in their relationship to God.

I wish every Muslim woman could listen in on Jesus's conversation with the adulteress that day. He peered straight into her thoughts and responded as if they were talking out loud about her innermost fears.

No longer miss the mark.

In that moment, she knew she was standing before God Himself. He set her free from shame. He was the guarantee that she would never miss the mark again.

Alone with the Savior, the woman was not further berated and abused. Rather, she was forgiven and restored, instructed and liberated. She left the place of humiliation with a new life sparkling with hope and value. She surely never expected that outcome in the terrible moments when she was seized and taken to the public square.

Examining this passage through the lenses of honor and shame challenges me. I am a follower of Christ. I have accepted His lordship over my life and the forgiveness of my sins. But have I fully understood that He also removes *my* secret shame? Am I still striving to hit the mark with my perfectionism or my performance? As I learn more about the burden my Muslim friends carry, I learn more about my own cumbersome load. The answer for both of us is one and the same: God's chosen liberator, Jesus Christ. Jesus is the restorer of honor for every woman in every culture.

∻ FOR FURTHER STUDY ∻

1. Read again the opening passage of this chapter, Zechariah 9:12.

   - What does it mean to be a "prisoner of hope"?
   - Who or what is the fortress referred to in this passage?

2. Read Joel 3:16. Underline the words that describe the Lord as a fortress. Have you trusted Him as your fortress? Have you become a "prisoner of hope"? You can do so today. Write a prayer below, asking God to be your fortress and give you hope.

3. Read Romans 4:18-21. God has promised honor instead of shame to those who will place their faith in Him.

   - What shame stood between Abraham and God's honor promises?
   - What role did hope play in Abraham's life?
   - What was the result?

Right There All Along

What is mankind that you are mindful of them, human
beings that you care for them? You have made them
a little lower than the angels and crowned them with
glory and honor. You made them rulers over the works
of your hands; you put everything under their feet.

PSALM 8:4-6

Those with a Western worldview read the Bible with a focus
on sin and forgiveness. Because of that mind-set, shame and
honor in the Old and New Testaments are commonly overlooked. Honor-shame language is ubiquitous in the Bible, but we often
skim right over it. Words such as *shame, disgrace, glory, honor, reputation, name, worthy, stranger, poor*, and many others reveal honor's
and shame's centrality to the biblical context and narrative. Learning
to recognize not only sin and forgiveness in the Bible but also shame
and honor will transform how we perceive and relate to those from an
honor-shame worldview, as well as change the way we look at ourselves.

Many people who fill the seats of Western churches today readily agree that they have been forgiven through Jesus Christ. Yet they
carry the weight of shame, hidden from view, and do not know how
to escape its condemnation. Shame is choking the Western church, yet
the gospel addresses it fully, if we only have eyes to see it.

COVERED FROM THE START

We already discussed shame's debut upon the stage of humanity.

After their disobedience, Adam and Eve realized they were naked and hid from God. Not wanting to be seen, they sewed fig leaves to cover their nakedness. Shame burned its way through their hearts as man and woman tried in vain to cover their sense of unworthiness. Humanity has been pursuing this goal ever since. Today we cover our shame in the neatly stitched garments of good works, Facebook friends, or health obsessions. No matter what we sew together and hide behind, we are still trying to keep ourselves from truly being seen and possibly rejected.

Adam and Eve were not only guilty of disobedience, they were also then shameful before God. Humiliation was not merely an emotion they felt in response to their sin: Humiliation was a fact that changed their position in relationship to God. Sin led to shame. Disobedience led to separation from God. The honored status bestowed upon Adam and Eve at creation was lost when a curse took its place. As a result, they would experience pain, hard work, hunger, and weakness, all signs of their new dishonored status. Their disgrace led to the disgrace of all mankind.

God, in His mercy, provided covering for their shame. Blood was shed for the first time, and animal skins would cover Adam and Eve's nakedness. This powerful picture of the coming Messiah, who would shed His blood to cover the disgrace of man and woman, is given to us from the start of God's great narrative so that we might have hope. God will provide a way out of our sin and shame. The story is not over when we seem to have destroyed everything. *There is hope.*

THE SUFFERING SERVANT

Christ's purpose was not only to forgive sin but also to display God's honor. *Honor* is another word for glory. Every time we see *glory* in the Bible, a bell should ring in our minds, declaring the honor of God. The Old Testament often uses the Hebrew word *kābôd* to describe the glory and honor of God, for the word embodies both meanings.[1] A beautiful example is found in Exodus 29:43, describing the beauty of God's meeting place with His people at the entrance to the Tent of Meeting: "There also I will meet with the Israelites, and the place will be consecrated by my glory."

In the New Testament, the Greek word *doxa* is an example of another word meaning both glory and honor. Luke used it in 9:32 to describe how Jesus appeared to Peter and his companions at the transfiguration. In this passage, it denotes the shining forth of a person and is used particularly of God, equivalent to *kābôd*.[2] Jesus was sinless, and He suffered God's wrath to achieve for us the forgiveness of sins. Fully God and fully man, He endured shame and was given honor by the Father so He could display the glory of God.

We may be uncomfortable with the image of the Lord's servant who had no beauty or majesty, nothing in His appearance that we should desire (Isaiah 53:2). Perhaps we cannot quite understand a God who was despised and rejected by men, a man of sorrows familiar with suffering. Like one from whom men hide their faces, Jesus was despised and not esteemed (verse 3). But this is the One foreshadowed from the beginning, as Adam and Eve stood ashamed and suffering before their merciful Creator. He was coming even then, from the start, to bring humanity back home to God. He would take up their infirmities and carry their sorrows. He would be crushed for their iniquities, and the punishment brought upon Him would bring all men and women peace. By His wounds they would be healed (verses 4-5). Finally, after the suffering of His soul, the servant of the Lord would see the light of life and be satisfied (verse 11). The glory and honor of God lies in His great, rescuing love of you and me. It has been displayed since the beginning and will bear us up to the end.

THE GOSPEL OF OPPOSITES

As stated above, Jesus was born into an honor-shame culture, and the gospel was accomplished within it. Emmanuel, God with us, left His place of honor to enter a world of man-made systems and distorted value. The honor-shame worldview is but one man-made system, imperfect and incomplete. Because the biblical writers were looking through honor-shame lenses, however, they saw no need to explain social values such as family, hospitality, community, ethnicity, and respect for elders. These values were intrinsic to honor-shame culture, and the biblical authors intuitively understood them. When modern readers now examine the ancient texts, they are influenced by Western values such as individuality, rationalism, legality, and egalitarianism, resulting in what Jayson Georges calls "cultural blindness."[3] Our understanding of the biblical texts is directly influenced by our culture and its values.

What I find fascinating is that, although the long-awaited Messiah was born into an honor-shame culture, what He did was absolutely contrary to that culture's understanding of the world and the Savior who would one day come to rescue them. From an honor viewpoint, the one true God, mighty and powerful, merciful and just, would never allow Himself to be shamed. He would never lay aside His majesty for the wooden cross of a criminal, dying in the place of a murderer. The One whom psalmists sang of giving life (Psalm 21:4; 91:16; 103:4) would never die the death of a life-taker.

Muslims hold the view that God would never permit Himself to be shamed so completely, and they take great issue with the thought that Jesus, whom they believe to be an honored prophet of God, would suffer such humiliating defeat. Was God not able to protect His prophet? Would that not bring shame to God? Along this line of logic, the Christian insistence that Jesus died on the cross is itself proof to Muslims that Jesus was not God. Islamic scholars give various explanations for what exactly happened to Jesus on the day of the crucifixion. Some teach that He was lifted up to heaven to escape persecution. Another Islamic tradition teaches that someone else died in His place, allowing His followers to secretly take Him away. The Qur'an itself states clearly "for of a surety they killed him (Jesus) not" (4:157-59).[4] Islam's adamant insistence on an alternate crucifixion narrative reflects the cultural view that one must avoid shame at all costs. Especially if that one is God. So they labor in a system not unlike Old Testament law, heaving the weight of sin and shame upon their own shoulders, trying to follow the rules, wearying themselves in an effort to be right, honorable, and accepted by God.

But Jesus had a habit of turning human customs and beliefs upside down and inside out, forcing humanity out of its stifled and limited way of thinking. The gospel is a message of humility and servanthood made evident in the life of God Himself as He laid aside His rights and chose obedience to a suffering He did not deserve, to rescue a people who deserved death instead of mercy.

> Let the same mind be in you that was in Christ Jesus, who, though he was in the form of God, did not regard equality with God as something to be exploited, but emptied himself, taking the form of a slave, being born in human likeness. And being found in human form, he humbled himself and became obedient to the point of death—even death on a cross. Therefore God also highly exalted him and gave him the name that is above every name (Philippians 2:5-9 NRSV).

The mystery of the gospel of opposites leaves us speechless. We fall on our knees in awe of Jesus, the One who bears the name that is above every name. God has done for us what we could not accomplish for ourselves, no matter our worldview. He has forgiven our sins, restored our honor, and given us power over fear. The upside-down gospel speaks into all worldviews and leads us in a right way.

JESUS'S HONOR PRAYER

Jesus openly prayed about His glory, the glory given to Him by the Father so that He in turn gives it to everyone who believes in Him. The Greek word *doxa* is once again used here to describe Jesus's glory. But Jesus took it a step further and asked the Father to give that *doxa* to those who believe in Him. When used to describe believers in Christ, the word signifies a state in which they are accorded the fullest enjoyment of the admiration and honor of God—the object of His highest regard and praise.[5] This is astounding. God now gives His children the full admiration, honor, regard, and praise reserved for His Son, Jesus. Jesus had a right to that glory. In God's mysterious love, He extended that right to us through Jesus's sacrifice.

The circle has closed. Man and woman began in a position of honor, enjoying mutual, reciprocal admiration and love in a secure relationship with God. Sin brought shame and severed that relationship, separating humanity from intimacy with God. God sent His Son, Jesus, to bear the shame and sin, abolishing it forever for those who would believe in Him.

In the Gospel of John we are privileged to eavesdrop on one of the most astonishing prayers ever prayed. The Rescuer was closing the loop, once again interceding for broken humanity so that they may believe that God has loved them since before the creation of the world. Jesus has restored honor and made unity with God and each other possible once again.

> I pray also for those who will believe in me through their [the disciples'] message, that all of them may be one, Father, just as you are in me and I am in you. May they also be in us so that the world may believe that you have sent me. I have given them the glory that you gave me, that they may be one as we are one—I in them and you in me—so that they may they be brought to complete unity. Then the world will know that you sent me and have loved them even as you have loved me. Father, I want those you have given me to be with me where I am, and to see my glory, the glory you have given me because you loved me before the creation of the world (17:20-24).

This passage is eye-opening to the glorious purpose for which Jesus came. What we know is that the Father loved Him and glorified Him. What we might not know is that God offers to us the exact same esteem, honor, and love that He gave to Jesus.

One morning my husband and I were driving through a small English village on our way to morning seminary classes where we were studying missiology and cultural anthropology. Through the car window I saw a flash of lovely lilac purple. It's my favorite color, and it drew my gaze immediately. A little girl was wearing a lilac coat as she walked to school. Her small hand was clasped firmly by the large, strong hand of her father. He looked down at her with love and laughter, and she returned his look of affection with chattered words I could not hear.

The pair was a charming sight. But deep in my heart, in the hidden place where we hide our shame, I felt a piercing pain. I have always wanted a father. Not knowing mine has been one of my life's great losses. Even as a grown woman, the grief catches me unawares, reminding me that I grew up fatherless. As I looked out at the girl and her daddy, I wished I were the one walking down the street, holding my father's strong, safe hand, basking in his delight as I wore a lovely lilac coat.

Over the years, my Father God has taken my hand in His strong, safe one, looked upon me with delight, and listened for hours to my chatter. That little English girl so long ago had a right to be loved and adored by her father. She was his own daughter. I know now that because of Jesus, I have a right to be loved and adored by my Father God as well, for I am His own daughter.

No matter our story, our worldview, or our culture, we have been offered the right to become God's own children, enjoying the full admiration, love, and delight of His Father heart. We no longer stand apart, alone, insecure, or unsafe. Jesus asked His Father to help us believe it is true and accept His gift of restoration.

BRIMMING OVER

Understanding that the Bible is brimming with honor themes will change our lives. We will discover something missing in our relationship with God and each other, and our hearts will weigh less as we lay shame aside. In later chapters, we will examine how to understand the gospel through the honor-shame framework so that we can share it from that worldview with those who are in our lives. But we must first understand it ourselves and closely inspect the unaddressed shame in our lives. As we begin to comprehend how deep and how wide is the love and honor bestowed upon us by the Father, our testimony will flow naturally out of us, drawing others to this life-changing truth.

In this chapter we have learned that the themes of honor and shame are found throughout the Old and New Testaments. Examine the following well-known passages for honor-shame themes. Underline any honor or shame vocabulary you find.

1. Read Genesis 6:5-10,18. In this passage, we learn that mankind can shame God.[6]

   • Describe mankind's actions, according to Genesis 6:5.

   • The behavior of humanity dishonored God and His creation. God's heart was filled with great pain and grief, and He was sorry He had made people. However, there was one man who honored God, and whom God honored in return. Their relationship of mutual honor prevented the complete destruction of humanity. Who was this man?

2. Read Psalm 62:7.

   • What is the source of all honor for women and men?

   • On whom do we depend for our value?

   • What promises are illustrated by the metaphors "rock" and "refuge" in this passage?

3. Read John 1:12-14.

   • In what must we believe in order to become children of God?

   • Why is the name so important?[7]

   • By whose authority do we gain the right to be children of God?

Instead of Hidden, Seen

You have searched me, Lord, and you know me.

PSALM 139:1

rresting in their beauty, her brown eyes were gracefully framed by long eyelashes and a carefully drawn line of kohl along the upper lids. I momentarily forgot I was at a surgical clinic to repair facial deformities. I saw no deformity in this beautiful young woman. But she had not yet removed the cobalt-blue scarf that draped over her hair and face, hiding her complete visage from view. I offered her a chair as I closed the door to my office. Most examinations were done in the open area of the lobby where children and adults with cleft lips and palates all clamored to get their names on the priority list. Shame about their condition was something they had left behind in their villages and cities. Now hope gusted through the motley crowd instead, punctuated by occasional outbursts of laughter or games of tag among the little ones. Today was a day of excitement and nervousness as people, dusty from their brave journeys, patiently anticipated the possibility of repair and new smiles.

By contrast, the woman in the striking blue scarf made a beeline for me through the bustling crowd and spoke in hushed tones. I leaned close to make out her request. "Peace be upon you and may God give long life to your parents," she said in greeting. "Could you have mercy on me and see me alone?" I sensed the shame and urgency in her manner. She held the posture of one who was risking everything, precariously balanced on the razor-sharp edge of despair and hope. I asked a colleague to cover me while I led her to a private space where we could speak without an audience.

Now here we were, alone in a room, her beautiful eyes looking straight at me as though measuring my trustworthiness. To break the ice, I began with customary, polite questions.

"Have you traveled far?"

"Yes. My village is many hours from here."

"What is your name?"

"Jameelah."

"You must be tired. May I get you a glass of water?"

"No, thank you."

I waited, saying a silent prayer that God would give me wisdom to know best how to assist Jameelah and to help her trust me.

"I am not like the people out there," she finally said, gesturing beyond the closed door.

"I was born complete, without any deformity. My father has been fiercely protective of me. He would not let men see my face because he did not want unworthy ones asking for my hand in marriage. He told me to wait and one day he would find the right husband for me. Father did find a man for me eventually, but he was as old as my father and I was not pleased with him. He came to our home and brought gold necklaces and beautiful dresses, but I was not impressed with his old face and wrinkled hands. I met a boy at school whom I loved, and I wanted to marry him." Jameelah paused here, nervously readjusting her scarf with henna-tipped fingers, making sure only her eyes were visible.

"Father and I had many fights about this. I cried and begged him not to make me marry the old man. When the old man came one day with sweets and perfume, I threw them at him and told him I would not marry him because I was in love with a handsome boy my own age. This humiliated my father, and my mother ran to her room weeping. The next week, as I was carrying food to the animals, a man with a covered face leapt out of the bushes with a machete and destroyed my beauty. He said, 'If I cannot have you, no one will.' He left me lying on the ground bleeding, until I passed out. When I woke up, I was in my bed. My mother and my aunts took care of me until the wound closed."

She stopped here and carefully removed her scarf. I had been trained to maintain my composure when working with those who have severe facial deformities. But in that moment, it was extremely difficult to withhold my distress at what had been done to this exquisitely lovely young woman. The face looking back at me appeared to be the image of a broken mirror. A jagged line ran from the top right corner of her cheekbone, across her nose, and down to the far edge of her opposite jawbone, creating a ghastly asymmetry of what had once been a perfectly balanced face. Jameelah's full lips were separated by a rutted purple ridge, the thick scar tissue making some sounds difficult to form as she spoke.

I let my eyes fill with the tears that demanded to flow. Reaching out my right hand, I took hers and murmured Arabic expressions of sorrow and disbelief. Her bravely squared shoulders relaxed and she leaned closer. "I know God sees me. Can you help me?"

We are not unlike the girl with a face like the image of a broken mirror. Who we were originally designed to be, our true image, is distorted to us. The archetype of humanity has been disfigured by sin and shame. The unblemished beauty of God's original creation has been marred. But God sees us, and help is here.

A wonderful Greek term, *paraklēsis*,[1] used in the Bible, describes the ministry of the Holy Spirit. Paraklēsis is the ministry of coming alongside that the Spirit of God provides us: helping, comforting, understanding, counseling, and strengthening us. Jesus called the Holy Spirit the "Paraclete," or helper (John 14:16). The Holy Spirit helps us understand who we were created to be. He reveals to us our true worth and identity, and He aids our understanding of the honor that is rightfully ours as children of God.

In the same way that He helps us in our own struggle to see clearly who we are in Christ, we have the opportunity to come alongside and help Muslim women. We lay down our own pain, our joys, our common experiences of womanhood alongside theirs and recognize our common need for a rescuer, the Lord Jesus. It is in this paraclete ministry that we see God's power to open a closed heart and give sight to blind eyes.

This ministry is not really possible, though, until we first understand our own need to be seen. We cannot minister effectively until we grapple with our own distorted image and our own need for the God who sees us. How can we declare honor and value to others if we have not fully believed and accepted it in our own lives?

HAGAR'S STORY

In the book of Genesis, at the beginning of God's story of love for us, we find an astonishing example of God's rescuing love for a woman in desperate circumstances. She was a woman hidden from view, cast out of her tribe and nation, made a slave in the house of foreigners and, eventually, expelled from that household.

The story of this woman, who would become the mother of the nation of people we now know as Muslims, is found in Genesis 16. Her name, Hagar, means "to flee." The Arabic word for Hagar is *Hajar*, and it has become a common female name in some parts of the Muslim world. Its Arabic root, *hijrah*, describes the migration of early Muslims from Mecca to Medina in 622 AD.[2] Seventh-century Muslims were not simply migrating; they were fleeing. Fleeing from persecution, harm, and oppression; seeking peace, safety, freedom, and justice. *Hijrah* is still happening today as Muslim refugees escape from their homelands by the hundreds of thousands, seeking the same things. In modern Arabic, *hijrah* has been used to describe uprooting, hurried departure that does not even allow people to take their belongings with them, abandoning and forsaking homes, communities, and nations. It implies leaving one's home and becoming a foreigner in a strange land, even forced homelessness. *Hijrah* means a breaking of relationships, a profound change in one's entire life systems.

I find it fascinating to think that this woman and her story right here in Genesis so widely influenced the Islamic culture we know today.

The story of Hagar is given in significant detail in the major *hadith* collection *Sahih al-Bukhari*.[3] Hagar's exile in the desert is central to the sacred pilgrimage to Mecca (*hajj*) each Muslim must make once in his or her lifetime. During their journey, pilgrims pay homage to Hagar by walking or running between the points symbolizing the Marwa and Safa mountains, the same path Hagar purportedly took according to the hadith.[4]

In the Genesis account, Hagar was a servant to Sarai, the wife of the man we now know as Abraham, the name God later gave him. But while he was still called Abram, he was promised by God that he would have a son and that his descendants would be as numerous as the stars in the sky. Time passed and Sarai did not conceive. So Sarai proposed that Abram sleep with her maidservant, Hagar, and build a family through her.

Remember, honor-shame culture is collectivist, and Hagar's story takes place in an honor-shame society. A person's identity was strongly attached to membership in one's group, and priority was placed on group over self. Because of what we have learned about the honor-shame context in which Hagar and Sarai lived, we can surmise that Hagar had already experienced the loss of her position in her original group; when she left Egypt, she lost her place among her family, her community, and her nation. Removal from the group equals shame in the honor-shame paradigm.

Hagar was already living a life shadowed by shame as an outsider in a family, a community, and a nation not her own. When commanded to sleep with her master, Hagar likely had to negotiate the lesser shame. Shame-sufferers have keen survival instincts. On the one hand was the shame that would result from losing her virginity, her marriage equity. On the other hand was the possibility of honor that would come with bearing her master the long-desired and promised son. As Sarai's servant, she knew about God's famous promise to Abram. She also observed Sarai's consequent impatience and despair as, month after month, her barrenness was displayed. Hagar possibly saw an opportunity to redeem herself, to remove some of her own shame through her union with Abraham.

When Hagar became pregnant, she must have thought she had succeeded. She became even more determined in her pursuit of shame removal. Did hatred for Sarai grow in Hagar's heart? Did she dream of supplanting her? We don't know for sure, but we do know that Hagar despised Sarai (Genesis 16:4). In turn, Sarai blocked Hagar's only way of redeeming herself from shame. Sarai complained to Abram and told him that he was responsible for the problem now looming between her and her servant. He then gave Sarai authority to do whatever she wanted with Hagar. Her response was to oppress Hagar, making her life unbearable. Hagar ran away, marking the first recorded *hijrah* in Muslim history.

This is when we find Hagar alone and on the brink of an encounter with God that would change her life.

> The angel of the LORD found Hagar near a spring in the desert; it was the spring that is beside the road to Shur. And he said, "Hagar, slave of Sarai, where have you come from, and where are you going?" "I'm running away from my mistress Sarai," she answered (Genesis 16:7-8).

The Lord found Hagar near a spring. In Hebrew, the word for spring is *'ayin*.[5] We discussed in chapter 3 that in Arabic, Hebrew's linguistic cousin, the word *'ayin* also exists but with a small difference in pronunciation. In both languages, the word has the same two primary meanings: It is defined as eye, vision, or eyesight, and spring.[6]

In the Arab country where I once lived for many years, I learned that in colloquial Arabic, *'ayin* has a third important meaning. It is also the source from which your family "springs." Today the word is commonly used to describe one's character, the quality of one's family, and the honor or shame for which that family is known.

The first time I understood this meaning clearly was in the market one day after I resisted the marriage proposal of a man who had been persistently following me. In angry response to my refusal, he sought to shame me in the street, shouting loudly, "It is better anyway for a man to find a wife from his own *'ayin* (spring)!" In other words, his race and family were superior to mine anyway; therefore, it was more honorable for him to seek marriage from within his own family rather than outside. To cover the shame my rejection caused him, the man publicly called out my position. The crowds gawked at me, and old ladies behind *niqabs* (veils that cover the lower face, allowing the eyes to peek out) tsk-tsked, shaking their heads derisively. *'Ayin,* or spring, can symbolize one's deepest identity, one's source of life. I was an outsider. I was ranked shameful on the street that day for refusing my chance to become an insider by marriage.[7] The source from which I sprang proved it.

We read in Jeremiah 2:13 that God is our *'ayin.* He is our spring of living water, our source of life, identity, and value. No other spring can fully validate our worth. "My people have committed two sins: They have forsaken me, the spring of living water, and have dug their own cisterns, broken cisterns that cannot hold water." Isaiah also used imagery of a spring, or well, of life-giving water to describe the source of life and salvation. Not only is God the source of our life; He also is the source of our strength, our defense, and our rescue.

> "Surely God is my salvation; I will trust and not be afraid.
> The LORD, the LORD himself, is my strength and my
> defense; he has become my salvation." With joy you will
> draw water from the wells of salvation (Isaiah 12:2-3).

One day Jesus intentionally rerouted His journey to Galilee to sit awhile and chat with an outcast woman in Samaria. She was living in shame and isolation from her community, forced to come to the village well at the hottest time of the day when no one else would be there. In this way she could avoid those who might jeer at her and criticize her for the wrong choices she had made in life. Jesus, during His encounter with her, used the metaphor of a spring to help her understand that He was the source of eternal life.

> Jesus answered, "Everyone who drinks this water will be
> thirsty again, but whoever drinks the water I give them
> will never thirst. Indeed, the water I give them will become
> in them a spring of water welling up to eternal life" (John
> 4:13-14).

Long before Jesus sat down to wait by the village spring in Samaria, God waited by a spring in the desert along another dusty road. To really grasp Hagar's experience with God, we must understand the crucial significance of the spring and the source of life. "The angel of the LORD found Hagar near a spring in the desert; it was the spring that is beside the road to Shur" (Genesis 16:7). Hagar was in a very real sense having an identity crisis. She had unwittingly drawn near the Source, the Spring of Life, the Creator God Himself. When God found her, Hagar was *near* the spring, not quite *at* it. If we examine this moment through the lenses of honor and shame, we might even say that without honor or family, Hagar was searching for herself, for meaning in her life, for *identity.* Hagar had no idea how *near* she was to the Source of all life, to an identity change that would impact all generations after her, including the Muslims you and I know.

If we read this passage allegorically, we can see ourselves on the journey from shame to honor. How good of the Lord to find us in our search, before we have even quite made it to our goal. His eyes see our pursuit of identity, and He meets us along the way. This is what He did for Hagar, and what He continues to do today for women everywhere.

Hagar's desert spring was beside the road to Shur. *Road* in Genesis 16:7 in Hebrew is *derek*, a word that can also mean "way of life, lot in life."[8] Hagar was doing what she had always done, her way of life, her lot in life, which for her was *running away.* That was, after all, what her name meant. She believed it was her identity.

God's question, "Where have you come from, and where are you going?" in verse 8 was a challenge. If God ever asks that question, get ready. He already knows where you and I have come from and where we are planning to go. He asked Adam and Eve a similar question framed in similar language when they were hiding from Him after eating the forbidden fruit. This revealing question is not intended to expose the answer to the Asker, but rather to reveal the truth to the one being asked. Something had blinded Hagar's heart. When God asked, "Where have you come from, and where are you going?" she answered truthfully, "I am running away." It was as if her bare statement of fact was also an honest confession: "I can't take it anymore."

Then the angel of the LORD told her, "Go back to your mistress and submit to her." The angel added, "I will increase your descendants so much that they will be too numerous to count." The angel of the LORD also said to her: "You are now pregnant and you will give birth to a son. You shall name him Ishmael, for the LORD has heard of your misery" (Genesis 16:9-11).

In the United States, it has become popular in recent years for expectant parents to have a "gender reveal party" where the proud mother and father announce to friends and family the gender of the coming baby. What an astonishing gender-reveal party Hagar had there on a dusty roadside with the angel of the Lord! God Himself told Hagar what was true about her, what she did not even know about herself. She was having a boy, ensuring her honor for all the generations to come.

In this passage, God answered Hagar's real need. God did not address how stressed out she was about Sarai's mistreatment of her. God did not attend to the matter of how unfair it all was that she had been used. Instead, God answered the pivotal question at the heart of the matter, the question of who Hagar was in relation to God. She might not even have been fully aware of that need, but God knew that every other need in her life depended on that one being met. It is the same for us today. If we do not know who we are in relation to God, our other needs cannot be completely met.

In Old Testament times a person's relationship with God was defined in terms of obedience or disobedience. God gave Hagar a command to obey, but He did not stop there. He gave her a command, and He gave her *helpers*. Hagar needed help to obey this command and change the entire course of her life. Have you ever felt that way? You have heard a command from God, but you need a little help obeying it. The good news is that God never leaves us helpless. He actually provides us help to obey. That is exactly what He did for Hagar. Hagar's helpers were called Hope and a Future—the same help He would promise to exiled Israelites a thousand years later (Jeremiah 29:11), and the same help He promises His children today. Furthermore, and perhaps most reassuring, He promised His own presence with her. The name of the son she carried was to be Ishmael, meaning "God, He heard me!"[9]

After God gave Hagar a preview of her future, something astonishing happened. Hagar's shame was removed. She was given the honor of authority and respect to actually *name* God. The privilege of giving God a name had never happened before. Adam had been given the task of naming the animals (Genesis 2:19). But here we see a woman, a slave, an indentured child bearer, the distant matriarch of Muslims today, given honor by God Himself. He allowed her to *know Him* and *name Him*.

> She gave this name to the LORD who spoke to her: "You are the God who sees me," for she said, "I have now seen the One who sees me" (Genesis 16:13).

In Hebrew, the word used here for *gave* is *qārā*, meaning to cry out, call; to name; to proclaim, preach.[10] *Rā'ah*, a Hebrew word for see, means particularly in this verse to ascertain.[11] With these meanings in mind, this sentence in Genesis 16:13 could be paraphrased something like this: *Hagar shouted out the name like a preacher. "You are the God who sees me," for she said, "I have now made sure of the One who has made sure of me."*

Many in the church today have placed their trust in God for salvation. But do we understand that He has made sure of us? Is our identity fully in Him? Women in our neighborhoods, our workplaces, our schools, and our cities have no idea that a woman much like them, part of their own ancient story, gave God that name. They might be struggling through their life circumstances, or not. But Muslim women each have the same heart need you and I do: the need for identity, to make sure of the One who has made sure of us. To be made right in our relationship with God, to be seen by the One who gave us life. To know Him. Christian women have an opportunity to show Muslim women that God sees them.

SEEN

When Jameelah came to our clinic so long ago for help and healing, she knew one thing for sure about God. She knew that God saw her. She had not yet, however, seen Him. Her heart, like her disfigured face, was hidden and covered in disgrace. But underneath was hope that because God saw her, help might come.

God offers more than help to us in our shame. He offers hope and a future and, to make us brave, He goes with us Himself on the healing journey. As I closed my hand around Jameelah's that morning in my office, we started a journey together toward the God who sees women everywhere. I showed her the way to the spring called *Beer Lahai Roi*, the Well of the Living One Who Sees Me. (This is what Hagar's spring came to be known as after her encounter with God that day. See Genesis 16:14.[12]) One day I hope we will rejoice together at another spring, called the River of Life.

> Then the angel showed me the river of the water of life, as clear as crystal, flowing from the throne of God and of the Lamb down the middle of the great street of the city. On each side of the river stood the tree of life, bearing twelve crops of fruit, yielding its fruit every month. And the leaves of the tree are for the healing of the nations. No longer will there be any curse (Revelation 22:1-3).

One day we will worship in heaven beside people from every worldview. Together, we will see for ourselves the spring that flows from the throne of God and gives eternal life and healing to the world. Shame will no longer mar the nations, for the curse will be no more.

⚘ **FOR FURTHER STUDY** ⚘

1. Read Isaiah 49:14-15. What strong promise does God make here?

2. Continue reading in verse 16. We are not forgotten by God. He sees past the walls men and women build to protect their hearts from pain, disgrace, rejection, from being seen.

3. Read Psalm 139:7-12. What do we learn from this passage about hiding from God?

4. Perhaps you are hiding from God today. He sees you and He is calling you. Let His light come into your darkness and help you. What are the walls that separate you from Him? List them below and write a prayer asking Him to give you courage and help to tear them down.

Instead of Broken, Healed

*He was pierced for our transgressions, he was crushed
for our iniquities; the punishment that brought us
peace was on him, and by his wounds we are healed.*

ISAIAH 53:5

Our footsteps echoed sharply off the walled passageways that wound through the old city like an intricate maze. We were headed to an early morning church service, to a nondescript apartment where we gathered each week to worship quietly, away from the peering eyes of informants and the secret police. My oldest son held his father's hand, leading the way for me and his two younger siblings. Not many people were out at this early hour. The winding streets were deserted and silent but for an occasional cat that darted across the cobbles to the cries of the cart-man plying his fresh mint for the morning tea.

As we rounded a corner, we almost tripped over a person sitting in the dust, half-shadowed by an overhanging doorway. "May God help me through you," she rasped, holding out her hand for alms. Wrapped in a blanket, the woman looked up at us hopefully, her two legs barely visible against the rough stones of the street. They ended abruptly right at the knees.

"Some small offering?" she asked again.

We fished in our pockets for a few coins and looked around, wishing the food shops were open so we could buy bread.

A cranking sound behind us signaled a small store opening its garage-like door. An old man in an embroidered *kufi*, the brimless, round cap worn by Muslim men, busily filled a glass case with fresh, hot baguettes. Standing on tiptoe, our son handed over the coins needed for three loaves as the woman in the dust patiently waited.

She was an amputee. Cultural mores constrained us from openly asking about her story of shame and how she ended up here at our feet begging for alms in a deserted alleyway. The distance between our circumstances and hers loomed between us like an uncrossable chasm. This morning, however, our lives touched between outstretched hands and the common human experience of freshly baked bread.

"May God give you goodness." She smiled gratefully through hearty bites.

"And may God make it easier for you," we rejoined with the customary Arabic blessing.

Saying goodbye, we continued on our way.

"Why didn't we ask Jesus to give her what she really needs?" our six-year-old asked, his question reverberating through the bright morning air and lodging in our hearts.

"What does she really need?" asked my husband.

"New legs. And a house. That's what she needs," he said, his face serious as his eyes probed his father's for affirmation.

As my husband and son quietly discussed the problem of brokenness all around us, I walked the rest of the way in silence, absorbed in my own thoughts about what exactly healing looks like and what the human heart really needs.

SPIRITUALLY BROKEN

Brokenness is a pervasive human problem. It vaunts in vulgar display among the poor and diseased, the disabled and discarded of the nations. It hides deceptively behind the wealthy and comfortable, the powerful and beautiful. Brokenness lurks in every life at some time or another.

To our young child, the woman on the street had two obvious needs: new legs and a roof over her head. Our son's unabashed faith in Jesus's ability to provide for those needs was not unreasonable.

Scripture brims with examples of Jesus's healing of the broken. We are instructed to be openhanded toward the poor and needy, to help them (Deuteronomy 15:11; Mark 14:7).

But to what end is brokenness if it does not lead us to realize our severed relationship with God? *This* is the primary brokenness that concerns humanity. *This* is the most critical issue across cultures and peoples of the world. This need for healing is the one to which all other needs we address must lead. If our doing, our service, and our giving does not lead to the healing of one's relationship with God, then we are offering incomplete restoration to a suffering world.

Complete restoration is impossible apart from Christ. The Healer described in Isaiah 61 peers directly into the souls of women and men and offers hope instead of despair, freedom instead of captivity, justice instead of oppression, beauty instead of ashes, joy instead of mourning, and praise instead of despair. His primary concern, it would appear, is healing for the soul and spirit of each person, not merely the physical condition.

In the 1953 movie *The Robe*, Roman centurion Marcellus Gallio is commanded to crucify Jesus of Nazareth. Afterward, he is tormented by guilt and embarks on a passionate retracing of Jesus's footsteps so that he might examine for himself the claims of the "King of the Jews." This journey takes him to the small village of Cana. That night, as he settles in his tent, the air begins to resonate with the most exquisite harp music and singing he has ever heard. Drawn through the shadowy village into a clearing, Gallio discovers a beautiful young woman sitting on a woven mat, playing the harp and singing the story of the resurrection morning. As Gallio enters, she looks directly into his eyes and sings the final refrain describing the empty tomb. From the centurion's startled expression, it appears this is the first he has heard of Jesus's resurrection after His death on the cross.

Gallio asks the village leader to tell him more about the intriguing singer. The leader explains that her name is Miriam and that, when she was 15, she was struck down with paralysis. Miriam became bitter and angry, poisoning all her relationships. One day there was a wedding and the whole village, except Miriam, went to join the celebration.

Instead, Miriam stayed home and wept over the bitter knowledge that because of her physical disability, she would never have her own wedding day. When Miriam's parents returned home, though, they found her smiling and singing, completely transformed. While the villagers were at the wedding, Jesus had visited with Miriam and healed her broken heart.

This story enrages Gallio, who demands to know why, if Jesus was a miracle worker, He did not heal her? The old, wise leader quietly replies that Jesus had. Gallio was confounded and silenced by the answer.

As the centurion is leaving the next morning, Miriam calls out to him from where she is sitting in a garden near the village square. Confronting his disquiet and confusion, the crippled woman describes with shining eyes the way Jesus healed her bitterness, her disappointment, and her shame. Her fractured heart was made whole, and she was given honor and new purpose. With haunting beauty, she exhorts Gallio to look beyond the physical to the spiritual healing essential to life.

Gallio was baffled by the peace and joy he saw in Miriam, the woman whose paralysis Jesus did not cure but whose heart was made completely new. Healing did not look logical to this Roman tribune visiting the small village of Cana, yet he could not deny the profound power of love he saw in its residents.

God does not always heal like we think He should. Sometimes physical healing does not come. New legs do not sprout for the amputee. The newborn baby does not always continue to breathe. The critically ill do not always rally. These are all physical examples, and perhaps that is our obstacle. Like Gallio, we are angry that God does not act according to our logic and heal the lame, the sick, and the dying. We do not have eyes to see that there is a deeper healing needed, a healing of the spirit within us.

WHAT IS REALLY NEEDED

In His time on earth, Jesus physically healed the lame, the sick, and the dying. But upon closer examination, we discover that His healing of the physical was enveloped in concern for the soul of the one He healed. He saw *completely* every person He met; He saw them mentally, spiritually, physically, and emotionally. With precise wisdom and knowledge of everything hidden, Jesus addressed their needs.

I have learned in my own life to yield to God's greater knowledge of the hidden. Many times, torn and tossed by difficult circumstances and overwhelming challenges, I have knelt and poured out to the Lord what I saw as my primary need. In His gentleness and wisdom, He has shone His light upon a deeper need of which I was not even aware. The raging storm in me calms, the peace of God covers me with comfort, and the next thing is clear. God is a revealing God, and He sees us *completely*.

He completely sees each Muslim woman and knows her greatest need. Her greatest need might not be your friendship or coats for her children. If she does not know Jesus Christ, she is spiritually, critically ill. A healed relationship with God through His Son, Jesus, will bring healing and wholeness to other areas of her life, but the heart is where healing begins. We must cultivate the habit of continually asking Him to reveal what is really needed. His healing might not seem logical or reasonable to us, but we can trust Him with all our needs, both seen and unseen.

UNDAUNTED HOPE

One day as crowds pressed around Jesus, a woman in desperate need of healing worked up the courage to touch the edge of His robe. She was seeking healing for what she saw as her primary need, what anyone who knew her would agree was her primary healing need. But when she touched the God who saw her completely, she received much more than she ever dared hope. The woman's name is unknown, but her story of healing speaks across the ages and will never be forgotten. Her story is found in Luke 8.

> As Jesus was on his way, the crowds almost crushed him. And a woman was there who had been subject to bleeding for twelve years, but no one could heal her. She came up behind him and touched the edge of his cloak, and immediately her bleeding stopped. "Who touched me?" Jesus asked. When they all denied it, Peter said, "Master, the

people are crowding and pressing against you." But Jesus said, "Someone touched me; I know that power has gone out from me." Then the woman, seeing that she could not go unnoticed, came trembling and fell at his feet. In the presence of all the people, she told why she had touched him and how she had been instantly healed. Then he said to her, "Daughter, your faith has healed you. Go in peace" (verses 42-48).

Twelve years is a long time to bleed. According to Levitical law, the woman's blood would have made her ceremonially unclean. This was a type of *positional shame*, alienating her from her family and community. We have previously discussed that, in honor-shame cultures both today and in the time of this Luke 8 encounter, shame was not merely a feeling; it was a position outside one's group. This understanding aids our comprehension of the extent of this woman's suffering. We can deduce that she had been socially restricted or separated for 12 long years. Her loneliness must have been profound, her misery accentuated by the fact that she lived in a collectivist society where one's identity was tied directly to one's relationship with the group. She had broken relationships and a broken identity.

No one could heal her. The story of this woman is also found in Matthew 9:18-26 and Mark 5:22-43. Mark tells us that "she had suffered a great deal under the care of many doctors and had spent all she had, yet instead of getting better she grew worse" (verse 26). Reading the text through the framework of an honor-shame culture, we can assume she was an outcast and had no money. Her situation could not have been bleaker. She had been stripped of all that gave one a position of honor in the society of the time: family, community, health, and money. To many of the onlookers ready to condemn her that day, she was a nobody. It was this nobody, devoid of stature, who had the courage to enter the throngs where she was prohibited and risk the little she had left to touch the garment of the Healer everyone was talking about.

Shame makes us feel like nobodies. We feel invisible, as though no one sees us. We pass through the crowds, obscure and unnoticed, suffering. But even a shamed heart can hold the small, bright flame of hope. Hope is what the suffering woman sheltered deep inside even after all she had endured.

At times in our lives we encounter a soul so shrouded in brokenness that it seems the flame of hope has been stifled permanently. At such times we must run to the God who sees what is hidden, the one who *completely* sees our cloistered soul, and cry out to Him to give that wounded heart courage to reach out and touch His robe.

This woman had courage, and her story offers courage to every woman living with the private brokenness of shame today. She reached out and touched Jesus. The Greek word *haptō*, used here for touch, refers to the kind of touch that is more than mere contact, the sort that creates "some kind of influence or effect...between the two subjects."[1] It is distinguished from the simpler Greek word for touch, *psēlaphaō*, which is a surface touch.[2] Many in the crowd that day pressed in for a look at the Messiah; many were simply touching the surface of Him. They jostled around Him, stepping on His robe, rudely hustling around Him trying to get a closer look. But that one touch, that one effecting, influencing, expectant touch, was distinctly different, and Jesus knew immediately. That touch expected something more from Him. The woman's touch called out like a cry for mercy and reached the depths of God's heart of love for His broken children. His response was immediate and public. "Who touched (*haptō*) me?" He exclaimed in Luke 8:45.

Dumbfounded by Jesus's question, Peter unnecessarily pointed out to the Lord that the people and the crowds were *all* pressing and crowding Him. Peter's implication was, "How can we know who touched You? *Everyone* is touching You."

We can be one of the crowds, curiously pressing on Jesus, the surface of Him, or we can be the nobody who takes the excruciating risk to reach out past our shame and *touch* Him because we cannot bear to remain as we are any longer. We can be assured that all who touch Him expectantly, seeking influence and an effect upon their lives, will reach the heart of God. And we will be changed.

"Someone touched me; I know that power has gone out from me" (Luke 8:46). Some have supposed that Jesus's question and following

statement in verses 45 and 46 indicate that He did not know who
touched Him, that He was ignorant of the person. I would like to suggest that Jesus knew exactly who she was and was trying to shield her
from shame. His mind was set on restoring her honor that day, and
He understood *completely* her utter brokenness—mentally, physically,
emotionally, and spiritually. From our view today, having heard the
complete gospel narrative, we know that the One who stopped her
blood that day would one day soon after hang upon a cross to eradicate
all our shame, His blood flowing for every woman and man. Through
the flowing of the Savior's blood, He would give His life and three days
later conquer death forever by rising from the dead. The Messiah walking among the pressing crowds that day knew very well who the "someone" was who had touched Him. He was about to restore her and give
her a new name.

HEALED AND RENAMED

Dirty. Outsider. Rejected. Impostor. Bad. Not Enough. The Savior
knows every name you believe about yourself. He weeps every time
shame pins a new badge on you and whispers its lies into your soul,
convincing you the lie is truth. As you bow lower and lower under the
burden of shame's condemnation, Jesus's arms stretch wide on the cross,
His mighty voice splitting the earth, declaring that Hope is on its way.
Life has conquered death. You were meant to *live*.

The suffering woman bowed low into the dusty, rocky road and
trembled at Jesus's feet. So many eyes were on her now, gawking at
the filthy, outcast woman who dared touch the Teacher. But one set of
eyes looked upon her with love and understanding. And to her astonishment, that One called her by the name she most wanted to hear.
"*Daughter*, your faith has healed you. Go in peace" (Luke 8:48, emphasis added).

Daughter. We do not know all the details of this woman's family life.
But we don't need to. In that single address, Jesus revealed to her and
to us the exact center of her pain. He confronted not only the physical pain of a bodily bleeding disorder but also tenderly exposed the
emotional, mental, and spiritual pain of rejection and the loss of her

relational position as a child of a loving parent. Due to the chronic severity of her condition, she had probably been expelled from worship and forced out of fellowship with her parents. Jesus's loving name for her discloses a deep desire to be loved and cherished, a desire surely unfulfilled in her present state of illness. Can you see how intimately the Savior knew her? Can you hear the intimacy in His voice, the knowledge of her most secret shame, her most private longing? The discovery that we are so personally known and understood by God is what convinces our wounded hearts that we can heal. To be known and loved by the Savior is to be set free from disgrace. Calling her "daughter" was a restoration of this woman's identity. She was restored to relationship with her heavenly Father that day. All other healing flowed from this essential, fundamental reinstatement.

And so it is with us and with our Muslim friends. All healing flows from that one most basic, fundamental restoration. When we are restored to relationship with our Father, we know who we truly are. We are His children, and we are loved. We are set free from shame. Instead of remaining broken, we are healed.

⚘ FOR FURTHER STUDY ⚘

1. Do you believe shame's names for you? Write them below, then next to them, write their opposites. For example, the opposite of *dirty* is *clean.*

2. Using a concordance in the back of your Bible or an online Bible study tool such as BibleGateway.com, look up the word *clean.* Ask God to speak to you through His Word from the verses containing *clean* and select one verse that describes a truth you want to believe is true about you. For example, Psalm 51:10 says, "Create in me a clean heart, O God, and put a new and right spirit within me" (NRSV). From this verse one might pray, "Lord, help me believe that You have the power to give me a clean heart and a new, right spirit. I am not destined to always feel dirty and embittered inside. With Your help I can be made new." Write your selected verse on a piece of paper and place it somewhere you can see it and memorize it. Using this method, replace the lies with truth, one by one.

3. Have you experienced the most fundamental need for healing, the need for a healed relationship with God? If you have not, you can become a follower of Jesus right now. Pray the following prayer alone or with a trusted friend:

> Dear God, my relationship with You is broken. Shame has separated me from You, and I am a sinner. I believe that You sent Your Son, Jesus, to remove my shame and forgive my sin. I believe that He died for my sin and shame and that You raised Him to life again. I want to trust Jesus as my Savior and follow Him as my Lord. Help me exchange lies for truth. In Jesus's name, Amen.

Instead of Abandoned, Treasured

You will no longer be called, "Abandoned"...Indeed,
you will be called "My Delight is in Her"...For the LORD
will take delight in you...As a bridegroom rejoices
over a bride, so your God will rejoice over you.

ISAIAH 62:4-5 NET

Ratna hummed to herself as she washed the dishes. The kitchen was small and sparse, but it was bright with sunshine today and it was hers. Recently married to a kind, gentle man, Ratna was the mistress of her own home. Her heart swelled with joy as she daydreamed about a little baby boy with dark curly hair like his daddy's.

Crack! The glass she was scrubbing slipped out of her soapy hands, glancing off the edge of the sink and jolting Ratna out of her reverie. Jagged shards sank beneath the bubbles out of sight. In alarm, she drained the water, carefully picking up the pieces and placing them on the counter. The happiness she had felt only moments before dissipated, replaced by creeping dread and fear. Taking a deep breath, she made herself stand taller and squared her shoulders bravely. She would have to face the consequences. Slowly drying the broken fragments, she put them aside and waited for her husband to come home.

A short while later, Lutfi inserted the key into the heavy lock on his apartment door. It always stuck and needed a shove just up to the right to make it open, but he barely noticed anymore. Removing his shoes, he tucked on house slippers, calling out to his wife. Their daily lunch at home together was one of the things he loved about being newlyweds.

But today, instead of her cheery welcome, he found Ratna sitting quietly at the table, a small pile of something sitting cautiously in front of her. Avoiding eye contact, she kept her head bowed down low. *Is she cowering from me?* he wondered.

"Dear one, what is wrong?" he asked.

She slowly looked up, and he could see she had been crying. Her eyes shone with a mixture of fear and courage. Pushing the pile across the table toward him, she replied, "Here. You can beat me now. Please do it quickly."

In Ratna and Lutfi's Muslim culture, the Qur'anic edict[1] placing men in charge of women was widely interpreted to give a husband the right to strike his wife if she displeased him. A particular superstition regarding broken glass urged men to beat their wives to cleanse the house of demonic influence. As a child, Ratna had witnessed her father beating her mother many times.

Now she sat immobilized, waiting for the generational pattern to repeat itself in her marriage. Lutfi stared at the broken shards of glass, carefully displayed on a soft towel, then looked at his young wife. She was beautiful, her brown eyes flecked with gold. Her hair lay softly against her flawless skin, the graceful outline of her face lovely to him. She sat stock-still, bracing herself for the customary punishment.

Lutfi placed his hands gently beneath her chin, lifting her face to his. "We know a better way now. We do not live by the old law any longer. We live by the law of love. Jesus the Messiah has taught us how to love one another. Do not be afraid. You are my treasure."

Ratna leaned toward her husband, relief and wonder filling her heart. Jesus had taught them a better way. She was cherished, by her God and by her husband. What God was this who, instead of abandoning women, treasured them?

Ratna and Lutfi's story is true. My husband and I were privileged to hear it retold the next Sunday evening as the couple came for the church meeting in our house. Lutfi looked away, a shy smile on his face, and allowed Ratna the full pleasure of relating to us the astounding tale. She bubbled over with joy, and Lutfi seemed to grow a little taller as she spoke.

The two had been married for less than three months. Their wedding had been an occasion for exceptional joy, for they were the first Christian couple in our small church of Muslim converts to be married. The tiny congregation of fewer than 20 members had celebrated for three full days, feasting and singing, dancing and praising God. Eyes sparkled with bright hope for a new generation of Christian families among the predominantly Muslim population of their homeland. Ratna and Lufti were leading the way to the New Way, the way of love between the Savior and His followers and between husbands and wives.

Transformed marriages in any culture are one of the most convincing proofs of the redemptive power of Jesus Christ. Marriage, in its origin, was intended to be a picture of God's great love for us. The love between husband and wife has the potential to reveal the deep and mysterious passion God has for His treasure, you and me. Tragically, in so many broken systems of humanity, marriage has fallen far from this ideal. But there is hope, for God is bent on rescuing the abandoned. It is the passion of His great heart, and there is no fear, no despair powerful enough to stop Him from rescuing us.

THE FEAR

Many women in the Muslim world today live in fear of abandonment. Abandonment comes in different forms. Widowhood leaves many women without means to support themselves. Shame and its resulting expulsion from the family or tribe leaves women alone as outsiders. Destruction and war rob Muslim women of their loved ones, leaving them destitute and frantic, in addition to being racked with grief.

Fear of abandonment is a common female experience. It can be observed in women around the globe. In parts of the world where women enjoy equal rights and access to education, this fear can sometimes be observed in the rigor with which women work to create a place for themselves in their societies. Armed with education, stature, and strength, they become their own rescuers, pursuing independence as insurance against abandonment. In cultures where women struggle under the burdens of illiteracy, injustice, and unfair legal systems, the fear of abandonment relegates women to manipulation of the system, desperate acts of self-sacrifice, and the pursuit of power over fear through supernatural means.

For a Muslim woman from an honor-shame worldview, where belonging to one's group is paramount to self-dignity and identity, abandonment can be an expected consequence if she breaks the group's rules. Many Muslim women in the world today live resigned to the reality that they must strive to earn their position of belonging. Even then, it is not guaranteed to last. They become industrious, willing to do anything to override the limitations set upon them. I have seen women in remote Muslim villages walk for days to find a special kind of food to please their husbands and keep them faithful. I have watched Muslim mothers severely scold their daughters for the misbehavior of younger brothers, knowing these little girls must be raised to follow the rules and bear honor for the next generation. If they don't, they may be rejected, cast outside the group, or disgraced. *Abandonment*, it turns out, is just one more word for shame.

A woman will do anything to survive, even risk her life to protect her family. We see a gripping example of the extremes to which she will go in the story of a woman named Rahab.

THE PROMISE

Scholars argue whether Rahab of Joshua 2 was a prostitute or an innkeeper at the time of the invasion of Jericho. In any case, her dwelling became center stage for one of God's most startling rescues of a woman and her family. Her entire existence and that of her family was shifting, on the verge of complete and utter change. Did she know it? Did Rahab have a clinching feeling in the pit of her stomach when she opened the door to those burly Israelite spies sent by their commander to look over the city? How did she know what she must do?

Rahab was surely unaware that, as one outside the tribe of the Lord Most High, she had been set apart, devoted, marked for divine service unto the one true God. But that is exactly what happened to her.

During a raid in which God commanded His people to devote the city of Jericho and all that was in it to the Lord, destroying every living thing within its walls, Rahab was both spared and set apart for divine service (Joshua 6:17). The Hebrew word *herem* translated in this verse as "devote" meant to destroy totally *or* to devote. It denoted something either devoted unto divine service or marked for destruction.[2] In Arabic, the similar word *haram*, also a derivative of the triliteral Semitic root H-R-M, is still used to mean something forbidden or sacred. Rahab was *herem*, set apart, marked by God, for divine service. Her destruction had been forbidden by God before the two spies ever struck a deal with her. Rahab was marked for divine service that would extend far beyond her actions during the fall of Jericho. Her story gives glorious insight into the words of 1 Corinthians 2:9: "'What no eye has seen, what no ear has heard, and what no human mind has conceived'—the things God has prepared for those who love him." Rahab chose the Lord, the God in heaven above and on the earth (Joshua 2:11, from her declaration of faith). She had no idea then what a beautiful story God had planned for her life.

Rahab would become an ancestor of the Messiah Himself, one of only five women listed in His genealogy as recorded by Matthew (1:5). But as she stood on the threshold of her house in the ancient wall, staring up at those strong warriors, she had no idea she was so treasured. Her only thought was how to avoid abandonment and death.

Like many women from an honor-shame worldview, she was willing to do whatever it took to preserve her family. She saw her opportunity for rescue and seized it, offering the Canaanites' enemies refuge and help. Her initial motives might not seem pure to a Western reader. They appear selfish, driven by fear and a desperate desire that she and her family survive pending destruction. Her concern was not for the glory of the God of Israel and the fulfillment of His promises to His chosen people. Rather, her thoughts were about herself and the people important to her. But no matter her starting point, Rahab was designated to reveal God's glory and honor. God drew her to Himself out of her concern for her loved ones.

Rahab's progression of knowledge is important to note. Much is said about what she *knew*. She began in Joshua 2:9 by telling her guests that she *knew* they had the favor and power of the Lord on their side. She and her people were terrified of the Israelites. She then detailed what she *knew* of the mighty deeds of their God. Their bold deeds and the extraordinary acts of their powerful God were interwoven as she described all she had seen and heard. Rahab *knew* she and all of Canaan were terrified of these men. She *knew* they carried the greatest power on earth, all because of the favor of their God. All of this knowledge had been revealed to Rahab by the customary human means of report and observation.

This knowledge had a fascinating effect on Rahab's own faith. Human knowledge had led to divine, God-given knowledge in her. In Joshua 2:11, she disclosed her own belief that the God of Israel was the one true God: "For the Lord your God is God in heaven above and on the earth below." Sometime during this terrifying ordeal, Rahab had taken a quiet step from unbeliever to believer in Elohim.

This is so often the pattern I have seen with Muslim women. They watch and observe; they listen and think deeply. They examine the gospel message and secretly wonder if it could be true. If they are brave, they ask questions and read the Bible. Then one day, quietly and with little fanfare, they make that life-changing step to belief in the saving power of the Rescuer, Jesus Christ. Their human knowledge and understanding are engulfed by the spiritual revelation that Jesus Christ is the Savior. They are convinced, and the honor burden transfers from their shoulders to the Messiah's. "Our lives for your lives!" the men assured Rahab in response to her request to be rescued (Joshua 2:14). "Jesus's life for your life!" we are assured in response to our cry to be delivered from shame and sin. "This is how we know what love is: Jesus Christ laid down his life for us" (1 John 3:16).

Rahab believed the warriors' promise, it resulted in her being included in the line of her ultimate Savior. She later became the wife of Salmon (a prince of Judah in the line of David), the mother of Boaz, and one of the ancestors of Christ (Matthew 1:5). The scarlet cord she tied in her window to identify her house in the chaos of the coming invasion was a picture of the scarlet sacrifice her descendant Jesus would one day make to identify His followers as *rescued, not abandoned.*

Rahab's faith was so significant that later, when Joshua, the commander of the Israelite army, finally shouted his declaration of war, he included her preservation in his instructions (Joshua 6:17). As he sent troops thundering forth in an adrenaline rush of built-up anticipation and certain victory, he reminded them of the covenant made to preserve Rahab and her household.

The battle for God's promises in our lives is thunderous and real, making His enemies tremble. But in the midst of the war, He remembers His covenant, He preserves His treasured ones, and He never leaves them abandoned in the tumult.

❧ FOR FURTHER STUDY ❧

1. Luke 18:27 says, "Jesus replied, 'What is impossible with man is possible with God.'" If you carry shame, it may seem impossible to ever believe you are treasured. Write Luke 18:27 on paper, put it where you will see it regularly, and memorize it. Ask God to change what you believe about yourself and to replace the lie that He has abandoned you with the truth that you are His treasure and He takes delight in you.

2. Read the following verses, and from each one write down what is true about those who place their faith in God. Ask God to help you believe what He says is true about you.

   - Isaiah 41:9-10
   - Isaiah 49:15-16
   - Joel 2:25-26
   - John 8:31-32

14

Instead of Uncertainty, Security

My sheep listen to my voice; I know them, and they
follow me. I give them eternal life, and they shall never
perish; no one will snatch them out of my hand.

JOHN 10:27-28

The sun had set and it was time for *salat-al-maghrib*.[1] The prayer
rugs had been carefully laid out to face Mecca, the Islamic
city that is revered and honored as the holiest city in the religion of Islam and the central place of prayer for Muslims. Seven-year-
old Areefa stood quietly beside her mother, listening for instructions.
Today she would officially begin praying *salat*. She had dressed carefully, making sure only her face, hands, and feet were visible.[2] "Stand
up straight and make sure your feet are close together, pointed toward
the *qiblah*,[3] my daughter," her mother reminded, demonstrating on
her own mat. "Now, let's make our intention."

I am going to pray salat, thought Areefa to herself, just as she had
been taught.

Her mother lifted her hands to either side of her chest, then crossed
them, her right hand over her left. Areefa imitated her slowly and carefully. In Arabic, Areefa's mother began the familiar chant, "God is the
greatest." For several more minutes, she quietly intoned the prescribed
prayers and positioned her body accordingly. Areefa joined in easily,

having watched and listened to this special time of prayer since she was a small girl. After the final prayer, Areefa and her mother looked at each other. Her mother's face was beaming.

"Well done, my daughter! You are a faithful girl."

Areefa smiled back shyly. She was a compliant, obedient child and always respected her parents. As Areefa grew older, she became adept at praying *salat*. One day when she was nine years old, after performing the required prayers, she asked her mother a question that had been burning in her mind for weeks.[4] "Mother, why must we pray in Arabic, and not our own language?" It made no sense to Areefa that God required her to pray in a language she did not understand. Didn't He create all languages? Perhaps it was shameful to even question Him.

Her mother looked up from the rice she was sorting, her face clouding with annoyance, and answered, "My daughter, this is how it has always been done. Do not ask questions." Areefa was dissatisfied with her mother's dismissal and silently determined to search until she found an answer that made sense. Areefa was a truth seeker. Her intellectual hunger was growing, and the questions inside her heart were also increasing. They would not go away even if she tried to ignore them.

Areefa had sensed God pursuing her since she was a small child. Deep down inside, she believed He didn't object to her inquisitive mind. She felt compelled to search for Him and find out everything possible about Him. She wanted to talk to God about all the details of her life, not only perform prescribed prayers at prescribed times every day in a language not her own. Surely God the Most Kind and the Most Merciful would not rebuke her for wanting to know Him as personally as possible.

Is He angry with me? she wondered. Areefa's mother constantly chastised her about the way she dressed, the way she played, the way she served tea. Her father always seemed to be concerned that she did not embarrass him by breaking the rules girls were supposed to live by. Was God like that? Areefa felt in her heart that He couldn't be. Looking to her parents for guidance, she grew more confused.

Areefa's father verbally assailed his daughters and wife regularly, calling them foul names and accusing them of shaming him. At the same time, Areefa began to notice that he would flirt with other women in front of her mother, telling women how beautiful they were and making lewd, admiring comments about their bodies. Eventually it became clear to Areefa that he was having affairs. During all of this, Areefa's mother remained silent. Areefa watched the imbalance in her parents' relationship with growing dismay. How could her mother allow this to continue? Again, her thoughts turned to God. Surely her father's behavior was wrong in God's sight.

As she grew into a young woman, Areefa's insecurity and confusion increased. All the rules she had learned about how to be righteous and how to gain God's favor seemed unstable and uncertain. They clearly were not working for her mother. Her mother followed all the rules carefully, yet she was not valued by her husband. Her life was miserable. As Areefa thought about it more, she concluded that her father's contradictory behavior must be against Islam. God surely could not approve.

She turned deeper into Islam, determined to find the true source of security for women. At age 19, she was accepted into a prestigious European University for Muslim students. She had a passion to learn about Islam and then teach it in Western societies. Areefa's greatest desire was to honor God and discover truth. Now she would become an Islamic seminary student, fully able to examine it for herself. Her plan was perfect, she thought. In the source texts of her religion, the Qur'an and hadith, she would discover truth that finally made sense. After she found it, she would teach truth to others and make the world a better place for women like her mother.

The Bible says, "Call to me and I will answer you and tell you great and unsearchable things you do not know" (Jeremiah 33:3). Areefa had no idea, but her cry to know the truth about God had been heard, and even then He was guiding her to Himself. The way would be a surprising one, a path she never could have expected. Areefa *would* find the truth, and she *would* teach it to others, making the world a better place for women like her mother. Since the first day when, as a tiny girl, Areefa began to desire a relationship with God, He was running toward her, overcoming every obstacle, every rough place, every crooked path to get to the one He loved. Areefa had no idea how near she was to the truth for which she longed.

A faithful student, she pursued knowledge with zeal, devouring everything her professors at the university could give her. But as she examined the life of her beloved prophet of Islam in the Qur'an and hadith, she was horrified to discover evidence that, instead of refuting the oppression and misuse of women, he actually supported it. The prophet's sexual life particularly disturbed Areefa. His marriage to Aisha took place when Aisha was six years old and was consummated shortly after her first menstruation at age nine.[5] Later, the leader of Islam took his adopted son's wife away from him.[6] Areefa's love for her prophet filled her with anguish as she discovered these passages. She had never been taught this. Rather, the prophet had been venerated as the example for all Muslims to follow. Well, she thought cynically, her father's behavior would have been approved by the prophet.

One day, as she labored through this crisis of faith, she came home to find her roommate texting with one of their married professors. With a guilty look, her roommate grabbed an overnight bag and dashed out the door. A few days later Areefa confronted her. "Were you meeting our instructor?" Eyes sparkling with false hope, her friend replied, "He loves me. And it's not forbidden, because we did *mut'a*." *Mut'a* is a temporary contract of marriage for the purpose of sexual pleasure.[7] Islam had made a way for the pleasure of men to override their marital obligation to their wife.

Areefa was flabbergasted. This same professor was one of the most admired and respected teachers of Islam in her university. She and her roommate had frequently stayed up late at night dreaming of their futures as college professors in the United States, dispelling the wrong impressions of Islam as a religion that devalued women and placed the burden of men's sexual impropriety upon them. But as her mind swirled, only one thing was clear to Areefa that night: Islam was no refuge for women.

The next morning she arranged a meeting with a male professor she trusted. She would present her findings in the Qur'an and hadith to him and ask him to help her understand. She had carefully compiled them in preparation for her dissertation on the topic of possible negative preconceptions in Muslim thought about female sexuality. She continued to uncover evidence that seemed to support a clear suppression of women's sexuality and value in Islam. Areefa was hanging on to a thread of hope she was wrong about her religion and her prophet.

The instructor looked at her title, and his face shadowed with grave concern. Glancing at her before quickly flipping through the texts she had cited, his eyes flashed a warning. *You are on shaky ground here,* they seemed to say.

Maybe I am just nervous, Areefa thought as she waited for his response. She was growing anxious and uncomfortable, the opposite of what she had expected to feel in the presence of this wise man's counsel. "This topic is unacceptable," he said seriously. "You are casting doubt upon our holy sources, and this cannot be done by one who is seeking to one day propagate our honorable religion to others." Areefa sat immobilized, unable to breathe. "You must choose a different topic for your dissertation," he concluded. With that, he rose to his feet from the ornate, red leather chair behind his dark cherry desk.

Areefa found her breath and felt a flash of courage surge through her. "But, sir, as a woman, I can offer a perspective men cannot. Please, help me understand these confusing texts."

"I have already given you my answer. You have until Friday to give me your new topic. If you choose not to, you may return home for a few weeks and reconsider how important your degree is to you."

With that, he walked to the door and opened it, gesturing for her to depart. Areefa stood in disbelief and walked slowly out, taking her unanswered questions with her. Two weeks later, Areefa was on a plane headed back to her childhood home, to the place it all began. She had refused to abandon the subject of her dissertation. She would never abandon her pursuit of truth and its impact on women.

Over the months that followed, she began to explore other religions and what they said about women. After reading a biographical book written by a former Muslim thinker who had become a follower of Christ, she began to read the Bible. What she found there astounded her. She was shocked to learn that Jesus showed compassion and love for women, even for prostitutes.

Jesus loves me even though I am a woman? Jesus sees me as an equal to any man? More questions flooded Areefa's heart and mind as she examined the life of the Messiah. Ravenous for answers, she read the Bible day and night, examining the Scriptures deeply. Jesus taught that everyone deserved to be loved, regardless of their sin and shame. He knew they needed love, not condemnation. This deeply impacted Areefa. The dirtiness and unworthiness she had carried for years began to slip away with each word she read. *I am God's daughter!* she thought to herself, overwhelmed. She could feel His great understanding of women's suffering. For the first time in her life, Areefa felt loved by God instead of condemned. The insecurity she had carried all her life was replaced with stability and certainty that was guaranteed to last. Jesus had said it Himself: No one could take her out of His hand. Strong and brave, Areefa could finally rest in the knowledge that she was safe and secure.

SEEKING SECURITY

Strength does not guarantee security. Throughout history, strong women have faced adversity, persevered, worked hard, searched high and low, and in the end found that God was the ultimate, unshakable source of stability in their lives. Ruth was one such woman. We spent time in chapter 7 examining her tenacious journey to the threshing floor, where she sought the protection of a kinsman redeemer named Boaz. Ruth was intimately acquainted with suffering, death, and abandonment. Her spirit was immovable, and with unflinching courage, she faced her circumstances and marched right into the center of God's story of rescue for humanity. In fact, she played a starring role in your security and mine.

The book of Ruth opens with the dramatic narrative of how an old woman named Naomi and her young daughter-in-law, Ruth, came to find themselves clinging to each other for survival. All of the men in the family, Naomi's husband and his two married sons, had died, leaving the women without home or protection, in the present or the future. In Naomi's mind, the solution was easy for her daughters-in-law. They were young and still had a chance at stability if they remarried. She implored each of them to return to their mother's home, declaring,

"May the LORD enable each of you to find security in the home of a new husband!" (Ruth 1:9 NET).

Grief had blinded Naomi to any hope for her own future. Left all alone and wracked with despair, she concluded that God's hand was against her. Despite their resistance, she urged her daughters-in-law to leave her. "At this they wept aloud again. Then Orpah kissed her mother-in-law goodbye, but Ruth clung to her" (Ruth 1:14).

The Hebrew phrase meaning "clung to" is used seven more times in the Old Testament, and every one of those times it is used in reference to holding fast to God.[8] The Israelites were exhorted repeatedly to hold fast to the Lord as their one security and identity. Deuteronomy states it beautifully: "Listen to his voice, and hold fast to him. For the LORD is your life" (30:20). How intriguing that the writer of Ruth, traditionally believed to be that great God-clinger Samuel, would use this poignant and meaningful phrase to describe Ruth's dependence upon Naomi.[9] If Samuel was indeed the author of the book of Ruth, then it is no surprise he knew commitment when he saw it. Samuel's life was a direct result of his mother Hannah's habit of holding fast to God (1 Samuel 1).

Ruth's security was firmly in her mother-in-law, and she was committed. Resourceful and overcoming, Ruth refused to give up, let go, or shut down. We do not know many details of Ruth and Naomi's relationship before this pivotal moment, but the evidence of the younger woman's deep love for and dependence upon Naomi is clear as she clings to her, refusing to find security elsewhere.

Ruth was an outsider. She was a Moabite, while Naomi's family was from the tribe of Judah. Ruth had not grown up worshipping the merciful and loving God of Abraham, Isaac, and Jacob. Her god was Chemosh, the god of the Moabites, a terrifying fish god who demanded human sacrifices (2 Kings 23:13).[10] Worshippers wouldn't cling to a god like this for security. Ruth must have watched the faith and practice of her husband's family with fascination. "Stop urging me to abandon you!" Ruth responded to Naomi's insistence she leave.

> For wherever you go, I will go. Wherever you live, I will live. Your people will become my people, and your God

will become my God. Wherever you die, I will die—and
there I will be buried. May the LORD punish me severely if
I do not keep my promise! Only death will be able to separate me from you! (Ruth 1:16-17 NET).

With that, the matter was settled. Ruth had clung to Naomi and
cemented her commitment with a declaration of faith in the God of
Israel. Maybe the thought of leaving Naomi triggered the realization
for Ruth that she would also be leaving the comfort of Naomi's faith.
It was time to make a decision, and Ruth chose faith in the God whose
strength and character she had come to understand through Naomi.
Reliance upon Naomi had grown into reliance upon Naomi's God.
Naomi's faith was now her own.

Ruth and Naomi turned their faces toward the future and headed
together down the road to Bethlehem, the tiny place where one day the
longed-for Messiah would be born. But they were not thinking of that
at the moment. They did not know how important Bethlehem would
eventually be to all of humankind. No, those two strong women were
fixated upon their own salvation and posterity, their survival together
without husbands or sons.

It was the beginning of the barley harvest when they arrived in
Bethlehem, and the fields were buzzing with activity. Servants worked
from sunrise to sunset collecting the harvest. Levitical law instructed
the Israelites to leave margins of their fields unharvested, as well as to
leave behind any produce that fell to the ground (Leviticus 19:9). This
was a way to allow the poor and those who were foreigners living in the
land to come along after the hired harvesters and collect provision from
the fields. Landowners oversaw this process carefully, deciding how
wide each field's margin would be and therefore how generous they
would be to those in need. This practice of working the fields behind
the laborers was called gleaning.

Ruth understood hard work, making it on her own. As both a
widow and a resident foreigner, Ruth was fully qualified to be a gleaner.
After seeking permission from Naomi to collect grain in this way, Ruth
went out to the fields to work. It just so happened she began in a field

belonging to one of Naomi's relatives, a man described in the Hebrew of Ruth 2:1 as a fortress, a safe place, mighty, strong, valiant, a man of substance and wealth.[11] His name was Boaz, and he was a compassionate man who practiced careful oversight of all he owned. When he saw Ruth, he immediately asked his foreman about her. After hearing that she was Naomi's daughter-in-law and a diligent worker, he quickly established her position in the group, saying, "Listen carefully, my dear! Do not leave to gather grain in another field. You need not go beyond the limits of this field. You may go along beside my female workers" (verse 8 NET). She was no longer a gleaner but a harvester, with all the protection Boaz's authority afforded.

Ruth was used to being an outsider. She was not accustomed to being shown favor and honor. Reminding him of her lesser value, she declared, "Why have I found such favor in your eyes that you notice me—a foreigner?" (verse 10). Those who know the shame of being outsiders are skeptical when they encounter honor. Some feel the necessity to remind others who they really are: less than. They have believed the lie so long that it has become their identity. Honor and value seem too good to be true. Ruth reminded Boaz of who she believed herself to be. What Ruth did not realize was that Boaz already knew everything about her, even her faith in the Lord, the God of Israel, under whose wings she had come to take refuge (verse 12). Boaz is a Christ-figure in this Old Testament story, foreshadowing for us the character of the Messiah who would one day come through his family line.

Like Ruth, we are skeptical when we encounter honor. Can it be trusted? What about my secret shame? Honor and value can seem too good to be true. Some of us have believed for so long that we are not important, that we are tarnished, dirty, or spoiled, that we think this is who we will always be. What we do not realize is that Jesus already knows everything about us, even the tiny firefly of hope that darts around in our dark thoughts on our most desperate days. He has already drawn the lines on the field of our freedom, and we have been given a position of honor, security, and protection in His name.

Ruth's encounter with Boaz that day was only the beginning of her security story. Theirs was the kind of love story that blows apart the tight seams of bondage that hold hearts in the grip of shame and inse-curity. As we learned in chapter 7, it turned out that Boaz was what the Bible calls a kinsman redeemer, one who was obligated to carry on a dead relative's name by purchasing his land and marrying his widow. Boaz not only gave Ruth a position of security in his harvest field, he married her. Three generations later, Ruth and Boaz's great-grandson David would slay a giant and become king. One day Ruth would be known as one of the ancestors of Jesus Christ, Savior of the world, guar-antor of security for all women and men.

❧ FOR FURTHER STUDY ❧

1. Read Deuteronomy 32:3-4. Describe the progression of praise in Moses's song. What names does Moses give God? What does each one signify?

2. Read 2 Samuel 22:1-4. What do Moses's and David's songs of praise have in common? Write your own song of praise to God.

3. What comfort do these verses offer the shamed?

Part Three

Honor
Shared

Stubbing My Toe Against Sin

This righteousness is given though faith in Jesus Christ to all who believe. There is no difference between Jew and Gentile, for all have sinned and fall short of the glory of God, and all are justified freely by his grace through the redemption that came by Christ Jesus.

ROMANS 3:22-24

We are all sinners. Our sin separates us from God," I earnestly explained to my friend Haifa. Her baby girl cooed softly as if she agreed, looking up at me with innocent, beautiful brown eyes. The infant's cleft lip was barely visible and would be simple to repair. We only had to work a bit to get her hemoglobin levels up enough for her to have surgery.

Haifa's friends had sent her to my door after seeing me on television at a recent cleft lip and palate project in the local hospital. The need that brought her to me originally had been eclipsed by something else I had to offer: a safe place to ask her private questions about God. I was a *Masihia*, or Christian. Haifa was hungry to know what I believed, and her questions challenged me.

"Don't worry about your sin," she interrupted me. "You are a good person and God is pleased with you. You help children. You pray and give God praise. You even fast!"

Confused, I paused mid-sentence. I was launching into the four spiritual laws I had always shared with those who were seeking God.[1] Haifa was lost and I was found. I was making it clear to her how to be saved. Didn't she realize her problem? I was giving her the answer! Frustration rose in me as I concluded that Haifa was not really listening. She had *missed the point*.

Islam told her that if she observed religious rules like prayer, fasting, and giving to the poor, she would gain favor with God. If she was compassionate and served those less fortunate than her, she surely would see her good deeds outweigh the bad, the scales tipping in her favor before Him. And if she was very, very good, she might gain entrance to heaven one day. But who knows? God had the final say, and He might change His mind. As for me, in her mind, I was fine. If anyone was secure in her position of favor with God, it was me. It was obvious, wasn't it? Any person who had left her parents, her home, and her culture to help provide children with free surgery was surely tipping heavily on God's good side. I even did some of the same things Muslims did, like praying and fasting. Heaven was probably a foregone conclusion for a *tabiba*,[2] or doctor, as everyone believed me to be. I was practically Muslim, according to Haifa's view. In fact, she often said, "You are much like a Muslim. You are getting close."

"No, you don't understand, my friend," I continued. "It doesn't matter how much good any of us do, we can never make ourselves sinless. We can't be good enough on our own to stand before a holy God."

"God will forgive *you*. You are a good person. Don't be anxious, my dear," she replied, patting my leg reassuringly. She thought I was worried about *my* salvation! Who was comforting whom and with what truth here? It was clear to me that I was the one *missing the point*.

My Western gospel appeal, founded on the paradigm of sin and forgiveness, was stubbing its toe right up against one of the most stubborn, foundational beliefs in Islam: work hard and you might be good enough to get into heaven. When I explained to Haifa that sin was the reason we were separated from God, she already had a solution, prescribed by her own beliefs. Do good works to solve the problem.

Many Muslims, when they encounter sincere followers of Christ, are initially surprised and confused to discover that Christ followers do many of the same things Islam holds in high regard. Faith, fasting, praying, and charity are four of the five pillars of Islam. The fifth is pilgrimage to the holy city of Mecca. Through her Islamic framework, Haifa interpreted my religious acts as signs that I was a person of true faith and perhaps even close to becoming a Muslim. The problem with my explanation of the gospel was that it did not seem relevant to any need Haifa felt she had. Islam resolves the sin problem with the option of doing good. Sin is rendered benign if you do it in secret without bringing shame to your group. And there are always good works if you need some extra equity against its effects in your life.

The approach I was using resulted in my defense of my own badness. The truth I most wanted her to understand was that Jesus is God's provision for man's sin and it is only through Him we can have a personal relationship with God. Instead, I found myself in the awkward position of convincing her that even a "good" person of faith like me was too bad to appear before God. Haifa refused to believe me. Her own worldview had persuaded her otherwise.

THE WESTERN WORLDVIEW:
SINNERS IN NEED OF A SAVIOR

The truth is, we have all sinned and fall short of the glory of God (Romans 3:23). When sin entered the world through mankind, humanity fell away from the unblemished honor and glory it once shared with God. Ever since, sin has held people like a tether, keeping them from reaching the glory of God on their own. The rope is too short, too tight, and leads to death instead of life. No matter our culture or worldview, we are separated from God because of sin.

The sin-forgiveness approach to the gospel is a valid one. We stand in need of forgiveness, a righteousness apart from the law. No amount of our doing good or obeying the law can make us right again. We need a Savior. Therefore, God has given us a way to righteousness through faith in His Son, Jesus. This is the gospel of Jesus Christ.

Two-thirds of the world today see everything through the lenses of honor and shame, not innocence and guilt. Through the honor-shame worldview, much sin can be overlooked as long as a person follows the rules of the group. My family experienced this firsthand living in the Arab world throughout the terms of three different American presidents. Americans are keenly interested in the private lives of their presidents and are often offended by their behavior and personal choices. It is wrong to commit adultery. It is right to give to charity. It is wrong to spend campaign money on personal comfort. It is right to meet with factory workers and listen to their concerns. Americans are pretty clearcut in our idea of what is right and wrong. We judge our leaders and form our opinions of them accordingly.

In contrast, our Muslim neighbors were unconcerned about the personal lives of American presidents, often excusing behaviors that incensed Americans. Instead, through the honor-shame worldview, leaders who were friendly and diplomatic with the Muslim world were admired no matter what their personal moral choices. Abiding by the rules of the group covered any personal infractions and even made the leader more endearing.

Approaching the gospel by appealing to one's sin burden and need for forgiveness can sound like unnecessary nonsense to a listener from an honor-shame worldview. Although those holding to this view would agree man's separation from God because of sin is true, it might not be understood as an impossible problem needing God's provision to resolve. Those from an honor-shame worldview need to know how the gospel addresses shame. How we begin our gospel discussion with the majority world could make a big difference in how the message of salvation is understood.

❦ FOR FURTHER STUDY ❦

1. Read Jeremiah 3:25 and answer the following questions.

    *   In this passage, Israel laments both her shame and her sin before God. What is Israel's response here to shame?

    *   Describe a time when shame made you want to hide.

    *   How does hiding from God affect our ability to obey Him?

    *   In your own words, describe how shame keeps us from confronting our sin or the sin of others.

2. How did Jesus Christ resolve both sin and shame?

16

The Trumpet Blast of Honor

"At that time I will deal with all who oppressed you.
I will rescue the lame; I will gather the exiles.
I will give them praise and honor in every land
where they have suffered shame. At that time I will gather
you; at that time I will bring you home. I will give you honor
and praise among all the peoples of the earth when I restore
your fortunes before your very eyes," says the LORD.

ZEPHANIAH 3:19-20

For 20 years, I worked with people with disfigurements, people with mobility impairments, and those whose natural beauty was distorted by forces beyond their control. Now I have laid aside my scrubs and surgical caps for a pen and paper, and I work with those who have been disfigured by the lies of shame. With these instruments, moved by the hand of God's Spirit, my prayer is that the gospel that offers forgiveness from sin, righteousness I cannot earn, will also offer honor in the place of shame for all who have been maimed by its dark power.

Jesus is the healer of the shamed, be they men or women. My friend tells the story of how he learned the honor gospel through the life of his disabled son. Born with cerebral palsy, his son James was a living declaration of the shame-removing gospel in their Arab community. In that culture the arrival of a firstborn son was cause for great celebration, exalting the father to a place of honor. The father would typically become known from that day on by his firstborn son's name. That son would grow into manhood, in turn carrying his father's name forward to the next generation, perpetuating the family honor. In the sad and unexpected event that a son was born with a disability, the restraints of disgrace would prevent that father from taking his firstborn's name, waiting instead for the birth of a second, unblemished son.

As a follower of Christ, however, my friend did not ascribe to that practice. From the beginning, he was known to all as Abu-James, the father of James. He rejoiced over his son and believed God had created him with value and purpose. Neighbors and all who met the family were fascinated to see that James had not brought shame upon his father. James and his family challenged the belief that a disability relegated one to a position of shame. It was clear to everyone that God honored, not rejected, James. That honor and value flowed into the lives of the community, changing it at the core. Hearts were opened and the message of Christ's love was demonstrated to a people who understood the problem of shame and its power to separate one from others and from God. My friend believes his son's impairment is God's manifest glory in the midst of his Arab community, declaring to a people devastated by shame that the Messiah removes disgrace and bestows honor instead.

OUR NAMES, AND HIS

Like James's father, our Father in heaven bears His children's names with love and compassion.

> Can a mother forget the baby at her breast and have no compassion on the child she has borne? Though she may forget, I will not forget you! See, I have engraved you on the palms of my hands; your walls are ever before me (Isaiah 49:15-16).

God will not forget us, no matter how high the walls shame has built around our hearts.

One ancient Jewish custom involved tattooing one's hands or arms with paintings of Jerusalem or the temple, creating a constant reminder for the bearer.[1] The imagery in Isaiah 49 is not only a reminder of God's love for Israel. It is also a promise to all who come to God through faith in Christ: *I will not forget you.* Later, the Messiah's wounds from the nails in His palms would become yet one more poignant illustration of God's constant remembrance of us. His thoughts are toward us.

God's name belongs to His children. He bears our names with tender remembrance and we bear His. This is a glimpse of the beautiful reciprocity, the giving and receiving, of value and honor that is integral to a healthy and loving relationship between God and people. Regardless of their station, physical form, weaknesses or strengths, or genders, all who believe in Jesus Christ have the right to be called children of God. With that noble right gained by faith, they are given honor and value, hope and a future. Relationship with God is restored, and they are no longer separated from Him.

God is a gatherer of His people. He longs to gather His children, to comfort them, to relieve their heavy burdens, and to heal their broken hearts. Through it all, He reveals His own honor and glory. The Bible overflows with beautiful imagery of God gathering those who have been scattered by sin and shame. Those once lost are found; those once rejected are accepted. For those from an honor-shame worldview, the image of God as a gatherer is particularly significant. Shame casts them outside. To be brought inside again is the essence of salvation.

For some women from honor-shame cultures, Muslim and non-Muslim alike, the shame they experience is a result of someone else's sin against them. One of the most horrific modern examples of this is the thousands of Yazidi women taken from their villages in northern Iraq and made *sabaya*, or sex slaves, by the Islamic State (ISIS). One woman who escaped from bondage reported that, as she was carried away to the slave market, she begged God to forgive her.[2] Shame does that to its victims. Shame makes its victims believe their expulsion is their fault. They believe they are inherently bad, and the responsibility of the true perpetrators is covered by this cunning lie.

The good news of the gospel for any woman victimized by another's sin is that God has sent a rescuer, Jesus Christ, to remove her shame and defend her honor. He is a God of deliverance and a God of justice.

She is loved and cherished by God. She has great value in His sight. He gathers her to Himself, to the refuge and safety of relationship with Him.

The honor gospel, as I called it in this chapter's title, is not a new and different gospel. Rather, it is one dimension of the liberating good news for all peoples of the earth. For some, the power of sin has immobilized them, and the message of forgiveness is the door through which they run to the arms of God. For others paralyzed by shame, the message of honor is the trumpet blast, signaling victory and homecoming. The gospel of Jesus Christ is multifaceted, for our God is a multifaceted, dynamic God. He meets every need of every person. Depending on our worldview, the starting point can make all the difference in understanding His great salvation.

FOR FURTHER STUDY

1. Read Zephaniah 3:19-20 and list everything God promises to do for those who trust Him.

2. Among these promises, is there one or more you long to see in your own life? Write it below.

17

The Hidden Room

There I will give her back her vineyards,
and will make the Valley of Achor a door of hope.

HOSEA 2:15

THE NATURE OF SHAME

The room was dank and musty, a tiled space beneath the family salon. You wouldn't know it was there if someone didn't show you. The present occupants lived in the house for many months before they discovered the door. Drab and hidden among the mosaic wall of the spacious and sunny courtyard, it concealed narrow stairs leading down to these sparse living quarters. The room had a feeling about it. It felt like terror.

The new owners asked around, seeking information about the purpose of the hidden room. Their questions were usually met with dismissal, or a *tsk-tsk* with wagging finger, warning them that the story was not a good one. But one day an old neighbor told the tale over a cup of hot tea. In a voice barely above a whisper, she explained that a young girl had lived in the room, brought from her country tribe in the far mountains. She had been sold to the wealthy urban family to be a servant, where her task was to serve the men of the household for their pleasure. In return, she was given the hidden room, food, and clothing.

The old lady leaned close and whispered, "I saw her one morning. She wore the night on her face. They took God's light from her eyes." In Arabic, there are two words for light: *daw'*, or man-made light, and *nour*, the light of God. This young servant girl was removed from her family and tribe and made a slave. She was covered in shame. The light of God was shrouded in darkness. Shame had concealed her core identity.

The first lie spoken to the first woman in the Garden of Eden was dripping with shame. The lie stripped woman of her position as honored and valued in relationship to her Creator. Shame, not animal skins, was Eve's first covering on that fateful day. The nature of shame is that it conceals what is true and good.

Since that pivotal moment in the history of mankind, a thief has crept through the generations, robbing souls of their most important asset, their value. The worth of humankind lies in the truth that we were created in the very image of God. Every woman and every man bear upon their souls the imprint of God Himself, His own reflection. Here is the birthplace of honor, the value of the human soul. Shame hides this intrinsic truth from those it harms.

With shame came the taking of value and, consequently, the veiling of true identity. The robbery of humankind's identity is at the center of shame's work. Humanity has been in desperate pursuit of identity every moment since. Their intended, created identity as people valued and loved by God has been obscured by shame.

Shame is a lie. Shame tells the bearer that she must hide. Shame persuades its listener that she is not important and never will be. It shouts that no matter how hard one works, worships, prays, and does right, one will never be *enough*. Shame levels the accusation that you are too broken, too damaged, or inherently bad. You are *outside the camp*. Go and hide yourself.

As we have learned, honor and shame are actual positions in society for those from the honor-shame worldview. Language reflects this positionality. In Arabic, the new title *Hajj* (for men) or *Haja* (for women) is earned when one has made the *hajj*, or sacred pilgrimage, to Mecca. In Pashto, the position of honor is described by the word *ghairat*. Sayed Naqibullah, Afghan author and linguist, explains on his cultural blog: "In Afghan culture, to tell someone that he/she does not have Ghairat is considered one of the biggest insults. If one doesn't have Ghairat in

Afghan society one will not be considered honorable; and if he/she is not honorable in this society, he/she could be alienated by most of the members and life can become very hard."[1] Words for one in a position of shame are unmentionable and frequently used as curse words.

One's honor or shame is directly dependent upon one's position in the group, be it a family, a tribe, or a nation. In the beginning of time God created one group, one family, one tribe, and one nation. Man and woman belonged with God, and their position was secure.

The shame carried by millions today has its origin in the beginning, when the deceiver proposed independence from God. A position outside the group. A "better" position. A more powerful one. In believing this lie, Adam and Eve lost, rather than gained, a better position. Separation from God led to separation from their true worth. Shame engulfed them and changed the course of their lives.

For those shrinking into the shadows of shame, identity is at the core of the crisis. The nature of shame has not changed. The deception it breathes continues in this era. Shame paralyzes its prey and makes her believe she is of no worth. The light of God, intended to shine in her, grows dim with despair. But there is hope. There is a power greater than deception, a power that overcomes the lie of shame. That power is love. The Creator, driven by blinding love, pursues the one He has created, offering her honor in the place of shame. She can belong again, safe and secure in her position of value, knowing for certain that she is loved. She can come out of hiding.

HIDING AT NOON

Anyone who has lived in the dry, arid parts of the world where water must be drawn from a village well understands that water is collected early in the morning before the heat grows to uncomfortable temperatures. Women and children rise with the sun and make their way to the well, jars and buckets balanced carefully on their heads or hips. The daily water collection is like a morning newscast, where all the events of the village are reported and discussed. For those in an honor-shame culture, this time of fellowship is a foundational part of community building and social bonding.

In the book of John, chapter 4, we find a woman who has come to the village well at the sixth hour. Time was counted from sunrise, making the sixth hour around noon. The woman was alone, laboring to fetch the day's necessary water at a time no one would gladly choose. No one ventured to the well at high noon except those who were avoiding their neighbors or who had been rejected from the group and pushed into hiding.

This particular woman was an outsider among outsiders. Her people, the Samaritans, claimed to worship the same God as the Jews, but disputed with them about the location of the chosen place they must worship. Samaritans believed it was Mount Gerizim, while Jews believed it was Mount Zion in Jerusalem. This conflict caused much division between Samaritans and Jews. Leaders from both groups taught that it was wrong to have any contact with one another.

As the woman made her way to the well alone, Jesus made His way up the winding road to Galilee. The road took Him right through the country of Samaria, nestled alongside the valley called Achor, or "trouble," which was named after the calamity Achan's sin brought upon all of Israel after the battle of Jericho (Joshua 7:1-26). Referring to God's promised redemption of His people, the Old Testament prophet Hosea beautifully referred to the Valley of Achor as a doorway of hope (Hosea 2:15). The hope's promise was closer than anyone could have imagined that day in the town of Sychar, in the country of Samaria, where a disgraced woman did the mundane daily work of going to the well for water.

The Samaritan woman lived a troubled life. She was about to meet the Doorway of Hope Himself, sitting quietly and wearily beside her village well. The Valley of Achor would indeed transform into a doorway of hope for her on this ordinary day of hiding in plain sight.

Jesus made His way to the woman's village and sat down at the well. He could have stopped somewhere else to rest and refresh Himself. But He did not, and I imagine this was because she was on His mind. I wonder if perhaps her emergence from the hiding place of shame was a priority in His heart that day. She mattered to the Savior. Perhaps He arranged His day to set her free.

Jesus did not avoid her. The Savior does not avoid our shame as we do. Instead, He quietly draws near and waits for us to open up about our darkest secret. There is no pressure, only His presence patiently waiting and loving us, knowing us better than we know ourselves, drawing us out of our shells. He is not constrained by time. He will wait as long as it takes.

Are you hiding? Do you believe Jesus intentionally pursues you? He might already be sitting on the wayside of your mundane task, waiting for you to lay aside your heavy vessels of burden and talk awhile. He is waiting with love, and He knows you better than you know yourself. Jesus is no harsh and abrasive confronter of our secrets. He is a gentle Savior, and your freedom is on His mind today. Shame hides from you what is most true about you: that you are loved by God and you matter. Draw near to the story of the woman at the well and learn what shame hides. It might surprise you.

LOVE

> When a Samaritan woman came to draw water, Jesus said
> to her, "Will you give me a drink?" he asked (John 4:7).

The irony! The Water of Life asked a woman, a Samaritan, for a drink! She was an outsider, in every way positionally dishonorable to Jesus the Jewish Rabbi. She was startled by His brazen request and reminded Him of her position. "You are a Jew and I am a Samaritan woman. How can you ask me for a drink?" (verse 9).

How often when approached by the Savior do the shamed try to convince Him they are unworthy! The false beliefs they hold about themselves are so deeply embedded that even when love draws near they cannot believe it is meant for them. The Samaritan woman thought there must have been some mistake, that somehow the thirsty man who sat at her ancestors' well had not heard how things were for Samaritans and women.

There was a time in my relationship with my husband, long before we were engaged, that I perceived his feelings for me were becoming more serious. One night as the snow fell all around us, we sat bundled in blankets under an ancient tree, sipping hot chocolate. I decided it was time for me to tell him about the trauma of my past and disclose how damaged I truly was. He deserved to know the truth about me, I thought, so that he could walk away before it was too late.

I will never forget the tangible quietness that came over him as he listened intently. When we parted that night, I was sure he would decide to stop seeing me. Shame had convinced me that I was worthy of abandonment. To my astonishment, he did not leave me, and we were married the following year. We will soon celebrate 25 years of marriage. When love draws near, shame insists we are unworthy. It is a cruel lie, hiding the truth that we were, in fact, *made to be loved.*

TRUTH

> Jesus answered her, "If you knew the gift of God and who it is that asks you for a drink, you would have asked him and he would have given you living water." "Sir," the woman said, "you have nothing to draw with and the well is deep. Where can you get this living water? Are you greater than our father Jacob, who gave us the well and drank from it himself, as did also his sons and his livestock?" Jesus answered, "Everyone who drinks this water will be thirsty again, but whoever drinks the water I give them will never thirst. Indeed, the water I give them will become in them a spring of water welling up to eternal life." The woman said to him, "Sir, give me this water so that I won't get thirsty and have to keep coming here to draw water" (John 4:10-15).

Shame hid the truth from this woman. She was unable to think beyond the concrete words Jesus said to her. Their wisdom was lost on her. She knew all about water and the drawing of water. She understood that one needed empty vessels to draw deep from the well, to fill and to carry back home for the day's work. She also knew that it was a necessary daily task. The one hidden in shame knows the daily toil of her burden. She was too tired to perceive anything beyond the physical and practical. Living was laborious. Anything to make it easier was welcome. Wasn't this man offering a quick fix, a magical solution to her daily labor? Listening with physical ears and looking with physical eyes, this was the only conclusion she could draw from His curious words.

Her lack of spiritual understanding did not deter Jesus. He was patient, because He had her freedom in mind. His next command would change her life. Well-placed and smack-dab in the middle of her ordinary day, it was the key that would unlock the door to all her secrets. "Go, call your husband and come back" (verse 16). Probing deeper, He began to reveal that He knew all about her. He knew her shameful past, the wrong decisions she had made, the reasons she had come slinking to the well at a time no respectable woman ever would. It is then, when shame in all its slippery darkness was confronted, that the woman's understanding made a dramatic shift. Light slipped into the conversation like a wedge intent on breaking through.

The truth was rising, no longer hidden. It had begun its crescendo, conducted by God Himself, and no one could stop it.

PURPOSE

That Jesus met the shamed woman exactly where she was is highly significant. He did not stand far off, send a messenger with special instructions for how she was to approach Him, and wait to see if she would show up. He intentionally came directly to her, right where she labored.

Jesus met the Samaritan woman geographically in her village of Sychar. He met her physically at a well, at the place where the common human experience of thirst is typically quenched. Jesus met her intellectually on her level of understanding, and from there He drew her higher. He met her where she was spiritually, affirmed what she already knew of salvation, and challenged her to learn more. He met her emotionally in her hiding place, exposing the secrets she was working hard at noon to cover.

Jesus comes to us exactly where we are and as we are. He meets each of us, all the way. We do not have to go to a special place to find Him. He is near us even now, waiting for us to notice, to engage, and to be courageous enough to talk to Him.

As the Samaritan woman bravely conversed with this stranger, she began to perceive that He was no mere man. His words shone with wisdom and truth no man could conjure.

> The woman said, "I know that Messiah" (called Christ) "is coming. When he comes, he will explain everything to us." Then Jesus declared, "I, the one speaking to you—I am he" (John 4:25-26).

In that instant, the woman was transformed from hider to proclaimer. The one who purposefully planned her day's work away from the prying eyes of her neighbors found her purpose. She didn't hide. Rather, she shouted to all who would listen, "I think I have found the Messiah!" The crowds grew and, before she knew it, they all followed her back to Jesus. She was not only in the group again, she was leading it. Her purpose was no longer hidden by shame.

The Bible records, "Many of the Samaritans from that town believed in him because of the woman's testimony," and "He told me everything I ever did!" (verse 39). What kind of Savior is this, who knows our secrets and loves us anyway? Shame cannot hide in the presence of the Savior. What has been carefully concealed is uncovered and what is secret becomes known. The result is healing and liberty.

As He approached Sychar that day, Jesus's eyes were certainly set upon the freedom of one disgraced woman. But He also knew that her freedom would lead to the freedom of many others. This is the glorious way of Christ, the way of the one who gives honor instead of shame.

❧ FOR FURTHER STUDY ❧

1. Read Luke 7:36-50 and answer the following questions:

   - What kind of woman came into the Pharisee's house? What was her reputation in town?

   - Where did she stand after she entered the house?

   - What did she do for Jesus, even as she stood in a position of shame and insecurity behind Him?

   - What was the response of the religious men to this woman?

   - In verse 44, Jesus turned toward the woman and addressed the men. In that moment, He changed her position with Himself. She was no longer behind Him, but face-to-face with Him. Then, looking at her, He addressed a man. What is the question He asked Simon?

   - How does Jesus's physical change in position illustrate the woman's spiritual change in position with Christ?

2. In what position do you stand with Jesus? Has shame forced you into hiding, afraid to face Jesus, but bravely longing to meet Him?

18

The Guarantee

For there is one God and one intermediary
between God and humanity, Christ Jesus, himself
human, who gave himself as a ransom for all,
revealing God's purpose at his appointed time.

1 TIMOTHY 2:5-6 NET

Isana met me at the door and quickly ushered me inside, pulling me through the pulsating crowds of men in the small front room of her family's apartment. Her face was shining with unwiped tears, and she had exchanged her typical, trendy European fashions for a dark *abaya* and headscarf. Her father had died. Nothing else really mattered that day. Now was the time for wailing and intercession. Would the prophet help her father reach heaven? The men chanted and shouted, their Arabic supplications punctuated with pleading phrases on behalf of Isana's father. They implored their mediator, the prophet of Islam, to bring the dead man safely into the presence of God.

Out of respect for my friend, my own hair was concealed by a scarf, my *abaya* covering everything except my hands and face. Isana led me into a second room in which all four walls were lined with couches covered in rich green and gold brocade. Women filled every seat, their sorrowful eyes peering curiously at me as I entered. The atmosphere in this room was starkly different. There was no shouting, no prayer. The air seemed to quiver with a mixture of fear, grief, and uncertainty. Whereas the men charged the gates of heaven like warriors on horseback, confident in their supplications, the women sat quiet, somber, anxious. Perhaps they were praying silently in the privacy of their own minds. I know I was. *God, let them know the only mediator between God and humanity, the man Jesus Christ, who has made their position in heaven sure,* I prayed.

THE GOSPEL OF CHRIST

The women in attendance that day were not only physically separated from the men by a wall but were also assigned to a different room. More importantly, they were spiritually separated from God by the belief that, even at the end of life, there is no guarantee they will be granted entrance to heaven. For my Muslim friends sitting in that room, solemn and downcast, hope for heaven lay in their ability to follow the rules. If they could do enough good deeds to outweigh the bad, they might be accepted by God on that final Judgment Day.

For followers of Jesus, hope lies in the grace of the Messiah Jesus. Because no one can stand blameless before a holy God, Jesus stands for us. The sinless, holy Savior has taken our place, making it possible for us to be reconciled to God. Through Christ, our place in heaven is guaranteed.

For Muslim or Christian, eternal separation from God is the ultimate loss of position, the ultimate disgrace. Without certainty of salvation, there is no resolution for shame or sin. No list of rules followed, no good behavior, no carefully observed religious practice can accomplish the holiness required to belong to the family of God. Salvation was accomplished one way, through one person, God incarnate, the man Jesus Christ. This is what honor reveals.

THE LOVE OF GOD

John 3:16 says, "For God so loved the world that he gave his one and only Son, that whoever believes in him shall not perish but have eternal life." Love is the beginning of honor's revelation. God loves you and me. For Western ears, this famous phrase from John 3 has become cheap, splashed on bumper stickers and billboards with bright yellow smiley faces, to be passed over and dismissed. But for the one who has spent her life trying to be righteous, striving like young Areefa in chapter 14 to follow religious rules dictating even how she holds her wrist when she approaches God in prayer, the message "God loves you" is nothing short of radical. Many Muslim and non-Muslim women alike conclude God is far away from their daily struggles.

One eloquent, university-educated Muslim woman I know spends her time poring over the names of God, examining how one might experience God's love personally. I have witnessed hope and joy illuminating the faces of Muslim women in both villages and cities as they considered for the first time that God might love them personally. At the heart of humanity is a desire to be loved. Muslim women are no different.

Islam is not without its concept of a loving God. One of His ninety-nine Islamic names is *Al-Wadud*, the Loving, the Kind One.[1] The Arabic word *wudd* means "love, affection."[2] Non-native Arabic speakers may be more familiar with the word *hubb*, which also means "love and affection."[3] In Muslim tradition and experience, *wudd* is love demonstrated by action, and *hubb* is love itself. According to Islam, God gave Himself the name *Al-Wadud*, the One who demonstrates His love by giving.[4]

The gospel of Christ underlines this belief with striking clarity: God indeed demonstrates His love for us by giving. He loves us so much that He gave His very life to restore us to loving relationship with Him. Our honor and value, distorted and misplaced when sin marred our friendship with God, were secured forever by this ultimate gift of sacrifice.

Al-Wadud of Islam requires service and works to gain His love, as demonstrated by the hadith writer Bukhari in Book 1, Hadith 386: "My slave keeps on coming closer to Me through performing Nawafil [voluntary prayers or doing extra deeds besides what is obligatory] *until I love him…*"[5] The same hadith goes on to describe an exquisitely beautiful love relationship between God and his slave, although such love is possible only after that condition of effort and labor on the slave's part is met.

The words "until I love him" haunt me. So many women, Muslim and non-Muslim, are trapped in the place of "until." Working for approval, striving for acceptance, they cherish a hope that one day they will be valued with a love so loyal, so fierce, that it can never be shaken. This desperate longing drives them to exhaustion, depression, sadness, perfectionism, and a plethora of other symptoms of the heart that does not know its value to God. The good news of the gospel is that there is no "until I love her" with Jesus Christ. He demonstrated His love for us when He laid down His life to secure ours for eternity.

The God of the Bible has already accomplished the labor, the effort, the death required to redeem us. There is no human endeavor worthy or capable of accomplishing the salvation of a human soul. As the psalmist writes, "No one can redeem the life of another or give to God a ransom for them—the ransom for a life is costly, no payment is ever enough" (Psalm 49:7-8). Life is costly. It is valuable, of great worth, a sum only its creator can fully measure and redeem.

We cannot work for God's love. We cannot earn it. *We have it through Jesus Christ.* Any attempt to reach God apart from His provided Mediator is futile. Those who have been harmed by shame's deception struggle greatly to believe this. Even as I write this book, I hear shame's voice mocking me, reminding me of what I used to believe about myself before Jesus's truth set me free. Shame is powerful and loud. It screams its lies, demanding we work faster, try harder. It demands that we strive and strain. Or, if you'd rather, just give up. Quit, exhausted, shrinking back into the shadows of rejection, accepting the lies that you are *bad.*

It bears repeating: Love is the beginning of honor's revelation. With honor comes defense and protection. The honor of Jesus offers security to those who accept His invitation to believe. They are brought into a safe place, a refuge, a sure and certain fortress that cannot be shaken. Men and women alike can know that the honor He gives is neither uncertain nor changing. It is eternal and unshakable. The time for wailing and intercession is past. The Mediator has made a way to heaven, guaranteed.

❧ FOR FURTHER STUDY ❧

1. Biblical honor reveals that we do not have to wait until we are good enough to be loved by God. Read 1 John 4:19. Who loved first, us or God? What is the significance?

2. Read Romans 5:6-8. How did God demonstrate His love for humanity? Describe what we were like when Christ died for us.

19

A Little Light for
the Journey Home

I did not see a temple in the city, because the Lord God
Almighty and the Lamb are its temple. The city does
not need the sun or the moon to shine on it, for the
glory of God gives it light, and the Lamb is its lamp. The
nations will walk by its light, and the kings of the earth
will bring their splendor into it. On no day will its gates
ever be shut, for there will be no night there. The glory
and the honor of the nations will be brought into it.

REVELATION 21:22-26

Wool rugs dyed in bright red, blue, yellow, and orange dotted the rocky riverbank like scattered quilt patches waiting for a giant to stitch them together. The women had spent the entire morning beating them, scrubbing them, rinsing them, and dipping them in the flowing stream to rinse away the all-purpose olive oil soap. These hard workers now gathered in clusters under shady trees, stewing hot tea over open fires and breaking soft, flat loaves of bread to share.

Like the laborers on the riverbank, we have beat the rug, scrubbed it, and rinsed it, so to speak. It is time to lay our subject out to dry and gather to discuss how to practically apply all we have learned.

The gospel of Jesus Christ removes our shame and bestows honor instead. This is the central message of this book. I have experienced it personally and have observed it in the lives of women around the world. It follows that understanding the honor-shame perspective could be an instrumental starting point of sharing the gospel with those harmed by shame, particularly if they are from a culture that holds the honor-shame worldview. The message of value, love, and honor is transformational for anyone who knows the cruel, silencing grip of disgrace and rejection.

A MESSAGE FOR EVERYONE

When I first began writing this book, my passion and purpose was to create a volume that contained tools I wish I had had in my many years living in an honor-shame culture among Muslims. No matter how fluent I became in Arabic, no matter how close my relationships or how immersed my family and I were in the ancient community, I was always aware that I could see only dimly the beautiful people around me. I could understand only in part their practices and perspectives, and was painfully aware of my imperfection as I shared with them the hope and freedom I had found in Christ. I was constantly disappointed in my own ability to understand and clearly express how great the love of Christ was for them in a way they could comprehend. Therefore, the idea of digging deep into themes of honor and shame in the Bible intrigued me and filled me with excitement and hope. Perhaps this was the missing strategy.

I increased my study, my conversations about honor and shame, and my exposure to wise Christians who are discussing the topic today. I began to pour out my heart on the subject at conferences and in publications and workshops. Across the globe, I met people who all were asking to know more about this worldview. The increasing conversation only fueled my passion and validated in my mind the goal of this book.

An American friend challenged me one day. "Can this perspective not also be for the many Western Christians covered in shame?" she questioned. "What about us? This is revelatory. How many Western Christians know they are forgiven, yet carry incredible burdens of hidden shame? And they have no idea how to remove it."

I realized that, in my zeal, I had overlooked my own culture. We all, regardless of our worldview, need *all* of the gospel. We need forgiveness. We need to know we are loved and have value. We need power over fear. We desperately need every single drop of the gospel and all its nuances and mysteries, its power to divide bone from marrow and reveal every last crevice of human weakness. Like blinding sunlight, it chases the darkness away and bleaches our stained souls. For some, that stain is called shame.

Naturally, as Westerners, we have historically read the Bible through our own innocence-guilt worldview. Yet God used people from an honor-shame worldview to write the sacred text, and it was injected into an honor-shame culture. The Bible does not need to be contextualized to be understood by those from that worldview today; our perspective does. As we look for honor-shame themes in the Bible, we will not only become better communicators of the gospel to Muslims, we will grow ourselves in our understanding of the gospel that not only forgives sin but *also* removes our shame and bestows honor instead.

Thus, my own purpose for this book has grown and expanded beyond my original intentions. Isaiah 55:9 reminds us that "as the heavens are higher than the earth, so are my ways higher than your ways and my thoughts than your thoughts." I am so thankful for wise and godly counselors who have stretched my thoughts toward God's and helped me find His higher way. This book is for you, whoever you are. May the Lord reveal His higher thoughts and higher ways for your life through its words.

LIGHT RECEIVED, LIGHT GIVEN

When we lived in the deep bush of East Africa, I was often asked for a little paraffin, also called kerosene, to light my neighbors' small, handmade tin lamps. I made sure to always have a supply of kerosene to give away in addition to what was necessary for my own lantern. I used to love the sight of a friend walking down the pathway from my house, the little light she had received from me flickering like hope in the blackness of the African night. Can you see the light in your mind's eye with me?

Maybe you want to share light with your neighbors and friends. You want them to know there is hope in Jesus Christ. Fill your own lantern first, then the overflow will be a constant supply for those who know you can be counted on for light and truth. If we want to reach Muslims or anyone writhing in the ropes of shame's lies, we must first come to the Savior and let Him deal with our own souls. We must choose to disclose to Him what He already knows about our hidden places, trusting the Savior to heal us. And *He will heal us.* He will show us a love so great it cannot be measured and will never be stolen from us. When we experience that love, that knowledge that we are valued by God Himself, we will not be able to see the end of the line of people at our door wanting a little light from our steadfast supply.

> Come, let us return to the LORD. He has torn us to pieces but he will heal us; he has injured us but he will bind up our wounds. After two days he will revive us; on the third day he will restore us, that we may live in his presence. Let us acknowledge the LORD; let us press on to acknowledge him. As surely as the sun rises, he will appear; he will come to us like the winter rains, like the spring rains that water the earth (Hosea 6:1-3).

Let us acknowledge the Lord. Let us *press on* to acknowledge Him. He chose to shroud His beauty and glory in our shame on the cross. Then, with all the power of heaven, He ripped it off like the discarded grave linens that could not hold Him in the tomb and secured our honor forever. We choose to trust Him, then we keep doing it every day of our lives, bringing as many with us into His presence as we possibly can. The gospel of Jesus Christ removes our shame and gives honor instead.

❧ FOR FURTHER STUDY ❧

1. Read 1 Corinthians 1:26-28 and answer the following questions.

   - In what condition are most people when God calls them to follow Him? In what condition were you?

2. How did God choose to reveal His wisdom to the world?

   - Do you believe that your life can be used by God to rescue others from shame? What steps do you need to take? Write your response.

Keys to Identifying Honor and Shame in Scripture

One of the best ways we can equip ourselves to understand honor and shame in the Bible and in turn share it with those from an honor-shame worldview is to read it for ourselves. This can be hard to do, though, when one has always read Scripture through a different cultural lens. I have developed the questions below to help you read the Bible through the lenses of honor and shame. The stories that follow will guide you through two examples of how to apply these keys.

1. Identify the hidden/covered issue: What does shame *conceal*?

2. Identify how God reveals and restores honor in this passage: What does honor *reveal*?

3. Identify how you can apply this to your own life or when sharing the message of honor with a friend: What is the *appeal*?

Honor and Shame
Key Applications

Read the following Scriptures and apply these keys:

- What does shame conceal?
- What does honor reveal?
- What is my appeal?

LUKE 7:36-50: JESUS IS ANOINTED BY A SINFUL WOMAN

What does shame conceal?

This account of "a sinful woman" illustrates the close relationship between sin and shame. In this passage a woman who had lived a sinful life, one described by the Greek word *hamartōlos* as heinous and habitual, had the courage to enter a Pharisee's house as Jesus dined there.[1] Her sinful choices in life had rendered this woman "sinful" in the eyes of the community, especially the religious leaders. We understand from the honor-shame culture of the time that her sinful choices and consequent disgraceful reputation also socially exiled her, placing her in a position of shame. She had an immoral reputation and had been rejected from society as a result. Her positional shame concealed from Simon, the Pharisee hosting the meal, the woman's potential for redemption and forgiveness. He could not see past her sin and shame.

He was appalled by her actions. Simon's reaction was appropriate within the context of his worldview. But Jesus, as we will see, challenges any worldview that devalues people, rendering them unredeemable.

We have learned that shame makes its bearer feel not only rejected but dirty and unworthy. In the culture of Luke 7, such a woman was also considered spiritually unclean. It is possible that shame also concealed in her heart an anguished hope that spiritual uncleanness did not equal permanent rejection from God Himself. Her tearful sacrifice of that item most precious to her, her costly alabaster jar of perfume, revealed how desperately she hoped for redemption, to be made clean again.

What does honor reveal?

Jesus restored honor by using the woman's sacrifice as an illustration to teach about forgiveness. He also gently rebuked the righteous, "right with God," Simon, pointing out that his love for Jesus was small compared to the "sinful" woman's. She understood clearly that she needed much forgiveness; she understood the value of Jesus's forgiveness and showed Him her faith by loving Him greatly in return. Simon was taking Jesus's forgiveness for granted and forgetting his own great need for forgiveness. To use a woman to teach a man a spiritual truth was shocking and potentially offensive in the male-led culture of that day. The underlying theme of this story is Jesus's restoration of the woman's honor by pointing out her value to God.

What is the appeal?

Women need to know they are valued by God. Nothing they have done has rendered them too unclean to be made clean or forgiven. It is never too late to surrender one's reputation to God. The sinful woman demonstrated courageous faith by going to the feet of Jesus in the presence of her accusers, those who had judged her a ruined person. Forgiveness is available for every person who makes this bold, risky step toward the Savior. But Jesus does not stop at forgiveness. His goal for you and me is complete freedom. Jesus removes our shame and gives honor in its place, for He sees our worth. What we have been hiding, the burden we have carried silently, shamefully, the Savior gently takes from us and declares us forgiven and honored. Our faith has saved us, and we are sent forth in peace.

Refugees and women in transit may not have not been able to do what Muslims normally do to make themselves "clean" before God. They have probably not been able to do ablutions, or ritual cleansing, before prayer. Maybe there has not been an acceptable place to pray. Maybe they have been forced, or have chosen, to commit shameful acts in order to survive. The message of acceptance and cleanness before God through Jesus Christ is a powerful truth for them.

1 SAMUEL 16:1-13: SAMUEL ANOINTS DAVID

What does shame conceal?

In the honor-shame culture of Samuel's time, honor was given to the oldest son. Outward strength and attractiveness made one more likely to gain the approval and esteem of one's group. This is still true today in many societies. In his search for God's chosen king, Samuel was following the cultural dictates of honor and shame. When he saw Jesse's firstborn son, Eliab, he thought he had found the next king. In this passage, human rules of honor and shame hid the truth from the man of God. The truth was disclosed when God said to Samuel in verse 7, "Do not consider his appearance or his height, for I have rejected him. The LORD does not look at the things man looks at. People look at the outward appearance, but the LORD looks at the heart."

This story turns the honor-shame paradigm upside down, from the value placed on birth order to the human tendency to bestow greater honor and esteem based upon one's outward appearance. Shame can conceal from even the wisest among us God's perspective about a person. It can conceal his worth to God, his gifts, and his future purpose. Shame can conceal wise judgment from us.

What does honor reveal?

Samuel, though he was God's servant, still needed God's help to see the true worth God saw in David. The Author of original honor knows what is in our hearts, and He reveals in this passage the source of true worth. Our hearts reveal our faith. David was the youngest and the smallest of his brothers, but his heart was full of faith in God. He was a worshipper and a poet. He hungered to know God. Honor also reveals that no matter how the world measures us outwardly, God measures our hearts. He sees our gifts, our purpose, our future. God sees our worth, and He loves us.

What is the appeal?

It can be either frightening or comforting to know that God sees our hearts. If we are hiding sin and shame, we might shrink back from His examination and hesitate to draw near. If we have been battered by the unfair judgment and rejection of others, the thought that God sees the truth about us might be liberating. No matter what one's response, fear or hope, it is never too late to bring our hearts to the One who can heal them, clean them, and make them strong again. He sees past the scars and scratches to who we were meant to be, and our future stretches out before us, upheld by a God who goes before us and loves us each step of the way.

Acknowledgments

To…

The One who leaves the 99 to take the lost lamb in His arms and bear it to safety, I thank you with all my heart for rescuing me from shame. Thank you, Jesus.

My best friend and teammate in all things, my husband, David. You have encouraged me and supported me every step of this journey. Thank you for believing in me more than I did myself at times and holding the vision of lives set free before me so I would run the race with endurance. You have shown my eyes what the honor and love of Jesus really look like.

My three children. Thank you for sharing your mom with Muslim women around the world and bearing with me when I pounded the keyboard at all hours of the day and night. Thank you for not minding cereal for dinner on deadline weeks, for your hugs at just the right time, and for telling me never to give up. I love you.

Dad K, thank you for speaking a father's blessing on this fatherless girl and showing me what honor looks like. I will always walk on the high road because you and Mom K showed me how. Thank you both for taking me in and making me yours.

My mother, who bravely faced the shame, thank you. Our story is still being written with grace.

Dr. Jarvis, you were the first to tell me I must, not should, write a book. Roland Muller, my mentor and encourager, I could never have done this without you. This book belongs to both of us. Hannah Thompson, my dear lifetime mentor, thank you for endless cups of tea and truth. You helped me heal. Edie Melson, my writing mentor, you have given so generously and patiently to me, and I am indebted to you for helping me become an author.

Jane, who opened the door.

The Bomb Squad, the prayer team behind this book, you know the private battles and victories it took to get this far.

My superior beta readers, Jen, Beth, Kit and the Muller family. You made the book readable and reachable.

Jami Staples. Thank you for becoming my fellow visionary, dreamer, friend, and colleague. I hope this book answers some of your nagging questions.

Fouad Masri, Werner Mischke, Jayson Georges, and Jackson Wu. Thank you for your leadership and guidance, and for the many emails and phone chats for your opinions and counsel.

To Floyd and Blackie's, my favorite coffee shop. Thanks for not charging me rent and for making me the best cup of coffee in three states.

David Van Diest, my literary agent. You have been a rock of wisdom and encouragement. Thank you.

The diligent and dedicated staff at Harvest House Publishers, especially Kathleen Kerr, Jessica Ballestrazze, Kyler Dougherty, and Betty Fletcher.

And finally, the many brave women who inspired this book's message. I will always be grateful to you for demanding to know the God who gives honor instead of shame.

Notes

INTRODUCTION

1. For further insight into Folk Islam, I recommend Dr. Rick Love's book *Muslims, Magic and the Kingdom of God* (Littleton, CO: William Carey Library, 2013).

2. In her dream, Jesus used words directly from Scripture, though she had never read the Bible. Muslims around the world consistently report dreams of Jesus speaking words they later discover are directly from the Bible. In this young woman's case, His words were a quote from John 14:6: "Jesus answered, 'I am the way and the truth and the life. No one comes to the Father except through me.'" The command "Follow me" is repeated numerous times in the New Testament when Jesus invited someone to become His disciple (see Matthew 4:19; 8:22; 9:9; 19:21; Mark 2:14; John 1:43; 21:19).

CHAPTER 1

1. Jon Ronson, "Monica Lewinsky: 'The Shame Sticks to You Like Tar,'" Guardian.com, April, 22, 2016, https://www.theguardian.com/technology/2016/apr/16/monica-lewinsky-shame-sticks -like-tar-jon-ronson.

2. Monica Lewinsky bravely addresses what she calls a "culture of humiliation" in her striking TED talk, "The Price of Shame," https://www.ted.com/talks/monica_lewinsky_the_price_of_shame.

3. This is a true scenario. During an afternoon gathering for tea with Muslim female friends one day, the women discussed the victim's guilt at length, much to my distress and attempted intervention. The verdict among them was firm: it was her fault, and she deserved whatever she got.

4. https://www.etymonline.com/word/shame.

CHAPTER 3

1. https://www.biblegateway.com/resources/matthew-henry/Isa.45.1-Isa.45.1-4.

2. https://www.biblegateway.com/resources/matthew-henry/Isa.45.1-Isa.45.4.

3. *The Cambridge Bible for Schools and Colleges* exegetical commentary, which looks at original biblical languages, describes the use of *surname* in Isaiah 45:4 as bestowing "honorable names" upon Cyrus (Cambridge University Press: 1882–1922), Isaiah 45. *The Pulpit Commentary* explains the surnames given to Cyrus in Isaiah 45 as "designations of honor" (Hendrickson Publishers, Peabody, MA: 1990), Isaiah 45.

4. Jayson Georges and Mark D. Baker, *Ministering in Honor-Shame Cultures* (Downers Grove, IL: IVP Academic, 2016), 17.

5. Malcolm Gladwell, *Outliers* (New York: Hachette Book Group, 2008), 167.

6. Hans Wehr, *The Hans Wehr Dictionary of Modern Written Arabic,* edited by J. M. Cowan (Urbana: Spoken Language Services, Inc., with permission of Otto Harrasowitz, 1994), 776.

7. Qur'an 4:11.

CHAPTER 4

1. Qur'an, Surah al-Baqarah 2:284.

2. *Al-Bukhari*, "Arabic-English Book Reference: Book 59, Hadith, 52, Vol. 4, Book 54, Hadith 464," https://sunnah.com/bukhari/59/52.

3. Jayson Georges, "The Three Kinds of Honor," http://honorshame.com/kinds-of-honor/.

CHAPTER 5

1. Werner Mischke, *The Global Gospel* (Mission ONE, 2015), 23.

CHAPTER 6

1. For an insightful discussion of this subject, see "Ascribed Honor Versus Achieved Honor: What Does it Mean for Cross-Cultural Partnerships?," http://wernermischke.org/2009/11/05/ascribed-honor-versus-achieved-honor-what-does-it-mean-for-cross-cultural-partnerships/.

2. Quran, Surah 3:45, 3:47, 2:136, 19:19, 3:55.

3. Fouad Masri, in *Unlock the Truth: Who Is Isa Bin Maryam* and *Do Christians Worship Three Gods?* (Colorado: Book Villages, 2014), provides a compelling examination of Jesus's identity as Son of God.

CHAPTER 7

1. Muller, Roland, 18.

2. Muller, 41-42.

3. William R. Nicoll, "Commentary on Genesis 3:21," Sermon Bible Commentary, https://www.studylight.org/commentaries/sbc/genesis-3.html.

4. Genesis 38:8; Leviticus 25:25; Deuteronomy 25:5-10.

CHAPTER 8

1. Aduruma tribe (Kenya); Sudan.

2. "Female Genital Mutilation: Key Facts," last modified January 31, 2018, http://www.who.int/news-room/fact-sheets/detail/female-genital-mutilation. According to the World Health Organization's definition, "female genital mutilation (FGM) includes procedures that intentionally alter or cause injury to the female genital organs for non-medical reasons."

3. http://www.who.int/news-room/fact-sheets/detail/female-genital-mutilation.

4. Kathy Gannon, "'I Had To:' Inside the Mind of an Honor Killer in Pakistan," APnews.com, accessed November 9, 2018, https://www.apnews.com/0ddcb44fe2b9416381e44ad35c07314b/%22I-had-to:%22-Inside-the-mind-of-an-'honor'-killer-in-Pakistan.

5. Psalm 107:7; Proverbs 3:6.

CHAPTER 9

1. John R. Kohlenberger III and James Swanson, *A Concise Dictionary of the Greek* (Michigan: Zondervan, 1996), 3666. John 1:14; 18; 3:16, 18; 1 John 4:9.

2. According to the *Amplified Bible* (La Habra, CA: Lockman Foundation, 2015), in footnote to Leviticus 16:8, the term means "goat of removal" or is otherwise a name. This goat's release (16:10) symbolized the carrying away of Israel's sin.

3. M.G. Easton MA, DD, *Illustrated Bible Dictionary*, 3rd ed. https://www.biblestudytools.com/dictionary/azazel/.

4. "Strong's #3371, (Greek) *meketi*," https://www.bibletools.org/index.cfm/fuseaction/Lexicon. show/ID/G3371/meketi.htm.

5. "Strong's #264, (Greek) hamartano," https://www.bibletools.org/index.cfm/fuseaction/Lexicon. show/ID/G264/hamartano.htm.

6. "The Rules of the Pharisees," pursueGOD.org, accessed November 9, 2018, http://www.pursue god.org/rules-pharisees/.

CHAPTER 10

1. Old Testament Lexical Aid, 3883, found also in Exodus 16:17; 1 Samuel 4:21-22; 2 Chronicles 5:14; Psalm 19:1; 57:5,11; Isaiah 40:5, *Hebrew Greek Key Word Study Bible*, NIV, AMG International, 1996.

2. New Testament Lexical Aid, 1518, *Hebrew Greek Key Word Study Bible*, NIV, AMG International, 1996.

3. Jayson Georges, "The Problem with Bible Translations: Your Culture," http://honorshame.com/ problem-of-culture.

4. For a more extensive discussion of the Muslim beliefs about the death of Jesus, see Fouad Masri's book *Who Died on the Cross?* Indianapolis IN: Crescent Projects n.d.

5. New Testament Lexical Aid, 1518, *Hebrew Greek Key Word Study Bible*, NIV, AMG International, 1996.

6. For an in-depth look at how man can shame God, read the article "Can You Shame God?" at HonorShame.com.

CHAPTER 11

1. John Kohlenberger and James Swanson, *A Concise Dictionary of the Greek* (Grand Rapids, MI: Zondervan, 1996) 4155.

2. Maher Khattab, "Lessons from Hijrah," Muslim Association of Britain, https://www.mabonline .net/about-islam/lessons-from-hijrah/.

3. *Sahih al Bukhari*, Book 15:9, Number 583.

4. Dr. Riffat Hassan, Pakistani-American theologian and Islamic feminist scholar, gives a fascinating exposition and commentary on who she calls her "foremother," Hagar (*Hajira* in Arabic) within the Abrahamic narrative of Islam in "Islamic Hagar and Her Family," *Hagar, Sarah and Their Children*, eds. Phyllis Trible and Letty M. Russel (Westminster Knox Press, 2006), 149-67.

5. Strong's Concordance, 5781a. 'ayin.

6. Wehr, Hans Wehr, *The Hans Wehr Dictionary of Modern Written Arabic*, ed. J. M. Cowan, (Urbana: Spoken Language Services, Inc., 1994), 776, with permission of Otto Harrasowitz, https://www.biblestudytools.com/dictionary/ayin/.

7. In Islam, it is permissible for Muslim men to marry Christian or Jewish women, called in Arabic *kitabiyyah*, "women of the Book" (see Qur'an Al-Ma'idah, 5). Muslim women, however, are not afforded the same right.

8. (Hebrew) *derek*, 1870: going, walk, journey, way, path, manner, way of life, lot in life. (Old Testament Lexical Aid, *Hebrew Greek Key Word Study Bible*, NASB, AMG International, 1996).

9. Study Notes on Genesis 16:11, *Hebrew Greek Key Word Study Bible*, NIV, AMG International, 1996.

10. (Hebrew) *qārā*, 7924. Old Testament Lexical Aid, *Hebrew Greek Key Word Study Bible*, NASB, AMG International, 1996.

11. (Hebrew) *rā'ah*, 8011. Old Testament Lexical Aid, *Hebrew Greek Key Word Study Bible*, NASB, AMG International, 1996.

12. John R. Kohlenberger III and James Swanson, *A Concise Dictionary of the Hebrew* (Grand Rapids, MI: Zondervan Publishing House, 1996), 936.

CHAPTER 12

1. "(Greek) *haptō:* implies a certain degree of involvement with the object on the part of the subject, more than mere contact or touch, but an engagement, handling, or use in which some kind of influence or effect is created between the items coming into contact." *New Testament Lexical Aid,* 721, *Hebrew Greek Key Word Study Bible,* NIV, AMG International, 1996.

2. (Greek) *psēlaphaō*, 6027, New Testament Lexical Aid, 721, *Hebrew Greek Key Word Study Bible,* NIV, AMG International, 1996.

CHAPTER 13

1. "Men are in charge of women by [right of] what Allah has given one over the other and what they spend [for maintenance] from their wealth. So righteous women are devoutly obedient, guarding in [the husband's] absence what Allah would have them guard. But those [wives] from whom you fear arrogance—[first] advise them; [then if they persist], forsake them in bed; and [finally], strike them. But if they obey you [once more], seek no means against them. Indeed, Allah is ever Exalted and Grand" (Qur'an 4:34). The interpretation of this passage is widely debated among contemporary Muslim apologists. Modern Muslims are hesitant to say that Islam promotes domestic violence. However, in many parts of the Muslim world, the practice is widespread and accepted without examination or question.

2. *herem* (Hebrew) 3051: from *haram*, to destroy totally, devote. Something devoted unto divine service; a person or thing marked for destruction. Often used in the sense of something forbidden, prohibited. (Old Testament Lexical Aid, *Hebrew Greek Key Word Study Bible,* NIV, AMG International, 1996).

CHAPTER 14

1. *Salat* is Arabic for obligatory, ritual prayer performed five times per day by Muslims. *Salat-al-maghrib* is the fourth prayer period of the day, occurring just after sunset. *Salat* is the second of the five pillars of Islam. From age seven, Muslim girls and boys are encouraged to pray the five daily prayers of *salat.*

2. *Salat* rules for girls and boys are different. Girls and women must perform ritual prayers with special consideration of concealment, or physical discretion. This principle dictates the covering of all body parts except face, hands, and feet, consequently requiring modified positions during praying such as only lifting the hands to the shoulders (which would risk exposure of the female's wrists or forearms) instead of extending them to the ears as males do.

3. The *qiblah* is Arabic for the direction of the Kaaba, a stone structure in Mecca. The Kaaba is the most sacred site in Islam. Muslims are to face the Kaaba when they perform *salat*, or prayer.

4. Some Islamic schools of thought encourage boys and girls as young as seven to begin their daily prayers.

5. Sahih al-Bukhari, Volume 5, Book 58, Number 234.

6. Qur'an 33:37.

7. Qur'an 4:24.

Notes

8. Deuteronomy 2:20; 11:22; 13:4; 30:20; Joshua 23:8; 2 Kings 18:6; Psalm 119:31-32.

9. Study Notes on Ruth, *Hebrew Greek Key Word Study Bible*, NIV, AMG International, 1996.

10. Monica Rey discusses Ruth's ethnical and religious background in her probing master's thesis "Intersectionality in the Book of Ruth: Constructing Ruth's Identity in Ancient Israel," Boston University School of Theology, 2012. Chemosh, god of the Moabites, is discussed extensively in other sources, including Britannica.com, christogea.org, and bible-history.com.

11. Ruth 2:1 (Hebrew) *hayil*, 2657 (Old Testament Lexical Aid, *Hebrew Greek Key Word Study Bible*, NIV, AMG International, 1996).

CHAPTER 15

1. Bill Bright, *The Four Spiritual Laws* (New Life Publications, 1993).

2. *Tabiba* is Arabic for doctor and is often used to describe various other medical workers. In my case, although I was not a doctor, it was the title I was given as a speech-language pathologist. My attempts to clarify my role were met with dismissal, and the name stuck whether I liked it or not. I examined patients, made decisions about their surgery, worked in the operating room, and wore scrubs. I carried children into surgery and delivered them to their mothers afterward. As far as the patients were concerned, I was a *tabiba*.

CHAPTER 16

1. https://www.bible-history.com/backd2/engraving_palms.html.

2. Nadia Murad, *The Last Girl* (New York: Tim Duggan Books, 2017), 115-16.

CHAPTER 17

1. Sayed Naqibullah, "What Does Ghairat Mean in Pashto," February 24, 2013, https://blogs .transparent.com/pashto/what-does-ghairat-mean-in-pashto/.

CHAPTER 18

1. Qur'an, Al Buruj 85:14.

2. Hans Wehr, *The Hans Wehr Dictionary of Modern Written Arabic*, ed. J.M. Cowan, 1241 (Urbana: Spoken Language Services, Inc., 1994), 1241, with permission of Otto Harrasowitz.

3. Wehr, 179.

4. Jinan Yousef, "Love Is in Giving: Al Wadud," http://www.virtualmosque.com/islam-studies/ islam-101/belief-and-worship/love-is-in-giving-al-wadud/.

5. Al-Bukhari, "Arabic-English Book Reference: Book 1, Hadith, 386," https://sunnah.com/riya dus-saliheen/1/386, emphasis added.

HONOR AND SHAME KEY APPLICATIONS

1. Luke 7:37 (Greek) *hamartōlos*, 283, New Testament Lexical Aid, *Hebrew Greek Key Word Study Bible*, NIV, AMG International, 1996.

Additional Resources

BOOKS:

Honor and Shame: Unlocking the Door by Roland Muller (Xlibris, 2001)

The 3D Gospel by Jayson Georges (Tim& 275 Press, 2014)

Ministering in Honor-Shame Cultures by Jayson Georges and Mark D. Baker (IVP, 2016)

The Global Gospel by Werner Mischke (Mission One, 2014)

Shame and Honor in the Book of Esther by Timothy Laniak (Society of Biblical Literature, 1998)

Honor, Patronage, Kinship, and Purity by David deSilva (IVP Academic, 2000)

Restoring the Shamed by Robin Stockitt (Wipf & Stock Publishers, 2012)

WEBSITES:

HonorShame.com

jacksonwu.org

RealHonour.com

www.audreyfrank.com

whenwomenspeak.net

Audrey Frank is an author, speaker, and storyteller. The stories she shares are brave and true. They give voice to those whose words are silenced by shame, the hard things in life that don't make sense, and the losses that leave us wondering if we will survive.

Audrey and her family have spent over 20 years living and working among Muslim cultures and various worldviews, and she has found that God's story of redemption spans every geography and culture. He is the God of *Instead*, giving honor *instead* of shame, gladness *instead* of mourning, hope *instead* of despair. Audrey holds a BS in communication disorders, an MA in speech-language pathology, and a BA in biblical and intercultural studies. However, her greatest credential is that she is known and loved by the One who made her.

You can also find Audrey at www.audreyfrank.com, as well as on Twitter (@audreycfrank) and Facebook.